WORLD FURNITURE

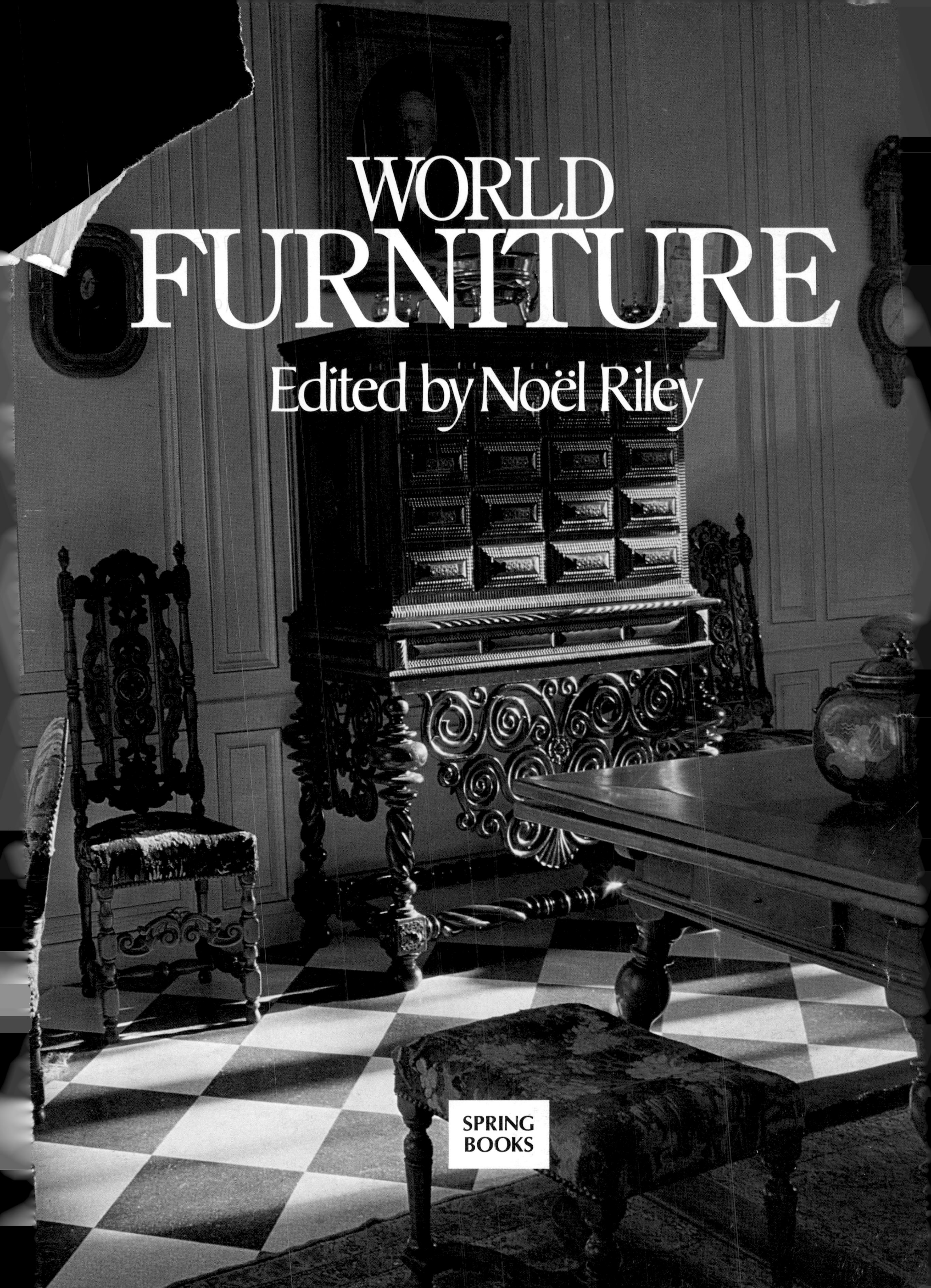
WORLD
FURNITURE
Edited by Noël Riley
SPRING
BOOKS

Contents

First published in 1980 by Octopus Books Limited

This edition published in 1989 by Spring Books
An imprint of Octopus Publishing Group plc
Michelin House
81 Fulham Road
London SW3 6RB

ISBN 0 600 56620 X

Printed and bound in Yugoslavia

Introduction

This book was conceived with a wide range of readers in mind: from those who know very little about antique furniture to those whose knowledge may be extensive in some fields but not in others. No book of this size can hope to cover all you need to know about furniture; indeed, no book on antiques should make any such claim. Practical experience must always go hand in hand with reading.

What a book of this kind can do, however, is to arm the interested with a thorough knowledge of styles, techniques and forms of decoration, to foster an ability to look, and to stimulate a feeling for design. Above all, it can whet the furniture collector's appetite. We hope to have achieved these aims and more besides.

Unlike many books on furniture, the subject is approached from an international standpoint, which gives an opportunity to trace the enormous cross-fertilization of ideas and the fascinating way in which furniture styles re-emerged in different places in different centuries. It shows how the furniture fashions of one country were taken up, often decades later, in another and then almost always adapted to fit an unmistakably national style.

French furniture, for example, was widely copied in other countries during the 18th century, but the subtleties of cabinet-making techniques and the kinds of woods used as well as the characteristically different interpretations of a particular design idiom nearly always proclaim a piece's true origins. Even a great master of style such as Chippendale, when he worked in the French taste, imparted a peculiarly English flavour to his chairs and commodes.

A rather different form of stylistic export took place between England and America where, for close on two centuries, English styles were regularly followed, often later and persisting for longer than in England. This can cause some confusion when these styles are given labels like 'Queen Anne' or 'Chippendale'. Although Queen Anne reigned from 1702–1714, a piece of American Queen Anne furniture would fall roughly into the 1720–1750 period. Likewise, American Chippendale was still in vogue in the 1770s and 80s by which time, in England, Chippendale had been eclipsed by Adam and Hepplewhite.

Another area of possible confusion in an internationally based book such as this one arises in the habit of labelling the centuries. Most Europeans refer to the years of the 1700s as the 18th century and those of the 1800s as the 19th. An Italian, on the other hand, talks of the 1600s as the seicento (16th century) and the 1700s as the settecento (17th).

It might appear superfluous that we have begun our story in the ancient world. After all, it is unlikely that furniture made before the Renaissance period at least will be available to the collector. Yet it is surprising how many furniture forms have their roots in ancient Egypt or Greece. The lion's paw foot, for example, is to be seen in the furniture of Tutankhamun and reappears frequently in the 18th and 19th centuries, while the Greek *klismos* chair with its sabre-shaped legs became a much favoured design in the late 18th century when the Neoclassical rage caused all kinds of ancient types to be resurrected.

Furniture from the medieval world is scanty, but it is clear from the few pieces that exist – and from contemporary illustrations – that the church was the dominant influence in both design and function. It is during the Renaissance period that the story of furniture begins to

Above: *A walnut sofa carved, gilt and upholstered in Beauvais tapestry, by Georges Jacob (1739–1814), one of the leading chair-makers in Paris in the late 18th century. Although he had worked for the* noblesse *in pre-revolutionary France, Jacob was later employed to make furniture for the Napoleonic palaces, and his work forms an interesting link between the Louis XVI and Empire styles.*
Far left: *An English oak hall cupboard of c.1600 with carved fluted supports and inlaid star motifs in the upper panels.*
Left: *An English mahogany armchair with caned seat and sides, and loose cushions upholstered in William Morris's 'Tulip' chintz. The chair was probably designed by George Jack and made, c.1893, by Morris & Co. It is a good example of the persistence of the caned bergère, a favoured English type since the early 19th century.*

assume a welcome familiarity. We can now understand the social factors that influenced its evolution, individual designers and makers start to emerge and the furniture itself, however scarce, is still around to be looked at. National and regional characteristics begin to play an important part in the identification process, and the growth of world communications through the opening up of trade routes, not just in Europe but with the East and, a little later, with America, meant that furniture began to move round the world. The result was a growing interchange of furniture styles and forms, and while national individuality was almost always maintained, influences and cross-influences can be discerned in all quarters.

Another important factor in this spread was the movement of craftsmen, especially round Europe. Royal and noble patrons in France and other countries of Europe

employed Italian and Flemish craftsmen, especially during the 16th and 17th centuries and, similarly, workers were sent by their patrons from one country to another to acquire new skills. Probably the most well known and certainly the most influential movement of labour came late in the 17th century when thousands of French Protestants – many of them skilled in the furniture trades – fled from persecution after the Revocation of the Edict of Nantes. They settled principally in Germany, the Netherlands and England, setting up workshops and introducing their expertise wherever they went.

The greater part of the book is concerned with furniture made after about 1750, that is, with pieces generally available to the modern collector. By this time one style tended to follow closely on the heels of another, sometimes overlapping chronologically and sometimes nationally. For example in England the Chippendale style incorporated the French Rococo taste, the Gothic and the Chinese, and although some of Chippendale's best work was in the Neoclassical style, Adam is generally the label given to English Neoclassical furniture of the 1760s and 1770s. Hepplewhite and Sheraton were in their way as eclectic as Chippendale and borrowed ideas from across the Channel as well as from earlier periods in England. Similarly, the links between the Regency style in England, the Directory style in America and the Directoire in France can be more clearly appreciated when it is realised that they are all rooted in Neoclassicism.

Left: *The state bed at Clandon Park, Surrey. It dates from the second quarter of the 18th century when enormous sums were still spent on bed-hangings and upholstery for state apartments.*
Right: *A sloping-front desk with delicately inlaid flowers and butterflies by Emile Gallé (1846–1904), one of the foremost exponents of the Art Nouveau style in both glass and furniture.*
Below: *An early 18th century bureau cabinet of wood inlaid with ivory, made in India for the European market.*

By the 19th century, styles and movements all over Europe and America are positively interlaced, so closely do they link with each other, and this situation has persisted up to our own day. We have attempted to show the many connecting strands in the evolution of furniture in the past 100 years and to pinpoint the designers who have made the most impact on changing fashions in furniture.

The chapter on upholstery provides valuable guidance for those faced with the problem of restoring old upholstered furniture. Upholstery is an avenue of furniture research that has only recently begun to be explored. Although it was the most important branch of furniture making throughout the 17th and 18th centuries – colossal sums were spent on bed-hangings in particular – it was also the most perishable, and it is now rare to find a chair with its original covering, still less a bed decked in the hangings with which it began life. The best we can do is to follow studied examples in restoring furniture, and a knowledge of upholstery techniques and textiles is essential.

Finally, we have included a section on oriental furniture, an important and hitherto rather neglected area which not only provides insights into the oriental way of living but reveals a fascinating range of collectable material.

Pre-Renaissance Furniture

The ancient world

If it is to be enjoyed to the full, the furniture of any particular period or place needs to be seen in the broader context of its relationship to other periods and other places. A chair made at about the time of Captain Cook's voyages, or a card table made in New York in the year of Waterloo, cannot be properly appreciated without reference to the source of its inspiration, which is to be found, as often as not, in classical antiquity. For this reason if for no other, it is worth learning about the furniture made in Egypt, Assyria, Greece, Etruria and Rome from about 1500 BC to 500 AD, even though the pieces known to have survived from that remote time are usually to be seen only in museums and could hardly be acquired by the private collector. Even so, for the enthusiast there is always the hope of finding a piece of pottery or a carving in stone that depicts one of these very early pieces.

Egypt

From the period of the New Kingdom (*c.*1575–1075 BC) a number of actual pieces have survived more or less intact, supplemented by painted or carved portrayals. Most extant examples have been found in the tombs of the Pharaohs, their families or officials of the Egyptian hierarchical government, so that our knowledge is confined mainly to the kind of furniture owned by the ruling classes.

This limitation however, applies to most furniture made anywhere before about 1500 AD because, before then, few could afford anything more or better than crude essentials. The extent to which the better pieces were status symbols as much as functional articles, is a theme that recurs in every country and in every period down to the present day.

The best-known hoard of Egyptian furniture to have come to light so far was found in the tomb of Tutankhamūn who died about 1350 BC, and includes couches, beds, chairs, stools, footstools, chests and small tables. Most of these are of sophisticated design and were made by techniques which, as excavations of older burial chambers have shown, were in use from much earlier times.

Left: *Highly sophisticated furniture existed in the Egypt of the Pharaohs. This portrayal of the young Tutankhamun seated on his throne appears on the back of the actual surviving throne. Dating from the mid-14th century BC, it is inlaid with lapis lazuli, cornelian and rock crystal into a ground of gold.*

Above: *Ancient Egyptian armchair from the tomb of Yuya and Tuyu, New Kingdom (c.1575–1075 BC). The wooden frame has a seat of interlaced cords, the back is veneered and decorated with gold foil laid over gesso. Similar gilding is found on the portrayals of human heads surmounting the legs, which are carved to represent those of animals.*

The chairs are throne-like, as might be expected, and were obviously meant to do more for the occupant's dignity than for his comfort – a tradition which was to persist in most societies for many centuries and which has still not entirely disappeared. A particular feature of the Egyptian throne-chair which has reappeared at intervals throughout the history of furniture is the chair leg fashioned in the form of an animal's leg, usually that of a lion. Similar legs occur on Egyptian couches and indeed, Tutankhamūn's funerary couches are themselves shaped to represent lions. His camp bed, which also has lion's paw feet, is ingeniously contrived to fold down into a compact space, as though intended for a modern bachelor apartment rather than an ancient burial pyramid. Another space-saving device from the same period is a folding stool with X-shaped supports. A different type of stool in fairly

Above: *Assyrian relief from the palace of King Assurbanipal (668–626 BC) at Nineveh, showing him taking his meal from a small table while reclining on a couch – a custom later adopted in Rome. The couch has a shaped end, to hold a pillow. The frame has carved decoration, and the legs are of the type that could have been turned on the lathe.*

common use had a 'dished' (slightly hollowed) seat of interlaced cords or strips of leather, on a rigid frame composed of four legs joined by stretchers and a well-engineered system of struts that gave added strength.

For the storage of valuables, box-like chests with domed lids were made from small pieces of wood cleverly joined together edge to edge, timber of any substantial width being in short supply in Pharaonic Egypt. This jigsaw foundation was then covered with ebony and ivory veneers and often decorated with marquetry, a technique of inlaying a pictorial design into a veneered surface, as distinct from solid inlay which involved only the inlaying of contrasting woods or other materials into hollows cut in the solid foundation. A cheaper alternative was to cover the foundation with gesso (a mixture of plaster and size) and paint it to imitate more luxurious materials. Even richer effects were achieved with gold and silver foil glued on to the surface.

Construction was by means of joints which are still favoured by good craftsmen today; the tenon, or tongue, fitting into the mortise, or slot to receive it; the dovetail, or wedge-shaped projection also fitting into a tailored space cut in the adjoining member; the mitre – a method of joining two pieces of wood which have to form an angle, as in a modern picture frame (there are several versions of the mitre, most of which were familiar to the Egyptian carpenter). Additional strength was provided by wooden pegs securing the joints, and from about the time of Tutankhamūn, metal nails were in use. For assembling those small, precious pieces of wood into large surfaces, there was the tongue-and-groove system, similar to that employed for modern matchboarding.

The Egyptians do not seem to have had any woodworking machinery except, at a later date than that so far discussed, the lathe. But they did have saws, chisels, drills, adzes and axes, and they managed quite well without planes, smoothing the surfaces first with the adze and finally with a stone.

Assyria and Persia

It was the Assyrian and Persian civilizations – Eastern rather than Western – which probably contributed to Mediterranean culture that most useful gadget, the lathe. Relief carvings in stone, dating from the 9th century BC onwards, show Assyrian kings seated on throne-stools or reclining on couches, the legs of which have clearly been 'thrown', i.e., turned on the lathe.

Skill in the use of this machine had reached a high point

in Persia by the 6th century BC. Contact between the Persian Empire, Egypt and European Greece was constant, in spite of intermittent wars and uprisings, and it is likely that the lathe-turning was one of the techniques that came with the natural flow of knowledge from East to West. Some authorities, however, credit Egypt with its invention. These early lathes consisted of two tree trunks with a spike in each; between these a length of wood was set horizontally and rotated to and fro, while the desired pattern was cut by placing a tool at given points along it.

Greece

Couches with legs turned by an unknown method are depicted on Greek pottery dating from the 8th century BC, and the lathe is thought to have been used in Greece from about the 7th century. After that date the turning of legs became increasingly delicate, even to the point of fragility – a weakness to be regretted in the work of turners far and wide, many centuries later. The legs at one end of the couch were extended upwards to form a head-rest, so that the couch could be used for reclining in the daytime and as a bed at night. Turning was also used for the throne-like chairs which were sometimes decorated with carvings of animals and snakes.

The Greeks developed a simpler, more portable chair, the *klismos*, in the making of which turning played little or no part. It was without arms and stood on inward-curving, sabre-shaped legs, with the back curved for comfort. Altogether, it was a most elegant and convenient article of seat furniture, yet it was allowed to disappear from the European home at the end of the classical period, and did not emerge again until late in the 18th century. It is a shape which enjoys great popularity today as a dining chair.

Stools of the X-shaped, folding kind were developed from Egyptian models but were often constructed as rigid pieces, with a boss carved as a human or animal mask at the point where the legs crossed each other. The seat-frame was sometimes decorated with a formal pattern such as the 'Greek key'.

Tables also followed Egyptian tradition in that they were mostly small stands on which individual dishes of food and cups of wine could be placed within easy reach of each guest. It was not customary, at least among the educated classes, for a group of people to eat sitting at the same table.

Cupboards do not seem to have been standard items either. The Greeks, again like the Egyptians, kept their valuables in chests, and anything that would not comfortably fit into them – cloak, hat, helmet, sword, musical instrument, wine-skin – was hung from a hook on the wall. The so-called 'trophies' of arms or instruments that were favourite motifs for artists and carvers in the 17th and 18th centuries may possibly owe their origin to ancient depictions of commonplace articles casually hung from walls.

Etruria

The Etruscans adopted a furnishing style somewhat similar to that of the Greeks, but with several interesting variations, of which the most important was their increased use of bronze for tripod tables, chests and even chairs, enabling them to be more adventurous in shaping and decorating their furniture. From about 400 BC they produced chests of bronze that were circular in form and richly engraved. Another innovation was a tub chair with a solid back curving round to form arms, riveted to a drum-shaped base. Their bronze candelabra and stands for oil-burning lamps were both practical and elegant, providing Roman craftsmen with models to follow.

Above: *Small terracotta figure of a Greek goddess seated on a throne, from Attica, 8th century BC – the early, 'geometric' period of Greek art. The full-scale original on which it was based was probably of painted wood and may have been more complicated in design. The gap between the goddess's feet and ground level indicates that there would have been a footstool – the usual accessory to a throne-chair.*

Rome

A chair of rather similar shape to the Etruscan bronze tub form, but made of a very different material, was popular during the later years of the Roman Empire. Made of wickerwork, it sometimes had a kind of hood surmounting the back and projecting forward over the seat. Some, at least, of these 'beehive' chairs were made in Britain and sent home by Roman officials as presents to their families in the capital. They appear to be the first recorded example of British-made furniture being exported to the continent of Europe. In their humble way these chairs demonstrate the comparative facility with which ideas and material objects were regularly exchanged between places far apart in the Roman Empire.

Rome took over much Greek, Egyptian and Middle Eastern culture, including designs for furniture, which they elaborated on and re-exported to the outposts of the Empire and beyond. The Roman couch, for example, developed from the Greek model with the addition of a back and arms so that with its turned legs, it came to serve as the model for the kind of sofa that graced almost every middle-class parlour in the West only 150 years ago; but 1,800 years before that it was fashionable as far north as the Rhineland.

The Romans used a variety of materials other than wood for furniture – bronze, iron, silver and marble being prominent among them. Like the Egyptians and the Greeks, they usually took their food from small tables while reclining on couches. They did produce larger tables, however, to serve as sideboards. Often made of carved marble, they were massive constructions with slabs forming supports at the ends. The slabs were shaped in profile and sculpted with mythological beasts forming the outlines and grotesque masks festooned with vines or honeysuckle (anthemion) at their centres. Like so much furniture of the ancient world, these tables are significant not only as symbols of the splendour in which the original owners lived, but as the prototypes for a series of revivals which began in the 16th century and continued at intervals down to comparatively modern times.

The early Middle Ages

Byzantium

In terms of art history the Christian era in Constantinople, which lasted for more than 1,000 years, is usually referred to as Byzantine. Although situated beyond the eastern shores of the Mediterranean, Byzantium was traditionally a Greek city, so that when it became Constantine's capital, the Roman influence was added to an already established classical heritage. Yet, by virtue of its geographical position, eastern ideas played a vital part in the development of its culture. Apart from a few notable exceptions such as the 6th century throne of Maximian – a remarkable piece of rectilinear form with box-like seat, made of intricately carved ivory, now at Ravenna – few substantial pieces of furniture have survived from the early Byzantine period. A fair idea of the standard achieved can however be gained from a study of the mosaics and carved panels that depict, mainly in biblical scenes, some of the types of furniture which – allowing for a little artistic licence – must have been in use.

Below: *Couch and stool reconstructed from remains found at Pompeii, a fashionable Roman resort until its destruction in 79 AD. The Roman couch developed from a Greek prototype. The legs on wooden couches of this design were turned on the lathe and carved, but rather similar ones were cast in bronze. They served for reclining in the daytime and for sleeping at night. In the late 18th century they inspired the chaise-longue in the Neoclassical style.*

As well as splendid-looking thrones, several types of chair were made, some with turned legs – turnery being a Byzantine speciality – others with X-shaped, folding frames. Fairly small, square-looking tables on straight legs with underframing are depicted, as well as large dining tables. Some of these are round or half-round, and can be seen in portrayals of the Last Supper, suggesting a mealtime custom different from the Greek and Roman habit of taking food from small, individual tables.

A number of richly carved ivory chests and caskets have survived, and in spite of being on a small scale, some are constructed on the panelled principle used for full-size chests. This method of making a piece of carcase furniture involved the insertion of panels, bevelled at their edges, into a surrounding framework while leaving sufficient play to allow for shrinkage and movement, thus reducing the danger of warping and splitting. Both the panels and framework were frequently overlaid with ivory and decorated with carving over their entire surfaces. Figures of saints would customarily occupy the panels, while the frame was covered with a complex pattern of animals and foliage in which the eastern influence is very marked.

There must, of course, have been a great deal of much simpler, more functional furniture. Cupboards, in the modern sense of the term, or more correctly, *armoires*, are known to have existed in plenty, as did bookshelves, both open and closed, for Byzantium was a centre of scholarship. But certain of the classic shapes such as the Greek chair with sabre-shaped legs and the Roman couch with back and scrolled arms – furniture which might have been expected to be continued in a city with a strong Graeco-Roman background – rather surprisingly disappear from view, to be replaced by pieces which possessed a more oriental splendour.

Precious as the Byzantine objects themselves are to posterity, what was of equal importance to later generations was that many arts and crafts were allowed to wither and die in Western Europe during the long and troubled period of the early Middle Ages, and were only kept alive in the eastern capital of Christendom, until that too fell victim to invaders in the 15th century. By that time though, Rome was once again ready to learn those skills anew.

Before that could happen however, the West had to survive a period when furniture, or the lack of it, was the least of most people's worries. Simply staying alive was more important. For some 600 years following the fall of Rome, large parts of Europe were in turn battlegrounds then wasteland. The great lords had a few pieces of furniture in their fortress homes – stately chairs to emphasize their authority, chests to hold their valuables, tables and beds which could usually be knocked apart and moved to another estate or refuge when danger threatened – but very little else.

Italy

When the Roman empire in the West collapsed, Rome came under the rule of the Goths – who were, it should be emphasized, in no way responsible for so-called 'Gothic' art, which came much later. Rome, Naples and Ravenna were all subsequently reconquered by an army sent by the Byzantine emperor Justinian in 536–540 but a fresh invasion from the north by the Lombards in 568–572 reduced a large part of the Italian population to near-slavery, and Rome was besieged. The Lombards were finally induced to raise the siege mainly by the efforts of Pope Gregory I, who employed all his diplomatic skill and a large sum out of church funds to buy them off. The immediate consequence of his efforts was a great gain in prestige, wealth and influence by the papacy, its power transcending national sovereignties as they slowly emerged from the chaos. Evidence concerning furniture at this time

Above: *Silver tripod table, Roman, 1st century AD. The scissor-like construction of the crossed braces allows the table to be folded up for easy portability. Stands of this type were used as supports for oil lamps, as well as for the serving of food and wine. The design was revived during the period of the French Empire in the early 19th century.*

Above: *The Byzantine ivory throne of Maximian at Ravenna, 6th century AD. The panels below the seat are carved with figures of four of the apostles and John the Baptist, the frame with animals and birds among scrolls of foliage. This contrast between classically draped figures and the intricacy of the borders demonstrates the merging of Western and Eastern influences on Byzantine art.*

is meagre, but what there is suggests that anything other than the crudest functional articles were made either for the church itself or, if for a rich layman, following a fashion dictated by ecclesiastical custom. This is broadly true of most European furniture throughout the Middle Ages.

The term 'Romanesque' is used in a variety of contexts, but in terms of furniture, it is used to describe a style – or rather a combination of styles – covering a period *c.*1000–1300, that resulted from the need of invaders from the north to adjust to their new Christianized environment. This they did by grafting elements of their own Nordic, Teutonic and Celtic cultures on to the remnants of the classical tradition. The distinction between Byzantine and Romanesque is not always too clear, strong eastern influence often being present in the decoration of medieval western artefacts. Furthermore, in its later phases the Romanesque style often overlapped with the Gothic.

The best medieval furniture was almost all related, to a greater or lesser extent, to church architecture, and perhaps the surest way of understanding the Romanesque style is to visit the outstanding buildings of the period: Pisa Cathedral; San Zeno Maggiore, Verona; Abbaye-aux-Dames, Caen; St Trophine, Arles; the Church of the Apostles, Cologne; Spires Cathedral; and Romsey Abbey.

It was in Italy that furniture displayed Romanesque architectural features most strongly: in particular, rounded arches supported on rather short, stumpy classical columns. It was in Italy, too, that Romanesque buildings from the 11th century show evidence of advanced sculptural technique, so the furniture intended for, or influenced by, those buildings is most skilfully carved. Colour also played an important part in the decoration, painting being extensively employed either in place of, or in addition to, carving. Byzantine craftsmen were constantly in demand in Rome to add a touch of oriental magnificence.

The classical tradition also remained strong in Tuscany, but Lombardy more or less abandoned quite early the attempt to imitate Ancient Rome. As early as the 8th century Lombardy's builders' guild, the *Maestri Comacini*, set to work in creating a building style more suited to the relatively crude techniques of the Lombards, but livened it with Byzantine effects derived through the Venetian region. Chests and armoires from this area exhibit the same characteristics, especially in the use of grotesque elements in the decoration, of a kind more often seen north of the Alps.

France

France is richly endowed with medieval churches, a number of which contain pieces of early furniture, as well as depictions in stone carvings. In the abbey church of St Etienne, Obazine, is an armoire (a large cupboard or wardrobe), dating from *c.*1176, which has a pair of arched doors set flush with the framework and relieved only by handsome iron strap hinges and locks. The ends are especially interesting, having two pairs of rounded arches set one above the other and slim, turned columns supporting them. This use of the arch as a decorative feature was often extended to form a continuous pattern, or run, across the entire width of a piece of furniture, when it is known as 'arcading'. Thus a 12th century carving depicts a footstool (a common adjunct to a throne-chair) with pierced arcading – that is, with the arches cut right through the thickness of the wood, not merely carved on its surface. Similar treatment has been accorded to a 12th century bed with square posts depicted in a stone carving at Chartres.

Arcading, both carved and pierced, is often to be seen on 13th century coffers in France and neighbouring countries. A well-known example with carved arcading on the front and pierced arches cut through the feet, is at the Musée de Valière, Sion, Switzerland.

Germany and Scandinavia

At the Cathedral Museum of Halberstadt in Germany, there is a Romanesque sacristy cupboard (an armoire for church plate and vestments), *c.*1200, which is massively constructed, the rather crude joinery being covered with

gesso (a type of plaster) and painted both inside and out with full-length figures of saints.

The Romanesque style was not only adopted by northern peoples who had originally moved southwards into Italy, but was fed back as far north as Scandinavia. There are more than 2,000 Romanesque churches in Denmark. Vallstena Church in Gotland, Sweden, contains a number of pieces of furniture including a desk with a chest-like carcase and sloping top, an armchair and a settle with slightly arched back, all believed to date from about 1200. On all three pieces, the craft of the turner has been taken to its limits. All the uprights have been turned, as have rows of spindles set between the rails of the seats (or in the case of the desk, the carcase) and the stretchers below, to form rudimentary Romanesque arches. The vertical surfaces are covered with turned billets of wood set edge to edge to form geometric patterns.

From earliest times the Norsemen were a sea-going people whose voyages and colonizations resulted in some of their cultural traditions being transplanted to distant places. Even as far away from home as Spain articles of 12th century furniture are to be found carved with animal's heads in a style suggesting Scandinavian influence. A more definite Norse flavour is to be seen in areas of the British Isles where Scandinavians settled.

Above: *Desk, bench and chair, c.1200, at Vallstena Church, Gotland, Sweden. All the uprights have been turned on the lathe and are morticed and tenoned to the flat, horizontal rails. Turned spindles act as columns to support arches arranged in series ('arcading').*

England

A chair in Hereford Cathedral bears strong resemblances to the Vallstena group of furniture previously described, being composed entirely of turned members with the exception of the seat, below which spindles join the front stretcher to form even more clearly-defined Romanesque arches. There is evidence that it originally had a footstool attachment and was thus a chair of 'estate' reserved for persons of authority.

'Estate' in this context meant 'status' and not class distinction. A man of low birth who served in a senior position in his master's household might well occupy the lord's chair in the latter's absence, as the symbol of continuing authority. The principle survives today in the practice of inviting someone to 'take the chair' or to be 'chairman' at a meeting when the usual incumbent is unable to attend.

The term 'Romanesque' is seldom used to describe English medieval furniture, perhaps because by the time the style arrived in England – largely as a side-effect of the

Above: *Walnut chest, c.1250, at Sion, Switzerland. Tongues of wood (tenons) projecting from the ends of the horizontal planks forming the front are housed in slots (mortices) cut in the stiles (uprights). The Romanesque arcading on the front, and also the roundels (circular motifs) are chip-carved without any modelling in relief.*

Norman conquest in the 11th century – it had become too diluted to have a very pronounced effect on the indigenous Anglo-Saxon tradition, which was probably somewhat primitive; yet the Normans were skilful, if somewhat sparing, in the furnishing of their homes and it is possible that their influence on English furniture-making may have been greater than is generally supposed. It is clearly present in pieces illustrated in illuminated manuscripts such as the 12th century Life of St Cuthbert, now at University College Library, Oxford, in which a chair and a long settle are shown, both with Romanesque arcading in the underframing.

As in other countries, the chest was the commonest article of furniture. Originally, the term 'coffer' (from the French *coffre*) or 'ark' was used to describe a type of chest with a domed or hipped lid, often without feet and used as a travelling chest – the shape of the top allowing rain water to run off while the vast amounts of baggage that people literally carted about with them were in transit. Other words, such as 'standard', were used to describe the flat-topped chest that was more in the nature of a permanent home fixture. The terms 'coffer' and 'chest' have now become more or less synonymous, but 'ark' is still reserved for the container with a detachable, hipped lid, of the kind that came to be used as a humble grain-holder.

The earliest chests were undoubtedly made from the trunks of trees that had become hollow and fallen, providing primitive men with useful places for storage. At some remote time, an inventive genius conceived the idea of hollowing out a log by means of flint tools and possibly fire. This kind of dug-out chest was common in the Middle Ages and continued to be made in some areas long after more sophisticated types were in use.

Several types of chest were made in 13th century England. A very simple variety – again proving most persistent – consisted of oak or elm boards forming the back, front, top and lid. The back and front boards, with the grain running horizontally, were set against end boards whose grain ran vertically; the boards were nailed together with iron nails. A larger and heavier version had thick boards housed into flat, wide corner-posts ('stiles') and was often strengthened with wrought-iron bands.

Many such chests were made for church use and fitted with three locks, the key of each being held by a different individual, so that they could be opened only when all the custodians were present. An example banded with iron, c.1280–1300, is at Merton College, Oxford.

In private homes, the chest usually had just one lock, the key of which was, by established custom, held by the lady of the house. In view of the fact that such a chest probably held all the family's portable assets in the way of coin, silver plate and fur robes, the practice suggests a rather greater degree of female emancipation than popular notions about medieval England take into account.

The later Middle Ages

France and Burgundy

The period 1200–1500 in Europe was one of awakening interest in learning accompanied by a sense of security that had not been possible for some centuries, and although these years were still marred by periodic outbreaks of international and civil wars, conditions were more conducive to a civilized way of life in which furniture could play a more significant role. While even large houses continued to be sparsely furnished a greater variety of articles were made and a fresh repertoire of ornamental decoration was introduced.

The first coherent style to emerge was the Gothic, which overlapped the Romanesque period and was itself to become modified by the Renaissance in Italy in the second half of the 15th century; it is not unusual to come across early pieces that combine Gothic with Romanesque detail, and later ones which show Renaissance features superimposed on Gothic forms. To suggest that there are precise dates for the ending of one style and the beginning of another would therefore be arbitrary and misleading.

The term 'Gothic' is itself misleading. It was first applied – or rather, misapplied – to late medieval buildings by Giorgio Vasari (1511–74), a pupil of Michelangelo and an enthusiast for the Renaissance style. He sought to pour scorn on the earlier buildings and labelled them 'Gothic' after the Goths who had been the conquerors of ancient Rome (in the same way destructive people are today called 'vandals' after an invading Germanic tribe of the 5th century). The power of the Goths themselves had been finally destroyed in 711, more than 400 years before the first 'Gothic' church was built in France. This was the abbey church of St Denis built in 1140–44 by Abbot Suger, which marked the first major transition from Romanesque to Gothic and set a fashion which by the 13th century was spreading across most of Europe and greatly influencing the design of furniture.

Suger set out to create the most beautiful church in France, and called in the finest artists and craftsmen available, thus bringing far more laymen into the church-building business than had been customary, the monks having hitherto operated what almost amounted to a closed shop. The practice spread and the experience gained from such employment increased the skills of the workmen, who were able to put them to good use on their return to private business. Craftsmanship in furniture-making greatly improved but the decoration of domestic pieces was more than ever influenced by the repertoire of ornament derived from ecclesiastical architecture and woodwork.

The most readily recognizable Gothic feature is the pointed arch, said to have been introduced to France by the Normans, who in turn had found it in Saracenic architecture in Sicily. The spaces in the arch are often occupied by delicate tracery, together with plant forms and animal and human figures, all rendered more naturalistically and with less emphasis on the grotesque than is often apparent in Romanesque work. Furniture with this kind of decoration was substantially made, usually in solid oak or walnut. The carving was frequently enriched with painting in vivid colours that created an effect far from the rather sombre appearance of surviving pieces, almost all of which lack their original colouration.

The chest remained the commonest article of furniture, the better French examples being enriched either with carving of the kind described above or with elaborately scrolled wrought-ironwork which both strengthened and beautified. So specialized did the construction of chests become that in 1254, the Provost of Paris, Etienne Boileau, ordained that their makers should have their own guild separate from that of the carpenters. The guild system was to prove a most important factor in the later development of the furniture trade, especially in France.

Two superficially similar articles in the 14th and 15th centuries were the *dressoir* and the *buffet*. Both seem to have begun as table-like bases over which stood a superstructure of shelving, but whereas the dressoir was a functional article used in the kitchen for dressing food and possibly in

Below: *Dome-topped Italian* cassone, *late 15th century. Carved and painted in tempera and with gilding over gesso, it displays the arms of the Montefeltro and Gonzago families, signifying that this was a dowry chest given on the occasion of a marriage.*

Above: *Full tester bed, French, early 15th century. The popular term 'four-poster' is very often a misnomer, as at this period it was more usual for there to be only two posts at the foot, the tester being supported at the other end by the panelled headboard, as in this example, which has linenfold decoration carved on the foot and panels of variously designed scrolls on the frieze.*

the hall (there being no 'dining room' as such) for serving it, the buffet was essentially a status symbol for the display of other status symbols. Its series of open shelves were draped with rich textiles on which stood silver plates and goblets – nominally for entertaining the guests but in reality to impress them with the wealth and in particular the rank of the host. The number of shelves was strictly regulated according to precedence. The Queen of France was permitted five shelves, the Countess of Amiens, three and lesser – but still noble – ladies, only one.

From the dressoir and the buffet a number of other pieces evolved. Various kinds of kitchen or farmhouse dresser of the type which later became known as a *vaisselier*, with a cupboard below and open shelves above, are descended from the medieval dressoir. The buffet, with its implications of 'estate', sired a long line of richly decorated armoires and cabinets. The earlier examples of these had doors carved or pierced with Gothic motifs.

In the 14th and 15th centuries, much of what is now France, Belgium and Holland had fallen under the rule of Burgundy, and it was in Burgundian Flanders that the old skill of panelled construction that had been practised by Byzantium was again revived, making the building of carcase furniture of a less unwieldy kind a practical possibility. Panelled doors of cupboards and the box-like seats of armchairs began, in France and elsewhere, to be carved with a formal pattern now known as 'linenfold' because of its fancied resemblance to folded linen but originally inspired by the effect created when parchment scrolls are unrolled. Linenfold was used also on the headboards of tester beds, on the fronts and ends of chests with panelled construction, and on the panelling of rooms.

Germany and Scandinavia

There is a 15th century German woodcarving in the Victoria and Albert Museum, London, which depicts the Holy Family resting on a settle which is similar in form to a church pew. The construction and decorative detail of a full-scale piece of furniture are faithfully reproduced, complete with linenfold carving on the panels and corner brackets of typical Gothic form which unite the rear seat-rail and the uprights of the ends. But more typical of the best German work of the period was the massively constructed armoire or press-cupboard which is often strangely impressive in spite of being surmounted by an exceptionally heavy, elaborately carved frieze and cornice that appear out of proportion to the small, carved panels at the centres of the doors. Heavy cornices and pediments were to remain a characteristic of much German and Scandinavian carcase furniture in subsequent periods.

England

The English devoted a substantial part of the later Middle Ages to fighting either their neighbours or each other, and this war-like spirit is reflected in several important chests carved with scenes that temper aggressiveness with chivalry. There is a 14th century tilting chest at the Victoria and Albert Museum, of crude plank construction and fitted with a handsome iron lock-plate, the front of which is carved in bold relief with a couple of jousting knights charging each other at full tilt. In the same museum another chest is carved, more skilfully, with the story of St George slaying the dragon. This theme occurs again on a chest of boarded construction with heavy stiles, dating from *c.*1380, at York Minster. The narrative style of the early chronicler who carved it is, to modern thinking, a little confusing, as the events in the tale are all combined in one overall design, with no clear indication of when one scene has ended and another begun. This chest might be regarded as one of the most important pieces of English Gothic furniture but for the fact that another very similar chest is at Bruges, and some authorities are of the opinion that both pieces are Flemish, not English.

Much more usual on early English furniture is a decorative device known as a chip-carved roundel. Chip-carving means exactly what it says – a design cut out in a series of small chips, with no attempt at modelling in relief. The word 'roundel' has a variety of meanings, but in this context it was simply a circular outline, anything from 5–25 cm (2–10 in) in diameter, within which a pattern of stylized stars, flowers or other formal devices was carved. It is not unusual to find three or four roundels, all carved with different motifs, on the same piece of furniture and arranged with little regard for symmetry. The roundel is sometimes said to have been inspired by the rose windows of Gothic cathedrals but it can be found on objects which

Above: *Oak* coffre *strengthened with iron bands and decorated with scrolls of wrought iron in typical French Gothic style, c.1250–1300. The solid planks are housed into vertical uprights, or 'stiles', at the corners. Other examples of the period have carved decoration.*

pre-date true Gothic architecture. It was by no means confined to Britain or to the Middle Ages, occurring on the artefacts of countries as far apart as Switzerland and Spain and as late as the 19th century.

The early English cupboard, or armoire, was the 'aumbry'. The French version of the word is still in regular use, while the use of 'aumbry' has died out in England but its original meaning is preserved in such words as 'alms' and 'almoner'. In the Middle Ages, and up to the time of the Reformation, the aumbry or 'almery' was a fitment with shelves, sometimes with doors, where food left over from a feast in a monastery or castle was put aside to give to the poor as alms. There is a fine example dating from the late 15th century, in York Minster, which has a castellated cornice and two pairs of doors with their original iron strap hinges. In other examples, the doors and ends are sometimes pierced, either crudely or with a conventional Gothic pattern, to provide ventilation for the food.

The word 'aumbry', variously spelled, persisted into the Elizabethan age in the later 16th century, until it was supplanted by 'cupboard'. Originally a 'cup board', literally for the display of silver cups, the Elizabethan version was an open structure on the lines of the French buffet and very much a prestige piece.

Armchairs in 15th-century England continued to enjoy respect when placed in the hall and especially during a meal served at a long table with detachable top, mounted on trestles and taken apart when the meal was over. The master of the house, his wife or perhaps a visitor of high rank would be accorded such a chair, while the rest of the company sat on stools or benches. The most prestigious type of chair however was the type with X-shaped supports, which had been promoted to the front rank by that champion of the Gothic style, Abbot Suger of St Denis. But a relatively crude chair, or even a stool, could be enhanced simply by placing it on a dais and draping it with a tapestry. There is also some evidence that chairs of various kinds were placed beside the bed in the chambers of powerful or well-to-do people. Some chairs had rudimentary upholstery.

The stools on which lesser mortals sat were fairly crude affairs of the three-legged type associated now with milkmaids. The legs of the stool were driven through holes in the seat and secured by wedges knocked down into the end grain. A stool which first appeared in England in the late 15th century had 'slab-end' supports which were slightly splayed and joined by a vertical board projecting through them and secured with wedges. The plain wooden top was softened by the addition of a cushion which was often embroidered by the women of the household in the wardrobe – a room in which clothes were stored in chests and behind curtains, with an area at the centre where the needlewomen were constantly at work.

Beds had frame constructions of a rather crude sort that were out of sight behind the hangings. A rich landowner with more than one house usually took the bed drapes with him on his manorial excursions and had them re-hung at the next port of call, where a framework awaited them.

Spain and Portugal

Spanish Gothic furniture tended to follow the international style, employing the usual shapes and decorative details but with certain striking embellishments provided by the Spanish-Moorish craftsmen who still employed Islamic motifs of a geometrical kind, in obedience – often only token – to the injunction of their old faith against the portrayal of animal or human forms.

The Moors were finally expelled from Spain in 1492, but some chose to remain and embrace the Christian faith. Their craftsmanship, especially in the art of inlay, was of a high order. It is known as Hispano-Moresque or *Mudéjar*, and was carried over from late Gothic to Renaissance.

Portuguese furniture in the Gothic style is perhaps the most difficult of all to estimate. What there is displays a love of intricate, ornate carving, but so much has been destroyed by earthquakes and other, man-made, disasters that little remains from before the 17th century.

Italy

Carving was not one of the arts in which Italian craftsmen excelled in the late Middle Ages, and the Gothic style, even in architecture, did not suit itself to the Italian climate or temperament. The great architects of Northern Gothic sought to lighten their cathedrals with great windows of stained glass to make the best of what sunshine there was in a cold climate. The Italians preferred smaller windows and large walls with painted decoration. It was painted decoration, rather than carving, that embellished their furniture, especially their version of the chest, the *cassone*.

It was natural enough that the Romanesque tradition lingered on in Italy, the country with more Roman remains than anywhere else. Concessions were made to the Gothic style but somewhat reluctantly, and for the most part Italy waited for her moment to come, as it did, towards the end of the 15th century. The Italian Renaissance really began about 1450, but the effect on furniture was not noticeable until about 1500, when its full force was released and a new furnishing style, at last more secular than ecclesiastical in inspiration, spread across Europe.

The Renaissance

Italy

Italian furniture is usually subdivided by regions rather than reigns. From *c.* 1350–1450 Italy was not one state but a number of small ones often at war with each other. The Italian League – a confederation founded in 1455 – fortunately led to a period of comparative unity, peace and prosperity in which the arts could flourish.

In its broad sense of 'the rebirth of learning', the Renaissance owed much to an attitude of mind cultivated a century earlier by the poet Petrarch (1304–74), who was passionately devoted to classical culture, collecting early manuscripts and other antiquities when few people bothered with such things. Although deeply religious, he was the founder of humanism, a philosophy which valued man's earthly existence and revived interest in the mythologies of Ancient Greece and Rome, finding in the legendary gods and goddesses many attractively human traits. A new style of architecture was inaugurated based on classical precepts, and eventually furniture was made to complement the new style.

Two major events contributed to the general awakening: first, the invention of printing in the West at about 1440, making books, including designs for craftsmen in wood, more widely available, and second, the fall of Constantinople to the Turks in 1453, which resulted in the transfer of the church's temporal power to Rome and an influx of skilled Byzantine workmen into that city.

The effect of all this on the furnishing of the Italian home – even the fairly prosperous ones – was only gradual. At first, richly decorated furniture in the new style was the exception rather than the rule and indeed the early effect of the Renaissance on Italian furniture was more negative than positive, the majority of pieces dating from *c.* 1450–80, being rather angular and plain. Traditional forms were preserved, and while Gothic ornament had been discarded, it had not yet been replaced by much Renaissance detail.

The true Renaissance man of studious inclination set aside a room for himself in which there were architecturally conceived, built-in shelves and cupboards to hold his precious books and manuscripts, collections of ancient coins, works of art and geological specimens. A chair to sit in, a table to work at and a portable desk with a sloping top which doubled as a lectern for heavy volumes – these were sufficient for his needs.

Left: *A 16th century room in the Palazzo Davanzati, Florence. The table has legs with shaped profiles which are echoed in the backs and slab fronts of the chairs. These are of the type known as* sgabello, *developed from the stool. The low cupboard against the back wall is a* credenza. *The settle against the right-hand wall is a* cassapanca, *developed from the* cassone *(chest) by the addition of a back and arms.*

Above: *St Jerome in his study, by Vincenzo di Biagio (called Catena), a painter of the Venetian school who died in 1531. The saint is shown at his desk which, like the bench seat and the cupboards for books, is architecturally conceived and built in as a permanent fixture – the kind of functional, dignified and angular furniture normally preferred by the scholar of the Italian Renaissance.*

If his taste ran to extravagant display, and he had the money to indulge it, the more public rooms of his house took on a new splendour to which, at first, rich textiles and finely-wrought silver contributed most. The piece of furniture on which he would be likely to lavish most expense was the Italian version of the chest, still known today by its old name of *cassone*. If he had married the daughter of a prosperous man, the cassone would have arrived with the bride, and would have held her dowry. In very rich families there was often a pair of such chests, one bearing the bride's coat-of-arms and the other, the bridegroom's.

This special use of the chest was adopted in many countries, and in some peasant communities it persisted as a tradition until well into the 19th century, complete with gaily painted decoration. In early 16th-century Italy, the cassone was often splendidly painted – in the north with biblical or other sacred subjects, in the south more often with pagan scenes taken from Roman mythology. Artists of the first rank did not consider it beneath their dignity to execute this work, with the result that some of the finest cassoni have been cut up to satisfy art collectors.

The woods most often used for painted furniture were pine and cypress overlaid with a coating of gesso. The texture of this type of plaster lent itself to delicate carving as well as painting, and many pieces – cassoni particularly – combine both forms of decoration. A plastic substance rather similar to gesso, called *pastiglia*, was used for crisply moulded decoration of panels and small caskets. The moulding was achieved with numerous small matrices which when pressed into the plaster, produced patterns of figures, plants and animals all over the surface.

The earlier cassoni were rectilinear in form, but by the middle of the 16th century enthusiasm for Roman remains led to the introduction of a chest based on the ancient sarcophagus, curved at the front and both ends, with a gentle swell that tapered inwards to the base. This type was usually made of walnut and was carved rather than painted. The degree of grandeur and sophistication varied from one region to another. In Tuscany, the carving usually followed formal, classical patterns of stylized leaves or scrolls, sometimes relieved with a figure of human or semi-human form at each of the two front corners. In Rome, the decoration of the cassone was more ambitious, the whole of the front often being occupied with a complex arrangement of human figures, more or less nude, disporting themselves among foliage or acting out a scene from an Olympian legend.

This use of the naked human form was, when the treatment remained naturalistic, a clear expression of both renewed interest in the classical ideal and a growing acceptance of the humanist regard for the dignity of mankind. Such decorative subjects, as well as the sarcophagus, the urn and various kinds of column were those which, in the early 16th century, were most often lifted piecemeal from the Roman repertoire.

The five 'orders' of architecture were codified by Sebastian Serlio in 1540: each is identified by a column with base, shaft, capital and entablature, and is decorated in one of the five styles known as Doric, Tuscan, Ionic, Corinthian and Composite. Both the decoration and the proportions often went wrong in the hands of Renaissance craftsmen, but some very satisfactory pieces in walnut, using these architectural devices with restraint, have survived in the form of the *credenza*, or sideboard, fitted with cupboards flanked by columns. The *cassapanca* – a cassone with box seat, fitted with a back and arms to make it into a handsome settle – sometimes looks like the prototype for a modern settee. It was probably inspired by Roman couches depicted in sculpture.

Roman-inspired designs were sometimes used for panels in chests and armoires decorated with intarsia, a kind of wood-mosaic or marquetry revived in the 15th century after hundreds of years of neglect, to be used at first for the panelling of churches and then for furniture in private houses. Piero della Francesca (*c.*1416–92) was one of the artists known to have provided designs for intarsia-work. The acknowledged expert in its execution was Fra Giovanni da Verona, who is thought to have decorated an armoire now at Monte Oliveto, Maggiore, near Siena, in 1502. At its best, intarsia work of this and slightly later dates, produced either in Italy, South Germany or the Netherlands, dazzles and confuses the spectator with *trompe l'oeil* effects. Architectural and still life subjects were so contrived as to appear three-dimensional. A related technique called *certosina* used small pieces of bone, metal and mother of pearl to form all-over geometrical patterns, especially popular in Lombardy and the Venice area.

Slab-ended tables of the kind described in the section on Ancient Rome were made in the second half of the 16th century, either of marble like the originals, or in walnut. The best-known extant marble table was made for the Farnese Palace in Rome about 1570, probably from a design by one of the finest architects of the day, Giacomo Barozzi da Vignola (1507–73).

The slab-end supports for these tables, especially those made of walnut, were often carved with grotesque, sphinx-

Left: *The X-shaped design of this 16th century Italian iron folding stool probably derives from the classical Roman curule or magistrate's stool. The supports and rails forming the arms are decorated with cast acanthus foliage, picked out with gilding and surmounted by brass finials. The seat has a cushion of scarlet and gold damask.*

Above right: *Northern Italian walnut* cassone *of panelled construction, early 17th century, carved with the kind of formally composed vases of flowers and carefully balanced, leafy scrolls often seen on the marble monuments of ancient Rome – an important source for the ornament, and occasionally the overall design, of furniture during the Renaissance period. This example fortunately retains its shaped and carved feet, often missing on* cassoni *of this kind.*

Right: *Commonly known by the French term* prie-dieu, *this Italian walnut praying-stool has the usual box-base on which the supplicant kneels, and a decorated superstructure providing an arm rest. The more usual type has a plainer superstructure fitted with drawers. In this example of c.1600, the Mannerist style of the late Renaissance employs caryatids – nude human figures serving as architectural supports – which strike a curiously pagan note in a piece intended for religious observance. This apparent contradiction is typical of the period.*

Above: *Although the high bed with its 'tester' or canopy continued in use in 16th century Italy, a fashion developed for a lower type, with headboard and posts but nothing overhead. This example of c.1550 was made in Tuscany.*

like figures. The word 'grotesque' is derived from *grotte* – the underground ruins in Rome where, in the late 15th century, ancient wall decorations were discovered that inspired such artists as Filippino Lippi (1457–1504) to use as features in their work the curious figures, half-animal, half-human, found in the decoration of houses such as that of Nero on the Esquiline Hill. Much fuller use of grotesques was made by Raphael (1483–1520) for interior decoration in a room at the Vatican and in the Villa Madama, Rome, both of which served as models for designers until about 1800.

A school of painting, now known as Mannerist (from the Italian *bella maniera*) originated in Rome and Florence in the 1520s. It made extensive use of grotesques, and engravings in the style, notably by Enea Vico (1523–67), were widely circulated throughout Europe and used as patterns by craftsmen in many materials – particularly silver and carved wood. The classical treatment of the human form, encouraged by the humanists, now combined with the extravagant exploitation of the semi-human and the monstrous to provide a furnishing style that was greeted enthusiastically north of the Alps.

France

French architecture, interior decoration and furniture – even the best – remained Gothic in spirit until the end of the 15th century, with cautious and uncertain borrowings of Renaissance ornament applied, often incongruously, to traditional forms. Italian cabinet work was much admired and imported by nobles who had seen it during military excursions. François I, King of France, was defeated and taken prisoner at the Battle of Pavia (1525) and to secure his release had to cede Burgundy and to give up the Italian territories he had previously claimed. This did not discourage him in the least from creating a magnificent palace and centre of culture at Fontainebleau where French and Italian talents combined to establish what is now known as the François I Style, or First Renaissance in France. This period is usually assumed to include the two previous reigns, when Italian influence began to have an effect, and so covers the period 1483–1547. It is very Italianate in feeling, the work at Fontainebleau being dominated by two Italian artists and designers of remarkable versatility, Giovanni Batista Rosso (1495–1540) and Francesco Primaticcio (1504–70).

They introduced Mannerist features into France – classical figures both draped and nude, architectural columns, garlands of flowers and *putti* (little naked boys, often referred to in English as 'cherubs'). Rosso is also credited with the invention of 'strapwork', an ornament of interlaced bands, angular or scrolled, rendered usually in flat, shallow carving – which was to become a very popular form of decoration not only in France but also in the Netherlands.

The palatial fashions of Fontainebleau gradually came to influence the furniture of the people throughout the 16th century, when a middle class comprised of tradesmen, farmers and merchants was creating homes for itself. During the first half of the 16th century, however, the variety of shapes and types of furniture did not greatly increase. The craftsman working at a modest level continued to produce coffers of the old kind, but decorated them with architectural pilasters dividing the panels. These were carved with isolated classical figures or, more often, with portrait medallions in profile, the latter sometimes attempts at portraying the owner and his wife. The dresser also maintained a Gothic form, with the cupboard above an open space and with arched or column supports. The carving again employs Renaissance motifs, sometimes in combination with linenfold panels.

A fresh treatment of the Renaissance idiom developed early in the next reign, which together with the two subsequent reigns covers the period called the Henri II Style, or High Renaissance in France spanning the years 1547–89. A group of designers and craftsmen who had worked at Fontainebleau set out with the deliberate intention of creating a 'national' style but the result was that while the visual language of the Renaissance remained basically Italian, only the accent was French.

Best remembered of these rebels is Jacques Androuet Du Cerceau the elder (*c.*1520–84), a designer who published the first French book of furniture designs about 1550. There is not a single piece of furniture in existence which entirely follows even one of his designs, the closest being a table at Hardwick Hall, England, which conforms at least partially to the published drawing.

Indirectly, however, the impact of Du Cerceau's highly personal interpretations of Renaissance styles must have been considerable. They cover two extremes, as well as what might be seen as a happy, or at least popular, compromise. He indulged in Mannerist fantasies of the most exaggerated kind, in which chimeras (grotesque monsters) often play a dominant rôle that can be interpreted as macabre, sensual or even comic. Yet many of his designs (and some of the extant pieces which, quite clearly, were based on them) are purely architectural, unrelieved by grotesques or, indeed, carved decoration of any kind.

Between these two limits of excess and purity there exist pieces of furniture numerous enough for examples to appear quite frequently on the open market, and which are of sensible, practical shapes, architecturally conceived, and are profusely carved with Mannerist subjects – though not in a way calculated to frighten anyone nervous.

Typical of this class is a two-stage cupboard, the *armoire-à-deux-corps*. In the late 16th century, this was made with the upper section narrower in width and shallower back to front than the lower. Both sections had panelled doors decorated with carving. Sometimes the centre portion of each panel was raised to form a slightly convex curve and was domed at the top. Against the uprights of the surrounding framework caryatids were applied – supports carved as human figures, male or female, usually naked to the waist and merging from there down into an architectural scroll, in rather the same way as a mermaid's form terminates in a fish's tail. The caryatid is a feature which appears from this time onwards on a variety of articles in many countries. The face often exhibits a horrific or horrified expression. The Ile de France was well known for its version of the *armoire-à-deux-corps* which was lavishly decorated with carving, particularly of Roman mythological figures. At one time the sculptor Jean Goujon (*d.*1567) was credited with the carving of many of these, but as he devoted much of his time to major sculpture in stone, it seems more likely that he influenced the design of provincial furniture but carved very little of it. The style continued in the more remote corners of the area until well into the 17th century.

Larger versions of the caryatid are called 'term' figures, and occur on full-length cupboards carved in the style of Hugues Sambin, a Burgundian who spent most of his life (*c.*1515–1600) at Dijon. In 1572 he published a book of designs devoted to *termes* which were no doubt used as copy books – not always very faithfully – by many craftsmen. Numerous pieces are attributed to his own hand, but none can be identified with certainty. Anything in his style is liable to have a Sambin label attached to it, including some good copies made in the late 19th century.

Chairs became more plentiful towards the end of the 16th century. One type, the *caquetoire* (gossip chair), was said to have been specially designed to accommodate women's skirts. It is an armchair which stands on simply-turned legs and has a seat that is very wide at the front,

Above right: *French Renaissance cabinet in walnut with carved and gilt decoration, c.1550, in the manner of Du Cerceau, whose designs illustrate similar pieces of classically inspired form.*
Right: *French cabinet in the style of François I c.1545. This type derives from the medieval* buffet *and* dressoir, *and is often called by one or other of these names. Although basically similar in construction to the example illustrated above, it is decorated with caryatid supports and other carved figures which define it as Mannerist in style.*

Above: *French cabinet, mid 16th century, in the manner of Du Cerceau, bought by Bess of Hardwick for Hardwick Hall, Derbyshire, which was finished in 1597. It is listed in the inventory of the contents made in 1601. The caryatid figures above and the sphinx-like harpies below are characteristic of the more bizarre Renaissance elements.*

Above: *Oak* caquetoire *(gossip chair), late 16th century, the back carved with a portrait medallion and scroll-work. The type was typically French, but examples were made in the Netherlands and in Scotland. It gets its name from the wide-fronted seat, which made it convenient for women in farthingale skirts.*

narrowing towards the high, panelled back. Another type, the *chaise lorraine*, is really a stool on turned front legs, but with the addition of a framed, open back. Often mistakenly called a child's chair, it was for general use and was a prototype for the standard chair without arms.

Beds developed in the later 16th century into a type with carved decoration on the posts and headboard so that interest was no longer centred entirely on the hangings which had, in the medieval period, disguised the crude framework. A French invention of the same period was the *lit de repos* or day-bed, which stood on six turned legs and had a slightly raked, panelled back. It may have been inspired by depictions of couches on Greek vases.

Several types of table, new to France, made their appearance. One, described as *à l'italienne*, was based on the Renaissance version of the Roman slab-ended marble table. It was usually made of walnut or chestnut, with the end-supports formed as pairs of fluted columns or draped figures. The feet are usually carved as beasts with yawning mouths. For extra stability, there is a line of turned legs coming down from under the table-top to a centre stretcher. They look impressive in Du Cerceau's drawings, but in practice the turnings are often clumsy and do not accord very well with the elaborate Renaissance decoration. A similar table, with an extending draw-leaf at each end, was based on an idea probably originating in the Netherlands.

The Netherlands

The dukes of Burgundy, who controlled large areas of the Netherlands from 1384 for almost a century, were celebrated for their rich collections of works of art including tapestries and furniture. Many of these were made by Netherlanders working in the Gothic tradition but coming increasingly under the influence of the Italian and French Renaissance styles introduced by the Burgundians. Foreign influences became even stronger and more varied after 1477, when Mary of Burgundy married the Austrian Emperor Maximilian of the House of Habsburg. Their grandsons Charles and Ferdinand eventually came to rule, between them, over a vast area of Europe and South America. Included in their territories were some 17 provinces of the Netherlands, which had to endure first an Austrian presence and then a Spanish occupying force.

Although the interlopers were strongly, even violently, resented over the years, the Netherlanders carried on with their work, absorbing ideas from many parts of the Habsburg empire and in return, made their own contribution to the design, construction and decoration of furniture, and exported not only the finished products but also several influential books of engravings. The draw-leaf table, mentioned in the section on France, probably originated in the Netherlands in the second half of the 16th century. Publications by Lucas van Leyden appearing *c.*1520–30 and those of Cornelis Floris and Cornelis Bos a few years later, included grotesque masks and particularly strapwork, which was a favourite device in the northern Netherlands, being rendered both as shallow-carved surface decoration and in fretted patterns for corner-brackets in the angles where the legs of tables joined the frames. An extended use of fretting is sometimes seen in the front stretchers of chairs.

Hans Vredeman de Vries (1527–1604) published a book of designs in Antwerp in 1565, many of which are concerned less with ornamentation than with shape and functional suitability. While some of his engravings – particularly of beds – are Mannerist and monumental, others are practical, fairly easy to follow and seemingly intended for the middle of the market rather than palaces. His son Paul (b.1567) issued two volumes of furniture designs in 1630, still Mannerist in style but more richly decorated and demonstrating the persistence of late Renaissance ornament in Northern Europe until well into the 17th century.

Coupled with the dislike by the Netherlanders of foreign rule was the conflict between Protestantism and Catholicism, which was not resolved until 1579 when a formal division was made between the Protestant Union of Utrecht in the north and the Roman Catholic League of Arras in the south. Regional differences occur in the furniture of every country and too much emphasis should not be placed on the effect of that arbitrary division; it is broadly true however, that the southern provinces tended to display a greater love of rich decoration, while those of the north leant towards a more sober style.

Antwerp was a centre for the production of large, two-stage cupboards, the upper stage recessed and supported on caryatids and with the panels of the doors inlaid with intarsia *trompe l'oeil* perspectives of buildings; of single-stage cupboards or sideboards derived from the Italian *credenza* but rather more chunky in proportion, well carved in solid oak and with ringed, Tuscan columns at the corners; and of cabinets with doors enclosing numerous small drawers, their fronts veneered in ebony or painted with mythological or biblical subjects. These were exported all over Europe.

Middelburg in Zeeland was equally celebrated for fine veneering and intarsia-work. In Holland, Amsterdam society was so highly organized that it had a guild of woodcarvers separate from that of the cabinetmakers, and members of both crafts would be needed to produce the local variant of the two-stage cupboard, the *Beeldenkast*,

Above: *Design for a bed in the Mannerist style by Hans Vredeman de Vries, whose* Differents pourtraicts de la menuiserie *were first published in Antwerp in 1565, the year in which he also issued* Architectura. *This includes designs for strapwork of the kind which ornaments the frieze on the canopy of this bed.*

so-called after the sculptural supports of caryatid type which characterize it.

Chairs in the Netherlands during the Renaissance displayed considerable variety, some of them following Italian or Spanish forms, the rectangular backs either upholstered in leather or left open with rows of delicately turned spindles. The legs on both these types are also turned to baluster shapes and often have two sets of stretchers, one above the other. The X-shaped frame, either folding or rigid, was also popular.

In spite of the de Vries extravaganzas, the Netherlands bed was often a dignified example of architectural furniture. It was sometimes built into the corner of the bedroom – which very often served also as a living room – and the back and one side were panelled to match the walls. A classical column would support the tester on the one exposed corner allowing curtains to be drawn at the foot and on the open side, giving privacy at night and hiding the bed from sight by day. In the early 17th century, the panelling was often set off with mouldings arranged in a variety of geometric patterns. This type of decoration

Above: *Spanish* vargueño *on* pie de punte *base. The writing-cabinet itself is late-16th or early-17th century, and is decorated in the Spanish-Moorish style known as* mudéjar, *derived from Islamic abstract patterns and practised by those Moors who became Christianized and remained in Spain after the end of Moorish rule.*

occurs on a wide range of furniture, the earliest examples being from the south, where Spanish influence was strongest.

Spain and Portugal

Mouldings applied geometrically to panels and drawer-fronts (in the style loosely known in England and America as 'Jacobean') probably owe their origin to abstract patterns introduced by Moors and Arabs into the Iberian peninsula which was in many ways, especially in the south from the 8th century to the final defeat of the Moors in 1492, more oriental than western.

The Portuguese added to this existing heritage by the establishment during the reigns of Manuel I (1495–1521) and John III (1521–57), of settlements and colonies as far to the East as India and Japan, from which furniture including lacquered beds was imported. What little Portuguese furniture survives from the period, taken together with written accounts of it, suggests that these mixed flavours from the Orient were combined during the earlier part of the 16th century with Italian and French Renaissance styles. Later, and especially after Spain and Portugal were technically united under Philip II of Spain in 1580, Spanish and Spanish-Moorish styles probably dominated the output of the Lisbon guild of furniture-makers, which was well established by the mid-16th century when the city was at the height of its wealth and power.

'Arabesque' was the name given to a complex pattern of inlaid scrolls, leaves and tendrils, probably deriving from Saracenic metalwork and forming part of the Spanish-Moorish repertoire of ornament that spread in the 16th century to many other countries, particularly those, like Spain, under Habsburg domination. In Spain, rich from conquests in South America, silver from that source was plentiful and was used for overlaying and inlaying furniture with arabesques and other devices. The style, known as 'plateresque' (from *plata*: silver), is extended to include pieces similarly decorated in other metals. A Moorish form of inlaid work, closely related to Italian *certosina* (described in the section on the Italian Renaissance), employed ivory or bone for formal, all-over patterns.

Carving was often of a high order, whether following Moorish abstract designs, or figurative Italianate motifs such as portrait medallions which were sometimes carried out in a peculiarly Spanish way by carving them in relief and fret-cutting around the profiles. The medallions were then mounted on a ground of richly-coloured velvet previously laid over the foundation. This kind of carved and pierced decoration was often gilded and further embellishment was provided by the addition of elaborate lock-plates, hinges and mounts, sometimes in silver, until economic crises made it necessary in the late 16th century to forbid such extravagance.

This kind of lavish treatment was accorded most often to a characteristically Spanish prestige piece, the *vargueño*, a chest with a hinged fall-front that could be used as a writing leaf and which, when lowered, reveals an elaborate fitment of small drawers. Frequently the top of the *vargueño* also opens. A version without the fall-front, in which the drawers are permanently exposed, is the *papileira*. Both types were normally supplied with stands, which take two main forms: one is the *taquillon* – essentially a chest-of-drawers, often with geometrically arranged mouldings on the drawer-fronts; the other is the *pie de puente* – a stand with trestle-ends for legs, strengthened either with a stretcher at the base and a line of turned uprights along it, or with a pair of finely-wrought bracing irons.

From the 16th century onwards, bracing irons occur on many Spanish tables having splayed trestle supports composed either of turnings or flat members shaped at their edges. Both types are mounted on 'sledge' feet, i.e. lengths of wood of square section which run from back to front at each end of the piece of furniture and with a substantial forward projection. Crude versions of these trestle-ended tables, often in pine or chestnut rather than the walnut found in the finer examples, continued to be made in peasant communities over a very long period and are often difficult, if not impossible, to date with certainty.

Several types of chair are characteristic of the Spanish Renaissance period, but sometimes lead to confusion because they were imitated or adapted in other countries, even in areas outside the wide dominions of the Habsburgs.

Above: *The bedroom of Philip II of Spain in the monastery of Escorial, built to fulfil a vow he made after the battle of St Quentin in 1557. The bed has simply turned posts, enriched with hangings. The armchairs are of the type known as* sillón de fraileros *(monk's chair), with square back and high front stretcher. A variation has 'sledge' feet – rails running from back to front under the legs.*

The term *sillón de fraileros* (monk's chair) is applied to an armchair with a rather square-looking frame. The legs rest on sledge feet and at the front have a wide stretcher linking them, relieved with pierced or carved decoration. Despite its name, the monk's chair was by no means confined to monastic use, as the secular coats-of-arms sometimes carved on the stretchers testify. The seat and rectangular back were covered either in velvet or finely tooled, coloured and gilded leatherwork called *guadamecil*, a Moorish speciality, its name deriving from Gadames in Tripolitania. The art was taken up elsewhere, especially in the Netherlands.

Another type of Spanish chair had no arms or upholstery. The seat was of solid wood, and the back was arcaded by the insertion of spindles below a shaped rail, in a way reminiscent of Romanesque decoration. This type – also known, a little confusingly, as a 'monk's chair' – may well have influenced the development of English chairs with arcaded backs made in Derbyshire and Yorkshire in the 17th and early 18th centuries.

Above: *Four-poster bed c.1580 from Schloss Amberg. The silk canopy is a modern replacement. The bedstead is of purplewood with inlays of ivory in ebony and ebony in ivory – a type of decoration which was very fashionable in the Germanic countries during the late 16th and 17th centuries, and which was partly due to Moorish influence filtering northwards from Spain.*

Above: *Nuremberg cupboard in oak and ash dated 1541 and made for the Holzschuhen family to a design by Peter Flötner, who worked in Nuremberg c.1522–46. The simple outline and the confining of carved decoration to panels within plain frames combines to produce a welcome sense of discipline at a time when enthusiasm for ornament often outweighed sound judgement.*

There is a type of chest made entirely of iron, with a multiple system of locks, popularly known as an 'armada chest'. Though German, these chests are often wrongly thought of as Spanish.

Austria, Germany, Switzerland and Scandinavia

The influence of the Renaissance on Germanic furniture became marked at about the same time as Charles, the Habsburg king of Spain, succeeded his grandfather as German king and head of the Holy Roman Empire in 1519. Impressive though his titles and the extent of his domains appear, the German kingship was little more than an honorary presidency over a number of states governed by princes who were no longer mere feudal lords but sovereigns in their own right, some of whom set up court with pretensions to grandeur. The older concept of fealty was undermined by Renaissance thinking, and the religious disturbances brought about by the Reformation disarrayed it even further. All these factors had some bearing on the development of furniture-making.

In Northern Germany where Protestantism was strongest, the styles of the Northern Netherlands (also Protestant) were influential. Carcase furniture, such as the two-stage cupboard and the armoire, displayed carved decoration in which the solid oak ground was often covered with strapwork, animal and human heads and closely-packed, scrolling leaf patterns in the manner of Heinrich Aldegrever (d.1561), who worked at Soest in Westphalia, producing woodcuts and engravings that provided woodworkers with patterns for Renaissance ornament. Westphalia – close to France and sometimes adopting French mannerisms – produced a distinctive class of furniture over a long period. Some fine chests of massive, housed construction, decorated with simple carving or left severely plain but for stout iron bands, have survived from the 16th century onwards in quantities large enough to be available to the private collector.

Scandinavia accepted with caution elements of Netherlandish and Germanic Renaissance decoration, applying it with discretion to Romanesque and Gothic forms. The restrained application of Renaissance ornament to Scandinavian furniture resulted in a graciousness not always evident elsewhere in northern Europe in the 16th century.

Shortly after 1600, Franz Pergo of Basle made furniture carved with Mannerist motifs. Switzerland adopted some styles from Italy and France but the birthplace of Calvin was strongly Protestant and tended to prefer furniture nearer in style to that of the Netherlands and North

England

The story of English furniture in the 16th century is the story of oak, that sturdy, durable, most English of woods, with which the country was richly stocked throughout medieval times thanks to the extensive mature forests which covered the land. The forests served England well, too well, in fact: generations plundered this natural resource with such abandon that consumption outstripped planting.

Oak was used for many purposes, not least furniture. Domestic walnut and elm partially augmented oak, and inlay of holly and bog oak – black-hued wood from ancient trees preserved in peat bogs – was used when the growth of affluence bred the desire for more ornamentation. But it was oak, employed in the solid, that saw the 16th century in, and as the principal material for furniture, it was oak that was still dominant when the Tudors handed over their reign to the Stuarts at the beginning of the 17th century.

There are more than 300 varieties of oak, the English species being *Quercus robur*, the common oak, and *Quercus sessiliflora*, fruited oak. The timber is hard and lasting, its colour varying from brown to white and, as the 17th century diarist and sylviculturist, John Evelyn, observed, it 'will not easily glew to other wood, nor not very well to its own kind'. There can be no greater tribute to its durability than the quantity of pieces of oak furniture which have survived, rich with the patina of age, to the present day.

Because mature oaks were felled in huge numbers, Henry VIII was moved to pass a law enforcing the preservation of oak woods. By the middle of Elizabeth's reign England was sufficiently alerted to the drain of its natural heritage that oak planting was widespread. Ironically, however, by the time these woods reached maturity one hundred years later in the reign of Charles II, the age of walnut was in full flower and oak was soon to be relegated to carcase construction and drawer linings – except in country areas, where it never lost its popularity for any and every type of furniture.

The importance of oak in the history of furniture has never been doubted, even by those who have contributed to its denigration as a furnishing material throughout most of the present century. Today, however, oak has regained its esteem among collectors, interior designers and all those who appreciate soundly made, practical and attractive furniture. Oak furniture is also a remarkably strong hedge against inflation; in the 1970s it increased in value at almost twice the average rate of all antique furniture, a rate which shows no sign of slackening in the 1980s.

There are several reasons for this popularity. Long considered too heavy and cumbersome in modern settings, oak received a fillip from the growth of the 'second home'

Left: *In its setting of a panelled room from Sizergh Castle, Westmorland, stands a buffet or court cupboard (from the French for 'short'), dating from about 1590. It is of the traditional sideboard type of three open shelves for the display of domestic vessels, but it is – for its time – uncommonly fashioned in walnut, inlaid with holly and bog oak.*

Below: *A magnificent draw leaf table of about 1600, in oak inlaid with sycamore, bog oak and other woods, dominates a panelled room section removed from the 'Old Palace' at Bromley-by-Bow. Heavy bulbous legs and floor level stretchers are characteristic. Oak is also the material for a decorative chest of 1637 and an early 17th century buffet.*

Above: *During Tudor times a new middle class prospered to enjoy the fruits of growing wealth. The home no longer necessarily centred round a single, huge dining table. Smaller tables were designed for a number of domestic purposes. A trestle type such as this from Barrington Court could be put against a wall when not in use.*

and 'country cottage' habit. It fitted in with new interior design standards and harmonized – surprisingly – with the light Scandinavian look. Interest in oak was also influenced by, as well as itself influencing a boom in collecting pewter, the latter looking best in an oak setting. In cool and temperate European climates and particularly in North America, where central heating has been found to play havoc with soft-wooded, veneered furniture, oak is liked because it resists the assault of temperature, just as it can resist the onset of time and wear. Above all, as the better furniture of the 18th century became popular with collectors, soared in value and became scarce, oak remained available – and underpriced.

Astonishing as it may seem, there is relatively more extant, top quality furniture from the century prior to 1650 than from the century which followed, simply because 'soft' walnut is so vulnerable in comparison with oak. Availability is patently an effective spur to collecting and oak furniture has the advantage of having been produced – by rural but nevertheless highly skilled joiners and cabinetmakers – long after the so-called age of oak ended towards the close of the 17th century. Later still, the Gothic revivalists of Victorian times turned to oak, adding to the fund of material available, although some of their work appeals only to certain tastes.

England celebrates in song its traditional 'hearts of oak', but there is more to this than sentimental patriotism and a nostalgic pride in an oak-armoured navy. A strong national element in furniture expressed itself by translating the vivid and decorative forms of the European late Renaissance into staid and simple terms. Changes in thought and living styles take time to spread and the Renaissance affected England much later than Italy or France; English furniture retained its natural and somewhat rough character longer than the French. It was as though England had more time to assimilate the results of the flowering of free thought, and ideas were put into practice at a time when social, economic and political changes had created a new background. In much the same manner, American furniture of later times developed in interesting, fresh ways by being subjected to a time lag; thus a European furniture style of one decade would be embraced and exploited in the Americas a decade or two later as a result of new climates of social and political feeling.

For England, therefore, the start of the 16th century and the reign of the Tudors marked a dividing line between the Middle Ages and the modern era. Europe was being influenced by the development of Renaissance free thought, education and nationalism – the last being a powerful factor in the progress of each country's furniture styles. Henry VII, intent on unifying the houses of York and Lancaster, was equally determined that their respective nobility, sadly debilitated by the Wars of the Roses, should never again wield the power of earlier days. The support he gave to commerce and foreign trade, his good husbandry of national finances and his choice of new men as ministers all helped to cement the allegiance of wealthy merchants, country gentry and yeomen farmers. A new middle class was being born to stimulate and enjoy innovations and improvements in living style. And furniture was at the forefront of this trend.

The affairs of the church dominated English politics during the 16th and part of the 17th centuries. It was the church, too, which had a profound effect on the course of furniture design and use. In no other area was this more apparent than that of coffers and chests, the earliest examples of case furniture.

Three forms of chest had existed in England before the dawn of the 16th century. In the days of Henry VII (1485–1509) they were all still in use and indeed two of them were to be made in their original forms until the early 17th century. Significantly, examples of each type have lasted to the present day, usually in the custody of churches or other ecclesiastical institutions, and are yet another tribute to the durability of stout oak.

The earliest and most crude form is made of a hollowed log, one example of which is at Milton Bryant Church, Bedfordshire. The chest is banded with iron to keep its shape, and is typical of medieval construction: an oak trunk would be split transversely and the lower section would then be hollowed out and banded; the section first removed would then be employed as the lid.

A later form was the boarded chest, composed of solid front, back and underpart, all of which fitted into ends which became the feet, thus raising it from the damp floor. Examples of these types were made until the early 17th century, although by that time the richer religious houses and the nobility and merchants were enjoying much more sophisticated items of chest furniture which developed with the growth of skilled craftsmanship and foreign

Left: *When the 16th century began oak and iron-bound caskets and boxes such as this were in common use in England. They were of simple joined construction and were traditionally employed in churches for the storage of relics, archives and valuables. This casket, about 18 inches wide, is carved in the Gothic style.*

influence. Yet another type was the chest of framed panels, joined together in simple but effective case-work. This type was made for some 300 years until it was relegated to the backwaters of 'country furniture' with the emergence of chests fitted with drawers and of cabinets.

The social structure of society inevitably meant that the ecclesiastical environment was the principal source for the development of boxes and chests whose earliest use was for the storage of books, religious writings being the most ancient of works. Even in some of the most exalted homes and families the priest might be the only literate member of the community. Therefore, by the beginning of the 'modern era' – England's true emergence from the Middle Ages – early 16th-century society regarded the storage of books and documents as an ecclesiastical function. There were however, many other reasons why the chest developed in more sophisticated forms under the aegis of the church.

Coffers and chests were employed in churches to hold regalia, jewels and vestments as well as archives, and were also in use as collection boxes. Large hinges and locks, with carved tracery in the old Gothic style, are characteristic of such boxes used in Henry VII's day. There are ecclesiastical records of these boxes and the purposes to which they were put. One collecting box of St Edmondsbury was to be placed 'near the door without the choir in the way of the people as that therein persons might put their contributions for the building of the tower'. By Henry's day a tradition of coffers with three locks had become established to ensure security, its principle being a 'failsafe' system of three custodians, none of which could open the coffer and gain access to the contents without agreement and participation of the other two.

A 16th-century Bishop of Chichester, worried about the effect of dampness on archives and vestments, urged the need for regular 'careful examination lest anything should perish by the boxes becoming old, or by the eating of worms, or in any other way'. The importance of boarded chests, raised above the ground on their end boards, was being given wider recognition.

The Wars of the Roses and the attendant unrest had fostered lawlessness on a grand scale and we have seen how Henry VII, determined to stamp this out, had taken measures to create a more ordered and peaceful life for his people. Yet old habits die hard and the very lawlessness of the age provided another reason why the church became associated with the development of case furniture.

Thievery and mayhem traditionally stopped short of the church doors, and domestic chests, vulnerable to pilfering in private homes, were entrusted to the church's care. There are examples of wills specifying that legacies of

Below: *By 1637 when this Renaissance style joined oak chest was made, such items of church and home furniture had long been customarily raised on board panel legs. The exuberance of the carving matched the mood of Charles I's day. Despite the growing use of cupboards for storage, chests were still popular for the laying down of linen.*

valuables such as plate or jewellery should be stored in abbeys or monasteries until the beneficiary came of age. On that date the valuables would be removed, but often the chests which had protected them would be left with the church. Thanks to careful husbandry by church officials through the centuries, these chests exist today as almost the only examples of types then in everyday use.

Boxes and chests however, were spreading beyond the domain of the church. On record is Henry VIII's passion for boxes or 'deskes', fitted with places for small implements such as 'sycssores and a payer of compas'. An inventory of the wardrobe of Catherine of Aragon referred to a 'desk covered with black velvette and garnysshed withe gilt nayles'. Other archives make mention of many boxes.

By the early 1500s the fronts of panelled chests were being divided into two and later three, sections, each panel being carved with scenes that were not always of religious origin. Designs of jousting knights for instance, might be used. As the improving quality of middle and upper-class life became apparent, the stock of household goods and utensils was growing, demanding special storage space. Chests were an obvious repository for plate but household linen – hangings, bedsheets and the richer clothes – was a factor increasingly to be considered. Carved panelling known as linenfold, executed to represent folds of linen, designated the purpose of many household chests. It was also profusely employed in the panelling of choir stalls and domestic apartments and became a popular feature of interior decoration throughout Elizabethan times.

Left: *Linenfold carving – fashioned in the form of folded linen – gave a clue to the function of storage coffers and chests in the early 16th century (although it was used extensively in room panelling as well). In this simple oak coffer linenfold appears in an unusual horizontal form.*
Below: *This oak inlaid chest was presented in 1588 to the church that is now Southwark Cathedral in London. Known as a Nonsuch chest, it bears architectural decoration in the style of one of Henry VIII's palaces built from designs by Toto del Nunziata (hence the popular corruption, Nonsuch). What makes the chest a landmark in furniture history, however, is the set of three small drawers in the lower part, evidence of a dramatic innovation in design.*

The panelling of the great halls of the early Tudor period displays these formal linenfold patterns and much of it bears evidence of the influence of a new breed of craftsmen who were being imported from the Continent to teach their English brothers. Peaceful times in England and the growth of domestic refinement required more comfortable surroundings. Royalty had its sumptuous palaces at Windsor and Richmond while elsewhere, feudal castles had given way to mansions which found ready employment for foreign craftsmen, artists and woodcarvers.

In Henry VIII's reign a traditional carving style which was a mixture of both Gothic and classic Renaissance was employed. A notable example of this transitional movement can be seen in the woodwork of King's College Chapel, Cambridge. Superb examples of the newly invigorated woodcarvers' skills can also be seen in the Great Hall at Hampton Court (dating from the end of the first quarter of the century). The roof and choir stalls of Henry VII's Chapel at Westminster Abbey are rich in the new art. Later the Elizabethan carvers took the ribbon decoration of the French and the intricately laced strapwork of the Flemish, and combined them with grotesque figurework – creatures that were half human, half monster – in a distinctive style adapted from foreign ideas.

These influences from abroad were of immense importance. The opening of new trade outlets with the East and West, the development of England's naval strength, first under Henry VIII and then under Elizabeth, and concurrent increases in prosperity at home, all meant the discovery of new horizons. Added to this background was the flight of Continental talent to Britain from European religious and political persecution, a factor that was to feed the furnishing and design industry of England for many years to come.

Italian influence was strong, both directly and indirectly (through movements from the Low Countries, where Italian Renaissance seeds had been quick to flower). In mid-Elizabethan times the country benefited from the flight of Antwerp merchants and their attendant craftsmen who were suffering at the hands of the Duke of Parma.

In Southwark Cathedral, London, there stands a magnificent treasure which owes its existence to the European influx into England during the 16th century. Not only is it yet another example of the church's part in furniture development, but it offers a rare opportunity to examine a piece which represents an important landmark in case furniture design: the transition from the lidded box to the chest of drawers as a storage unit.

What had begun as the Church of St Mary Overie in 1106, probably on the site of an earlier religious establishment, became in 1540 the parish church of St Saviour, and in 1905 the Cathedral of Southwark. In 1588 the church received from Hugh Offley, Lord Mayor of London, and his father-in-law, Richard Harding, an oak chest which stands 0.99 m (3 ft 3 in) high and 1.98 m (6 ft 6 in) wide. The architecturally representative decoration in coloured wood on the front gives the chest its name – Nonsuch. Nonsuch chests, many of which were made in southern England in the mid- to late-16th century, are so named from a corruption of Toto del Nunziata, an Italian artist

Above: *Throughout the period in which oak dominated English furniture making it was found in no sturdier or more useful form than as the ubiquitous joint or joined stool. This example with carved and turned legs of fluted baluster type has broad stretchers characteristically placed at floor level.*

who was responsible for designs from which Henry VIII had a palace built at Cheam in Surrey. Late 16th century Nonsuch chests usually bore a resemblance in their decoration to the palace's appearance as depicted in contemporary illustrations. The Southwark piece is so decorated and it is believed to have been the work of German immigrant craftsmen, to whom similar chests have been attributed.

The Southwark chest is on an arcaded stand of probably later date and sports characteristic subsidiary decoration of floral arabesques. But what sets it apart as the harbinger of a new and exciting development in case furniture is the existence of three small drawers in its lower portion. It is without doubt an extremely early example of a chest with drawers, although it is not claimed to be the first or even among the first such examples. Nevertheless chests with drawers did not become common in England for a decade or two after Offley and Harding made their presentation to the church.

When Margaret, daughter of Henry VII, travelled to Scotland to marry James IV in 1503 she attended a prenuptial supper in the course of which she complained that the stool given to her was 'not for hyr Ease', whereupon the king offered her his 'Chayre', clearly the only one in the great hall of the castle.

The anecdote, recorded by the herald who accompanied Margaret, is more than just a tale of royal gallantry. It tells

Above: *Basic styles of oak stool and settle laid down in Henry VIII's and Elizabeth's reigns survived in country workshops for many years afterwards. A box stool of James I period has a rising lid with hasp lock. The mid-18th century settle has seat storage facilities.*

us much about the furnishing styles of the day. While the head of the house sat in the chair (probably the only one), benches, forms and simple joined stools sufficed for the less exalted. However, during the reign of the Tudors, seat furniture was to undergo a revolution. Indeed, it was already well under way in England at the time the Scottish James was attempting to show his bride that he could keep her in the manner to which she was accustomed.

In the early years of the 16th century three types of chair were in existence. The first was a simple development of the lidded chest, which was given panelled sides and back to form seating of the settle type but which still retained its box-seat compartment for the storage of linen. A similar natural progression had been witnessed in Italy, home of the Renaissance and many furniture innovations, where the massive, elaborately carved chest known as a *cassone* had been given low arms and a back to become a *cassapanca*. It was a piece that could seat several persons and though still retaining its chest, the *cassapanca* now fulfilled the principal function of the settle. It is interesting to note that while sunny Italy opted for low back and arms, the English settle developed a distinctive tall style which offered more comfort and protection in the draughty halls and chambers of northern climes.

The English settle was not, of course, a child of Tudor times. Its origins dated back some two centuries or more. Indeed, the styles of this particular type of seating in the 16th century deviated from the established Gothic only in details of ornamentation. It was translated into a 16th century product through the carver's vocabulary: Tudor roses, scrolls and dolphins, zigzags and interlaced strap-work, as well as linenfold. It was a happy repository for this last style of carving, which was ideally suited to recti-linear forms and Elizabethan examples of such chairs are among the aristocrats of early oak, commanding astro-nomic prices when (rarely) they appear on the market today. The Victoria and Albert Museum in London has an example of a type known as a 'joyned chair', high backed, but with sides at arm level. Italianate Renaissance carving decorates a head panel, but the remainder of the chair back and the front of the seat are carved in linenfold, the two styles harmonizing perfectly.

The settle type of chair has met with mixed fortunes in modern markets. Understandably, anything from the 16th century, which is frequently termed for convenience 'Elizabethan', and pieces from a similarly wide-embracing 'Jacobean' period command a high price. But settles, like some of the chests described in the earlier chapter, continued to be made throughout successive centuries. They epitomize country furniture and their simple, joined construction offers no great challenge to the unsophisticated carpenter. They belong to the farmhouse kitchen but are equally at home in the country pub. But, as a Sussex auctioneer remarked after a sale in which half a dozen settles had provided the only downbeat note in a catalogue of scintillating prices for oak furniture, 'what do you do with a settle in a home?' Its high-backed form dictates that the settle be placed against a wall to prevent it becoming a troublesome room divider.

In a more exalted form, the 'joyned chair' had existed in the 15th century as a canopied piece of great height which stood on a small raised platform in the hall and from which the master could survey his household ranged on benches below. Sometimes they were made to be dismantled and were provided with leather packing cases into which the chair could be placed when the owner travelled from house to house. By the time of the Tudors, this travelling function had necessitated the emergence of a second type of chair, the X-frame, similar in construction to the modern camp stool and of a convenient form which lent itself to campaign and travelling furniture of wood and metal through several centuries up to the present. Originally of simple construction, with loose cushions provided for comfort, the X-frame was given a new lease of popularity in the mid-16th century, by which time it had developed into a luxurious piece in keeping with the mood of the time. The woodwork was completely clothed in velvet, damask or silk and the loose cushions rested on a webbing support attached at each side to the rails of the frame. There is evidence of such chairs being provided in numbers for Henry VIII, wide, substantial examples ideally suited to the king's ample girth and weight, and richly fringed with gold silk. In the early years of Elizabeth's reign the court coterie vied with each other by ordering immensely costly examples in emulation of the queen's taste for X-frame chairs. They had frames which were gilded, painted and carved and often revealed the influence of the Italian style.

Winchester Cathedral possesses an oak X-frame chair, somewhat bare in its unrestored state, but which once was covered in blue velvet secured with gilt-headed nails and capped with metal finials. It dates from about 1550, the decade in which Elizabeth came to the throne. In this traditional form, the X shape is viewable from the front and rear. An oak armchair in the Victoria and Albert Museum, on the other hand, has X-shaped legs at the sides and the whole is meant to fold somewhat like a modern garden chair. It is a remarkably early example of travelling convenience, dating from the turn of the 16th century.

The 'turned' chair was the third type which made enormous strides in design during the century and became the basic form of seating in Elizabethan England. It was constructed of separate pieces, socketed together and the turning was of the knobbed or ringed variety. Its construction had become more open and the seat was usually of ample dimensions to take the voluminous clothing of the time. Frequently it had a raked back for comfort and embodied four plain, stout stretchers. These were now about two inches above the floor, earlier stretchers having been at floor level. Originally designed as a foot rest and a protection from the cold of stone floors whose only covering would have been rushes, stretchers were gradually raised as carpets became more prevalent. By the 17th century the function of stretchers as foot rests had disappeared completely and they remained as essential units of construction and vehicles for decoration. The discerning collector knows that the faker can never successfully reproduce the scuffed, worn look of early oak stretchers, caused by the feet of generations; stools and chairs, benches and forms sold as examples of 15th and 16th century oak furniture are immediately suspect if the stretchers present a telltale unused appearance.

Above: *Sturdy and functional – an oak chair of 1641 with the date carved into its slightly raked back. Its form offers no encumbrance to the ample skirts of the day. The stretchers by this time have risen some two or three inches above floor level, and economy dictates that the turned leg decoration is reserved only for the front members.*

A common feature of chairs was their display of two turned legs at the front and plain ones at the back. There are records of many with triangular seats, a style which continued into the 17th century, and often sloping arms swept down from the top corners of the back. All chairs had

Above: *Triangular seats were not uncommon during the 16th century and well into the 17th. They were convenient for voluminous clothing and would stand attractively in the corner of a room. The seat of this ash framed chair is rushed and the absence of turning and its somewhat rustic appearance suggests it was made by an English country joiner.*

loose cushions; upholstered chairs began to appear late in Elizabeth's reign, although strictly this was a development of the 17th century. A contemporary observer wrote in 1597 that 'the fashion of cushioned chayrs is taken up in every merchant's house'. Large cushions, satin embroidered and edged with gold or silver lace, were used extensively for window seats in Elizabethan mansions.

Clues to everyday life in Elizabethan times have come down to us through invoices, household books and, frequently, from contemporary diarists. A prolific writer was William Harrison, topographer, chronologist, parson and scholar (1534–93), who, in *The Description of England*, ranged over a wide variety of topics. On the subject of domestic life-styles in the steadily prospering upper and middle class society of England he is at his most enlightening:

> The furniture of our houses also exceedeth and is grown in manner even to passing delicacy: and herein I do not speak of the nobility and gentry only, but likewise of the lowest sort in most places of our south country that have anything at all to take to. Certes in noblemen's houses it is not rare to see abundance of arras, rich hangings of tapestry, silver vessel and so much other plate as may furnish sundry cupboards to the sum oftentimes of a thousand or two thousand pounds at the least, whereby the value of this and the rest of their stuff doth grow to be almost inestimable. Likewise in the houses of knights, gentlemen, merchantmen and some other wealthy citizens it is not geson (rare) to behold generally their great provision of tapestry, Turkey work, pewter, brass, fine linen, and thereto costly cupboards of plate.

Harrison is using the term 'cupboard' – literally cup board – in its widest sense to denote any wooden structure with open display spaces on which to place plate and other utensils. In many Elizabethan inventories the words cupboard, aumbry and press seem to have been interchangeable.

Harrison provides interesting background information about developments in household fashions – many of which affected the progress of furniture design – when he touches on the question of glassware. Amid the increasing affluence of the more fortunate classes, glassware was apparently very fashionable, infinitely more fashionable than everyday gold and silver.

Tables had an important part to play in the advancement to more luxurious styles of living. The chimney corner was taking the place of the open hearth and the large, public hall was giving way to smaller private rooms. Wealth led to the search for privacy and at dining times more intimacy was demanded. The design of the Englishman's table reflected these changes.

Medieval tables had been solid baulks of timber placed on trestles, the whole being removed and stacked against a side wall when the hall had to be cleared for dancing or other purposes. From these beginnings, Tudor England inherited the long refectory table, which had a rectangular top with fixed, simple supports united by four stretchers used as foot rests. The mid-16th century saw carving appearing on the legs and on the frieze below the table top. Only rarely was there inlay of holly and bog oak. When not in use, the tables were covered with what William Harrison has referred to as 'Turkey work', which was a type of heavy fabric woven with knotted pile in imitation of carpets from Asia Minor and Persia. Similar pieces continued to be used as table coverings and drapes for chair backs and seats until well into the seventeenth century.

Table legs were carved in baluster form or bulbous shapes, the latter being of enormous proportions in Elizabeth's time and giving oak tables of that period a very distinctive appearance.

Expanding tables appeared in Italy and France and then England early in the 16th century, the draw-top being among the commonest. Later came centre-opening tables and towards the close of the century, the new, more intimate living styles produced the drop-leaf type. Also introduced was the gate-leg table, a species which, however, has more in common with Stuart times than Tudor. Side tables were extremely rare, the buffet and court cupboard fulfilling the function of serving surfaces.

In all the new variations of the table, the carver of Elizabethan England was finding new and exciting opportunities to show off his talents. The vase-shaped and massively bulbous legs showed Flemish and German origin. On rare occasions mythical beasts formed the supports of tables. An elaborate, draw-top table from about 1600, now in a private collection, has intricately carved supports of winged monsters to which lion cubs have been added on the four corners at floor level. In the Burrell Collection of the Glasgow Art Gallery and Museum there is an oak hall table bearing the typical six legs of bulbous form and sporting a very 'avant garde' set of claw-like feet which predate the claw and ball foot by well over a century. Elizabethan exploration was not limited to sea-going ventures in gold-laden hemispheres.

Nowhere was 16th century experiment and change more apparent from the cabinetmaker's point of view than in the making of storage furniture, which was used as an adjunct to the dining table and the bed chamber. As before, the church had played an important role. The cupboard of today owes its early development to a very large degree to ecclesiastical requirements and usages. A board for cups was originally an open structure of shelves. The idea of a closed structure, to which access was by a door or doors in the front, was expressed in the French term *armoire*. Differing and sometimes quite arbitrary translations have helped confuse the issue and early invoices and household accounts juggle with such words as ambry, aumbry, aumbrie, cupboard, book-presse, and press. The French *dressoir*, denoting a closed cupboard on a stand, gives us the dresser which developed from Jacobean origins in Britain.

The word aumbry was most frequently used for a type of wardrobe before Tudor times. It had several compartments with hinged doors and was used in churches as a safe. In a bewildering variety of spellings, a nunnery at Boston in Lincolnshire recorded in a 1534 inventory 'a playne arombry' with 'two lockes' for altar utensils, while a Durham monastery had 'almeryes of fine wenscote (boarding), beinge varnished and finely painted and guilted finely over with little images, verye seemly and beautiful to behould, for the Reliques belonging to Saint Cuthbert to lye in'. Such pieces continued to be used in churches for books, vestments and relics until the Reformation, after which they gained a wider domestic use.

In the second half of the 16th century it was becoming increasingly common to place the cupboard in the dining

Below: *By the time of James I, who used this group of furniture in a hunting lodge, the draw leaf table was in use. This oak example, inlaid with bog oak, sycamore and other woods, can be extended to twice the closed length. It is complemented by a carved oak bench with turned legs and a pair of joined stools.*

room. It was either a structure of three open shelves on carved supports, or a combination of shelves and a cupboard as we know the term today. Usually it was of oak, although examples in solid walnut are not unknown. The open type, known sometimes as a buffet or a court cupboard ('court' from the French word for 'short'), usually had three open shelves, the lowest being supported on short block feet. The back supports were plain, being hidden when in use by the display of plate. The front supports were heavily carved in Elizabethan days and much play was made of the huge bulbous shapes which by then were decorating table legs. The Elizabethan oak court cupboard and its later Jacobean descendants are beautiful pieces of furniture much in demand today; a key attraction is their relatively small size compared with the longer and more cumbersome dimensions of what we have come to call the Welsh dresser.

All these types of furniture were intended for the display of plate and other items used at meals. In addition there was the livery cupboard, placed in the sleeping quarters and containing refreshments which could be taken after retiring. In order to provide ventilation the front was carved in tracery or pierced with a network of holes through which the air could pass. Some hung on the wall, while others were placed on small stands. Similar food hutches stood in the dining and kitchen quarters of Tudor England. As so often the requirements of the church had a hand in their development for they were widely used for the storage of communion wine and bread.

Above: *No bed has been the subject of as many literary references as the Great Bed of Ware. Designed in the late 16th century and housed variously in bedrooms at Ware, Hertfordshire, it is renowned for its extraordinary dimensions (3.25 m/10 ft 8 in square), but it remains a superb example of Elizabethan bed style, with its richly carved posts, panels and canopy.*

Right: *An English 16th century oak cupboard has developed significantly from the three open shelves form of the court cupboard or buffet and now has a central section enclosed by doors.*

The Baroque Era

Italy

Shellfish and other sea-creatures formed an important element in the connection between the auricular style of the late Renaissance and the complex imagery of the Baroque. The word 'baroque' comes from an Italian word meaning 'irregular pearl', and the oyster shell has a long history as a symbol of beauty and sensuality. It was the container of the pearl itself and the source of mother-of-pearl (a material greatly valued by furniture-makers for inlay work). Aphrodite herself, Greek goddess of love, is often shown rising from the sea-foam (*aphros*) in a shell.

At the Palazzo Reale, Turin, is a console table dating from *c.*1680 in carved and gilt wood which depicts a mermaid and a merman with a huge shell between them, putti behind them and a tangled mass of vines around them. Such pieces as this – with or without shells – typify the High Baroque style in Italy, where it had originated and became fully developed by *c.*1620. When fully expressed, it was a palatial manner, adopted by rich merchants and bankers often to impress their friends and clients and so was confined mainly to rooms used for entertaining. A much simpler, homelier atmosphere existed in those parts of the house reserved for family life. The difference is most clearly seen in the contrast between the elaborately carved thrones, composed almost entirely of scrolls and sculptural features, and the dignified chairs and armchairs with square legs, sometimes relieved with a little turning but always rectilinear in form, their padded seats and backs covered in tapestry, which were made both for the rich in their private quarters and for the not-so-rich in their homes generally. Both the palatial and the domestic types of Italian furniture continued to be made with little change over a long period. Filippo Juvarra (1678–1736), the leading Italian architect of his day, was still designing handsome Baroque pieces in the 1730s for the court at Turin.

The simpler type of chair described above was really a continuation of the Renaissance style. Likewise, numerous pieces of handsome if rather provincial-looking furniture such as cupboards and chests continued to be made of walnut throughout the 17th and well into the 18th century, and maintained the earlier traditions of classical proportions and simply carved decoration. Applied mouldings arranged geometrically, and columns or pilasters of the 'barley sugar' twist type – a characteristic symptom of Baroque restlessness occuring after 1625 – relieved the otherwise austere appearance of many functional pieces.

Left: *Interior of an early 17th century French château. The Louis XIII table, covered with a cloth as was the custom, has turned legs with H-shaped stretchers. The armchair in the foreground also has turned members and is of the same period, while that a little to its left has scrolled legs and shaped stretchers – a later feature more typical of the Louis XIV style.*

Above: *Carved and gilt console table with sculptural figures forming the supports. This early-18th century North Italian example is a comparatively late expression of the Baroque style, which lingered on in this form, especially for palatial furnishing schemes, long after other fashions had come and gone.*

The greatest master of the sculptural style was Andrea Brustolon (1662–1732) who was born at Belluno, an Alpine town long celebrated for the craft of woodcarving, particularly church carving, and to which he eventually returned, taking up again the carving of crucifixes he had learned as a boy. Much of his life was spent in Venice, where he made suites of furniture such as that produced for the Venier family, now at the Palazzo Rezzonico, which has chairs composed of realistic tree-branches supported by black boys, and pedestals formed as negro slaves. The traffic in slaves became a major industry in the 17th century and prompted a vogue for tables and candlestands with supports taking this form. The fashion spread across Europe. Other skilled exponents of the style in Italy were Domenico and Francesco Stainhart, who in 1678–80 produced a cabinet designed by Carlo Fontana with kneeling negroes supporting a piece of architecture in miniature – classical columns flanking drawers faced with delicately carved ivory panels, the whole surmounted by an elaborate pediment.

Above: *Florentine cabinet of drawers in ebony, 17th century, mounted on a later stand. This historic example belonged to the English diarist John Evelyn (1620–1706) who recorded that during a visit to Florence in 1644, he bought the* pietre dure *(inlaid marble) panels for the drawer fronts from Domenico Benotti. The bronze mounts were cast by Francesco Fanelli, who later worked in Paris c.1649–52.*

This kind of cabinet-on-stand, variously decorated, was a standard item of prestige furniture in the late 17th and early 18th centuries throughout Europe. Nominally intended to hold collected specimens, but almost as impressive even if empty, the numerous small drawers were faced with ivory, bronze, tortoiseshell, ebony or designs – pictorial or formal – composed of coloured marble and other hard stones. This technique, known as *pietre dure*, was a speciality of Florence, where the Grand Duke had established a studio to practise the craft in 1588, as well as of Milan. It can take two main forms: the flat-surfaced version, known sometimes as Florentine mosaic, and the type which employs coloured stones in relief to form a pattern, very often of fruit or flowers, used for cabinet doors. When only one kind of stone is used, along with inlaid silver, gold or enamel, the correct grammatical term is in the singular – *pietra dura*. *Pietre dure* panels for table-tops and drawer-fronts were very widely exported and made up into furniture in the countries importing them.

Another popular export was mirror-glass – a commodity in which Venice held a virtual monopoly from the early 16th to the late 17th century. Carved and gilt frames for looking-glasses were produced in Venice and also in Florence. The frame-making craft has continued in Florence down to the present day, just as the glass industry has been maintained on the island of Murano, Venice. In the 17th century however, Venetian mirrors were of blown glass and consequently rather small. The initiative passed to France where, at the Saint-Gobain glasshouse, a casting and grinding process for making large sheets of plate glass was invented late in the 17th century.

France

Earlier in the 17th century France had been inundated with imported furniture and immigrant craftsmen. Following the upheaval caused by the accession of the Bourbon king Henri IV in 1589, efforts were made to revive the flagging spirits of the French. The Edict of Nantes in 1598 guaranteed freedom of worship to the Huguenots (originally a nickname for the Protestants). Many craftsmen in the furniture and allied trades were Huguenots, and their improved situation created a far healthier atmosphere in which to work. But during the recent troubles their creativity had suffered, and their skills had fallen behind those of tradesmen in other countries. To correct this, Henri sent a number of cabinetmakers abroad to improve their skills, and in 1608 he set up workshops at the Louvre where others could learn under the tuition of Italian and Flemish masters. Henri was not to see the fruits of these efforts for in 1610 he was assassinated.

Most of the furniture made in France during Henri's reign had continued in Renaissance traditions, using familiar shapes such as the *armoire-à-deux-corps* decorated with conventional Mannerist figures set in isolation in the middle of panels. During the reign of his son, Louis XIII, this was to change gradually in favour of a fluid style of carving more in keeping with the vigour of Baroque. The new king had not yet come of age and taste at court was dominated by his mother, Marie de' Medici who, in spite of having been born a Florentine, had a preference for Flemish art and encouraged skilled Flemings to settle in France.

A weak ruler, her method was to buy political support with money and titles, thus creating a *nouveau riche* class who set themselves up in fine houses and furnished them in the grand manner, partly with pieces imported from the Netherlands and Italy, but partly with native products. Marie performed a valuable service by recalling to France from the Netherlands a craftsman, Jean Macé, whose techniques were ultimately to revolutionize French furniture-making. Macé had spent two years at Middelburg in Zeeland, where he learned the art of veneering before returning to France about 1620 to take up employment in the workshops of the Louvre, where he remained as a royal cabinetmaker until his death in 1672.

Veneering, though an ancient craft, was new to France. In principle, it consists of glueing a thin sheet of finely-figured wood over a solid foundation. All the sheets cut parallel to each other from the same piece of wood, exhibit nearly identical figurations in the grain. By reversing or twisting and turning them until they match, it is thus

Above: *Late 16th century walnut* armoire-à-deux-corps, *probably Burgundian, of a type which continued to be made well into the 17th century. Earlier examples are usually carved with Renaissance subjects placed at the centres of the doors, but here the panels are carved over their entire surfaces with scenes from the parable of the Prodigal Son.*

possible to create symmetrical patterns that could hardly be achieved if solid timber were used. Other effects made possible were 'cross-banding' – setting a narrow band of veneer around the outer edge of a panel or table-top with the grain running at right angles to that of the central area; and 'oyster' patterns, contrived by setting cross-cuts of veneer, from the branches of such trees as laburnum, side by side. The veneers on antique furniture were saw-cut by hand, and are much thicker than the modern, knife-cut product.

Once the basic technique of veneering is mastered, marquetry and parquetry decoration become possible. Marquetry can be executed in several ways, but it is essentially the creation of a decorative design by inlaying one veneer into another. One method is to veneer the solid surface, then to cut out a design and fill the gaps with veneers of contrasting grain or colour. Another way is to glue sheets of contrasting veneers lightly together with sheets of paper between them to form a pack, which is held in a special type of vice. The design is then cut through the entire thickness using a saw, and the individual sheets are separated. The designs in one wood – say, the darker – can then be fitted into the pattern cut into the lighter and *vice versa*. Other materials besides wood, such as tortoiseshell, can be used as veneers.

To understand parquetry it is necessary only to think of a parquet floor. Small squares, rhomboids and other geometric shapes are cut from a variety of contrasting veneers and are assembled, edge to edge, to form a pattern. Ingenious juxtapositioning can produce remarkable *trompe l'oeil* effects, making the pattern appear as a pyramid of cubes or a tiled floor seen in perspective.

Veneering has acquired a dubious reputation because it has often been employed to give a showy finish to a shoddy article, but in the hands of a master, it can be raised to a degree of artistry little short of miraculous. This fact was recognized in France early in the 17th century, and the ability to handle veneers – particularly those in the highly fashionable ebony – distinguished the cabinetmaker (*ébéniste*) from the worker in solid wood, the joiner (*menuisier*).

When Louis XIII was still a boy, a marriage of alliance was arranged between him and Anne of Austria, who later developed an enthusiasm for Italian styles. This was to some extent balanced by the influence on Louis, when he grew up and ruled in his own right, of his prime minister, Cardinal Richelieu, who was a great collector himself and did all he could to encourage the arts in France.

The craft of veneering was at first employed only on the more important pieces of prestige furniture, such as the cabinet-on-stand with its elaborately fitted interior. The upper stage was usually veneered, but the stand was a table-like construction mainly in solid wood, with turned legs of columnar form or twist shape. At first the twist had to be carved by hand, until the turners later learned to produce it on the lathe using a jig and tool. Elaborate variations of double and hollow twists were evolved in the course of the 17th century.

Turning of a similar kind was extensively used on tables and chairs of the Louis XIII period. The styles established continued in many country districts, with little change, throughout the 17th century. Dining tables do not play a leading part in the story of French furniture – at least not until the end of the 18th century. The French for long preserved the old tradition of eating at a simple table spread with a cloth. Small rectangular tables began to be made in greater numbers in the first half of the 17th century and were intended for individual meals, as writing tables or simply for displaying personal possessions. They were made in solid wood – oak, walnut or fruitwood – and were mounted on turned legs with stretchers below. Quite often, the under-edge of the frieze (the framework under the top) was shaped. Stools and backstools of the *chaise-lorraine* type were constructed on much the same lines, and it is probable that many were made to match the tables, for it was at this time that furniture began to be made in suites. The trend became more marked during the reign of Louis XIV.

Chairs, too, were being made in sets. The backs were low, square and upholstered to match the seats. The legs were turned, either spirally or to baluster or bobbin profiles. It was an age that showed an increasing awareness of comfort, and some of the armchairs have backs that are

Above: *Flat-topped, knee-hole desk c.1680 of the type later known as a* bureau-Mazarin, *after the statesman who virtually ruled France during the minority of Louis XIV. Contemporary prints demonstrate that it was also used as a dressing-table, with a mirror hung on the wall over it. This example is veneered in transparent tortoiseshell backed with coloured mica and inlaid with brass marquetry.*

slightly pitched. The arms themselves begin to take on an agreeable curve and the seats are well padded. Though still imposing, such chairs are no longer 'seats of estate' only, but make some concession to the idea of relaxation. Such ideas were not only confined to court circles. Much Louis XIII furniture is clearly not very sophisticated and doubtless originated in country districts. As such, it is the earliest group in the great tradition of French Provincial furniture to have survived in any quantity, and to be suitable for use in the less pretentious modern home.

The two-part cabinet or *armoire-à-deux-corps* continued to be made but was gradually superseded by a full-length cupboard or armoire in the usually accepted sense. The earlier examples of the latter show a reluctance on the designer's part to break with tradition. The doors are in fact full length, but each is divided into an upper and lower section by a rail, giving an appearance of four small doors, each one decorated with multiple mouldings forming an octagonal or diamond-shaped frame around a central panel. The stiles, or vertical corner-posts of the frame, are ornamented with columns of turnery sometimes in the round, but more often with one flat side glued to the frame. This method of decoration, which was extensively used in many countries, is known as split turnery. It was achieved by lightly glueing together two lengths of wood, with a paper divider between them. The resulting package was turned on the lathe to the desired pattern and then split open again down the middle, providing two identical pieces, each decorated on one face and flat on the other, ready to be attached to the frame.

Split turnery was a favourite form of decoration on furniture constructed in the solid, and occasionally on pieces partly or wholly veneered. It is to be found on early commodes (chests-of-drawers) which by the mid-17th century were gradually replacing the *coffre* or lidded chest in popularity. They have survived in large numbers in France and elsewhere, and are still found to be as convenient and useful as when they were first made.

Richelieu died in December 1642 and was replaced by his protégé Mazarin. Louis XIII also died in May of the following year, leaving a five-year-old son as heir to the throne. Once again, France was to be ruled, nominally at least, by a queen mother in the person of Anne, but in reality by Jules Mazarin (1602–61), an Italian by birth, a Frenchman by adoption and a cosmopolitan by instinct. In taste, however, he remained true to his land of origin, and as Anne was very much under his influence, Italianate furniture and decoration dominated the court during these twenty years.

Native French traditions meant little to Mazarin. In his determination to destroy the last vestiges of feudal power still wielded by the nobles, he seized on every opportunity to demolish a medieval castle. That he was a collector of art

Below: *Louis XIV armchair,* c.1660–70, *the frame carved in gilt, with scrolled arms and crossed stretchers joining the legs to provide greater strength as well as decorative value. The padded seat and back, covered in a rich brocade with a floral design, make concessions to comfort while maintaining the traditional significance of the armchair as a 'seat of estate'.*

and of fine furniture, is proved by the inventory of his effects made in 1653. He imported tables with *pietre dure* tops from Italy, cabinets-on-stands from the Netherlands and Germany; he introduced talented cabinetmakers such as Cucci from Italy and Golle from the Netherlands (see below).

Mazarin is immortalized in the history of furniture by having had a particular type of desk named after him. The *bureau Mazarin* is a writing table composed of two pedestals, each with three drawers one above the other and four legs to each section, with a kneehole between them and a flat top over them. It is usually decorated with arabesques of brass inlaid into a ground of tortoiseshell veneer in the style known as 'Boulle' (see below). Ironically, this type of desk does not seem to have been invented in Mazarin's lifetime – all examples known appear to date from after his death – and his name only came to be attached to it in the 19th century.

Following Mazarin's death in 1661, Louis XIV assumed personal power for the first time at the age of 23, and set about creating at Versailles a palace which would symbolize the greatness of France and its king. He was aided in this by his minister, Jean-Baptiste Colbert (1619–83), a patron of the arts who presided over the first exhibition of paintings by living artists in 1673. Colbert appointed Charles Le Brun (1619–90) to the post of first director of the royal factory, the *Manufacture des Gobelins*, in 1663. Le Brun had trained as an artist in Rome where he had cultivated a High Baroque style modified and disciplined by classical principles. It was this splendid but rather solemn version of the Baroque which is known today as the Louis XIV style.

A capable designer himself, especially of tapestries, Le Brun's real genius lay in his ability to organize the creations of others into a magnificent, harmonious whole that unashamedly acknowledged foreign contributions but emerged first as a national and then as an international style, imitated and emulated even in the countries that had supplied the initial ingredients. Versailles was finally made ready for the court in 1682, when the king took up residence. Colbert died in the following year and Le Brun fell from royal favour.

Louis' chief designer of furniture was Jean Le Pautre (1618–82), who left over 2,000 engraved designs that included beds with canopies (which gave maximum opportunity to the upholsterer), console tables and other gilt furniture that employ the full range of Baroque imagery. His earlier work is heavy with sculptural figures of nymphs trapped in jungles of foliage. His later designs are less

Below: *Writing table of* bureau-Mazarin *type, late 17th century, differing significantly from the example illustrated on the previous page, the legs of which are scrolled, and which has Boulle inlay of the intricate, tightly packed kind. This example has square tapered legs and the floral marquetry is bolder and more freely executed.*

oppressive and anticipate the lighter style of Jean Bérain *père* (1637–1711), whose son (also Jean) adopted his father's style, one which frequently exhibits a sense of humour not quite in tune with Versailles at its most grandiloquent. He took over from Le Brun and in 1690 moved into an apartment in the Louvre, near that of André-Charles Boulle (1642–1732), the *maitre-ébéniste* famous for his metal marquetry in a ground of tortoiseshell veneer. By making up a pack of alternating sheets of brass and tortoiseshell and sawing a pattern in them all simultaneously, it was possible to inlay pieces of brass into the spaces cut into the tortoiseshell ('Boullework') and pieces of shell into the spaces cut in the brass ('counter-Boulle'). Recent research, however, casts doubt on whether Boulle himself adopted this ingeniously economic method. It seems more likely that he started from scratch for each type.

Bérain's designs included arabesques, grotesques and the increasingly popular chinoiseries. Colbert had founded the *Compagnie des Indes* in 1664, which now imported oriental lacquer, porcelain and other works of art. These

Below: *Marquetry cabinet made for Louis XIV and attributed to A.-C. Boulle, with a medallion by J. Manger, late 17th century. The supports take the form of* termes *– large-scale caryatids. Although Boulle is known to have produced many pieces of fine furniture while occupying workshops at the Louvre, only two are fully authenticated.*

almost certainly influenced both the shapes and the decoration of some of Boulle's work, and possibly that of Domenico Cucci (*c.*1635–1704) and Pierre Golle (*fl.*1670–90), both of whom decorated furniture with rich marquetry in exotic woods, tortoiseshell, metal and lapis lazuli, embellished with gilt bronze mounts which were cast and chiselled. Known in English as 'ormolu mounts', they were first intended as protective pieces on the corners of furniture, but gradually came to be used for purely decorative purposes as well. Curvilinear shapes began to replace rectilinear forms, and vertical legs slowly gave way to scrolled outlines.

In 1685 the king issued an order requiring all furniture arriving in the royal palaces to be entered in a day-book (*Journal du Garde-Meubles*), which was maintained more or less consistently until the outbreak of the Revolution, and provides a fund of information about the pieces and their makers. Sadly, not all the furniture itself has survived. All that is known to exist from the output of Cucci, for example, is a pair of ebony cabinets made in 1681–83 for Versailles and now at Alnwick Castle in England. Most of his work was sold in the 18th century and broken up, to be cannibalized by other cabinetmakers – a not uncommon practice.

Although there are thousands of pieces in existence which go by the name of 'Boulle' because they are decorated in the style he made famous, the vast majority are of a much later date, the technique being continued both in France and elsewhere during the 18th and 19th centuries. A few pieces can be attributed fairly confidently to Boulle himself but the only fully documented examples are two commodes made for the king in 1708–9. The commode of *bombé* (blown out, swollen) form, which was to become so important a feature of Continental furniture in the 18th century, was at least partly invented by Boulle. He retired in 1718 but a fire destroyed his workshops, stock and collection of art, ruining him financially and forcing him to return to work.

Louis XIV issued another order in 1685, revoking the Edict of Nantes and thereby withdrawing protection from the Huguenots. This had a profound effect on the arts and crafts in Europe. Thousands of French Protestants sought refuge abroad. Among those to flee were Pierre Golle and his brother Adrian, also a skilled cabinetmaker, who returned to Holland. Their nephew, Daniel Marot (1663–1752), who probably worked for Boulle, was Paris-born but also left for the Netherlands. These were just a few of the most distinguished craftsmen of their time to leave France hurriedly, after lending their talents to the creation of the Louis XIV style. France's loss was the rest of Europe's gain.

The Netherlands

The long struggle for the independence of the Netherlands was won in 1609, when the seven northern provinces formed a republic. The Dutch East India Company had already been established in 1602. These two events occurring in the first decade of the 17th century helped to create the climate for a long period of successful free enterprise at home and abroad, in which the Dutch and Flemish furniture industry fully shared.

From about 1650, carcase pieces, especially various kinds of cupboards with doors, developed flat panels free of carving, the emphasis being placed on finely-figured exotic woods, which became available through the activities of the East India Company and were used either in the solid or as veneers. Carving was sometimes employed to decorate the arched framework of doors and panels, and often follows the soft, meaty manner known as auricular.

This treatment is common on the tall cupboards with rounded arches on doors and end panels made in the north, especially in the province of Holland. Arched doors with plain panels occur also on the two-stage cupboards popular in Zeeland at about the same time (*c.* 1650), but on these, the carving echoes the earlier Renaissance style of Mannerist figures and animal masks. Pieces of this type, together

Above: *Oak armoire, northern Flanders, mid 17th century, with overhanging cornice and convex frieze above two doors decorated with applied pilasters and carvings of scrolling foliage. The architectural quality is emphasized by the three Corinthian columns. The turned feet are ebonized and small tablets of ebony are deployed at intervals on the front. The end shows the typical panelled construction of the period.*

Below: *Walnut armchair, North Netherlands, c.1660–80, with caned seat and back. This use of split cane had only recently been learned from the Chinese when this chair was made. The carving and piercing of the frame, and use of 'barley sugar twists' are typical of the period.*

with chests-of-drawers with decoration composed of geometrically arranged mouldings, almost always stood on boldly turned 'bun' feet, which were made of oak but were often stained and polished black to imitate ebony. Ebony or 'ebonized' pearwood was also used for mouldings, beadings and narrow strips of veneer employed to emphasize the line of a piece, giving it a dramatic, dignified but slightly mournful appearance. Ebonized mouldings were often chiselled on their surface to produce a rippled effect which reflected light in subtle ways.

Ebony played an even more important rôle in the cabinets-on-stands for which Antwerp in the south continued to be famous, combining the dark veneers with contrasting materials – ivory, silver, tortoiseshell and painted plaques. From about 1660, completed pieces of ebony furniture, particularly chairs, were imported from Dutch colonies in the East Indies and Ceylon. They are usually worked in solid wood rather than in veneers, and display remarkable skill in fashioning this hard material into legs and spindles of twist shape, as well as in carving the cresting rails of chairs with much the same patterns of masks and foliage as are found on Dutch silver of the period. Chairs of this kind had seats of woven cane – the first to appear in Europe.

Left: *Dutch marquetry cabinet-on-stand c.1690 made by Jan van Mekeren of Amsterdam. The composition of the floral marquetry derives inspiration from Dutch flower painting of the period and is finely executed in a variety of woods on a ground of ebony veneer. The square tapered legs are a Dutch adaptation of a Louis XIV type and are united by a shaped stretcher.*

Right: *Cabinet-on-stand, Antwerp, early to mid 17th century. Antwerp was celebrated for cabinets of this type, their drawer-fronts variously decorated with painting, carved ivory or ebony, wrought silver or* pietre dure. *Rightly regarded as works of art in their own right, the cabinets were often exported without stands. They ceased to be fashionable c.1700.*

The precise origin of this kind of colonial furniture is often difficult to decide, especially when more than one European power was in occupation simultaneously with, or closely following upon, another, as in the case of Ceylon, first colonized by the Portuguese who were not expelled by the Dutch until 1658, and who left their mark on local interpretations of European requirements long after their departure.

Towards the end of the 17th century a taste for woods more colourful than ebony began to exert itself in the Netherlands. This was fostered by the influence of the Baroque style, especially the French version of it which was given an added boost when, following the exodus of the Huguenots in 1685, many highly skilled craftsmen, some of them Dutch or Flemish by origin, came to the Low Countries. Included among these was Daniel Marot who became chief designer to William, Prince of Orange, and worked on the interior decoration and furnishing of the royal palace at Het Loo. His style, as demonstrated in his published designs, was a personal interpretation of the Louis XIV manner, with a strong emphasis on luxuriously upholstered beds, chairs and stools. The chairs have high, rather narrow backs, either padded or elaborately fretted and carved with scroll patterns. The seats may be stuffed and upholstered or caned to receive squab cushions. The legs are either vertical and turned – often to a distinctive shape having a bold protuberance like an upturned cup near the top – or have a hook-like scroll which anticipates the S-shaped curve of the fully developed cabriole leg, which was soon to emerge.

Like many other chairs, stools and tables of the period, particularly Dutch ones, Marot's designs frequently employ stretchers of X or H shape joining the legs to give added strength as well as providing a decorative feature. Some of the grander versions of his style are gilded, but walnut was now the principal wood for fashionable furniture in Holland, used both in veneers and in the solid. When William of Orange went to rule England jointly with his wife Mary, Marot followed his master to work there, returning to Holland in 1698. He was especially clever in his use of draped fabrics to create opulent effects, particularly on a type of bed with no posts at the foot but with flounced testers, cantilevered from the wall and suspended from the ceiling.

Two passions of the Dutch from the second half of the 17th century onwards, were for flowers and ceramics. The first of these loves is reflected in furniture painted with flower subjects, and more especially in floral marquetry patterns employing woods of many colours either natural or stained. The latter was used to decorate the doors of large cabinets on dwarf stands and the tops of tables intended to occupy the centre of a room and to be admired as works of art rather than used as pieces of furniture. One of the leading practitioners in this field was Jan van Mekeren (*fl.*1690–*c.*1735), whose floral panels were based on contemporary still-life paintings.

Above: *Centre table, Antwerp, late 17th century, veneered with tortoiseshell and inlaid with pewter – a variant of the more usual 'Boullework' in brass. The construction employs the combination of square tapered legs and flat, shaped stretcher that was often used for Netherlands cabinet stands of the type illustrated on the previous page.*

The preoccupation with floral marquetry was a long-standing feature of much Dutch furniture, though not all of it reaches the high standard set by the style's early exponents. In the 19th century, many pieces which had started life as honest, plain articles were embellished with rather coarse floral decoration.

The second obsession of the Dutch in the later 17th century was Chinese porcelain which they collected avidly, mixing it with their own Delft pottery. To house their collections, they invented the display cabinet, with glazed

Above: *South German* Barockschrank *(Baroque cupboard) dated 1723, in walnut and stained pine, decorated with mouldings and enriched with carving. The bobbin-turned columns add to the sense of solid, houseproud respectability possessed by many regional variations of such cupboards.*

doors divided into rectangular panes in the upper stage, and a cupboard below with panelled doors. The panels are often decorated with marquetry. A distinctive feature of these cabinets is the canting of the ends to show the contents of the glazed section to better advantage. The top is usually shaped – not merely the doors and cornice, but the ceiling of the carcase too – in a rounded arch.

The bureau and the bureau-cabinet (known in America as a 'secretary' and 'secretary cabinet' respectively) were English in origin and enjoyed wide popularity in many Continental countries, especially Holland. In Dutch variations the upper stage, or cabinet section, of the bureau-cabinet was usually shaped as a double dome and the ceiling followed the outline of the front elevation. These pieces were either in oak for the burgher home, or veneered on oak in walnut with marquetry or parquetry for the wealthier customer. Another finish was 'japanning' in imitation of oriental lacquer.

Lacquer cabinets were imported from both China and Japan by the East India Company. The Dutch succeeded in maintaining a foothold in Japan after the Portuguese had been expelled in the 17th century as a result of their missionary zeal, and Holland was the chief Western contact with the Japanese until the second half of the 19th century. In Europe, the lacquer cabinets were mounted on carved and gilt stands in the Baroque style, with little or no attempt in most cases, at an Eastern flavour. Lacquer soon came to be imitated in the West, with various varnishes substituting for the authentic oriental product, which was derived from the sap of the tree *Rhus vernicifera*.

Spa, near Liège, was an important centre for japanning, and the Flemish and Dutch imitations of lacquer are so good as to be difficult to distinguish from the real thing. Spa was a watering-place (its name becoming a generic term for all such resorts) and consequently its japanned wares were sold to visitors from all over Europe. One of its native practitioners, Gerhard Dagly (*fl.*1687–1714), went to Germany and became Director of Ornaments to Friedrich Wilhelm, Elector of Brandenburg.

Germany, Austria, Scandinavia and Switzerland

When Gerhard Dagly went from Spa to Berlin in 1688, the Baroque style had been flourishing in Germany for about 50 years, and was to persist there for another 70. Its heavy grandeur seemed to settle itself immovably in palace and farmhouse, town and country. The most typical piece was the *Schrank*, or large cupboard, which while displaying regional variations was always of architectural form, massive construction and such generous proportions that it was usually accommodated in the entrance hall to save space in the living rooms. It is probable, too, that it was placed there strategically, as the status symbol to be encountered on first entering the house.

Frankfurt was especially noted for its handsome version of the *Schrank* which was unrelieved by carving and depended for its effect on the series of mouldings arranged geometrically, like picture-frames set one inside another, in long narrow rectangles on each of its two doors. In some examples the corners are canted and similarly treated. The play of light on the mouldings produces a wave-like effect. This type is also known as a *Wellenschrank* (from *Wellen*: waves, shafts). The *Schrank* is usually fitted with two drawers in the base, and most regional types have heavy cornices. The exceptions are some Austrian examples, which do not always have drawers, and on which the cornices are frequently of modest proportions.

A related type is the *Geschirrschrank* (china cupboard) made in North Germany. This is a dwarf cupboard, with moulded or carved decoration on the doors and fitted with a rack of shelves for china above. The *Stollenschrank* (cabinet-on-stand) was also made with a surface composed entirely of mouldings, like the *Wellenschrank*. It usually stood on twist legs joined by X-shaped stretchers.

Bavaria at this time was allied by marriage to Savoy, and thus Italian influence was strong in the later 17th century. Palatial furniture in the High Baroque style was made for the court and its imitators at Munich until that city began to rival Augsburg and Nuremberg in the production of luxurious pieces, such as marble-topped tables on gilt stands with supports formed as carved figures.

Paul Decker (1677–1713) was a native of Nuremberg who went to work as a designer in Berlin. His designs included some for lacquerwork and it is possible that he was associated with Gerhard Dagly, who was there at the same time. Dagly's work for Friedrich Wilhelm and the latter's successor, Frederick I, was chiefly the decoration of furniture in chinoiseries of an unusual kind. Decorators

Below: *German writing cabinet on stand, the upper stage of* Tabernakel *type, on which a variety of woodworking skills have been lavished. The doors and drawer fronts are veneered and edged with 'ripple' mouldings. The hinges and lock plates are elaborately fretted. The stand is a piece of figurative sculpture in the round, in a Germanic version of the Baroque which has survived down to the 20th century in the woodcarving of Bavaria and Switzerland.*

Above: *A 17th century panelled study in Strassburg. The table with its turned, boldly splayed legs joined by flat stretchers, and the chair with simple peg-legs in contrast to the elaborately shaped back, are both characteristic Germanic types made from the late 16th century onwards until well into the 19th century.*

in lacquer mostly imitated the Chinese and Japanese standard products, using gold figures on a black, red or green ground. Dagly brought a welcome airiness to the heavy Baroque atmosphere by working on pale-coloured grounds, achieving effects that were light-hearted and charming. He was nevertheless dismissed from his post in 1713, and his chief assistant, Martin Schnell (*fl.* 1703–40) returned to his birthplace, Dresden.

Schnell worked for Augustus the Strong (the King of Poland and Elector of Saxony) as a painter of porcelain at Meissen. He also painted furniture and seems to have specialized in decorating bureaux (*Schreibkommoden*). The German fall-front bureau in the late 17th and early 18th centuries was sometimes inspired by Anglo-Dutch models, and when it was given a cabinet above, this had doors fitted with arched panels of wood or mirror-glass (not, at that time, clear glass).

In the South, Italian influence helped to dictate the design of a three-stage article that, by the middle of the 18th century, had developed into a characteristic German form, the *Tabernakel-Schreibkommode* or *Tabernakel-Sekretär*. The base consisted of a three-drawer chest or commode with serpentine front. Above this was the desk section, with sloping fall-front enclosing a fitted interior. On top again was the *Tabernakel*, consisting of a central cupboard flanked by a bank of small drawers, usually four or five each side. Despite the relatively late date, the style is still Baroque in spirit. The wood is usually walnut veneer with wide cross-banding and linear marquetry. This type was also made in Austria, and given as a wedding gift.

Switzerland, in spite of the infiltration of ideas from surrounding countries, nevertheless evolved a national style. Pine was the principal timber for those carcase pieces intended to be painted in cheerful colours with flowers. All the Alpine countries cultivated this type of peasant tradition, sometimes using the paint to imitate the grain of expensive woods.

For grand furniture, the workshops of Geneva and Berne adopted the Louis XIV style, but some interesting middle-class pieces were made in walnut, particularly a composite buffet (*Aufsatzbüfett*) of asymmetrical form. The design varied, but in principle it consisted of a low cupboard of sideboard height with two doors. Above this was another cupboard, raised at the front on turned columns and with a panelled back behind the open space between the upper and lower stages. To one side only of this main structure was attached a narrower unit of similar construction which was often fitted with a pewter bowl and water cistern in the open space, for washing utensils. Fine examples carved in Renaissance style were still being made in the mid-17th century, and versions in painted pine continued to be produced until the early 19th century, still retaining the asymmetrical shape.

In Scandinavia, German princes had come to rule over Norway, Denmark and, from 1654, Sweden. Inevitably, a strong German influence was exercised over much, though not all, of the furniture. In the main, it follows North German and Netherlands styles, until *c.*1675 when Sweden began to adopt the Louis XIV manner. Again, it is to the folk culture of the peasantry that one must look for native inventiveness. Cupboards, chairs and simple trestle tables with X-shaped supports, mostly in pine – sometimes painted, sometimes scrubbed to a brilliant cleanliness – often display a love of intricate shapes both in outline and

Below: *The office of Linnaeus (Carl von Linné, 1707–78), Swedish botanist, at Uppsala. The furniture is mid-18th century and a rather stiff version of the cabriole leg is in evidence, but earlier features from the Baroque period have been retained in the high backs, turned rear legs and stretchers of the side chairs.*

Above: *Spanish walnut table c. 1600 in the style known as* Herrera *after Juan de Herrera, architect to Philip II. The deep, moulded drawers, the heavily turned legs and the projections supporting the front of the top are all characteristic features of a style which persisted in country districts of Spain and in the colonies – especially Mexico – until the 19th century.*

fretted designs. Chip-carving of roundels sometimes occurs on primitive chests.

The traditional painting on Norwegian furniture is known as *rosemaling*. Flowers, animals and birds were the stock ingredients, but a fresh approach taken by succeeding generations kept this form of folk culture alive and well. It was once a Norwegian custom for the house and principal items of furniture to be built at the same time. The process began with the careful selection of pine trees in the spring, then in late summer or autumn they were felled and allowed to season for four years before construction began. Characteristic Norwegian pieces included the *klappbord*, an ingeniously contrived table, folding flat against the wall when not in use, and the *bandestol*, a three-legged chair with a semicircular seat, its arms often terminating in dragons' heads – not unlike the prows of Viking ships.

A popular type of cupboard in Denmark, known as a 'pillar cupboard', had an upper stage supported by columns and stood on a platform in the corner of the room with a bench or form at its side. These pieces are often dated, but it was the custom to repaint the article and alter the date when it was handed on to another generation.

Spain, Portugal and their Colonies in America and India

At its most extravagant, Spanish Baroque seems to be trying to rival and outdo even the more extreme interpretations found in the rest of Europe. The style employed architectural features and the human figure in the emotional, eccentric style known as Churrigueresque, after the chief practitioner of this fantastic manner, Don José Churriguera (d. 1725). It was as if the style was a last defiant gesture by a dying empire. During the reigns of Philip III (1596–1621), Philip IV (1621–65) and Charles II (1665–1700), Spain was growing both poorer and politically weaker. Nevertheless Spanish society seemed determined to keep up appearances, and as always, furniture was one of the main props in the drama.

At a time when few could afford it, the writing-cabinet or *vargueño* came into wider use – a symbol, now, not so much of nobility as of respectability. Its interior façade of colonnaded intricacy became an essay in miniature of the Churrigueresque, with little twisted columns and elaborate marquetry on the drawer-fronts. The *papileira*, having no writing leaf to conceal the façade, followed closely on the heels of the cabinets of Cologne and Antwerp, but added a fretted gallery of gilded metal to the top, and adopted the fashionable twist legs for the stand.

Twist legs, or less elaborately turned ones, were also a feature of long, narrow tables which appeared in addition to, but not entirely in place of, those with trestle ends and iron braces. The new type had drawers in the frieze, carved with roundels or later foliage, and usually fitted with iron ring handles. A boldly projecting moulding extended around the frieze on its bottom edge. This type of table occurs in varying qualities. The best are of walnut or chestnut, but cheaper versions, which continued to be made for the peasantry for at least another century, were in pine. Simple chairs with no upholstery, the cross-rails of the back shaped and finished with a little carving, were similarly produced from this time onwards in large numbers.

Even the traditional 'monk's chair' (*sillón de fraileros*) was given a new look by being fitted out with the ubiquitous twist legs. In the second half of the 17th century, a Portuguese type of chair became popular in Spain. It had a Moorish medallion-shaped back which, like the seat, was covered in embossed leather. The legs were turned and on Spanish examples, the foot was often scrolled and fluted. It was transmitted to other countries, notably England, where it is still known as a 'Spanish' or 'Braganza' foot.

The 17th century was not an especially prosperous period for Portugal but independence from Spain with the accession of the Duke of Braganza as King John IV (1640–56), and the recovery of Brazil from the Dutch in 1654, all contributed to a raising of national morale which expressed itself in the arts, including furniture-making.

The chair with the medallion-shaped back which was copied in Spain developed on very similar lines at home. The feet were usually turned rather than scrolled but added interest was provided by the front stretcher, which was wide, arched and pierced with a design of interlaced curves. It was covered in embossed leather nailed to a frame of native oak or walnut, or sometimes jacaranda, a very hard material related to rosewood and imported from Brazil.

The legs on tables and related objects were turned with very bold protuberances refined by multiple rings. Drawer-fronts and lock-plates on doors were in fretted and engraved brass. All these distinctive features were displayed on the *contador*, the Portuguese version of the cabinet-on-stand.

A two-stage cupboard, with a pair of doors top and bottom, showed Dutch influence (probably derived from the earlier occupation of Brazil by the Dutch, rather than by direct European contact), especially in the treatment of mouldings, which were rippled on their surface. The effect is known in Portuguese as *tremidos*. Unlike Spain, where

Below: *Spanish armchair, mid 17th century. The squareness of the design, and the use of leather for the seat and back, fixed with decoratively headed nails, are in the tradition of the 16th century 'monk's chair', but twist legs, uprights and stretchers have now appeared to provide a thoroughly Baroque flavour.*

Below: *Portuguese* contador *(cabinet of drawers on stand) in rosewood, second half of the 17th century. The drawer fronts have fretted escutcheons to the keyholes, surrounded by a geometric arrangement of mouldings displaying the* tremidos *effect. The bold turning of the legs and the carved frieze are typical of 17th century Portuguese taste.*

Left: *Portuguese walnut chair, late 17th century, with medallion-shaped back and front stretcher carved to represent interlaced scrolls. The finely embossed leather on back and seat, fixed to the frame with brass-headed nails, is of the kind which originated in Moorish Spain, probably in the region of Cordova and known as* guadamecil, *or Cordovan leatherwork. It was, however, made in many other centres. This type of Portuguese chair became very fashionable in Spain also.*

cupboards were rapidly ousting the traditional chest, in Portugal it remained popular at least until the end of the 17th century.

Portugal produced several distinctive types of bed, of which the most impressive was the *cama de bilros* – a posted bed with an open framework, on which the turner clearly delighted to exercise his skills. The posts and the framework are all turned with twist and bobbin patterns, but in a way which lightens the otherwise excessive heaviness of much Baroque turnery.

In the north of both Spain and Portugal but particularly in the Portuguese province of Minho, there was a prosperous industry in richly carved furniture, mainly chestnut, which survived as a form of folk culture, catering for local needs and preserving traditional styles long after they had ceased to be fashionable in more sophisticated areas.

Portuguese craftsmen settled in Brazil and catered for their countrymen in occupation there. Apart from the influence of the earlier Dutch occupation, Brazilian furniture remains fairly close to the original Portuguese types. Colonization in the Orient, however, resulted in a strange grafting of the decorative techniques of India, particularly Goa, on to basically European shapes. A typical example of the Indo-Portuguese style is a *contador* or cabinet of small drawers, profusely inlaid with bone or ivory, and mounted on a stand with mermaid supports. This type of article was made for Portuguese residents in the colonies and also for export to Lisbon.

The Spanish colonies in South and Central America produced a curious mixture of Spanish and native traditions. At Cuzco in Peru, the centre of the ancient Inca civilization, furniture was made for both church and domestic use, and displays several features of construction which differentiate it from its Spanish equivalents. Dovetails are exposed to form a pattern on the surface, which is never veneered. Tenons project through mortises and their ends are left exposed. Although elaborate turning was practised, the lathe cannot always have been readily available and some bulbous projections were made by splicing pieces of wood together and smoothing them into a rounded shape. Leatherwork is often embossed with coats-of-arms, including royal ones, but these can be most misleading. The badge of Charles V of Spain even appears occasionally on chairs made about 200 years after his reign ended in 1556.

Poland and Russia

In the early 17th century, Danzig (Gdańsk), a port on the Baltic, was a thriving town with upwards of 40,000 inhabitants, where the country squires sold their produce and bought luxury goods imported from the West, as well as paintings and engravings produced locally, and various other artefacts that included the typical *Schapp* or *Schrank* – a heavily Baroque cupboard with doors having cartouche-shaped panels, drawers below and a characteristic gabled cornice above. This same type of cornice is found on the unusually tall Danzig cabinet-on-stand with twist legs and a third tier above the customary enclosed nest of drawers. This gabled cornice is so closely identified with Danzig that pieces exhibiting it are often attributed to that city when they may well have been made elsewhere, such as Frankfurt.

In the south, elements of folk culture were incorporated in more sophisticated furniture. Motifs drawn from nature

– birds and flowers – were used for marquetry decoration on other versions of the cabinet-on-stand. The legs are relatively slim and look too slender to support the bulky carcase. There was in fact a structural weakness in this type of article, for the same problem seems to have arisen in cabinets produced in many countries by many different makers, and many stands have had to be heavily restored or entirely replaced.

Russian furniture of the Baroque period inevitably tends to have a provincial flavour. Most of it was made by country craftsmen bound for life, unless freed by their masters, to the estates on which they worked. These labourers drew their inspiration partly from their own folk culture and partly from French imports. The result was a palace style that, however carefully executed, tends to look out of proportion and clumsy when seen out of context but no doubt suited the buildings for which it was intended. Owing to their dispersal following the Russian Revolution, such pieces appear on the market from time to time but often go unrecognized for what they are, and it is not unknown for them to have been dismissed as 19th century copies of French or Italian period pieces.

Above: *Massive cupboard of the type known as a* Schapp *with the heavy, gabled cornice particularly associated with Danzig (Gdańsk) in the late 17th and early 18th centuries, but also produced in other centres. As well as the peculiarity of the gable, this piece is remarkable for the elaboration of the mouldings and the carving in the full-blown Baroque style that characterized Polish furniture of the period.*

England

The reign of the unlucky Stuarts, which began in 1603 with the accession of James I, saw much refinement in English furniture styles. The course of politics and international and national events, as well as foreign religious intolerance and natural and man-provoked disasters all had their influence on art and design in 17th century England. The effects of certain traumatic happenings were obvious and immediate.

The Great Plague – which in London reached its peak in 1665 – covered Europe with a darkness unknown since the Middle Ages. When the cloud was lifted a universal reaction showed itself in a spontaneous plunge into gaiety, extravagance and escapism. It was reflected in clothing fashion, living styles, and not least, furniture. Shortly after the plague an event occurred in England which produced a watershed in furniture history.

In 1666 the Great Fire of London, although a fearful disaster to those involved, was responsible for long-term beneficial effects. The holocaust destroyed 89 churches and 13,000 homes. Much of the superb artistry of Inigo Jones was lost. As surveyor of works to Charles I, he had influenced furniture and interior decoration through his love of Italian classicism and the result had been a chaster style, thrusting out the decorative excesses of the late Elizabethan period. After the fire many city churches were rebuilt under the genius of Sir Christopher Wren; the London renaissance was responsible for the building of St Paul's Cathedral, as well as many other buildings.

A new London grew up on the site of the fire, which, undeniably, had disposed of many rat-infested, disease ridden slums. To a large extent, English furniture faced a rebirth, and the reason was simple: London represented the heartland of the country's furniture inventiveness and production; it housed much of the entire stock of the nation's fine furniture, no other centre even approaching the capital's importance in this respect. With the destruction of so many homes and the furniture they contained, the fire gave great impetus to new styles in the escapist aftermath of the plague.

Other people's misfortunes on the continent of Europe had similarly beneficial effects on art and design in 17th century England. A typical example came in 1685 when Louis XIV revoked the Edict of Nantes, which had given Protestants some degree of protection against religious persecution. The event drove thousands of French weavers, cabinetmakers and glassworkers to exile in Holland and England. Silk workers who settled in Spitalfields, London, built a silk and brocade-making industry which enriched the trend in furniture upholstery. Wren eagerly employed the talents of French craftsmen to produce crystal glass chandeliers in palace settings that were to rival the luxuries of Versailles.

Left: *Furniture and interior design flowered after the Restoration of the monarchy. An inventory of 1679 of the Duke and Duchess of Lauderdale's possessions at Ham House, Surrey (of which a portion of the north drawing room is shown here) spoke of a proliferation of small tables and many types of upholstered chairs. Such pieces were used in juxtaposition with tapestries and elaborately carved walls and ceilings.*

Above: *Marquetry – delicate patterns formed by woods of different types and colours – decorates this late 17th century side table. The spirally turned legs are typical of the period. Eventually the Dutch cabinetmakers were to dominate the marquetry field and England began to import their richly decorated products in very large quantities.*

Furniture followed a clear evolutionary pattern during the century. Under James I, style and simplicity followed the late Elizabethan indulgence in grotesque ornamentation. The oak chest experienced a decline in favour of more sophisticated furniture. The lathe was an important factor in this evolution and the craft of the chairmaker began to separate itself from that of the cabinetmaker. Turning gradually replaced carving and the lathe's use spread into rural areas, raising the quality and widening the range of country furniture. The century was also to see the birth of the Windsor chair, with its seat of elm, legs and uprights of beech and hoops of ash, beech, yew or fruitwood. Restrained use of inlay became popular but in the early years of the century marquetry had not yet reached any degree of perfection. The time was approaching when furniture was to be designed primarily for its utility. Ostentation was frowned upon if it interfered with functionalism.

In the reign of Charles I, who was a great patron of the arts, a tapestry factory flourished at Mortlake on the Thames (it had been set up by James in 1619) and Vandyck was installed in London under royal patronage. Refined lines and well balanced proportions were a keynote of the best furniture. The Commonwealth of Oliver Cromwell cannot claim to have produced its own furniture styles; one type of chair on severe lines and with a leather back and seat is sometimes dubbed Cromwellian, but really it owed its origins to the Dutch. In Puritan England styles merely continued the pattern established under Charles.

After the Restoration of the monarchy in 1660, furniture styles were guided by the court of Charles II, whose exile overseas had imbued him with exotic tastes. French, Dutch and Italian furniture mingled with that introduced by his Portuguese queen, Catherine of Braganza. With the marriage had come the dowry of Bombay and Eastern influences began to show in English furniture in the form of carved ebony chairs, inlaid with ivory. Exquisite leather work became a feature of English chairs, similar in design to those high-backed favourites in Catherine's homeland.

An epoch-making event was the introduction, *c.*1680, of the cabriole or goat's leg from France. This outwardly curved style, which first appeared on chairs and later on tables, was to bring about a revolution in furniture. As a result the basic wood of English choice was to change, for curves and flowing lines demanded a softer wood than oak. The age was fast approaching when the sturdy oak of England had to give way to walnut. The new age was ushered in towards the close of the 17th century. It was developed under William and Mary and was in full flower by the reign of Queen Anne.

It was inevitable that Dutch influence should predominate during the reign of William of Orange and his wife at the end of the century. It is arguable that Holland

Below: *This carved oak open chair dates from 1656 as the panel at the top of the back denotes. It is an example of furniture from the Commonwealth period, but, like much produced in that era, it owes its lines to Charles I styling. Nevertheless the appearance of seat and supports is thoroughly in keeping with the austere and sober climate of the times.*

was equally as responsible as France for England's introduction to the cabriole leg. Certainly Dutch influence led to the adoption about 1700 of the claw and ball foot style of carving which became the characteristic terminal feature of the cabriole legs of chairs and tables throughout the 18th century. The Dutch had imported this style, which was based on the symbol of a dragon's claw holding a pearl, from China.

Yet another Dutch legacy was the custom of collecting china jars, bowls and dishes, which led to the introduction of display cabinets in the reign of William and Mary. From Holland, too, came the fashion for marquetry, an art raised to the highest levels by the Dutch cabinetmakers of the 18th century. The taste for long case clocks also owes much to the stimulus given by William's countrymen.

The development of furniture from the reign of James I to the end of the 17th century is best traced through its component types. Early Stuart chairs, still oak, were assuming more comfortable proportions, with lightly padded seats, small back panels and often plain legs. Stretchers were gradually being placed higher above floor level. The armless farthingale chair was so named because it afforded a lady the opportunity to spread out and show off the dress of that name. The X-frame chair was given a new lease of life in a more richly upholstered form, which made the best use of existing talents in the embroidery of damask, velvet and brocade.

After the dog days of the Commonwealth, Restoration furniture moved into new areas, with walnut and beech sometimes replacing the traditional oak. Upholstery became more common. Tall backs, in the Dutch style, acquired attractive panels of cane, which was also used extensively in seats. The front stretcher, now abandoning completely its earlier function as a foot rest, became the vehicle for elaborate carving, an important decorative feature of the finished chair. Arms, on those chairs which possessed them, often ended in a downward scroll. Carving generally became open – pierced instead of the solid form of the previous century. Settees to seat two and three people, with cane or open splat backs gained favour in the last quarter of the century. Under William and Mary, some of the more elaborate carving of Charles II's day was

Below: *Contrasting styles of turning and carving are seen in these 17th century oak chairs. The turned version has a characteristically shaped triangular seat. The carved chair displays a Garden of Eden scene in the back panel and is heavily ornamented elsewhere with scrolls, figures and grotesque beasts. Already, however, the front stretcher has begun to lose its function and is becoming a vehicle for decoration.*

Above: *A farthingale chair, an armless type so termed because it was designed to accommodate the hooped petticoat of that name. This oak version of about 1645 still retains its original upholstery of 'Turkey work', heavy fabric woven with knotted pile in imitation of Middle Eastern carpets. The simple chamfered legs are typical of such chairs.*

Above: *Described in the 1679 inventory of Ham House as a 'scriptor', this silver-mounted writing cabinet (c.1675) is veneered with kingwood and rests on a turned and carved stand of the same wood. The flap lets down to provide a writing surface and reveals a nest of drawers. Age has lightened the exterior veneer to a golden brown.*

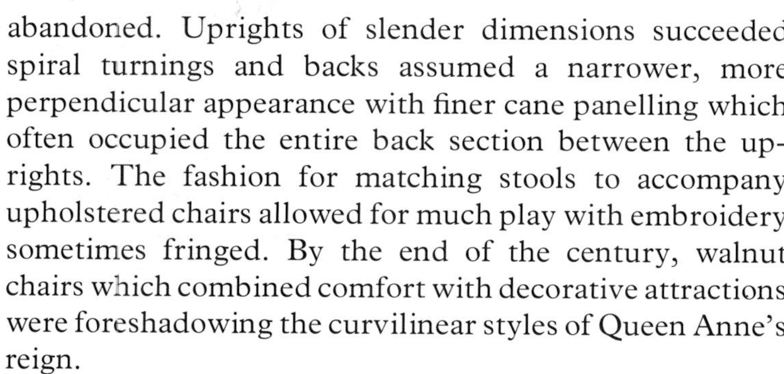

abandoned. Uprights of slender dimensions succeeded spiral turnings and backs assumed a narrower, more perpendicular appearance with finer cane panelling which often occupied the entire back section between the uprights. The fashion for matching stools to accompany upholstered chairs allowed for much play with embroidery sometimes fringed. By the end of the century, walnut chairs which combined comfort with decorative attractions were foreshadowing the curvilinear styles of Queen Anne's reign.

Tables became progressively smaller as the century progressed. It was the day of the gate-leg table, a type ideally suited to the custom of dining at a series of individual tables rather than at one long refectory table. An innovation was the fitting of small drawers to the ends of such tables. Small rectangular tables on turned legs, with flat curved stretchers, were dotted round the room. After the Restoration, these were designed to go *en suite* with mirrors and wall sconces (the latter to hold candles, which were increasingly effective in good decoration thanks to the reflecting qualities of mirrors). Spirally turned, early Stuart legs were gradually replaced by tapering baluster legs and by the end of the century corporate design – involving architecture, interior decoration and furnishing – had led to the introduction of gilded tables with tops of marble or scagliola, a composition used to imitate marble. These were known as pier tables, standing as they did against the pier or wall section between two windows, and often surmounted by elaborately framed pier glasses or mirrors.

Chests, which had begun to accommodate drawers in a modest way, during the 16th century, developed quickly in early Stuart days. By the Restoration chests of drawers were in everyday use throughout England. The fashion for dainty clothing necessitated a profusion of small drawers and such chests frequently stood on stands with spirally turned legs. Later, these legs assumed the cabriole form which was affecting the design of chairs and tables. Inlays of ivory, mother-of-pearl and increasing use of marquetry and the geometrical parquetry added to the decorative qualities of this type of furniture.

In the dining room, the buffet and court cupboard were coming into widespread use as utilitarian pieces of furniture and not merely for the ostentatious display of plate (much of which had been lost through melting down during the Civil War). The sideboard, as it became known, had its main working surface at a convenient height for carving. Of similar derivation was the Stuart dresser, the lower part with a cupboard and row of drawers beneath ranks of narrow shelves on which plates and other vessels could be arranged ready for use. The so-called Welsh dresser was not a native of that area but Wales took eagerly to the developing style and distinctive variations emerged. North Wales dressers had a base completely enclosed with cupboards and drawers, while those from west Wales had three drawers and two cupboards with a 'dog kennel' space between; south Wales favoured a type with drawers below and an open pot board above. By the end of the 17th century the country yeomanry was becoming increasingly prosperous and a rich tradition of finely carved oak dressers was growing up in Yorkshire, Derbyshire, Sussex and Suffolk, as well as Wales. These pieces of furniture are in high demand today.

Desks, which had previously been little more than portable boxes, began to evolve in the form in which we know them today. When Charles II revived the monarchy in 1660 they were beginning to assume a more sophisticated form consisting of two parts. The upper secretaire might have a sloping, hinged lid opening downwards, or be in the shape of a cabinet with a fall front. This upper section stood on a separate stand with spirally turned or baluster legs. Such pieces of furniture were among the earliest to be made in walnut, often in the form of fine veneers. Later the traditional English bureau was to evolve, with a chest of drawers surmounted by a slope-top writing compartment containing nests of small drawers. In a time of plotting and counter-plotting, secret drawers with hidden locks and catches became a feature of these bureaux and secretaires.

Below: *Walnut oyster veneer – cut as cross sections of roots and branches and resembling oyster shells – decorates a side table of about 1680, together with floral marquetry of other woods. Beech forms the frame. The marquetry is repeated in the centre of the stretcher. Legs of spirally turned shape complete this elegant piece.*

Above: *Functionalism and the minimum of ornamentation are immediately obvious in this Charles II oak side table. The stretchers, uniting the simply turned legs, are plain, flat pieces of wood. Nevertheless the symmetry of its design makes it a highly desirable piece in the saleroom market today.*
Left: *This James II side table, of a type sometimes known as a credence table, has an octagonal hinged top, which may be opened up and supported on a gate-leg. It has a decoratively carved apron, bulbous turned legs and stands on simple block feet. The wood is oak, still in favour at the time, but gradually bowing out to walnut.*
Right: *In honest oak – a tridarn, a Welsh term for a cupboard or press in three sections. Dating from the 17th century, this is an example of a typical regional variety which developed its own lines and styling from the Elizabethan court cupboard.*

As aids to writing developed with the spread of literacy, so there grew the demand for the storage of books. The first rooms to be designated as libraries were a feature of post-Restoration days. In London the Victoria and Albert Museum has one of the earliest English bookcases. It is in solid oak, stands on five bun feet and dates from about 1675. Shelves compose the upper and lower parts, both of which are enclosed by glazed doors. Heavy glazing bars are a feature of bookcases of this period and the more delicate tracery which was eventually to cover the fronts of bookcases was not to be seen until the late 18th century. Lacquered and japanned cabinets of Restoration days were rectangular in shape and were mounted on elaborately carved stands. Other cabinets stood on chests of drawers and were cousins of the tallboy to be found in the bedroom areas of the house.

Of the vast fund of skill and talent which contributed to English furniture and decorative design in the 17th century, there is no more romantic story than that of the wood-carver *par excellence*, Grinling Gibbons (1648–1721). Born in Rotterdam, and much influenced by the Dutch carving style, he became the leader of a highly talented school of wood-carvers which flowered initially in England at the court of Charles II – although Gibbons served successive monarchs equally faithfully. His 'discovery' is the stuff of legend. The diarist John Evelyn has described how, one day when he was out walking near the marshes at Deptford in south-east London, he found Gibbons at work in a thatched cottage. The subject was an elaborate carving of Tintoretto's *Crucifixion*, a priceless work which is today housed on loan at the Victoria and Albert Museum. Gibbons was brought to the attention of Charles II and a long and successful royal connection ensued. The carver most liked to work in soft limewood, but examples of his incomparable carvings are to be found in oak and pearwood. He excelled in natural chains of fruit, flowers, foliage, birds and cherubs' heads. One of his finest works is the frame of a portrait of Henry VIII after Holbein at Petworth, Sussex. It is carved in limewood and was executed between 1689 and 1692. Horace Walpole described it as 'the most superb monument to Grinling Gibbons' skill'.

Left: *Over the altar of St James in Piccadilly stands this, one of the many memorials in London churches to the incomparable carving skill of Grinling Gibbons (1648–1721), an artist whose fame was advanced by the patronage of Charles II and other influential people. Gibbons excelled in the creation of elaborate festoons of flowers, foliage, game and cherubs.*

His work abounds in London and neighbouring counties and much of it is documented by contemporary invoices and letters between carver and clients. There is one communication from Grinling Gibbons, dated 1686, to which a dramatic postscript was written two and a half centuries later. The letter was to a church dignitary and concerned an altarpiece or reredos (a screen), which Gibbons carved for the Wren church of St Mary Abchurch in the City of London. It reads:

> I would beg the faver from You to send me the 30 1. (£30) due of the olter pees but if the Gentellmen consarnd does not beleave it to be not folle (full) Anof of worck then obleage to send 20 1. by this baerer and as soen as I kane kome in toune Agane I will waet one You and sattisfy You Youer desire.
>
> Sor I am Youer sarvt
> Grinling Gibbons

In 1940 a German bomb wrecked the church and the Grinling reredos. A salvage team led by a woman verger combed the debris and gathered together 2,000 pieces of the shattered carving. Today, like the church, the reredos has been restored, a tribute to the master craftsman Grinling Gibbons and a remarkable example of links between 17th and 20th century skills.

Queen Anne was the last of the Stuart monarchs, reigning from 1702 to 1714. Even though her line had suffered more than its share of misfortunes, the Stuarts' legacy to England was not inconsiderable. At home, their reigns had been marked by growing toleration for nonconformists and the arts, sciences and literature had prospered. Milton had written *Paradise Lost* and Bunyan *Pilgrim's Progress*. Abroad there had been significant progress to new paradises. England, competing with Holland and France, had staked rich claims; the trading stations of the East India Company had been established, the American colonies were set up and Gibraltar and Minorca had been placed under the flag. Increased power and prestige in Europe led to a fervent British nationalism. Its effects were clearly seen in furniture development under Queen Anne, her name being used in furniture annals to describe her own reign and also the early Georgian period until about 1730.

Left: *A close-up of oyster veneering, showing the dramatic effect it has on the surface of a Queen Anne chest on stand when combined with concentric stringing – narrow bands of inlaid wood in contrasting tones. The variety of colours of walnut was one of the wood's attractions which appealed to furniture makers, who relied on tones and configurations, rather than carving, popular in earlier periods, for decorative effect.*

Walnut, of course, reigned supreme. Although widely used in Italy, Spain, France, Flanders, the Low Countries and South Germany during the Renaissance movements, it had found only minor acceptance in England until the Restoration. Once regarded as a luxury wood for the wealthy, it was in general use by Anne's day. It has strength without excessive weight, cuts and carves well and takes a high polish. Both as a solid and as a veneer it has variety of colour, texture and configuration, producing interesting patterns. Europe first used its own species, *Juglans regia*, which is pale brown in colour with brown and black veinings. Grown in large quantities on the eastern seaboard of America, and eventually imported into Europe as the walnut age flowered, was the species *Juglans nigra* – black walnut, having a darker brown colour, with even darker markings – a beautiful wood much favoured by cabinetmakers. England relied on Continental imports to supplement the production of its own walnut plantations, but the severe winter of 1709 killed many trees in central Europe and in 1720 France forbade any export of walnut. These setbacks encouraged the trade with Virginia and may well have speeded the progression towards mahogany.

Walnut was a wood ideally suited to the gracious curves of Anne's time epitomized by the cabriole leg. The curving line was echoed in the swan's neck shaping of the chair back around splats which were frequently vase-shaped. The era was marked by a general move towards comfort. There was

Right: *English, walnut, early 18th century, and typical. The chair has a characteristic vase-shaped splat and the front cabriole legs display a restrained amount of knee carving. They end in the renowned claw and ball feet, a type derived from China via the Netherlands. By Queen Anne's day walnut was in general use, in town and country, among English furniture makers.*

Above: *The Windsor chair, traditionally made in the beech woods of Buckinghamshire of beech, elm and yew, demonstrates its ability to make advantageous and harmonious use of the cabriole leg, so popular in Queen Anne's day. Here, the front legs are united by a bow-shaped stretcher. The Windsor had many varieties, and American chair makers produced their own characteristic versions.*

developed of importing marquetry cabinets from Holland that was to last throughout the century.

The home-produced cabinet was mounted at first on a stand with the turned spiral legs of Jacobean days; later, the stand adopted the universal cabriole legs terminating in claw and ball feet (the last feature being often the only place where the carver could show his skills). The cabinet became a natural vehicle for growing experiments in lacquering, although English attempts at this oriental art were generally not very successful. Nevertheless, as trade with the east increased, Chinese and Japanese lacquered cabinets were imported through Holland. Bastardized versions exist which are the products of Chinese craftsmen who supplied do-it-yourself panels to the cabinetmakers of the Netherlands, France and occasionally England.

Chairs lost their stretchers completely when the adoption of the cabriole leg made them redundant. Seats had a gently rounded front rail. Legs ended in the claw and ball or club foot. Armchairs had their arms supported by an upright a little way back from the front of the seat because the cabriole leg made it difficult to continue leg and arm support in one flowing movement. Chairs generally became less tall and had rounded or hoop-shaped backs in harmonious proportions with the curves of seats and legs. Country chairs, too, were changing. The Windsor chair prospered, most being made in the beech woods found around High Wycombe, Buckinghamshire. In Lancashire, Yorkshire and other country areas, typical chairs developed with ladder or upright splat backs. Such chairs were unfashionable in London but today early 18th century examples vie with the most expensive aristocrats of the international salerooms.

Card playing became fashionable – almost a vice said some. The craze resulted in a flood of Queen Anne card

elegance of an inornate quality, without severity; dignity and balanced proportion graced a period which lasted the better part of half a century. Above all, English furniture developed an insularity that almost consciously rejected the styles and movements of France and other continental countries. The European influences which had prospered under the patronage of Charles II and William and Mary were being systematically anglicized by a new generation of native craftsmen who were now specialists in their own right.

Carving was restrained, being limited to a minimum amount of decoration on the knee of a leg. Much use was made of improved techniques in veneering. Reliance was placed on wood's natural configuration as decoration; thus, we find widespread favour for burr walnut, a type of veneer displaying attractive patterns produced by sawing transversely through knots and boughs of the original gnarled wood. Marquetry was less in favour, but it did appear occasionally on chairs and small tables and a tradition

tables of walnut veneer, with folding tops and frequently tills or candle sconces at each corner. A development of the gate leg enabled these tables to be condensed in size and placed against a wall when not in use. Their cabriole legs were generally plain, but they became the recipients of more carving when mahogany was introduced later in the century.

The reigns of Queen Anne, George I (1714–27) and the early years of George II saw the introduction of small tables for taking tea or the display of porcelain but their development owes more to the period after 1730. Similarly, heavy console tables, fixed to the wall by a bracket were soon to appear, but their greatest popularity was achieved a little later under the direction of architect and designer William Kent, who was responsible for an extravagant Baroque style in the second quarter of the century.

The double chest, or tallboy, which had appeared at the end of the 17th century, rose to a height of about two metres (six feet) and in Anne's time it was often embellished with burr walnut veneers. This fine finish was sometimes complemented by fluted pilasters at the front. A version of the tallboy entered the territory of the secretaire and bureau when it was provided with a middle section complete with fall front and compartmented area for writing materials. In this field, however, perhaps the most characteristic product of Queen Anne furniture styling was the essentially English bureau, which consisted of a sloping front upper section, mounted on a chest of drawers. It took little for this construction to be surmounted by a cabinet to form the traditional English bureau cabinet and subsequently the bureau bookcase. Simultaneously the bookcase proper developed in more sophisticated directions; in early Georgian times it was frequently topped by the type of architectural, triangular pediment found on classical temples.

The fashion for collecting porcelain had become very widespread thanks to the new trading links with the East and display cabinets with glazed doors were found in the homes of the wealthy, placed in the dining room now rather than the drawing room. As a furniture accessory to the service of meals, the sideboard table was replacing the shelved sideboard of the 17th century. It tended to be a fairly simple object consisting of a marble top placed on a cabriole-legged structure. Refinement of storage facilities and function were to come in the later days of mahogany in the second half of the century.

Across the Atlantic the colonial version of the Queen Anne style enjoyed a lease of life that far outlasted its parent style in the home country. Indeed, the graceful curved line that epitomized the movement lingered on American furniture until the end of the century, spanning the Revolution and overlapping into what is now known as the Federal period in American furniture. This time-lag, experienced with every style of European furniture, is a fascinating aspect of American furniture history and has resulted in a rich field of study for collectors. For example, the claw and ball foot was not popular in the American colonies until about 1750 and even then it was very much the adopted style of the New York area only. By that time, however, Europe had moved on to fresh fields. In England, from about 1730, walnut was bowing out to the newly fashionable mahogany. The transition once again opened the door to the wood-carver and signalled the beginning of one of the most glorious phases of English furniture history.

Left: *For decoration, this Queen Anne bachelor chest relies almost entirely on the fine configuration of the walnut, a technique which was widespread in the period. It has a fold-out top, with extending slides to support it.*
Right: *A double-domed bureau bookcase of Queen Anne's time has the typical lines of the day, but it is made in oak, whereas walnut was being extensively used for this most English of furniture pieces. Slides support the drop flap of the secretaire compartment.*

The Age of Rococo

France

The word 'Rococo' is a term coined in the 19th century and derived from the French *rocaille*, a word which originally described the rock and shell work of the artificially constructed grottoes in the grounds of Versailles and they came to mean any decoration of this type. Many pieces of carved furniture dating from the 18th century – in particular, mirror frames – depict rocks, shells and dripping water in their composition, frequently in association with Chinese figures and pagodas. A similar concept of the romantic landscapes is characteristic of much authentic Chinese painting.

Chinoiseries however, were popular in France before the Rococo style began, appearing in the designs of Bérain and in Boulle marquetry in the late 17th century, when French Baroque was beginning to display signs of relaxing a little from its customary rigidity but was still preserving an essential symmetry. One of the first to rebel against this discipline was Pierre Le Pautre (*c.*1648–1716), the son of Jean (chief designer of furniture under Le Brun: see page 53). Pierre worked as a designer at Versailles (under J.H. Mansart) from 1699 until his death, a period which covered the last years of Louis XIV, when the king himself was growing a little weary of the ornate grandeur with which he had surrounded himself.

Even so, it was not until after the death of Louis in 1715 that any fundamental changes were permitted to happen, other than a gradual replacement of vertical legs with those of scroll or S-shape which had made their appearance in the 1680s. When the king died, his heir was his great-grandson, Louis XV, then a child of five, and a regency under Philippe, Duke of Orléans, was established. Stylistically, the term Régence is usually extended to cover the last years of Louis XIV and the early ones of Louis XV – *c.*1700–35 – and was a period when the heavy, male splendour of the Baroque was slowly giving way to the light, feminine charm of the Rococo.

The femininity however, may not always be apparent in typical pieces of the Régence period. The Boulle commode was at first either *en tombeau* (sarcophagus form), or serpentine-fronted. Next to appear was the bombé (swollen) form, which was difficult to create because it involved a complexity of curves on both the horizontal and the vertical planes. This had three drawers, the bottom one extending almost to the ground. It was often decorated with parquetry, and fitted with massively cast bronze handles and mounts.

Left: *The Mars salon at Versailles, with furniture of the Louis XV period. The* bureau-plat *(flat-topped writing table) on four cabriole legs has replaced the eight-legged* bureau-Mazarin *of the Louis XIV period. The* fauteuils *(armchairs) and the* canapé *(sofa) also have elegant cabriole legs and are made comfortable with fine upholstery.*

Above: *Commode of* bombé *shape, c.1760–70, decorated with marquetry in various woods and mounted with gilded, chiselled bronze – known in England as 'ormolu' (literally, ground gold). The top is of marble. The maker is thought to have been Pierre Langlois, a cabinetmaker of French origin who settled in London c.1760.*

The cabinetmakers chiefly responsible for these developments were probably Boulle himself and Charles Cressent (1685–1758), the son of a sculptor who, in 1719, married the widow of Joseph Poitou, Boulle's chief rival and cabinetmaker to the Regent. Cressent gave up his father's profession, which he had been following, and adopted his grandfather's, which happened to be cabinet-making – or rather, he combined the two. His furniture, especially the bronze mounts, are highly sculptural. He became cabinetmaker to the Regent in Poitou's place, and developed a rich, flowing, curvaceous style. Boulle was probably the first to reduce the bulk of the commode by dispensing with the bottom drawer and raising the carcase on curved legs; but Cressent was probably responsible for creating the typical Louis XV commode of bombé form in which the two drawer-fronts appear as one uninterrupted surface, and are decorated as such, with no apparent dividing rail between them. The type is known as *sans*

Left: *Louis XV* bureau-de-dame *(lady's bureau) with scarlet decoration in imitation of Chinese lacquer, achieved by painting with* vernis Martin, *a patent varnish invented by the family whose name it commemorates. Authentic 18th century examples such as this are prized by collectors and command very high prices.*

traverse. Cressent's early work is characterized by relatively plain veneers in fine woods, ornamented by fine mounts which he made himself – much to the annoyance of the guilds, who insisted on demarcation lines between the crafts of woodwork and metalwork. Although eminently successful, he nevertheless got into financial difficulties in 1748 and thereafter cut down on the expensive bronze mounts which had to be cast, chiselled, gilded with an amalgam of mercury and pure gold and finally burnished. Cressent's later pieces were decorated with floral marquetry.

There are some who contend that Antoine-Robert Gaudreau (or Gaudreaux, *c.*1680–1751) was the inventor of the *commode sans traverse.* He worked for Louis XV from 1726 and was a competitor of Cressent, employing a most sumptuous style. A commode he produced for the king's bedroom at Versailles (now in the Wallace Collection, London) had bronze mounts by Jacques Caffiéri (1673–1755), the greatest master in this medium, and was made to a design by Antoine-Sébastien Slodtz (*c.*1695–1754), whose versatility extended to designing for the theatre.

The honour for inventing the fully developed Rococo style is shared by two designers, both of them well-travelled in widely separated parts of Europe. Juste-Aurèle Meissonier (*c.* 1693–1750) was born in Turin and went to Paris about 1720 where he succeeded Bérain in 1725 as architect-designer to the king. He designed a wide range of objects and cultivated the second phase of Rococo, known as the *genre pittoresque.* This movement totally rejected classical principles, ignored the orders of architecture and favoured an asymmetrical fantasy of C-scrolls, flowers, rocks, shells, Chinamen and putti, all of which had been used before but never in such charming and sometimes absurd arrangements. He actually worked as a silversmith and some of his furniture-designs give the impression of having been intended to be cast in that metal rather than fashioned out of wood. He worked in Poland and Portugal as an architect, and published a series of highly influential designs for complete interiors, bronzes, silver and furniture.

The other leading light of the *genre pittoresque* was Nicolas Pineau (1684–1754), who was born in Paris but worked in Russia from 1716 to 1726, designing for Peter the Great at the Peterhof, *c.*1720. On returning to Paris he became a fashionable creator of elegant furnishing schemes at a time when the city rather than Versailles had become the smart place to live. (Louis XIV had insisted on his court living most of their lives in the palace.) Cressent was among the makers who worked to his designs, six of which were pirated in England by Thomas Langley, without acknowledgement.

The vogue for chinoiseries encouraged the perfecting of substitutes for oriental lacquer that could be used effectively for patterns in low relief. Success in this was achieved by the four brothers Martin: Guillaume (d.1749), Etiènne-Simon (d.1770), Julien (d.1783) and Robert (1706–66). In 1730 Guillaume and Etiènne were granted a monopoly, renewed in 1744, for the production of a varnish that was good enough to be used in association with authentic Japanese lacquer panels. Robert specialized in a variation of this varnish which produced a monochrome, gold-dusted finish. It was derived from a varnish called *cipolin* which contains garlic. Following the technique which originated in the Far East, up to 40 coats were applied to the surface, each one being rubbed down before the next was applied. Martin brothers' varnish was widely known as *vernis Martin* and the term has come to be applied to a particular type of decoration on furniture in the Louis XV style – particularly the Watteau-like scenes painted on *vitrines* (display cabinets); most of those seen today are 19th century or later.

Robert Martin enjoyed the patronage of Madame la Marquise de Pompadour (1721–64) who became *maîtresse-en-titre* to Louis XV in 1745, when she was given that title and the estate that went with it. She was created a *duchesse* in 1752 and until her death at the age of 42 exercised great power over the king, his court, and all the arts including the creation of fine furniture. Most of the results were beneficial. It was partly her influence – although the trend was already evident – that led to the fashion for smaller, more intimate rooms both in palaces and private houses. A whole new range of comparatively small, elegant pieces of furniture – desks, stools, small tables and other pieces – was created to equip apartments that were frequently panelled and painted in the Rococo style.

Among the many cabinetmakers of the period now known by name was Bernard II van Risenburgh (*c.*1700–65). Both his father and his son were cabinet-makers, and they are referred to as Bernard I and III respectively. Bernard II used *vernis Martin* very cleverly to decorate the frames of small tables to match, as exactly as possible, the colours and patterns of Sèvres porcelain plaques inserted into the tops. The Sèvres factory was one of the enterprises which owed its continued existence largely to the support of Madame de Pompadour, and plaques of various shapes and sizes were frequently used in this way for embellishing furniture. It was an activity governed to some extent by the middlemen or dealers known as *marchand-merciers* who obtained commissions from clients and placed orders with the makers, in rather the same way as a modern interior decorator works. They had much to contend with, reconciling the whims of their clients with the obstructive practices of the various *corporations* (guilds) and the royal monopolies limiting the sale of

Right: *Detail of the decoration in European lacquer on a bureau bookcase* c.*1730. The fashion for oriental lacquer and for the many imitations of it which had begun during the Baroque period in the 17th century, continued during the 18th century, finding expression in light-hearted depictions of birds, flowers, trees, figures in rocky landscapes, all perfectly suited to the element of fantasy in Rococo design.*
Below: *Bombé commode lacquered in the oriental style, probably by Bernard van Risenburgh II, a leading exponent of this style of decoration who sometimes used panels of genuine Chinese or Japanese lacquer in combination with a skilful imitation achieved with* vernis Martin, *a substitute produced in France. Bernard's son, van Risenburgh III, probably made some of the mounts for his father's furniture.*

Above: *A sumptuous Louis XV commode made by Antoine-Robert Gaudreau (c.1680–1751) who is credited with inventing the construction which dispensed with, or concealed, the dividing rail between the drawers of the commode so that the whole frontal surface could be treated, for decorative purposes, as one area. The feature is known as* sans traverse *when eliminated, and as* traverse perdue *when disguised.*

such things as Sèvres porcelain. Van Risenburgh seems always to have worked through a *marchand-mercier* – usually either Hébert or Poirier who were among the most influential.

Until 1957, Bernard van Risenburgh (or Risen Burgh) was known only by his initials as they appeared on pieces of his workmanship – B.V.R.B. The stamping of a personal mark became obligatory for every cabinetmaker and joiner in the Paris guild from 1743 until 1791, with the exceptions of those working directly for the royal household, as well as a privileged group of foreign craftsmen with premises in the Faubourg St Antoine area. The mark usually consists of the surname followed by the letters 'JME' (*juré des menuisiers et ébénistes*) stamped into the wood in an inconspicuous place. On a commode, it is usually to be found in the unpolished wood below the marble top. Research has brought to light not only fairly complete lists of the members of the guild working during the second half of the 18th century until all guilds were abolished following the Revolution, but also a remarkable fund of information concerning the relationships between whole tribes of craftsmen. The official guild system was backed up by an unofficial dynastic one resulting from intermarriage between families in the furniture trade. Large provincial centres, such as Lyons, also had their guilds and their systems of applying *estampilles* (stamped names) but much less is known about them. Some of them achieved high standards and it should be emphasized that merely because a piece bears no mark, it does not follow that it is not genuinely 18th century – it may be a good provincial article, or one made in Paris before 1751 when the stamp became a legal requirement and not merely, as in 1743, a guild regulation that was often defied. The object of the system was to maintain high standards of workmanship by requiring the craftsman to put his name to his products, thus putting his reputation to the test.

The recorded names of 18th century French cabinetmakers and joiners, and those practising related crafts, are far too numerous to be listed here. The majority are listed by J. Nicolay in *L'art des maîtres Ebénistes Français* (1959) and much detailed information concerning their working and family relationships is provided by Guillaume Janneau's *Les Ateliers Parisiens d'Ebénistes et de Menuisiers* (1975), together with facsimile reproductions of their *estampilles.* The names of a few of the best-known craftsmen are mentioned below in relation to the types of product in which they specialized.

Sophisticated French furniture is conveniently divided into two main groups – *ébénisterie*, i.e. pieces which were veneered, such as commodes; and *menuiserie*, i.e. pieces not veneered, such as chairs and settees. A characteristic of most sophisticated pieces, whether solid or veneered, during the Louis XV period was the elimination of the straight line wherever possible. Not only the decoration but the pieces themselves followed graceful lines, of which the S-shaped curve of the cabriole leg, often embodied in the outline of the carcase, was consistently present. The word 'cabriole' was not used to describe this type of leg until the 19th century and is derived from the Latin *capra* (goat).

The cabriole leg evolved from ancient shapes found on furniture in Egypt, Greece and Rome that were modelled on the legs of animals (see page 13). The correct French

Right: *Louis XV* encoignure *(corner cabinet) richly ornamented in gilded bronze and surmounted by a clock in a case of the same material. This very rare piece was made c.1740 by Jacques Dubois (c.1693–1763) to a design by Nicolas Pineau (1684–1754), one of the principal creators of the more frivolous elements in the Rococo style. It was more usual for an* encoignure *to be waist-high, with no superstructure.*

term for the shape is *pied-de-biche* (foot of a hind, or female deer). The French version of the leg usually joined the under-edge of the frame in an uninterrupted concave curve (In some other versions, a convex bulge appeared at this point). The leg terminated in a carved, upward-turning scroll on *menuiserie*, or was shod with a gilt bronze *sabot* cast in the form of a hoof, paw or foliate scroll on *ébénisterie*. In such a position, the bronze is serving a protective function for the wood underneath as well as providing a decorative finish.

This kind of protection was not needed on 18th century French chairs and settees. Almost without exception, they were made in solid oak, walnut or beech and were either left in the natural state and wax-polished or provided with a painted or gilt finish. They were seldom veneered. The flowing lines of the cabriole legs were continued along the under-edge of the seat-frame, up through the *os-de-mouton* (ram's horn) arm-supports and along to the cartouche-shaped back. Carved decoration of flowers and shells were employed at carefully spaced intervals on some examples but many were relieved only with carved mouldings (*décor en mouluration*) that emphasized the rhythmic sweep. Seat and back were usually upholstered in silk or tapestry. If the arms of an armchair are enclosed, and if the seat is supplied with a loose cushion, the type is properly known as a *bergère*. (This term is traditionally used differently on English furniture, to mean a chair with canework on arms and back). When the arms of the chair are left open, and there is no cushion for the seat, then the armchair is termed a *fauteuil*.

There is an extensive vocabulary to cover the variety of settees or sofas. Collectively they are known as *canapés*. The *canapé-à-confident* was curved so that two people could half-face each other in conversation. Alternative names are *causeuse* and *tête-à-tête*. The *marquise* was a straight-fronted type, while the *duchesse* consisted of two or three separate items that could be put together: a long-seated *bergère* could be combined with a *bergère* of normal proportions, or two *bergères* could face each other with a stool between them; either system resulted in a form of day-bed. There are many other terms for types of settees, though each name may not always be used to mean exactly the same type. The Rue de Cléry was a centre for the making of seat furniture in the mid-18th century, and housed several generations of important makers including the Foliot, Cresson and Blanchard families.

Stools (*tabourets*) had a special significance at court, being occupied by ladies while in the king's presence. Madame de Pompadour was accorded her *tabouret* only on becoming a duchess. Less formally, stools were made *en suite* with chairs and settees.

The cabinet-on-stand went out of fashion during the Louis XV period, as did most tall pieces of salon furniture. The most important prestige piece was the commode, reaching only up to dado level so that a mirror or picture could be hung over it. Although it usually conformed to the type with two drawers already described, it was sometimes fitted as a cupboard with two doors decorated with marquetry or lacquer, the panels framed in complex, opposing C-scrolls of gilded bronze. A variation on the cabinet-commode, which was also an exception to the general preference for low wall-pieces, was the *cartonnier*, a dwarf cabinet with an upper stage of open shelves, sometimes surmounted by a clock built into the frame. A clock was also a feature in the superstructure of a corner

Above: *Rolltop desk – probably the first ever – made for Louis XV in the years 1760–9. It was begun by J.-F. Oeben who had become cabinetmaker to the king in 1754 but died before finishing it. The work was completed by J.-H. Riesener, one of his assistants who succeeded him, marrying the widow Oeben and taking over the business.*

cabinet (*encoignure*) with cupboard-base and open shelves above in a design by Pineau, closely followed *c.* 1750 by Jacques Dubois (*c.*1693–1763). More often, however, the *encoignure* was a dwarf piece with no superstructure. It was sometimes veneered or lacquered, or made in the solid and panelled to match the walls of the room.

The *cartonnier* also appeared in another form as an adjunct to a flat-topped writing table, the *bureau-plat*, which replaced the heavier-looking *bureau-Mazarin* of the Louis XIV period. The bureau-plat was basically a simple construction of a table top on four cabriole legs, with drawers concealed in the frieze; in practice it became a highly impressive item of furniture, the top of separate shape on all four sides, the legs mounted in gilded bronze, with matching handles to the drawers. The type was much copied, often extremely well, in the 19th century. A notable mid-18th century example by Pierre Roussel (1723–82) is in the Louvre.

Many pieces of furniture were made expressly for the use of women, the ladies' equivalent of the *bureau-plat* was the *bureau-de-dame*, a small desk with sloping fall-front, whose entire exterior sometimes consisted of gently undulating curves. Closely related was the *secrétaire-à-capucin* with 'tumble over' top. When closed, it appears to be a small table with an exceptionally deep frieze which concealed a nest of drawers; the fold-over top is opened forwards, and a spring mechanism releases the bank of drawers which spring up into position. Makers of these ingenious mechanical contrivances including Roger van der Cruse, who was admitted to the guild as a master cabinetmaker in 1755, and his brother-in-law J.F. Oeben (*c.*1720–63), a South German who settled in Paris, becoming *ébéniste-du-roi* in 1754, a post he held until his death. Nevertheless he died bankrupt. Two of his assistants, J.-F. Leleu and J.-H. Riesener, both paid court to the widow Oeben. Riesener (1734–1806) was the successful suitor and took over the business.

A wide variety of small tables came into being, some as toilet tables with mirrors which conveniently disappeared from view when, as was the fashion, the bedchamber was being used for entertaining guests. This type was known as a *bureau-de-toilette* and doubled as a dressing and writing table. Lighting depended on candles, and a special stand for the candelabrum, called a *guéridon*, was deemed essential in a well-appointed room. The *guéridon* evolved from the Baroque stands carved to represent negro slaves, which were popular in 17th century Italy. 'Gueridon' was the name of a Moorish slave whose exploits were celebrated in Provençal folk songs.

An occasional table, small enough to be portable (although often proving surprisingly heavy to lift) was the *table ambulante*. A celebrated maker of these small pieces was Charles Topino (*c.*1725–*c.*1789), who was born at Arras in Northern France and settled in the Faubourg St Antoine about 1745, where he is said to have lived a bohemian way of life. He specialized in a distinctive kind of marquetry in which flower vases and inkstands with quill pens are featured. By the time he had started work in Paris, there was already a reaction developing against the frivolity of the Rococo, and most of his work belongs to the transitional period between the styles associated with the reigns of Louis XV and Louis XVI. Topino was among the last of the great Louis XV cabinetmakers to abandon the cabriole leg. Typical of these transitional pieces was the *bonheur-du-jour*, a lady's writing-table with a superstructure of little drawers.

Styles did not change as rapidly in country places as they did in Paris. Armoires in the Louis XIV style, with 'bun' feet, continued to be made as late as the mid-18th century, and those in the Louis XV style with cabriole feet were still being produced in the early 19th century. The Rococo style did however, lend itself to the carvers of what is now termed *meubles regionaux* or *meubles provinciaux* (not to be confused with Provençal, which implies Provence as the source). 'Regional' or 'Provincial' furniture, then, has to be considered in its own right, and judged mainly on how well the maker handled his wood in the solid – oak, walnut or fruitwood, largely depending on local availability.

Almost all of it is anonymous, and while certain types were more popular in some areas than in others, it is dangerous to assume that because a particular piece is found in, say, Normandy, it necessarily started life there. The words used by the French for 'furniture' mean, literally, 'movable', and even the *grande armoire* with its double doors hung on pin hinges of steel or brass was easily taken apart by knocking out the dowel pins that held it together. The doors are, in the best examples, elaborately shaped, with flowers and foliage crisply carved on the frames and frequently on the cornice. Normandy examples

Below: Bonheur-du-jour *or lady's desk with a superstructure, in the transitional style that retained elements of Louis XV Rococo while moving towards the Neoclassicism of the Louis XVI period. The bronze mounts were the first feature to reflect the new preference for symmetry. Many makers were reluctant to abandon the carbriole leg.*

Below: *Like the* bonheur-du-jour *(left) this* bureau de toilette, *concealing a mirror under the hinged top and combining the functions of dressing table and desk, belongs to the transitional period linking the Louis XV and Louis XVI styles. The marquetry and cabriole legs are essentially Rococo, but the gilt metal mounts are Neoclassical.*

are noted for carving in high relief of baskets of flowers and pairs of lovebirds on armoires given as marriage cupboards.

In western France in particular, the single-door *petite armoire* or *bonnetière* was favoured by the women of those districts where exceptionally wide-brimmed hats were worn. Also in the west, in the Vendée and the Nantes region, the *homme debout* with a cupboard above, a drawer in the centre and another cupboard below, was popular. The *buffet-à-deux-corps* had a two-door cupboard of considerable height, which rested on another only about half its height. Late 18th-century Normandy examples show a slight reduction in Rococo exuberance but otherwise concede little to Neoclassical influence. The *pantalonnière*, seen in the south-west, is rather similar but has as its base a chest of two short and one long drawers.

The *buffet bas* is a low sideboard with cupboards and (usually) drawers above them. In large houses, the buffet was often of great length with four or five cupboard doors ranged side by side. When fitted with a rack of shelves above, it is known as a *buffet-vaisselier* or simply a *vaisselier*, and is equivalent to the English or Welsh dresser. Primitive examples in pine with painted decoration of formal lozenges come from Alsace-Lorraine. By contrast, a highly elaborate type with cupboards flanking the rack of shelves and a clock case at the centre, was produced in the Bourg-en-Bresse area in eastern France.

Perhaps the most highly prized French provincial pieces of all are the commodes which, to a greater or lesser extent, imitate the fashions set by the Parisian makers. They range from fairly simple rectilinear forms relieved by the most elementary attempts at carving, to the full bombé shapes, some with marble tops, produced in the region of Bordeaux. On the vast majority, bronze is employed only for handles, and veneer hardly at all. Certain centres, such as Grenoble, were more sophisticated. Marseilles imported mahogany which was used in the solid more generously than by most mid-18th century Paris makers. Full-blooded carving in the Rococo style takes the place of bronze mounts. Shaped or 'block' fronts occur more frequently than the full bombé curves. But the wood is rich in colour and the proportions are right. The Rococo style has been brought down to earth.

Left: *French Provincial child's armchair, mid 18th century, in fruitwood and pine, with shaped seat rail and cabriole legs inspired by a Louis XV* fauteuil. *The method of securing the tenon and mortice joints with pegs, the heads of which are clearly seen here, follows the same principle of construction used on sophisticated, full-scale chairs.*

Above: *Oak cabinet in two stages, mid 18th century. The doors, hung on pin hinges and easy to lift off, have panels shaped to correspond with the panelling of rooms of the Louis XV period. The quality of the carving suggests that this piece was made at Liège in the Netherlands, usually considered a centre of the French Provincial style at this period.*

Italy

Far from coming down to earth, Italian Rococo furniture often indulged in flights of fancy undreamed of in France. Venice produced some of the most lively confections. The typical Venetian commode in the mid-18th century was of exaggerated bombé shape, with a bold swelling towards the top, making the small cabriole feet appear inadequate. Asymmetrically arranged C-scrolls edged the drawers. The whole was painted in bright colours with either chinoiseries or, more often, flowers. The quality of the interior usually failed to live up to the high standards of Italian workmanship in the earlier periods and the *lacca* (painted or lacquered decoration) is not equal to that of some other countries.

A substitute for painted decoration was *lacca povera* ('poor man's lacquer'), for which specially-produced prints were cut out, glued on to the painted surface and varnished over. Bureaux based on English prototypes were treated in this way and sometimes employed in pairs at country retreats. Good examples today are fairly expensive. Another Venetian speciality was a sofa of exceptional length for use in ballrooms. It had cabriole legs and an open back supported at the centre by a fretted splat which often shows Anglo-Dutch influence, although the carving of scrolls and shells is very French in feeling. Similar carving, picked out in gold, frames painted panels on bed-heads which are sometimes shaped as enormous scallop shells. The Baroque tradition is perpetuated, with a touch of Rococo light-heartedness, in the carved and gilt throne chairs which continued to be made in Venice until the middle of the 18th century. An example in the Palazzo Rezzonico is believed to be the work of the sculptor Antonio Corradini, *c.*1730.

Relatively little Italian furniture of the period can be attributed with certainty to particular makers, but some of the best produced in Turin is credited to Pietro Piffetti (*c.*1700–77). Born in Rome, he settled in Turin in 1731 and produced ecclesiastical pieces for the next four years under the influence of Filippo Juvarra (see page 49). Piffetti then adopted a highly ornate Rococo manner, producing

Below: *French Provincial commode in solid walnut, Louis XV period. The shaping of the apron below the drawers, the carved shell at its centre and the cabriole feet are all countrified expressions of the Rococo style, but other features, such as the shaping of the end panels, are in the Louis XIV style and show the conservatism of rural craftsmen.*

cabinets-on-stands and bureau-cabinets richly decorated with inlaid ivory, tortoiseshell and mother-of-pearl, and mounted with bronzes of humans or animals specially made by Francesco Ladetti (1706–87), who was Paris-trained and interpreted the Rococo style in a subtle way. After about 1750, Piffetti also employed the style with more restraint.

Florence still produced its famous table-tops in *pietre dure*, but a less expensive substitute, *scagliola*, was developed by Enrico Hugford, Laberto Cristiano Gori and Pietro Belloni. Known since Roman times, *scagliola* was a paste made from ground selenite set in wet plaster. It was then coloured and polished to resemble various kinds of hard stone. Like *lacca povera*, it catered for a middle-class customer who loved the operatic richness of the Italian Rococo, but could not afford the best.

Left: *Venetian commode of* bombé *form with the swell towards the top and a painted surface with floral decoration – both characteristic features of the Rococo style in Venice in the mid-18th century. It was customary for the commode, in most continental countries, to reach to the dado on the wall, and to be surmounted, as in this case, by a mirror in an elaborate carved and gilded Rococo frame.*

Spain, Portugal and Latin America

Spain was torn by the wars of the Spanish Succession from 1700–13. Philip V was a Bourbon, married first to Maria Louisa of Savoy then, following her death in 1714, to Isabella Farnese, daughter of the Duke of Parma. Isabella was a strong-minded woman who encouraged her husband to break his ties with France. In spite of this, it was the French version of Rococo that influenced Spain most during the first half of the 18th century. A good example of this is La Granja Palace at Segovia, which Philip began to build in 1721, to remind him of Versailles.

Armchairs were based on the Louis XV *fauteuil*, but with an interesting difference. An example is a suite of chairs and settees designed for the Royal Palace at Madrid by a Neapolitan, Gasparini, which are veneered in rosewood with ebony inlay, whereas French seat furniture of the period was hardly ever veneered. Other chairs display English influence. Considerable quantities of English furniture were imported into Spain and Portugal in the first half of the 18th century and Spanish craftsmen copied the Queen Anne and Early Georgian versions of the cabriole leg and the mid-Georgian 'ribbon' back. A wholly Spanish flavour was often provided however, by painting these chairs black and picking out the carving in gold.

Gilding was also used lavishly on ornate console tables and the frames of the mirrors above them, the glass for which was produced in a factory at San Ildefonso set up by the king in 1736. At about the same time, commodes resembling French Provincial ones came to be made. Early examples were not veneered or mounted in gilt bronze, but made in the solid and decorated with carving, which was picked out in gilt – presumably to create the effect of bronze mounts. In France they would have been regarded as rustic but in Spain they represented sophisticated taste. Truly rustic pieces were based on much earlier models of chairs, chests and tables, and were made colourful with a coat of paint in imitation of Italian *lacca*.

Portugal was strongly under English influence during the first half of the 18th century, following the signing of the Treaty of Methuen in 1703 which, in return for preferential rates of duty on Portuguese wines exported to England (encouraging a long-lasting British predilection for a glass of 'port'), the Portuguese undertook to import quantities of goods of English manufacture – woollens in particular. During the reign of John V (1706–50), many pieces of furniture found their way from London to Lisbon. Bureau-cabinets decorated in red japanning were a particular favourite. The Portuguese themselves were good at imitating the oriental lacquer which their East India Company imported. They also had a warehouse in Paris where they sold oriental, Portuguese and probably English lacquer too, with very confusing results for the modern furniture historian to unravel. The main influence however, was oriental rather than English.

Left: *Venetian carved and gilt settee in the Rococo style, mid-18th century. The rather high back, divided into three panels, is typically Italian. The carving of the shells and scrolls is executed with an agreeably light touch and is more restrained than is usual on Italian furniture of this period.*

Above: *Portuguese chair, c.1725, made of jacaranda wood imported from Brazil. Some English influence is to be seen in the shaping of the splat in the back, but the flat stretchers are closer to those on French* Régence *chairs. The pronounced curves of the outside frame of the back, and the fretted cresting rail, are typically Portuguese.*

As in Spain, a more truly English flavour is found in many Portuguese chairs on cabriole legs with shaped and sometimes fretted splats in the backs. The legs are usually united by turned stretchers – a feature eliminated on fashionable English cabriole-legged chairs quite early in the 18th century. The old preference for high-backed chairs in Portugal also asserts itself, the back legs as well as the front are often of cabriole shape, and the continental Rococo love of asymmetrical motifs in carved decoration is inclined to be marked on pieces that might otherwise pass as English. In some armchairs with padded backs, both English Chippendale, Louis XV Rococo and traditional Portuguese proportions combine to produce dignity, luxury and the perfection of Portuguese carving at its best.

The Portuguese commode is usually four drawers in depth, making it rather high, and is serpentine-fronted with a distinct central bulge. Corners are canted and carved with foliage. The top is normally of the same wood as the carcase and seldom made of marble. A distinctive type of gaming table was made in the 1750s with a basically circular top but with a wavy edge, and was fitted with

Above: *Portuguese* bombé *commode, mid 18th century, in jacaranda, a wood imported from Brazil. Rococo carving takes the place of gilded bronze on the angles, but the moulding of the drawers remains Baroque in feeling. This feature, together with the low-bellied effect created by the three drawers, shows an affinity with the French commode of the Régence period, rather than with the fully developed Louis XV style.*

reversible panels inlaid for chess and other games. The frieze is fitted with drawers and has four cabriole legs.

The Portuguese were among the most adventurous designers of beds in the mid-18th century, discarding the tester and posts entirely and creating a panelled headboard in a carved Rococo frame. In place of the traditional posts, the foot has cabriole legs with reverse cabrioles pointing upwards.

In Brazil, many of the characteristics of Portuguese furniture in the mid-18th century were taken up by local craftsmen to create – often a generation later – an authentic colonial style with occasional flourishes of exaggerated Rococo. The style was introduced to Peru by the Spanish viceroy, Don Manuel Afat, and was given an extra sparkle by the use of silver for decorative purposes, instead of the bronze or gilded carving that would have sufficed in Europe. Silver was employed in this way in Mexico, too, but the most interesting pieces of Mexican furniture are a curious combination of Renaissance shapes with a blend of Baroque and Rococo ornament. Into this remarkable mixture, a distinct element of native culture was often added, with masks carved on the knees of cabriole legs as they often were in Europe but here they are more reminiscent of the old Indian gods than of Mannerist satyrs.

The Netherlands

Holland had made a significant contribution to the development of English furniture in the last years of the 17th century, and in first half of the 18th century this was reciprocated to such an extent that there is a substantial group of furniture, most of it veneered with burr walnut, that is conveniently described as 'Anglo-Dutch'. The influence of the French Régence style was also marked, especially on armchairs, and many Dutch examples combine the cartouche-shaped, padded back of the French type with cabriole legs having the typically English convex bulge at the junction with the seat rail. Quite often, these legs are joined by shaped stretchers in the Régence manner. This kind of stretcher also appears on chairs with English-style claw-and-ball feet and vase-shaped splats in the backs but decorated in an uncompromisingly Dutch way with floral marquetry.

By about 1750 the Rococo style was well established in the Netherlands. In the south, fine oak armoires were made at Liége, their doors and cornices carved with formal cartouches relieved by delicate, asymmetrically arranged, leafy tendrils and shells. In the north, walnut-veneered commodes of bombé shape with marquetry decoration were produced in the Louis XV manner, usually with wooden rather than marble tops. The swell of the Dutch bombé form is often low in the belly of the carcase. Another piece, the 'tallboy' or 'highboy', evolved from the bombé commode, using the shape of the latter as the base beneath a two-door clothes-press, which was fitted inside with sliding trays and rose to a stepped cornice that provided ledges for Chinese or Delft vases.

While the general tendency was for French influence to increase in the mid-18th century, some tables and lowboys (side-tables with several drawers) owe something to English designs of the period. In spite of these foreign fashions, the furniture of the Netherlands developed a strong national character which the guilds fought hard to preserve, while maintaining high standards of workmanship. Each large town had its own guild, and the records of some have been preserved, but as relatively few pieces were signed it is difficult to attribute pieces to particular makers.

Poland and Russia

The Rococo style reached Poland through Saxony, early in the reign (1733–63) of Augustus III, who was also Elector of Saxony and who entrusted what he found to be the boring business of government to his all-powerful minister of state, Count Heinrich von Brühl. One of Brühl's responsibilities was the Meissen porcelain factory near Dresden, the capital city of Saxony, and it is probable that Dresden china figures – the perfect expression of the late Baroque and Rococo styles – originated as table ornaments for the banquets von Brühl delighted in giving. With such an enthusiast for rich decoration supervising the country, it is hardly surprising that Polish Rococo was both colourful and a little florid in its interpretation of the Louis XV style; the carved motifs on *fauteuils* and *canapés* for instance, were sometimes picked out in colour against a gilt ground. By contrast, the furniture of the countryside was often left plain, primitive shapes being employed without even carved decoration. In the region of Cracow in the south – 'Little Poland' – there was however a long tradition of making marriage chests painted with a single floral composition. It was general practice in Poland throughout the 18th century for landlords to have large workshops on their estates, where the furniture for their own homes was made, often to a high standard.

A rather similar system obtained in Russia, where most of the furniture was made on country estates by serf craftsmen who were often highly-skilled, especially in the field of wood-carving. A lush and vivid version of the Rococo suited to their talents, was developed during the reign (1741–62) of Elizabeth, daughter of Peter the Great. It was a promising period for the arts, and saw the fruition of Peter's plans for a Russian university in Moscow, the establishment of a theatre and the encouragement of literature. In this atmosphere, the leading architect of the time, Count Bartolommeo Rastrelli, designed Rococo pieces in carved and gilt wood that display a magnificent self-confidence. The Count, Russian-born but of Italian descent, was responsible for the Peterhof and other great Baroque buildings.

Norway and Denmark

English influence is also evident in some Scandinavian furniture in the 18th century. This stemmed partly from the export of timber from Norway to England. Dutch styles, too, were taken up by the middle classes. For political and commercial reasons, both the English and the Dutch took a keen interest in Scandinavian affairs, at a time when Norway was under Danish rule and obliged to support Denmark against Sweden. Copenhagen was the capital from which Norway and Denmark were governed.

Below: *Walnut armchair, Danish or possibly North German, c.1725–50. A characteristic Scandinavian feature is provided by the asymmetrical shaping of the cresting rail. This is echoed in the carved motif at the centre of the seat rail. The knee of the cabriole leg is also less pronounced than it would be in an English example, with which a chair of this type might easily be confused.*

Above: *Danish bridal cupboard dated 1759, painted to simulate exotic materials. The style is still, at this comparatively late date, essentially Baroque, but the horns of plenty on the doors have an asymmetrical Rococo flavour. Marriage cupboards, chests and beds were an essential part of the Scandinavian peasant home and its folk culture.*

It had a guild of chairmakers separate from, and more conservative than that of the cabinetmakers. Chairs with the English type of cabriole legs continued to be made with turned stretchers bracing them long after this precaution had been dispensed with in Britain. The curve of the leg also differs from the English form, the knee being less pronounced. A rather exaggerated Rococo flavour is sometimes imparted by an asymmetrical crest at the centre of the top rail of the back.

Peasant furniture was little affected by these foreign influences. The Norwegian peasantry had a strong tradition of freedom, but serfdom was not ended in Denmark until 1702, and even after this the obligation of *stavnsbaand* was revived, providing landowners with free labour by farmers' sons born on their estates. In spite of the ensuing differences, the old traditions of folk culture persisted both in Norway and Denmark. In Norway, they were symbolized by the dowry chest being carried in procession from the bride's home; it was made of pine, painted with flowers and an inscription and held personal clothing she would keep for the rest of her life. Other painted furniture, including the marriage bed, which sometimes incorporated a cupboard overhead, was borne along with equal ceremony.

A slightly more sophisticated version of this kind of decoration, deriving from peasant roots but affected by the fashion for lacquer in Holland and Germany, was employed on chests-of-drawers with shaped fronts and mounted on cabriole-legged stands for the homes of the Danish nobility. Members of the Copenhagen guild produced more luxurious pieces to special order, but only one member, Mathias Ortmann, is known to have carried large stocks in the mid-18th century. Most of his work shows strong Germanic influence, especially in his treatment of the bombé shape for commodes and bureau-cabinets. His work is better identified than most because of his practice of attaching a trade label to each piece and numbering it.

Sweden

Some Anglo-Dutch influence is seen in Swedish furniture, particularly chairs, made in the first half of the 18th century but a Franco-German flavour gradually gained in strength. From this confluence a national style emerged, best seen in cupboards with panelled doors on bombé bases which were the test-pieces that had to be made by all cabinetmakers aspiring to membership of the Stockholm guild. Without this passport to freedom, the craftsman could not become self-employed unless he chose to isolate himself well away from the centres where the guilds operated.

The cupboards varied in details of design over the years according to the current fashions. In the Rococo period the base had a vase-shaped projection at the centre, forming a 'break-front'. The panels of the doors were framed with carved and gilded tendrils, the imposing cornice had two opposed curves of the kind called 'swan neck', and between them there is often an elaborate finial in the form of an asymmetrical ornament, also carved and gilded.

Above: *Swedish table, mid 18th century, constructed like a stool with drop-in seat. The top is a tile of Rörstrand faience, a type of pottery made in Stockholm and similar to Delftware. The cabriole legs display Anglo-Dutch influence, joining the seat frame with a convex curve.*
Right: *Secretaire cabinet, Mainz, c.1758 attributed to Franz Anton Hermann. The Mainz guild was noted for cabinets of this kind, a number of which have survived. Typical features are the curved surface of the exterior of the writing leaf; the elaborate volutes at the angles; the mouldings around the doors; the imposing cresting piece; the carved apron below; and the relationship of the marquetry to the overall design.*

A formative influence on the Swedish Rococo style was Christian Precht (1706–79), the son of a German cabinetmaker from Bremen. By trade he was a silversmith but he also designed furniture. Another influential designer, Carl Harleman (1700–53), studied in Paris and became architect to the Swedish Court. A master of the Rococo style, his console tables employed opposing C-scrolls, not merely to create surface decoration (as on the carving for a panelled door) but to form organic shapes.

These curving shapes were immensely liked in Sweden, the bombé commode reaching the height of its popularity after 1760 (by which date it was already outmoded in France). The Swedish version was always three drawers deep like the French Régence prototype from the early years of the century. A peculiarity of the commode was a channel cut into the wood on the rails between the drawers, which was usually gilded or sometimes lined with sheet brass. The gilt metal handles were delicate and the walnut veneers carefully matched. Swedish commodes are often mistakenly thought to be Dutch, but the swell of the curve on Swedish examples is usually higher, and the top is usually of marble, not wood.

Germany, Austria and Switzerland

Baroque palaces built in the late 17th and early 18th centuries in the capitals of Germanic states in imitation of Versailles, helped to preserve that style from the unsettling effects of Rococo. But by about 1750, thanks largely to the circulation of French, Italian and English designs printed in Nuremberg and Augsburg, Rococo curlicues were attaching themselves to ponderous Baroque forms. Soon, carcase shapes were beginning to assume a livelier and more curvaceous appearance. As is often the way with converts, German designers, once having embraced the new faith, carried it to unprecedented extremes.

The cousins Spindler (Johann Friedrich, 1726–*c.*1799 and Heinrich Wilhelm, 1738-*c.*1799) were the sons of two brothers noted for marquetry work at Bayreuth. The younger generation both went to work for Frederick the Great at Sans Souci, producing some magnificent pieces, notably commodes of bombé form with very deep apron-fronts, lavishly decorated with marquetry and mounted in gilt bronze by the Swiss-born Johann Melchior Kambli (1718–73). Kambli, a cabinetmaker in his own right, was inspired by the Louis XV Rococo style but was one of those responsible for creating the distinctive Potsdam style. Another important contributor to the Potsdam style was Johann August Nahl (1710–85), whose confections have an air of fantasy unrivalled by anything made in France. He was succeeded as Director of Ornaments by Johann Christian Hoppenhaupt (1719–86), whose elder brother, Johann Michael Hoppenhaupt (1709–69) trained at Dresden and Vienna, and settled in Potsdam in 1740 where between 1751 and 1755 he published some remarkable designs for commodes, console tables and sedan chairs.

At Würzburg, capital of Mainz, the episcopal residence began as a Baroque palace but was eventually given a Rococo interior of great brilliance, for which Ferdinand Hundt (*c.*1704–58) produced some exceptionally well-carved furniture – particularly firescreens and guéridons. Sadly, much of his authenticated work was destroyed in World War II, but enough survives to demonstrate the great delicacy achieved by the finest German craftsmen. The trend to lightness was encouraged by the work of François Cuvilliés (1695–1768), a Fleming of diminutive

Right: *A gaming table with fold-over top in three parts, opening up to provide amenities for various games – cards, chess, backgammon. Under the top is a well to hold the cards and chessmen. The rear legs are hinged and swing out to support the top when open. It is the work of Abraham Roentgen and is distinguished by the intricacy of the carving.*
Below: *Commode made for Frederick the Great by Heinrich Wilhelm Spindler c.1765. The lavish mounts in gilded bronze were very probably produced by the Swiss-born Johann Melchior Kambli. Like much German furniture of the Rococo period, an element of Baroque grandeur lingers on, and the shape of this piece – especially the depth of the apron front – is a little reminiscent of Boulle's early commodes.*

size whose first appointment was as Court Dwarf to the Elector Max Emanuel of Bavaria. He studied in Paris and then became Court Architect at Munich, designing furniture fit for a fairy palace, which is what his 'Mirror Room' at Nymphenburg resembles.

A number of other pieces of palace furniture can be identified with the men who made them. Unfortunately, furniture made for more modest homes is largely anonymous, for the German guilds did not insist on the signing of pieces and in fact actively discouraged the practice. Thus the handsome oak cupboards of Aachen (Aix-la-Chapelle), carved in the Rococo style with a masterly and delicate touch that rivals the best carved armoires of Liège, usually defy the attempts of scholars to link them with particular makers of whom little is known but their names.

J.P. Schotte's name is noted as a maker to the Court at Dresden. He specialized in chairs in the English style in the 1730s. Both French and English fashions were followed in Saxony, French taste becoming dominant by about 1740.

Another important cabinetmaker was Abraham Roentgen (1711–93). Born at Mühlheim, he was a Protestant belonging to the strict Moravian sect. He went to England at the age of 20 and worked there as a cabinetmaker for about seven years before returning to Germany. He then set sail for Carolina as a missionary, but his ship foundered off the Irish coast. He found employment for a time in Galway, then went back to his home country and set up in business in Neuwied, near Coblenz, where there was a Moravian colony, in 1750. His workshops were noted for fine marquetry work which is reminiscent of the architectural subjects of Renaissance craftsmen in South Germany. Roentgen, however, had to some extent been influenced by his years in England, and English craftsmanship commanded sufficient respect in Germany for him to describe himself as an *Englischer Kabinettmacher*. Some of his work in the Rococo style may perhaps justify this, in so far as it is more restrained than most German work of the period.

The business he built up in Neuwied was taken over by his son David, who was to become a major figure internationally in the creation of fine furniture during the Neoclassical period.

England

One of the fascinating aspects of the study of the history of English furniture is the process of rapid evolution that took place. A couple of decades – and sometimes less – were often enough to see dramatic winds of change sweeping through design, blowing away yesterday's cherished tenets and altering the course of popular taste. The short period between about 1725 and 1750, spanning the major part of George II's reign (1727–60) is a good example of such rapid evolution.

These years represent a milestone in the nomenclature of English furniture periods. Previously, phases of furniture design gained their description from reigning monarchs – from the Tudors, through the Stuarts and ending with Queen Anne. After the latter reign the picture changes. Admittedly we often use terms such as mid- or late Georgian or resort to more specific descriptions, such as George II, III or Regency, when referring to pieces of the 18th and early 19th century periods respectively, but the main movements of England's golden age of furniture come to life for us in the names of cabinetmaking commoners, rather than kings and queens. This age was preceded by a short period, the second quarter of the 18th century, which had a profound effect on what was to follow. The most important factor in this transition was the establishment of mahogany as the English cabinetmaker's principal material. Secondly, the period was notable for the contribution of architects such as William Kent, who was probably the first of his profession to make a practice of designing the movable as well as the fixed furniture of his rooms as part of unified schemes.

American furniture historians have occasionally claimed that the colonies had the distinction of leading the world in the use of mahogany for furniture making. The justification for this is the existence of inventories and other records in the New York and Philadelphia areas referring to the use of the wood between 1690 and 1708, some long time before the 1720s, a period which is generally accepted as the beginning of England's age of mahogany.

Apart, however, from the fact that Elizabeth I is reputed to have been mildly interested in the wood when Sir Walter Raleigh imported some mahogany from the West Indies and used it to repair his ships, it is known that the pioneering use of mahogany in furniture occurred in England in the latter half of the 17th century. In fact, Spain, with its strong bonds in the Caribbean area, the home of mahogany, had had recourse to the wood much earlier. But records of such occasions were few and far between, and it was the relaxation of import duties on Jamaican supplies in the third decade of the 18th century that opened the way to the general use of mahogany in Britain. Further lifting of tariff restrictions in 1733 gave the 'new' wood an enormous boost and led to its competing with walnut on a grand scale.

Left: *A Georgian room at the Geffrye Museum, London, illustrates the use to which furniture was being put in the pursuit of a leisured and cultural life. Music had its important place. Examples of chair and table developments all mirror the advancement to an age of elegance.*

Above: *Mirrors served an important function in the room settings of the designer-architects of George II's reign. Their moulding often matched that of cornices and door and window surrounds. Gesso, a hard-setting preparation which was an ideal carving medium, was often used in the frames. This carved gilt mirror in the style of William Kent displays several of his characteristic decorative forms – human masks, ostrich feathers, scrolls and foliage.*

Mahogany was to be the perfect material for the Georgian cabinetmakers. It was excellent for carving and the earliest supplies from San Domingo, Jamaica and Cuba had a light colour which gradually changed to a deep, lustrous patina. It had a variety of grain which lent itself to veneers, seasoned easily and was possessed of a strength unknown in walnut. Furthermore, cabinetmakers discovered in it a quality which was to influence important aspects of furniture design towards the middle of the 18th century: it was about that time that the expansive widths of mahogany board then being offered made its use ideal for large areas such as the doors of wardrobes and cabinets and the leaves of table tops, which could be made in one piece instead of in sections as in the age of walnut.

In the period to about 1750 it was the mahogany from San Domingo that was the most popular. San Domingo mahogany, from the tree *Swietenia mahogani*, was more lightly figured than types in later use, and appealed to craftsmen because of its denseness and suitability for carving. As supplies became scarcer, Cuban wood from the same tree was employed. Later still, in the latter years of the century, *Swietenia macrophylla*, a softer wood from Honduras and other parts of Central America, was widely used especially in furniture carcases.

To follow the fortunes of mahogany through furniture design into the 19th century is to record the eventual introduction of an inferior type from Africa; it was lighter in weight and softer, but it frequently displayed interesting striped effects in its figure.

Coinciding with the adoption of mahogany, there was a trend towards decorative magnificence in furniture bred by a new prosperity in England. The new style denied the simple elegance of earlier work and its exponents have often been said to have been responsible for 'architects' furniture' – a term used sometimes in admiration, sometimes in denigration.

William Kent, an archpriest of the new movement, so burdened his furniture with ornament that Horace Walpole called some of his designs 'immeasurably ponderous'. Despite such strictures, however, Kent was one of a band of architects who played a key role in the annals of English interior design during the formative years up to the middle of the century.

Their nourishment was Palladianism, a style that prevailed in English architecture from about 1715 to 1760. It was classical by nature – a style essentially based on ideas and precepts about proportion and planning evolved by the Italian architect Andrea Palladio (1508–1580) in his buildings in Venice and Vicenza. Palladianism was seen in the work of his immediate followers in Italy, and in England in the masterpieces of Inigo Jones in the late 16th and early 17th centuries. The style was characterized by symmetry and the addition of classical columns to the façades.

Between the years of 1715 and 1724, the architect Colen Campbell (who died in 1729) set up the architectural models on which the whole of the new Palladianism in England was to depend. He illustrated these designs in *Vitruvius Britannicus*, named after the classical scholar who had been Palladio's own inspiration.

William Kent (1686–1748) was heavily influenced by the styles of Palladio, Inigo Jones, Christopher Wren and, subsequently, Campbell. An allegorical painter, he was sent to Italy in 1709 by a group of friends and admirers to study art. On his return ten years later he found a passionate and constant patronage in the support of the artistically talented Richard, third Earl of Burlington, known as 'The Apollo of the Arts'.

Together they redesigned the fronts of the Treasury Buildings in Whitehall, and Burlington House. Horse Guards was Kent's own creation. He combined the talents of painter, architect, interior decorator and landscape gardener, and in the latter role his work was seen in the gardens of several great houses, drawing on an unusually natural style which contrasted dramatically with the lavishly ornamental flavour of much of his furniture and room settings. So well did he succeed in developing the natural attributes of these gardens that the critic Walpole – he of the 'immeasurably ponderous' jibe – was moved to describe Kent as the 'Father of Modern Gardening'.

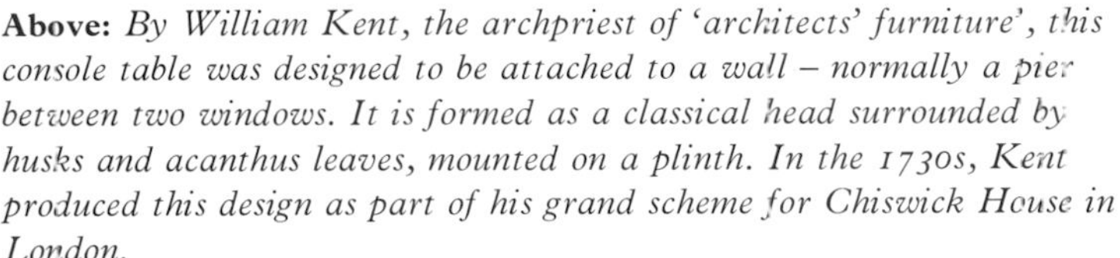

Above: *By William Kent, the archpriest of 'architects' furniture', this console table was designed to be attached to a wall – normally a pier between two windows. It is formed as a classical head surrounded by husks and acanthus leaves, mounted on a plinth. In the 1730s, Kent produced this design as part of his grand scheme for Chiswick House in London.*

Above right: *It is the mid-18th century and the drop leaf table pictured here shows a style in stark contrast to the preceding florid era of William Kent (who died in 1748). Unadorned and sturdy, on simple tapering legs and pad feet, the table is utterly utilitarian. It would be used for a meal, then placed against the wall when not in use.*

It was little wonder therefore that when turning to furniture, a man of such all-embracing talents as Kent's should design it as part of the unified scheme in a house. His furniture designs ushered in the day when architecture and furniture joined hands. His authority dominated public taste and his name was law in matters of design ranging from tables and chairs, mirrors and frames to the dresses that people wore when they used his furniture and his rooms. The child of fashion-conscious parents would sleep in a cradle based on a Kent design, and if there is no record of Kent's having designed a gravestone or a catafalque there can be no doubt that such churchyard monuments of his time frequently owed their form to the architectural principles which he embraced in stone and wood. His writ even extended to Britain's waterways, where his work was seen in the design of barges.

Florid or pompous, depending on your point of view, Kent's furniture revelled in ornamentation. It was furniture for the rich. Cabriole legs were embellished with animal details such as lion, eagle, owl and human masks, claw and ball feet and eagles' talons. Foliated scrolls, lion manes, rocks and shells, satyrs and other mythological beasts . . . these were all in his vocabulary of design, as were dominant architectural pediments, columns and statuary.

Above: *William Kent, who borrowed heavily from Palladianism and the Baroque, designed this mahogany kneehole desk about 1730. It is heavily decorated with lions' heads, claws and carved and gilded borders.*

Such magnificence often demanded the final touch of opulence supplied by gilding, and this was never stinted by Kent and his confrères. Selectively borrowing from various sources and periods, he both influenced and mirrored the trends of design through many departments of domestic and ceremonial furniture, as more detailed study of these developments reveals below.

We have seen how Kent as an architect pioneered the practice of designing the movable as well as the fixed furniture of his room settings. There was yet another role played by him which illustrates the importance in transitional terms of the second quarter of the 18th century. He took part in a development – the growing use of the printed word, accompanied by designs – which was to herald the age of furniture dictionaries and drawing books. Before that time, much of what cabinetmakers learned and put into practice depended on word of mouth. The propagation of design books to a receptive, large and often distant (for example, transatlantic) readership was soon to revolutionize the way furniture styles affected populations.

As early as 1727 Kent had published two folio volumes which illustrated works of Inigo Jones, several by the Earl of Burlington, and some of his own room sections and chimney pieces; inevitably a few designs by Palladio were included. In 1744 he published another work containing examples from the designs of former masters and some of his own.

In the meantime (1739) there had been significant circulation in limited but influential quarters of a treatise by William Jones, the *Gentleman's or Builder's Companion.* It contained 20 designs of side tables and pier glasses (large mirrors fixed to the pier or wall between two windows), representative of furniture designed for Georgian homes by architects.

Above: *The 18th century rage for playing cards led to the creation of many varieties of the card table. When opened out, the top reveals slightly dished recesses at the four corners to hold candles. Although in walnut and of Queen Anne's time, it foreshadows the advent of more elaborate carving in the decoration on the knees of its cabriole legs.*

Prior to these publications there had rarely been any literature on interior decoration available for study, copy or adaptation. Such literature speeded furniture evolution to such an extent that within 20 or 30 years the ponderous lines of Kent's day, epitomized by massive and ornamental chimney pieces as well as furniture, were superseded by designs in light and fanciful proportions that were eventually to be the inspiration for masters like Thomas Chippendale.

An innovation which lent itself admirably to widespread employment in 'architects' furniture' was gesso, from the Italian word for plaster or chalk. It was a mixture of whiting and parchment size, and was applied layer after layer as each coat dried. Thus a form was built up from which the background could be carved away to produce a pattern in relief. The next stage was burnishing followed by the application of gold leaf.

Gesso provided a convenient medium for the florid Baroque ornamentation beloved of William Kent and his architectural contemporaries. No less fitting was the opportunity it offered for gilding. Gesso had appeared before 1700, but the years up to about 1740 saw it in high fashionable demand, particularly on chairs, certain types of tables, and the lavishly decorated mirrors which were to become characteristic of the period. Although the carvers sometimes resorted to softwood to create their Baroque extravaganzas, gesso with its remarkable plasticity was used universally together with walnut and the all-conquering mahogany.

After the plain elegance of Queen Anne, chairs were among the first types of furniture to become vehicles for the new ornamental styles. Hoof feet were popular at an early stage. Between 1720 and 1735 there was widespread carving of the lion mask on chair legs and arms, with manes frequently covering the arm supports. Fish scales were another motif used to decorate legs which might end in dolphin heads. In the homes of the rich, whose rooms were designed by fashionable architects, chairs formed a wild menagerie of fur and feather.

Just as important as the lion motif was the eagle whose head terminated arms and legs and surmounted back rails and whose feathers sometimes swathed the whole of the carvable surfaces which were then finished in parcel (partial) gilt. These animal forms found a perfect framework in the sinuous lines of the cabriole leg which stayed at the forefront of furniture fashion throughout the entire period.

Human masks, usually female, were employed extensively on the 'knees' of chairs; Kent also made effective use of American Indian heads, which provided fertile opportunity for the lavish addition of feather headdresses.

An important feature of the chair – undoubtedly because of the scope it provided for carving – was the apron provided by the seat's front rail. Shellwork and scrolling were to be found in profusion on these aprons. A popular form of carving was the acanthus whose leaf has strongly serrated edges; it was a design found on Corinthian capitals and therefore much in harmony with the classical flavour of the new Palladianism. Elaborately carved aprons were a feature of the work of Giles Grendey (1693–1780), a London master joiner who produced many pieces for export.

While chairs were undergoing this decorative transition, they were becoming wider – some, indeed, assuming extraordinarily wide proportions – to accommodate the large hooped skirts of the time. Similarly, the arm supports were being raked, the upper end being considerably farther back than the lower, for the same reasons.

Gilt chairs proliferated and none were more splendid than those designed by Kent as parts of a unified scheme of interior decoration. Typical were a set of twelve mahogany armchairs carved in gilt about 1730 for a room at Houghton Hall, Norfolk. The seat rails are centred by a double carved shell, a favourite motif of Kent's. The seats are covered in a Spitalfields velvet which matches the covering of the walls. Such unity of design might seem unremarkable now, but it was an early English example of such thought.

Left: *Fast losing the feminine grace of Anne's day, the cabriole leg becomes ponderous and forbidding in this mahogany, leather upholstered chair of about 1739, designed for the Old Treasury Buildings in London. Lion mask and claw feet are typical of the time.*

Below: *Eagle heads decorate the arms of these George II carved walnut armchairs, upholstered in gros and petit point needlework. Again, note the open character of the chair's forward part for the comfort and convenience of heavily gowned ladies.*

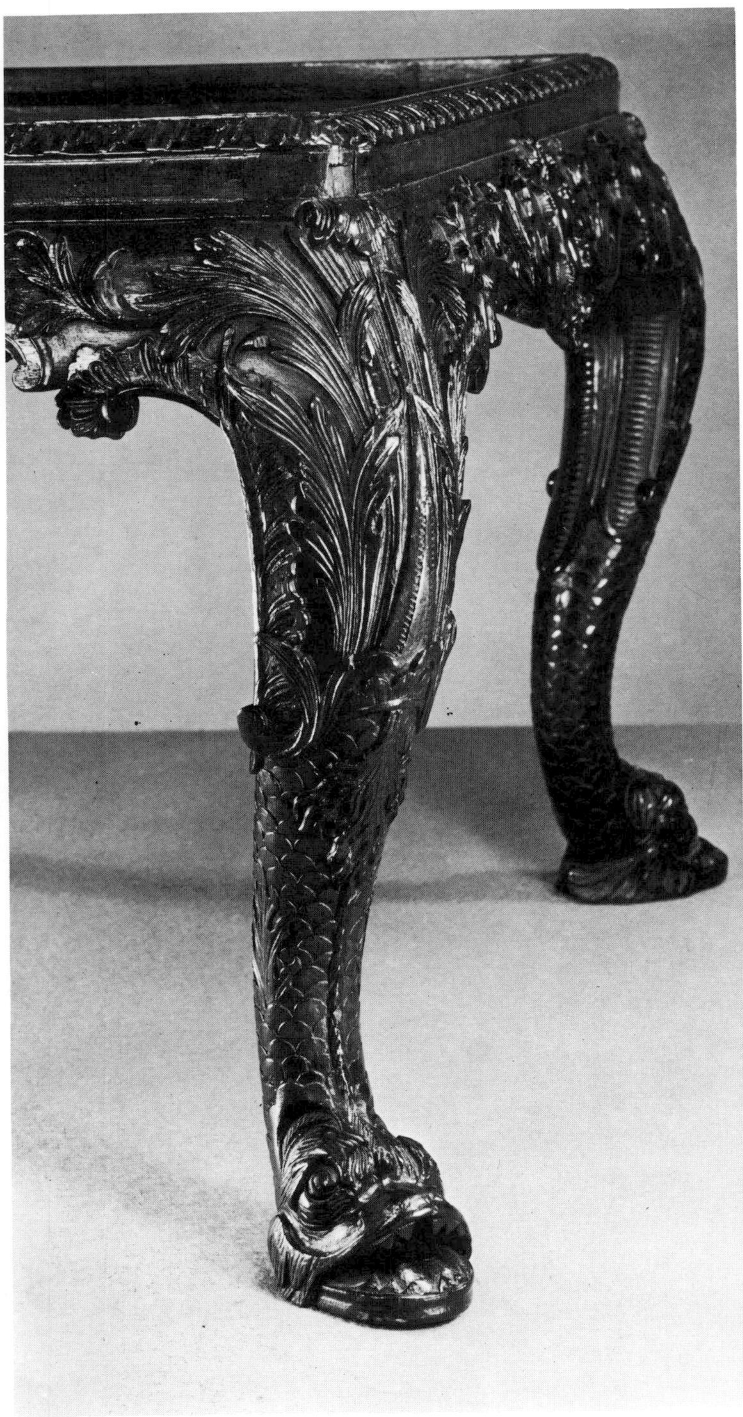

Left: *Extravagance of carving was in full spate in the two decades leading to the mid 18th century. This mahogany stool has dolphin and foliage decoration. In close-up can be seen details of the dolphin head and the scaling with which the joiner covered the lower part of the cabriole legs, thus leaving no part of the woodwork unadorned.*

When one considers some of Kent's experiments with his favoured Italian style – particularly in the use of Italian X-frame construction – one is tempted to agree with some of the more caustic of Horace Walpole's criticisms. Between 1730 and 1750 the old medieval X form experienced some revival, and not always happily. It was sometimes used for the forelegs of a chair, where of course it was the vehicle for heavy carving, and was combined with cabriole legs at the rear. The hybrid result is not to everyone's taste, and certainly far from the harmonious discipline of Palladian symmetry.

French Rococo began to show its influence in chairs (and other furniture) from about 1745. The style gained its name from the French word *rocaille*, rockwork, which was a common motif used in carving in conjunction with shells and leafy C-scrolls. It was a lighter, more fanciful style, infinitely more feminine than the overbearing mood of Baroque. It led to less full-blooded low relief carving and to more graceful curves. The splats between the uprights on the backs of chairs showed a tendency to open in strapwork and tracery. Vase and hoop shaped backs were gradually giving way to more upright and square shaped backs, or outlines formed by uprights curving gently outwards to meet the top rail, foreshadowing shapes of the latter half of the 18th century.

Among tables, the console above all others epitomized the aims and aspirations of the architect-decorators of the second quarter of the 18th century. This is a side table introduced as a permanent fixture projecting from the wall. The back is fixed to the wall, needing in some circumstances no legs, and the result is a sturdy and exceptionally rigid table surface, ideal for displaying a treasured ornament or vast flower arrangement. The bracket supports of such tables offered ample opportunity for the talents of the Baroque designers. A variation was the console table standing squarely on four legs, but which nevertheless was intended to be placed in a permanent position against the wall.

The console table often stood against the pier between two windows of a room or saloon and was topped by a mirror in matching style, the whole ensemble being embellished by the addition of candle brackets. The terms pier table and pier glass are frequently used in this context in furniture books of the period, such as the *Gentleman's or Builder's Companion* of William Jones.

Those who wished to remain in the van of fashion paid enormous sums for console tables surmounted by superb marble slabs imported from Italy. Less expensive versions carried slabs of scagliola, a hard-setting paste flecked with chips of coloured marble, or tops of mosaic and gesso. When not used for purely decorative purposes, consoles served as sideboards on which food and utensils could be marshalled for the dinner table – otherwise the sideboard – as the cupboard and drawer type of furniture in which form it became known later in the century – was non-existent.

With their main construction of plain walnut, giltwood, or wood embellished by gesso, these tables were ideally suited to the popular adaptations of the Italian style. They embodied the full repertoire of motifs that were to be found on chairs – animal and human heads, sphinxes, putti and family coats of arms.

Many bracket designs required attractively carved side aprons to mask the unsightly supporting struts that were necessary to carry the immense weight of the marble tops. In some forms of console table however, these side aprons were not needed; an example was the spectacular use of an eagle's body as a bracket – in which case the outstretched wings sloped backwards – both for support and in strut concealment. Eagle consoles are rare and fabulously expensive today. Towards the mid-century the trend for refinement of line and decoration affected console tables as much as chairs and their ornamental character gradually became less extravagant.

Above: *A carved and parcel gilt mahogany settee from a set of 10 chairs and two settees formerly at Wroxton Abbey, Oxfordshire, and attributed to William Kent. Designed about 1730 to 1740, the settee shows, in the open tracery of the back, signs of the eventual trend to a lighter approach in fashionable furniture.*

Below: *The double shell motif, used on the front apron of tables, was a favourite motif of William Kent and it is seen here on one of his small tables in carved giltwood, surmounted by a marble top. Vast amounts were paid to import the best marble from Italy. The less well-to-do settled for scagliola, a hard-setting paste flecked with marble chips.*

Above: *The architectural pediment, in open emulation of the new Palladian style influencing building in contemporary England, dominates this George II gilt mirror. Glass was so expensive that it often sufficed for several frames as the fashions in the latter changed, decade by decade.*

Before examining developments in other types of tables, we must turn to the mirrors which were so much a part of the console table concept of unified design. From 1725, the design of mirrors was directly inspired by their architectural setting. Mouldings frequently corresponded with those on pier tables, doors, cornices and around windows. The high cost of glass meant that frames were often replaced time and time again – even through several decades of evolving styles and fashions – while the original glass was treasured from generation to generation of taste. During the 1720–40 period, frames followed the highly decorative path taken by furniture, thereafter moving into the lighter Rococo direction.

New effects were being created by the larger expanses of wood available in mahogany. The gate-leg table was made generally with circular or oval top of fairly large surface area, one cabriole leg swinging out either side to support the flaps. Stretchers had long since vanished. Other gate-leg tables were made with square flaps so that several could be placed together when a large company was dining. Such a composite affair might have as many as 32 legs: the result was a magnificent, long expanse of mahogany of rich patina, a perfect setting for an important banquet.

The 'big' look of mahogany was equally at home in the library, a room without which no great home was complete in George II's day. Giant library tables sported elaborate mouldings, carved pendants of flowers and lion masks, often combined with architectural columns. The owl, symbol of learning, was a popular motif here. These tables had a profusion of cupboards and drawers and almost without exception those found in Palladian homes were part of the integral design of bookshelves and other internal fixtures of the library.

In the overall design were included small kneehole desks which had moved on from plain Queen Anne styles to accommodate the architectural trimmings of the new fashions, and small tables bearing three drawers in the frieze. The latter were used by ladies who, in their private apartments, had kneehole varieties of the dressing table in figured walnut and mahogany, lavishly equipped with fittings to hold beauty aids and all those accoutrements and preparations necessary to maintain the elaborate hair styles of the day.

Occasional tables, too, became a receptacle for the trend towards ponderous decoration. Square centre tables were richly carved on all sides and the lion and the human masks were freely used on their legs. Again, gilt and gesso were much used and the marble quarries of Italy did a roaring trade with the British importers.

Below: *A mahogany kneehole dressing table shows how the new, simpler tastes were taking over. Architectural columns, surmounted by acanthus leaf carving, are now a feature of its canted corners. The frieze drawer is fitted with an adjustable mirror and lidded compartments to contain beauty aids and all the paraphernalia to cope with the elaborate hair styles then in fashion.*

In chests of drawers walnut found a longer lease of life than in other types of furniture and we find the wood in widespread use until the mid-century. Notably, chests escaped the more outrageous excesses of the Baroque fever, although in the double form as tallboys they were sometimes given the 'architectural' treatment of dominant cornices and broken pediments. So, too, were china cabinets which, through the heyday of Kent's influence, were hardly distinguishable from bookcases. It is often difficult to tell for which purpose a cabinet was intended, both having a glazed upper stage and a pronounced architectural character. In the 1740s when the Rococo influence introduced carved floral ornaments and other more feminine refinements, the china cabinet slimmed down to a more individualistic and recognizable piece of drawing room furniture.

Throughout the whole of the second quarter of the century demand was strong for cabinets – and many other pieces of furniture – decorated in lacquer or, more likely, the home-based japanning.

The sap of a tree, *Rhus vernicifera* (the lacquer tree or 'lac-tree'), found in Japan, China and Malaya, is the basis of lacquering. The sap is tapped like that of the rubber tree and when dry forms a semi-hard transparent film. The hard, dense result achieved in Oriental lacquering comes from tedious putting on and rubbing down of many successive coats. It is a process which has little in common with modern lacquer, a compound of cellulose derivatives sprayed on by means of compressed air.

The original process dates from remote antiquity in the Far East, but it reached Europe, probably first in decorated panels, only about the end of the 16th century. The sap of the lac-tree was not available in Europe and imitation of lacquer was attempted by a method essentially different from the Oriental techniques: thus in English the term 'japanning' is much more appropriate when describing the European version of lacquer. In the mid-18th century an English authority on the subject described japanning as 'the art of covering bodies by grounds of opake colours in varnish; which may be afterwards decorated by painting or gilding, or left in a plain state'.

The wood is first treated with a mixture of size and whiting and then coated with two or more applications of varnish composed of gum-lac, seed-lac or shellac. These are different preparations of the resin squeezed from twigs on which it is deposited by an insect. Before the resin is ready for the process it is dissolved in spirits of wine and other gums and substances are added.

In France imitations of lacquer attained excellence under Louis XIV (1643–1715), who installed artists in the Gobelins factory to manufacture Oriental styles which they called *laquage*. The Dutch had a long tradition of trade in lacquer work, the first examples of which were boxes sent home from the East by Dutch merchants. Like the French, they employed in furniture whole panels shipped from the East; they also tried their hand at producing lacquerwork. From Holland – and later from England – made-up furniture was shipped out to China to be lacquered and the Dutch took the trade a step further by sending joiners out East to make furniture on the spot, to be lacquered and then

Above: *A crimson japanned cabinet in the style of Giles Grendey, on a George II giltwood stand which embodies the spirit of the age's heavily ornamented taste. The cabinet is decorated with Chinese scenes in gold, black and grey, and contains ten drawers behind the prominently hinged doors.*

transported to an eager market in Europe. Chinese artists were brought to the Low Countries and this venture appeared to be somewhat more successful than the movement of craftsmen in the opposite direction.

In the 17th century the extensive traffic between the Dutch and the English and the bonds between the courts of Charles II and Louis XIV created a vogue for japanned work in this country, particularly towards the end of Charles's reign. It produced quantities of japanned cabinets, screens, mirrors and tables.

Under Queen Anne, the strengthening of trade links with China laid the groundwork for a passionate demand for lacquered objects during the second quarter of the 18th century. Different in form from the current trends in Baroque furniture, lacquered items nevertheless met the

Above: *Giles Grendey (1693–1780) was a London cabinetmaker who specialised in the export business and was skilled in the imitation of Oriental lacquerwork, a technique known as japanning in the West. He made this day bed in red japanned beech, with silver and gilt decoration, about 1730, as part of a very large suite.*

desire for ostentation in decoration and furnishings. It was to be seen in a profusion of japanned cabinets, bureaux, tables, chairs and even whole rooms made up of finely decorated panels. The very wealthy had panels of eastern origin, the moderately wealthy made do with the products of home-based japanners who now formed a flourishing industry in London. Their products were of three varieties: there was the basic flat lacquerwork – plain panels of tinted varnish; secondly, there was raised lacquerwork in which the ground was coloured blue, green, black or vermilion with a raised motif gilded on to it; thirdly, there was a type of incised lacquerwork called Bantam work, named after a port in the Dutch East Indies from which the first examples had been shipped in the 17th century.

A skilful exponent of japanning was Giles Grendey, to whom earlier reference has been made in connection with chairs and exports. So highly was his work prized that he found no shortage of ready buyers abroad for his imitations of the Oriental style. One such export consignment to Spain was a set of furniture japanned in a brilliant sealing wax colour, decorated with gold and silver. It consisted of a day bed (now in the Victoria and Albert Museum), six armchairs and twenty single chairs.

We have seen how the Oriental and European grounds of lacquerwork differed because of the nature of the basic materials available and the techniques used to apply them. The respective appearances of the finished products are also different in the way they are decorated. In Oriental examples costumes and faces are unmistakably eastern in character, and western designs have a stilted quality which is the inevitable result of copying from original Chinese and Japanese patterns.

Some of the finest examples of English japanned work may suffer in comparison with their Oriental equivalents, and the vast majority of pieces existing today from the period under review – the height of the fashion up to the mid-18th century – are perforce English in origin. The reason, as so often happens in furniture history, was a matter of commerce and politics.

In England, the commercial history of lacquer had roughly followed the pattern of the Dutch: first, the importation of lacquer boxes and panels (there are invoices from around 1700 which inform us of such purchases as 'twelve leaves of cutt Jappan Skreens'); then English merchants exported patterns and models of all kinds of furniture, the completed goods being lacquered and sent back from the East; finally, some merchants adopted the practice of shipping out made-up furniture to be treated and reimported into this country.

Many cabinetmakers, however, felt that the practice of sending out goods to be lacquered was unfair competition, and in 1701 a widely representative body of cabinetmakers and allied tradesmen petitioned parliament to curb this trade. The result of political pressure was a punitive import tax on lacquered goods which gave added impetus to the home trade in japanning.

In George II's reign the japanning of boxes and the painting of japanwork became a fashionable pastime for ladies in society. These amateur efforts account partly for the large amount of indifferent japanning that has come down to us through the years and have undoubtedly nourished the view that, on the whole, English imitations of lacquerwork were lamentable.

By the middle of the 18th century furniture-making in England would seem to have been dominated by a handful of individuals – Chippendale, Adam, Hepplewhite, Sheraton. Indeed they were men of stature in the history of furniture and they lent their names to conveniently labelled styles, but it would be wrong to imagine that there were so few figures on the stage. There were literally hundreds of cabinetmakers working in London and the main provincial centres, and while records of most may be scanty or non-existent, there can be no doubt that they provided a strong supporting cast for the great names, or those who worked for the grandest patrons.

The sheer numbers of craftsmen involved in furniture-making during the second part of the 18th century is a reflection of demand, especially by the well-heeled middle classes. Fashion was a relentless dictator and a family's status was affirmed by its ability to reflect the trends of the time. This often meant emulating the French and in France, according to Horace Walpole, writing in 1766, 'No fashion is meant to last longer than a lover'. The English were always strongly if sometimes uneasily influenced by the French; they admired their refinement and love of luxury, and many of the richest bought their furnishings direct from France. Others managed with English furniture 'in the French taste', or at least by changing their decorations and furniture almost as often as their clothes.

Another major influence on the demand for furniture was the changing pattern of living habits among the middle classes. Throughout the 18th century there was a steady progress away from the harshness of preceding centuries towards a better mannered, more refined way of life. This was reflected in, among other things, the architecture of houses and in the furnishing of their rooms. There was time for conversation, for long and enjoyable meals, for reading and writing, for card games and needlework, and a great deal of furniture was made to meet these varied demands of daily life and leisure among the moneyed classes.

No one was more perspicacious in recognizing the furniture needs or in meeting the stylistic fancies of his clients – and potential clients – than Thomas Chippendale. Little is known of his early life except that he came from a family of joiners from the Yorkshire village of Otley and that he was born in 1718. By 1748 he was married in London. In the following year he acquired premises in Conduit Court, Long Acre. He later took premises – probably not workshops – in Somerset Court in the Strand (*c.*1752). Two years later, in 1754, he had a cabinet and upholstery warehouse at The Sign of the Chair in St Martin's Lane, an address he held until his death in 1779. By the time he had acquired his St Martin's Lane premises he had also taken on a partner, James Rannie, who died in

Above: *A rosewood dressing-table in the Chippendale Rococo style, with gilt decoration, c.1760.* The Gentleman and Cabinetmaker's Director *includes a design for a similar 'Dressing-Table for a Lady; the Drawer above the Recess hath all the Conveniences for Dressing, and the Top of it is a Dressing-Glass, which comes forward with folding Hinges.'*

1766. Chippendale then managed his business single-handed until 1771 when he took another partner, Thomas Haig, apparently to supervise the business in London while he was away – often in the north of England – dealing with his more prestigious commissions. A third partner, of whom little is known, was Henry Ferguson. The firm was thenceforward known as Chippendale, Haig and Co. His son, also Thomas Chippendale, continued the family business into the 19th century, and kept up his father's high standards of craftsmanship, but eventually became bankrupt. The firm was always in financial difficulties, partly because many of its customers were bad payers.

In 1754 the first edition of the work which immortalized Chippendale appeared – *The Gentleman and Cabinet-Maker's Director*. This became a best-seller and was without doubt responsible for Chippendale's success both in his lifetime and in the eyes of posterity. A second edition was published in 1755 and a third in 1762. Many of his contemporaries also produced cabinet work of the highest quality but *The Director* brought fame and prominence to Chippendale above the rest. Craftsmen all over Britain and America copied the designs he published and thus propagated the 'Chippendale style' far beyond the bounds of his own workshop. A French translation of the descriptions of the designs was advertised in 1763. Copies of it are very rare. Whereas others among the most famous designers, like William Kent before him and Robert Adam a little later, were chiefly concerned with the furnishing of the stately homes of the nobility, Chippendale's aim was to make good furniture in the latest styles 'suited to the fancy and circumstances of persons in all degrees of life'. In this respect, *The Director* must be seen as a great achievement.

While many of its designs are elaborate and fanciful in the extreme, *The Director* is an unparalleled guide to mid-18th century furniture, both as regards style and the kinds of objects used by the well-heeled. For whatever Chippendale's assertions about 'persons in all degrees of life', these pieces could only have been bought by the wealthier classes. While Chippendale emphasized in his preface that he could undertake to make any of the designs in the book in his workshop, many of them were actually carried out in pruned down, plainer form, as often for economic reasons as from choice.

The French taste is, in *The Director*, subtly translated into an unmistakably English form. The Rococo was still having its day, and Chippendale succeeded in giving it as much heady exuberance as any Englishman dared: there were ribbon-backed chairs, mirrors and girandoles carved with asymmetrical leaves and curlicues, and surmounted by phoenixes; cabriole-legged sofas and commodes bordered with acanthus and shell decoration. But unlike truly French furniture of the period, many of Chippendale's designs were most suitably executed in mahogany, with decoration carved in the wood rather than applied in the form of metal mounts. He recommended japanning for a number of the designs, particularly for the lighter furniture intended for ladies' rooms. Gilding, too, he suggested for smaller items such as stands, firescreens, chandeliers and brackets.

He provides designs for furniture in the 'Gothick' taste and, more exuberant than ever, in the Chinese, both of which were the rage at this time. Of these, the Gothick (spelt that way to distinguish it from medieval Gothic) was a style of considerable dignity and grandeur, yet in its way it was as frivolous as the Chinese. Its most famous enthusiast was Horace Walpole to whose Gothick villa, Strawberry Hill, Twickenham, the fashionable multitudes flocked. Gothick had little academic basis, but made use of the clustered columns and pointed arches and even, occasionally, rose windows of medieval stonework in the shapes of chair backs and the legs of tables, chairs and other furniture. Gothic tracery was carved in mahogany on cupboard doors or the sides of desks, while medieval turrets and pinnacles surmounted bookcases. Sometimes Gothick decoration was married, most incongruously, to Chinese and even then the style undoubtedly worked. Of all historical pastiches, mid-18th century Gothick was one of the most elegant and exciting.

The Chinese taste, when executed with restraint, also had much charm. Its usual manifestations on furniture were geometric trellis work, known as Chinese railing, in the backs and sides of chairs, fret-cut patterns in friezes and borders, and pagodas surmounting beds, cabinets and bookcases. Eighteenth century chinoiserie was very much part of the international Rococo style – a frolicsome search for the fantastic and exotic rather than a serious copying of Chinese originals. Like the Gothick, it had little basis in either history or geography.

Chippendale's essays in chinoiserie range from far-fetched confections like his design for a japanned china case – carved, canopied and dripping with icicles and bells – to chunky sideboards and library tables, plain except for blind

Left: *A giltwood armchair upholstered in damask designed by Adam and made in Chippendale's workshops. It is part of a suite of 10 chairs and three sofas made for Sir Lawrence Dundas in about 1764. Its early Georgian form – cabriole legs, wide seat, bow-shaped back rail and lion-paw feet – contrasts strongly with the classically inspired ornament of sphinxes, honeysuckle and formal leaf and scroll designs.*

Left: *A view of the Chinese bedroom at Saltram House. The bed is based on designs in the* Director, *and the two chairs are typical of the 'Chinese Chippendale' style.*
Right: *A design for a 'Dome Bed' from Chippendale's* Director. *Its Rococo flavour is particularly strong in the carved decoration of the back and the tester.*

fret-cutting in the friezes, and fretted brackets of a faintly Chinese flavour.

The Director includes drawings of beds and pillars for beds, cornices, picture-frames, organ cases, lanterns and stove-grates; dressing tables, writing tables, commode tables, sideboard tables, china tables, breakfast tables and shaving tables; for basin stands, candle stands, clock cases and tea caddies. There are even designs for 'Handles and Escutcheons for Brass Work' and patterns of Chinese railings for 'genteel Fences for Gardens, etc'.

Chippendale borrowed his ideas from all quarters and, on the whole, illustrated furniture forms which had been in use for some time. His designs for 'Bason Stands' and 'A Shaving Table' are among the few new ideas, and herald the more sophisticated washstands and toilet tables of the later 18th century. It is noteworthy that Chippendale illustrated a number of sideboard tables, but no sideboards – this was another item that evolved much later in the 18th century. Large dining tables are also absent; in this period people generally took their meals in small groups, often from the square, oval or round flap table known as a Pembroke which was used for various purposes throughout the second half of the 18th century. It was not until the last quarter of the century that the dining room, furnished with an extendable table which could seat a dozen or so, became commonplace.

Chippendale was undoubtedly a well known figure in cultured circles. He was a member of the Society of Arts, and among the 308 subscribers to *The Director* were some of the most cultivated men of the day as well as a procession of cabinetmakers, upholsterers and chairmakers. His most accomplished furniture was in the Neoclassical style and in this he carried out the decoration for some of the grand houses of the period, among them Nostell Priory and Harewood House in Yorkshire, and Mersham-le-Hatch in Kent, whose interiors were designed by Robert Adam. At the same time, his workshops turned out a vast range of quite ordinary but well-made furniture for the homes of the middle classes; he was in business as an upholsterer, undertaker and paperhanger, and was not above importing unfinished furniture from France, and getting into trouble from customs officers for not declaring its full value. Comparatively few pieces can be attributed to his workshop with certainty, and of these the plain and elegant designs carried out for Ninian Home at Paxton House, Berwickshire, are probably far more representative of his usual work than his virtuoso performances for Harewood House.

Chippendale's *Director* was followed by several other cabinetmakers' publications during the next few years. Among these were designs by Thomas Johnson, a carver and gilder who, in spite of affirming a fashionable Francophobia (on account of the Seven Years' War) did more than any other furniture designer to promote the Rococo – an essentially French style – in its most fanciful form. In 1755 he published designs for *Twelve Girandoles* and these were followed by a *Collection of Designs*, issued in monthly instalments from 1756–58 and subsequently republished. All his engravings are for 'carver's pieces' – girandoles, brackets, looking glasses, kettle stands, console tables, candlestands and so on, and most of them were evidently intended to be gilded. They are highly elaborate confections owing a great deal to French fashions but with an unmistakably English flavour. Several, for instance, incorporate animals taken from Francis Barlow's illustrations of *Aesop's Fables*, and most of them lack the polished finesse of French designs. Johnson's publications were probably intended mainly for furniture makers and carvers rather than prospective clients, and a number of pieces have been found which correspond to his designs.

Between 1759 and 1762 *The Universal System of Household Furniture* appeared, issued in parts by William Ince and John Mayhew, cabinetmakers and upholsterers of Soho. Their book added little to Chippendale's, except for some designs for 'Claw Tables', or tripod-based tea tables of a type popular for many years to come. Like Chippendale, they purveyed a mixture of French, Chinese and Gothic styles.

A little later, in 1765, *The Cabinet and Chairmaker's Real Friend and Companion, or the Whole System of Chair-making made plain and easy* was published by Robert Manwaring. This consisted of 100 or so designs for chairs, also in the French, Gothic and Chinese styles, and was followed a year later by *The Chairmakers' Guide*, a similar but larger work consisting of about 'two hundred New and Genteel Designs, both Decorative and Plain'.

One route to fame for a cabinetmaker was to publish a design book; another was to enjoy the patronage of royalty, and several of Chippendale's contemporaries gained prestige in this way. Among them was William Vile who, with his partner John Cobb, had premises close to Chippendale's in St Martin's Lane in the 1750s and 1760s. He produced a number of pieces for the royal family in the 1760s – some of them are still at Buckingham Palace and

Below: *A mahogany settee of 'ribbon-back' design, with elaborately carved cabriole legs. Chippendale included several designs for 'Ribband Back Chairs' in the* Director *and they epitomize the English Rococo at its most vivacious.*

Windsor Castle. His characteristic furniture was of mahogany of grand proportions and notable for its superb carving in the Rococo manner. Vile's prices were notoriously high, but the quality of his cabinet work as well as the prestige of his clients sets him apart from most of his contemporaries.

After Vile's retirement in 1765 the business was carried on, most successfully, by his partner, John Cobb 'perhaps one of the proudest men in England', according to an early 19th century writer. Cobb is known to have executed furniture of greater flamboyance than Vile's but of similarly impeccable workmanship. Several of his designs in the French manner have survived. Some have elaborate marquetry veneers while others rely for their effect on the natural figure of the wood. A particularly French feature was his use of elaborate metal mounts, especially on the corners of commodes.

John Cobb has been credited with the invention of the type of drawing, writing and reading table which has an adjustable rising top. The artist Nathaniel Dance Holland is said to have painted Cobb's portrait in return for one of these tables – 'with upper and inward rising desks, so healthy for those who stand to write, read or draw', and they are sometimes known as Cobb's tables. Whether Cobb actually invented such a table or merely popularized his variation of a well-established idea is open to question.

Pierre Langlois was a Frenchman who, by 1759–60, had established a business in London for making 'all sorts of Fine Cabinets and Commodes made and inlaid in the Politest manner with Brass and Tortoiseshell'. His work in the Louis XV and Louis XVI styles, with marquetry decoration and gilt-bronze mounts, was of the highest quality, and was much admired by the fashionable aristocracy. According to Ambrose Heal 'he appears to have been patronized extensively by the nobility and gentry both here and in France'.

At the other end of the scale was the steady and almost timeless production of country furniture. All over England single craftsmen (sometimes estate carpenters for the nobility) or small groups of workers continued to turn out serviceable furniture for the less well off or for the unimportant rooms of important houses. They used oak, fruitwoods, ash, elm and yew – whatever was locally available – and maintained a tradition of vernacular furniture of unpretentious charm. Most of it is impossible to date accurately because styles changed so slowly, but regional differences in design and construction are often apparent. The Windsor chair is probably the most celebrated representative of the country tradition. The type was made all over Britain (although its chief centre of production was High Wycombe) and took many forms, from smart versions with Gothic arches and carved knees suitable for libraries, to rustic chairs for use in the garden.

Another form of seating, the settle of ancient origin, persisted in its usefulness in country taverns and farmhouses long after being outmoded in grander situations. Its draughtproof qualities were undoubtedly the main reason for its popularity in the country, and many were permanently fixed into chimney corners where they were sometimes known as ingle-benches. Low-backed wooden

Above: *An oak dresser with an attractive and elaborate arrangement of drawers and cupboards. It is typical of those produced in North Wales or the border counties and was probably made c.1770.*

settles, generally of oak, were country cousins of the more luxurious upholstered settee.

The dresser – an extremely useful piece of furniture combining the functions of sideboard and plate rack – was another product of country craftsmen, though not exclusively those of Wales. A typical 18th century dresser is made of oak and has three drawers in the top of the base, with cupboards below the two side drawers and a panel in the central section. In the top tier the two, and sometimes three, shelves for pottery or pewter are surmounted by a protecting canopy. But there are many variants of this scheme: some dressers are smaller, with two drawers and cupboards and some, designed perhaps for large farmhouse kitchens, have four, while drawers sometimes replace the central cupboard panel in the triple-fronted type.

Many indeed, especially those made before the late 18th century, had no cupboards in their bases; instead a shelf known as a potboard extended between the customary six legs (two at each end and two as extra front supports). Others had no superstructure, and consisted of a sideboard table with a variable arrangement of drawers and cupboards below.

The space-saving corner cupboard was another favourite in the country. Many were made of oak or painted pine and most consisted simply of two double-doored cupboards, one on top of the other. In the best examples the upper storey has a rounded back and domed top, sometimes with a shell motif carved inside it. Other, smaller, types have single doors, and some were designed without base sections to hang on the wall.

Neoclassicism

Italy

Neoclassicism is a rather inelegant word, but useful for describing a nevertheless elegant style, based on a fresh interest in 'antique' architectural ornament, that came into fashion *c.*1750–90. By 'antique' was meant the Greek, Roman, Etruscan, Egyptian and even Assyrian civilizations described in the section on the ancient world. A second phase of Neoclassicism developed at the end of the 18th century and ultimately became closely associated with the first French Empire under Napoleon, usually being known as the Empire style. Interest in classical architecture had been maintained ever since the Renaissance, and even during the Rococo period there were some furniture designers who never abandoned classical principles.

The Neoclassical movement was, to some extent, a reaction against the frivolity of the Rococo style, just as the Rococo itself had been a rebellion against the pomposity of the High Baroque (especially that of Louis XIV). In the mid-18th century, a need was felt for a return to greater discipline and architects, artists, designers and men of reason turned again for inspiration to the apparent, if in some ways illusory, sense of order manifest in what had survived from the Ancient World. From the start, it was an international movement.

J. Soufflot (1709–80) had designed the Hôtel-Dieu at Lyons in classical style as early as 1737, and in 1749–51 he was in Rome with the engraver, Charles-Nicolas Cochin the Younger (*c.*1715–90), a rebel against the excesses of the Rococo. Also in the party was Madame de Pompadour's brother who, as the Marquis de Marigny, was to become Director General of Buildings to Louis XV. The Comte de Caylus (1692–1765), better known in some circles for his disreputable tales of Parisian life, began to publish his perfectly respectable *Recueil d'antiquités* in 1752. By 1755, a brilliant group of enthusiasts had gathered in Rome. Among them were a painter of Danish origin from Bohemia, Anthony Raphael Mengs (1728–79); Johann Joachim Winckelmann (1717–68) who had started life as a shoemaker's son in Saxony and became an archaeologist, and whose *History of Ancient Art* (1764) proved of lasting worth; Robert Adam, destined to become the leading British architect of his time and major designer of furniture; and the French architect Jacques-Louis Clérisseau (1722–1820) whose future commissions took him as far afield as St Petersburg.

Left: *Jewel cabinet made in 1787 for Marie-Antoinette by J.F. Schwerdfeger and others. P.P. Thomire probably contributed the four caryatid figures and other bronze mounts. Sèvres plaques vie for attention with mother-of-pearl and painted glass against the mahogany framework. It was commissioned by the aldermen of Paris.*

Many others came and went, some making their stay in Rome a long one. Of the whole circle, one of the liveliest personalities and, at least indirectly, one of the most influential was the Venetian, Giovanni Battista Piranesi (1720–78). His etchings of Roman buildings began to appear in 1756 under the title of *Le antichità Romane.* His own designs were, like himself, rather exaggerated and theatrical – he had worked as a stage-designer – and Robert Adam described him as 'the most extraordinary fellow I ever saw'. He was a great enthusiast of Roman and Etruscan art and architecture, but actively disliked Greek arts. He did not conform to classical ideas entirely however, and even challenged the principles of the classical Roman architect Vitruvius, suggesting that designers should take what they wished from the classical repertoire and use it as they pleased, with their own good taste as the sole criterion.

Practising what he preached, he designed furniture for Cardinal Rezzonico in Venice, 1764–9, some of it Rococo but mostly Neoclassical with a lavish use of sphinxes, palmettes, lion monopod supports and bucrania (ox skulls). The only surviving examples of furniture carried out exactly to his design, however, are a pair of side-tables, one of which is now at the Minneapolis Institute of Fine Arts and the other at the Rijksmuseum, Amsterdam. At the time he was working on his designs, relatively little was known about Roman furniture, beyond what was depicted in sculpture; yet some of his designs are remarkably close to pieces subsequently excavated at Pompeii.

Pompeii and Herculaneum – Roman towns not far from Naples – had both been badly damaged by an earthquake in AD 63 and obliterated by the eruption of Vesuvius in AD 79. The ruins of Pompeii were discovered in 1594–1600 by Domenico Fontana during the building of an aqueduct, and at various times pieces of sculpture were unearthed from the layers of ashes and loose cinders covering the site. More careful inspections were made in 1748 and systematic excavations began in 1763. At Herculaneum the task was more difficult, as the deposits of ash had been drenched with water at the time of the disaster, causing them to solidify, but work there began in 1738 and continued until 1780, when interest shifted to Pompeii. Publications on the discoveries appeared from 1757 to 1792.

Left: *Piedmontese chair – one of a set of eight with matching settee – of the late 18th century. The frame is simply carved with fluting and spiral bands, and is painted. The draped upholstery is typical of the period. Piedmont was a centre for the production of Neoclassical furniture, taking the Louis XVI style as a basis on which to elaborate.*

The Pompeiian style, particularly as it was expressed in wall-paintings found in the ancient buildings, was taken up by many designers internationally, being used not only for interior decoration but as a source of inspiration for marquetry and painting on furniture. In the main, 18th-century designers interpreted Neoclassicism in the spirit of free adaptation advocated by Piranesi. It was the decorative range of rams' heads, Vitruvian scrolls, urns, lion masks, classical columns, paterae, swags and laurel wreaths that appealed to designers, who at first applied them to the existing Rococo shapes and, a little later, to more suitable forms. Such forms, however, were not inspired by actual Greek or Roman furniture until a more pedantic approach was made in the late 18th and early 19th centuries.

In the earlier approach to Neoclassicism, the general principle was to replace the curvaceous, S-shaped curves and C-scrolls of the Rococo with geometrical contours: rectangles, squares, ovals and circles. The cabriole leg was slow to depart but was eventually superseded by various vertical types of square or round section, often tapered and sometimes fluted or relieved with delicate carving. Those of round section were turned on a lathe and decoration was provided in the process by breaking the line with protuberances in low relief, frequently no more than a neat ring.

The bombé commode, so popular in most continental countries (much less so in England and America), gave way to the 'break-front' form of rectilinear outline, its front having a central portion that projected slightly. A similar plan was sometimes followed for certain other pieces of carcase furniture, for instance, the cupboard-bases of bookcases and vitrines. These changes came about very gradually in some places but quite abruptly in others, depending on a variety of factors, not least of which was the balance achieved between adventurousness and conservatism on the part of both designer and customer. This balance varied not only from place to place, but from one cabinetmaker to another and from one customer to another.

Although Italy provided the source-material for the Neoclassical style, it was not in the forefront of the movement so far as the production of furniture was concerned, tending rather to follow the lead of French and English designers.

Much Italian furniture that was made in the French manner of the Louis XVI period is very ornate and is inclined to retain Rococo elements, such as asymmetrical flourishes in carved decoration. For the middle-class home, chairs were being produced in the 1780s and 1790s, particularly in Naples but also in Florence and Venice, which show the open shield backs favoured by London cabinetmakers at that time. In the country districts, especially Tuscany, some excellent furniture was made along traditional lines, including ladder-back (slat-back) chairs, simple stools and drop-leaf tables, usually in solid pine, cypress or walnut. Chairs and chests of this peasant class are sometimes decorated with naive versions of Neoclassical motifs.

A more thoroughly Italian version of Neoclassicism occurred in sophisticated furniture. Slab-ended tables of the type made in ancient Rome, and reproduced during the Renaissance, make another appearance, with tops of marble, porphyry or *pietre dure*. The sculptural possibilities provided by stands for tables always appealed to the Italian genius, and many were designed by men who were not really members of the furniture trade at all. The sculptor Vincenzo Pacetti supplied, *c.*1789, 12 supports cast in bronze, all representing Hercules in various poses, for a table designed by Giuseppe Valadier (1762–1839) who was one of a family of silversmiths in Rome, but who also worked as an architect and designer.

Giuseppe Maggiolini (1738–1814), who began as a carpenter in a monastery and worked in Milan from 1771, is celebrated for his commodes, often made in pairs and following rectilinear shapes. The typical Milanese commode has two drawers with a concealed traverse so that the gap between the upper and lower drawers is all but invisible; it is thus capable of supporting decoration of a pictorial kind – often a Roman portrait medallion – centred on the front. Maggiolini executed this kind of marquetry on veneered grounds of ebony, satinwood, citruswood and palisander, to name but a few. He is said to have used 85 different kinds of wood in the year 1795, all in their natural, unstained state. Very few pieces are signed by him compared with the vast number attributed to him.

Ignazio Revelli (*b.*1756) and his son Luigi (*b.*1776) were natives of Vercelli, in Piedmont. They settled in Turin and specialised in making the half-round commodes for which that town was noted. Other Turin makers of these commodes largely concentrated on lacquered decoration. The Revellis became famous for pictorial marquetry of a standard second only to that of Maggiolini in Milan. Not content with the hackneyed repertoire of Neoclassical motifs, the Revellis created original designs for their intarsia pictures, and were patronised by the royal family of Sardinia.

Much of the furniture made in Turin at the end of the 18th century was decorated with lush carving of foliage, painted

Above: *Transitional Louis XV/Louis XVI commode made in Paris by Louis-Noël Malle (b.1734). The leg is still basically cabriole but the curve is minimal. The bombé shape has been abandoned in favour of a rectilinear carcase with a projection at the centre ('breakfront'). The marquetry achieves a* trompe l'oeil *effect by the use of perspective for the architectural view, particularly for the paved foreground.*
Far left: *Bureau veneered in walnut, southern Italy, late 18th century. Gentle curves add interest to the outside of the writing leaf and the drawer fronts. Apart from a single band of geometric pattern, no marquetry is employed, but the main areas are surrounded by a narrow crossbanding with the grain at right angles to its edges, and by a wide banding with the grain used diagonally.*

HEYDEN
202 BUYING FISH ADRIAEN VAN OSTADE (1610-1685) SIGNED AND DATED 1661

and gilded. The leading exponent of this Italian version of the Neoclassical style was Giuseppe Maria Bonzanigo (1745–1820), who was born as Asti and settled in Turin in 1773, where he worked for the Sardinian royal family for 20 years and was appointed woodcarver to the Crown in 1787. His output of console tables and firescreens, bureaux and commodes – mostly for the royal household – provided him with a splendid pretext for lavishly carved fruit, flowers and urns, as well as portrait busts of his patrons, with which his studio was well stocked until Napoleon's army arrived in 1796; being a survivor, Bonzanigo swiftly replaced the existing stock with busts of Napoleon, the Empress and their little son, the King of Rome. He even went so far as to make a tactful alteration to a piece of furniture, replacing a royal portrait with one of the Emperor.

France

The Neoclassical style was introduced into France only gradually, bronze mounts and handles being the first details to be affected by the return to symmetry, and the cabriole leg the last Rococo feature to be ousted in favour of vertical types. French Neoclassicism is commonly associated with the reign of Louis XVI but Cochin, who had been in Italy *c.*1750, was decrying the wastefulness of the Rococo in a supplication addressed to goldsmiths and sculptors in 1754 – the year that the future Louis XVI was born, and 20 years before he became king.

The first designs for Neoclassical furniture to be published in France were those of Jean-François Neufforge (1714–91), which appeared in 1765 and 1768. His 'medal cabinets' are monumental constructions and suggest a revival of the Louis XIV style at its most opulent. One such cabinet has draped figures as term supports and a pediment composed of two Grecian maidens flanking a bust. Neufforge also used sphinxes and other Egyptian motifs but the style was known to fashionable Parisian society as *gout grec*, 'the Greek taste'. Another designer of this heavy style was Jean-Charles Delafosse (1734–91), who made great play with Greek key patterns and laurel wreaths in his engravings, published in 1768, 1773, 1776 and 1785.

Boulle marquetry, a technique which had been rather neglected for some years, was now used again, as was *pietre dure*. Panels of this work in inlaid, coloured stones were not infrequently taken from Louis XIV pieces and re-used on break-front commodes of the Louis XVI period. One of the eminent cabinetmakers who adopted this practice was Adam Weisweiler (*c.*1750–*c.*1810), who was among the many Germans who settled in Paris in response to the great demand there for expensive furniture. There is little or no evidence that they were actively encouraged to come by the Queen, Marie Antoinette, as is sometimes suggested, but the extravagance of court circles was no doubt a sufficient inducement. Weisweiler worked for the Roentgen family

Left: Encoignure *(corner cabinet) made by Gilles Joubert (1689–1775) for the palace of Versailles. The door is decorated with parquetry – small diamond-shaped sections of tulipwood veneer fitted edge to edge on a foundation of oak. The gilded bronze mounts in the Neoclassical style are particularly fine. Joubert was 74 when he became cabinetmaker to the king, and retained the post until he retired at 85.*

Above: *Small gilt armchair, c.1775. Although employing curves to good advantage, especially in the shaping of the arms, the design is essentially geometrical and fully in accord with the Louis XVI style. The delicate spiral fluting of the legs, and the treatment of the back as a trimmed circle flanked by* oreilles, *suggest that this may have been made by J.-B.-C. Sené, who supplied chairs to the Crown.*

at Neuwied before settling in Paris in 1778, where he operated mainly through the dealer Dominique Daguerre.

Weisweiler seldom executed marquetry, preferring plain mahogany in combination with sheer black lacquer, sometimes inset with Sèvres porcelain plaques. He specialized in small, delicate pieces such as the *chiffonière*, originally a narrow chest-of-drawers, known as a *semainier* when it was seven drawers – one for every day of the week.

Characteristic features of Weisweiler's work are legs which revive in a highly refined way the barley-sugar twist, and which are often joined by curiously interlaced stretchers. He used bronze mounts, including some in the form of sphinx heads, which were of exceptional quality. The mounts were frequently supplied by Pierre Gouthière (1732–*c.*1812), one of the finest makers of bronze mounts, clock-cases and ornaments, who perfected a process whereby part of the surface was left matt while the rest was polished. He seldom signed his work, although objects of art bearing bogus signatures are not uncommon. He went

Above: Fauteuil *(armchair) c.1785 by Jean-Baptiste-Claude Sené (1748–1803) son of Claude Sené (1724–92), also a distinguished chairmaker. This example of the son's work includes typical features – columns flanking the panel of the back, and arms which sweep away from them in a graceful curve to be supported by caryatid figures. The draped upholstery was a fashionable flourish in the Louis XVI period.*

bankrupt in 1788 and was irretrievably ruined by the Revolution in the following year. It is probable that he supplied mounts to J.-H. Riesener, the successor to J.F. Oeben. Riesener completed two desks begun by his predecessor, one for Louis XV which is now at Versailles, and the other for the exiled king of Poland, Stanislaw Leszczynski, who was the father-in-law of Louis. This latter desk is now in the Wallace Collection, and it is one of the very first roll-top desks. It is a type known as a *bureau-cylindre*, the large kneehole writing-table having a semi-cylindrical cover which encloses the top. These magnificent specimens served as models for later, less sumptuous pieces. Riesener is generally held to be the greatest *ébéniste* working in Paris during the Louis XVI period, the years 1780–89 being his most productive, when he supplied a great deal of furniture at enormously high prices to Marie Antoinette. He continued to employ marquetry decoration throughout this period, especially on the central panels of break-front commodes, while at the same time producing much plainer pieces with mahogany and satinwood veneers relieved with bronze of an unsurpassed quality.

Riesener's prices proved a little too much for the King, whose chief interest in furniture lay in any mechanical devices or gadgetry forming part of a piece. (He was better at repairing clocks and locks than in affairs of state.) In 1785, Riesener lost his appointment as cabinetmaker to the King, although the Queen continued to patronize him to the end. He was replaced as *ébéniste-du-Roi* by another German, Guillaume Beneman (*fl.*1784–1811), whose prices were more competitive and who was not above revamping other men's work, if it was considered a little old-fashioned, by giving it a new look in the 'Roman' style. An adaptable man, he survived the Revolution and continued to work during the Empire period.

Not all the important makers of the Louis XVI era were German. René Dubois (1737–99), belonged to an established French family of craftsmen that included his father, Jacques (*c.*1693–1763) and a brother, Louis (1732–90). René was given a royal appointment by the Queen in 1779 and produced the famous 'Tilsit' table carved with figures (probably by his brother Louis) which was given by the king to the Empress of Russia, Catherine II. It is now in the Wallace Collection in London.

Although the name sounds French, Martin Carlin was in fact of German origin. He had worked under Oeben and had married Oeben's sister, Marie-Catherine. Carlin was more artist than craftsman, specializing in small, feminine pieces such as the *bonheur-du-jour* on which he used Sèvres plaques against a ground of ebony. His work is original in conception and refined in execution, but he died relatively poor in 1785.

David Roentgen supplied large quantities of furniture both to the Crown and to fashionable society in Paris, but as he never had workshops in France, preferring to remain at Neuwied, his career is discussed in the section on Germany.

It was a Frenchman, the artist Jacques-Louis David (1748–1825), who was one of the first to design furniture which attempted to reproduce as exactly as possible actual pieces of Ancient Roman and Greek work – couches on turned feet, tripod stands, chairs of *klismos* form with sabre legs, stools of Roman *curule* shape on X-curved supports. Many of these ideas were no doubt derived from Greek pots, of the red-figure or black-figure kind, which sometimes depicted figures of people using furniture; it may be significant that in having these designs executed for his own use and for the Comte d'Artois, David's colour scheme was mainly black and red. David was trained by J.M. Vien (1716–1809), with whom he went to Rome and who was a pioneer of Neoclassical painting. It is perhaps not altogether irrelevant that some of those – David among them – who adopted this later, more pedantic Neoclassical style in France were equally revolutionary in their politics, supporting the anti-monarchist movement and going on to serve the Directoire and the Empire of Napoleon.

David's furniture *à la grecque* was made for him by Georges Jacob (1739–1814) who was of Burgundian peasant stock. He was appointed a *maître* of the guild in 1765 and acknowledged as a leading maker of seat furniture by *c.*1780. His chairs in the earlier Louis XVI style have rectangular backs, and the frames are finely carved with flowers and classical motifs. He was especially fond of carving a marguerite on the seat-rail. He avoided painting and gilding whenever possible, preferring natural wood, particularly mahogany which had not previously been fashionable in France. It was well suited to the later, more severe Louis XVI style initiated by David, and Jacob employed it for X-framed stools and chairs, lyre-backed chairs, sabre-legged seats of various kinds and for furniture other than seats. Although not much employed by the court, he was owed large sums of money by the aristocracy when the Revolution began; he was never paid, many of his clients having gone to the guillotine. Thanks to the support of David, he was given an entrée into the austere world of the new régime.

The chairmaker preferred by the Crown was Jean-Baptiste-Claude Sené (1748–1803) who became *maître* in 1769 and *fournisseur de la Coronne* in 1785, making lyre-back chairs and others in mahogany. He often placed a fluted column at each side of the central panel on gilt examples, accompanied by a leg with a neat barley-sugar twist. Jean-Démosthène Dugourc, a leading exponent of the archaeological approach to Neoclassicism, designed for him. Sené provided furniture for the bedroom of Marie Antoinette at Fontainebleau in 1787, which proved to be one of the last major royal commissions before the Revolution, after which he was employed in the production of office furniture for bureaucrats.

These were but a few of the many craftsmen working in the age of Louis XVI, producing most of the principal types of furniture current in the previous reign but modifying them to conform first with the highly decorated early Neoclassical style, and then with the plainer fashion which anticipated the *Directoire*. Some of them exploited all the succeeding fashions from Rococo through Neoclassical to Empire. During the Louis XVI period, several types of furniture either appeared for the first time or came into much more general use.

Intimate dining rooms for small parties came to be furnished with circular tables on centre pedestals. Food was placed on a kind of open sideboard, the *console desserte*, supplemented by a 'dumb waiter' with two or three tiers, the *serviteur fidèle*, from which diners helped themselves after the servants had been discreetly dismissed. The break-front commode of rectilinear form, which replaced the bombé version, sometimes had drawers or cupboard-space concealed by sliding panels. For bow-fronted cabinets or roll-top desks, the *tambour* became a popular method of enclosure. It consisted of narrow fillets of wood laid close together and glued onto a canvas backing which travelled within grooved guides. The *secrétaire-à-abattant*

Below: *Dwarf cabinet made by Adam Weisweiler (c.1750–c.1810), one of the most distinguished German cabinetmakers to settle in Paris during the Louis XVI period. He seldom executed marquetry but frequently recycled panels of boullework and* pietre dure *taken from Louis XIV cabinets. He was fond of using the distinctive type of foot seen here.*

Below: Bonheur-du-jour *(lady's writing table with superstructure) veneered in tulipwood and mounted with Sèvres porcelain plaques which are dated 1766 – the year in which the cabinetmaker who made this piece, Martin Carlin, was admitted to the guild as a master. He is believed to have worked sometimes to designs by G.-P. Cauvet (1731–88).*

(fall-front secretaire), though by no means a new invention, gained in popularity. The upper stage had a writing-leaf which occupied a vertical position when the desk was closed. The lower stage was either a carcase with drawers or cupboard enclosed by doors, or was a table-like, open framework of legs and stretchers. Fine examples were produced in lacquer, marquetry or plain mahogany.

Notable among smaller pieces of furniture were glass-fronted vitrines for the display of porcelain (especially Sèvres), which became more austere, not merely in accord with the general trend towards the end of the Louis XVI period, but also on the principle that the porcelain was sufficiently decorative in itself.

To offset the increasing severity of the furniture, flower arrangements gained in importance, and rectangular or oval *jardinières* were produced with removable tops that could drop into position, forming a small table when flowers were not available.

Bourgeois furniture followed closely the fashions set by the court, the elaboration of veneering and mounting in bronze being imitated in less costly forms. The regional furniture of the countryside – the armoires and commodes in fruitwood, oak and walnut – continued to be made much as before. Near the larger provincial towns, the commodes became more rectilinear, and the doors of armoires were sometimes carved with Neoclassical motifs – occasionally the whole area of the door was carved to represent an oval Greek shield. On the whole however, the Louis XV style continued to be used with only minor modifications. Long, narrow tables were made in ever-increasing numbers, standing on square, tapered legs and with one or two drawers in the frieze. Occasionally there is an extension-leaf at one end. Provided the frieze is not too deep, they make excellent dining tables, but many were made as side-tables in farmhouse kitchens and are too low to sit at in comfort. The woods used were usually from fruit trees and polished to a fine, warm colour, *merisier* (wild cherry) being especially attractive. Those meant to be sat at were originally provided with pairs of benches.

The more sophisticated, veneered furniture is usually constructed of oak, with drawer-sides and bottoms of the same timber. In country furniture, the secondary wood is very often chestnut or poplar. Mortise-and-tenon joints on 18th-century French furniture are normally secured with dowel pins and the heads of these are visible on the surface of most pieces that are not veneered.

Spain

The Neoclassical style reached Spain during the reign of Charles III (reigned 1759–88) and continued during that of Charles IV (reigned 1788–1802) in a composite version derived from Italy, France and England. A recognizable Spanish flavour nevertheless emerged.

Matias Gasparini, a Neapolitan, became director of the royal workshops at Madrid in 1768, after which date commodes of both curvilinear (sarcophagus-shape) and rectilinear (break-front) types are decorated with marquetry in the Milanese manner, often with profiles of Roman emperors on their fronts, or with painting of grotesque masks, figures and wreaths in the 'Pompeiian' style of Naples. Another favourite form of embellishment was the countersinking of small pieces of mirror glass. Mahogany pieces were seldom left plain, but decorated with marquetry on rectangular or diamond-shaped panels.

There was a great demand for small tables suitable for writing, gaming or taking refreshment. These stood on square tapered legs, their surfaces being covered in marquetry. Where bronze mounts would be used on a French equivalent – as at the tops of the legs – on Spanish examples they are simulated in marquetry.

Chairs with open backs, also standing on square tapered legs, show English influence, while others are of the French *en gondole* type, derived from ancient Greek originals, in which the backs are composed of panels, rounded laterally to receive the human frame in comfort and painted or inlaid with Neoclassical motifs. The

Left: *Many small tables with a feminine charm were produced for the salons of the Louis XV and Louis XVI periods. This late Louis XV example is composed of elegant curves and decorated with floral marquetry, but the angular fretting of the metal gallery, the gilt bronze mounts of classical flavour, and the pendant husks inlaid in the legs herald the approach of the Louis XVI style.*

Right: *Louis XVI* secrétaire-à-abattant *(fall-front secretaire), the outside of the writing-leaf with an amusing* trompe l'oeil *portrayal of books and writing implements in marquetry, over which hangs a plaited swag suspended from equally illusory ring handles, imitating the real ones on the drawer above. The doors below are decorated with parquetry.*

Above: *Portuguese breakfront commode in the 'Donna Maria' style, late 18th century. Distinctive features are the deep apron below the central projection, enamelled handles and the use of symmetrically patterned quartered veneers for the drawer fronts.*

proportions of Spanish chairs are often strikingly exaggerated: very narrow, lyre-shaped backs are perched over very large, round seats which rest on turned and tapered legs. A complex result emerged from Spanish interpretations of Neapolitan adaptations of basically English types, as in the case of chair-backs composed of interlaced geometric patterns. These were usually painted and 'parcel gilt' – i.e. details of turning and carving were picked out in gold leaf.

Beds became structurally simpler, the tester being dispensed with entirely and the headboard taking on a new importance with painted decoration, often lavish, in the Pompeiian style.

Peasant furniture was little affected by these fashionable developments, although there was more of it, at least during the earlier years of this period, thanks to social reforms carried out by Charles III. This improvement was largely nullified by Charles IV.

Portugal and Latin America

Following a disastrous earthquake in 1755, the government of Portugal was largely in the hands of Sebastiao José de Carvalho (later Marquess of Pombal, by which name he is best known), who took charge of the necessary reorganization and gained complete ascendancy over the King, Joseph I (reigned 1750–77). Employing arbitrary and at times ruthless methods, Pombal succeeded in building up the economic strength of the country and limiting the power of British merchants in Portugal. In spite of this last reform, English influence on Portuguese furniture, already quite marked, tended to increase. An early form of the convertible bed-settee, of which relatively few English examples exist, became popular in Portugal and was known as a *leito a inglesa*.

The true Portuguese bed, however, owed little to any other country and certainly nothing to England. Having long ago discarded the posts and tester, the Portuguese adapted their beds to the Neoclassical style of making them more architectural in form and by decorating the headboards with fine marquetry employing Pompeiian features.

Among articles of seat furniture, the influence of late 18th century English styles was evident. During the earlier years of the melancholic Queen Maria I (reigned 1777–1816), there was a marked absence of comfortable, French-style armchairs. Instead, there was a fashion for suites of chairs and settees (*doiradinhas*) of framed construction. They were very prim-looking, the settees formed on the principle of three rectangular chair-backs joined together, standing on square tapered legs, in the manner of Hepplewhite or Sheraton. They were painted with urns, pendant husks and flowers *en grisaille* – a French term describing painting in tones of grey, green and buff, and originally used on walls to simulate architectural details and sculpture but often employed on furniture for depicting other subjects.

The 'Donna Maria' commode was rectilinear and breakfronted with an unusually deep apron below the break. It was three drawers deep, each drawer being fitted with enamelled handles. The top was of marble. Semicircular shapes were also popular for small commodes, made in pairs, and for gaming tables. It was a prosperous period in Portugal and money was available for such luxurious pieces as the cylinder-top commode enriched with parquetry on the cylinder, marquetry on the drawer-fronts and quartered veneers on the ends.

One of the few Lisbon makers who was in the habit of signing his work was Domingos Tenuta who flourished in the last years of the century and who sometimes embossed his name on leather tablets concealed in one of the secret drawers with which 18th-century bureaux abounded.

In 1808 the court exiled itself to Brazil and the Neoclassical style was introduced into that country. Neoclassicism was very late arriving in Latin America; Father Joseph Schmidt is said to have introduced it to Peru. Immigrants from many lands arrived with ideas and varying ability to execute them. The more sophisticated pieces are decorated with rather old-fashioned-looking marquetry, more Baroque than Neoclassical in spirit but the new style was observed in the increased use of straight lines for actual shapes, where previously a delight in curves had triumphed.

The Netherlands

The demand for fashionable English and French furniture became so great in Holland in the 1760s that the prosperity of Dutch craftsmen was seriously threatened and in 1771 all imports were banned except a limited quantity permitted for an annual fair. Craftsmen benefited from this measure of protection and Dutch furniture in the Neoclassical style reached a high standard. To distinguish Dutch pieces from foreign imports, members of the Amsterdam guild of St Joseph had to mark each piece with the arms of the city and the initials 'J.G.' (Joseph's Guild).

Above: *Dutch octagonal tea table in pine, mid-18th century, the top with moulded edges and painted with a still life subject, the tripod base painted and grained to simulate rosewood. Painted furniture was produced in rural areas in many countries, but this example, inspired by Dutch pictures, displays a higher degree of artistry than was usual.*

The Dutch woodworkers digested styles from abroad, blending them to produce one that was characteristically their own. Armchairs with rectangular backs followed Louis XVI types but were made in mahogany and carved in the English manner. Carcase pieces such as commodes are mounted on rather heavy, square tapered feet. The typical Dutch commode of the period is rectilinear and has a wood top, around which runs a low gallery, veneered with alternating pieces of ebony and light-coloured wood, set diagonally to produce a striped effect. Satinwood was extensively used in association with oriental lacquer, or with the excellent Dutch imitation of it.

A characteristically Dutch piece of the period was a low cabinet or commode with a hinged top. When opened, the inside of the lid has shelves which are also hinged and can be made rigid. Set in these shelves is a pewter cistern for water. A pair of extension leaves, hinged to the ends, can be opened out sideways to form a working top and to reveal a pewter bowl in a cut-out space below. The function of this luxurious sink unit was to provide facilities for washing glasses in the drawing-room.

Left: *Table made by the leading Swedish cabinetmaker of the late 18th century, Georg Haupt (1741–84), who trained in Germany, Holland, Paris and London before returning to Stockholm in 1769 – the year in which this table was made. The swags on the frieze and the turning of the legs show some English influence – a trend which became more apparent in Swedish work after Haupt's death, when the leading makers were Iwersson and the brothers Masreliez.*

The bombé-based wardrobe continued for a time with fashionable modifications to the decoration but was ultimately replaced with a rectilinear form. The traditional *kas*, or cupboard, continued to be made, especially in farming areas, with decoration either of flowers in polychrome or Neoclassical subjects *en grisaille* on a pine structure. Pine was also used for oval and octagonal tea tables on tripod bases, again with painted decoration that occasionally reached a high artistic level.

Denmark and Norway

The formal introduction of Neoclassical decoration to Denmark occurred in 1757 when the French architect Nicolas Jardin employed it in a scheme for a room in the palace of a Copenhagen nobleman. His pupil, C.F. Harsdorff (1735–99), subsequently designed some agreeable furniture in rather plain mahogany relieved with classical columns set at the corners of carcase pieces and with deep friezes carved with Greek key and anthemion patterns.

High standards of craftsmanship were maintained by the guilds and by the Academy of Copenhagen, set up in the 1750s under the direction of the sculptor Jacques-François Saly (1717–76). The system whereby a 'masterpiece' has to be submitted to the guild before its maker was accepted as a member was made more strict, designs for the piece first having to be approved by the Academy. Saly, who had first come to Denmark in 1753 to make a statue of King Frederick V (reigned 1746–66), did not return to Paris until 1774.

Three years later, the *Kongelige Meubel Magazin* (Royal Furniture Emporium) was established. Georg Roentgen, one of the famous family of German cabinetmakers, made a visit to this factory and although his stay was a short one, he helped to revive interest in the neglected art of floral marquetry. The directorship was taken over in 1781 by the Norwegian statesman Carsten Anker. Norway was still tied politically to Denmark and contributed many men of great ability to the government as well as the cultures of the two countries. Perhaps due partly to the influence of the Queen (who was a sister of the English King George III, and not very happily married to Denmark's Christian VII, who reigned 1766–1808), Anker was an enthusiast for English styles and despatched craftsmen from the Emporium to London to improve their skills. Jens Brøtterup was one such craftsman who, on his return to Copenhagen, passed on his knowledge to others. The result was the production of a great deal of furniture of basically English design (especially chairs with square backs having vertical struts and standing on square tapered legs), but which also demonstrated the Danish liking for clean lines uncluttered by excessive decoration.

Norwegian furniture of the period tends to follow Danish styles very closely, but the proportions are a little different, resulting in a heavier, more sturdy style.

Sweden

The leading Swedish cabinetmaker of the Neoclassical period was Georg Haupt (1741–84), who was born in Stockholm. He was the son of a carpenter from Nuremberg and was apprenticed in Germany until 1763. He then worked in Holland for a time before moving on to Paris, where a desk at the *Institut Géographique* bears an inscription stating that he made it in 1767. In 1769 he visited London, returning in the same year to Stockholm. In 1770 he submitted his masterpiece to the guild – a splendid writing-table topped with a *cartonnier* at one end. The table stands on square tapered legs and has a generally severe outline, relieved with restrained marquetry decoration with its main feature a panel depicting books, pens and scattered papers. This became the property of the new King, Gustav III (reigned 1771–92) and is still in the Royal Palace, Stockholm. In 1773–74, Haupt made an equally magnificent cabinet for a mineralogical collection for the king to give to the Prince de Condé. It is preserved at the Musée Condé, Chantilly.

Above: *Mahogany secretaire in the later Neoclassical style which abandoned charm in favour of solemnity. The columns, plaques and mounts make this piece into a miniature Greek temple. It was one of several supplied by David Roentgen from his workshops in Neuwied near Coblenz to Catherine II following his visit to Russia in 1783.*

The Swedish court continued to adopt, quite consciously, the Louis XVI style but at less august levels German and English influences were also felt. In the early 1790s Gotlob Iwersson, who had been a follower of Haupt's style, began to adopt a more severe manner with an English flavour to it; his bureaux however, have drawer-fronts with a framed effect achieved with wide beadings, much more pronounced than the English style of cock-beading. The feet on his carcase pieces are turned and tapered and look too delicate for the weight they have to support.

Oval chair-backs, certainly, of the late 1790s are reminiscent of the Hepplewhite style, but a characteristic Swedish feature, a transverse channel cut into the seat rails, is seen on many of them. The same detail is found on various other items of furniture. Chairs made in Stockholm after 1765 were required by the guild to bear a stamped label but this has survived on comparatively few examples.

Germany and Austria

The greatest German furniture-maker of the Neoclassical period, David Roentgen (1743–1807), seldom stamped or signed his products, even though officially required to do so after becoming, under pressure, a member of the Paris guild in 1789. He is often classed with the German cabinetmakers who settled in Paris but after taking over control of the family business at Neuwied, near Coblenz, in 1770, he never transferred his workshops elsewhere. As a shrewd businessman, one of his first acts was to raise capital by running a lottery with furniture as the prizes, which proved highly successful.

In 1774 he visited Paris for the first time, returning five years later with a large consignment of furniture, and thereafter maintaining a depôt in the city from which he supplied his customers including Louis XVI and Marie Antoinette. Both spent huge sums with Roentgen, the King finding something to interest him in the ingenious mechanical contrivances devised for Roentgen by Peter Kintzing, who also made clocks, and the Queen being attracted to elaborate marquetry based on the careful drawings of Januarius Zick (1730–97).

Roentgen spent much of his time travelling abroad, cultivating his rich customers and setting up other depôts. He visited Italy and the Netherlands and made seven trips to Russia, supplying many pieces to the Empress Catherine II. In 1791 he was appointed 'Court Furnisher' to Wilhelm II in Berlin, which helped him to survive the disaster of the French Revolution when he lost not only the vast sums of money owing to him in France but all the stock he had in store there.

Below: *Upright secretaire with fall front* (secrétaire-à-abattant) *made by David Roentgen c.1780 – about three years before he supplied the mahogany desk to Catherine of Russia shown on page 125. A comparison of these two shows the essential differences between the earlier, more decorative Neoclassicism and the later, more architectural version.*

The contrast between early, highly decorated Louis XVI furniture and the much simpler, later style in mahogany relieved only with bronze mounts is clearly seen in the development of Roentgen's products. Marquetry dominated his work from 1770–80 and mahogany from 1780–90. Unquestionably, until faced with ruin in France, Roentgen was the most successful manufacturer of furniture in Europe before 1800.

The phenomenon of the Roentgen organization apart, Germany was rather cautious in its acceptance of the Neoclassical style. Even allowing for the customary time-lag between the establishment of a fashion in any metropolis and its acceptance in the provinces, there was a marked inclination at such centres as the Prussian Court to retain the Rococo style. Strong elements of the Rococo are present for instance, in furniture made by J.C. Fiedler for Frederick the Great in 1775. It was not until 1787 that a magazine published in Weimar presented a fully developed Neoclassical style which shows English rather than Louis XVI influence.

Neoclassicism was adopted more readily in the north of Germany, especially along the Lower Rhine, where some good-quality furniture for the middle range of the market was made in solid walnut, carved with pendant husks, mounted with neat ring handles and resting on turned and tapered legs. Austria, during the reign of Joseph II (1780–90), produced some elegant pieces, the slightly exaggerated height of the legs on tables and desks sometimes giving them a rather stilted appearance. The Viennese guild insisted on high quality, not only for princely pieces but for those intended for modest homes. At this time also a preference for light-coloured woods, such as cherry, began to emerge.

Away from the capital cities and especially in the Alpine areas, the tradition of gaily painted marriage beds and cupboards, often inscribed and dated, continued. In the Upper Rhine area of Germany and Switzerland, this practice of commemorating marriages with specially made articles of furniture extended to chairs, usually with busily turned members in the backs and with a rail suitably inscribed.

Poland

In most countries, furniture made on country estates has an honest but naive flavour. In Poland, estate-made pieces reached a remarkable degree of sophistication. Bureaux, commodes and sideboards were among the many things veneered in walnut, with wide crossbanding dividing the ground into rectangular panels which in turn are decorated with neat floral marquetry. It is known collectively as *Kolbuszowa* work, after one of the estates near Rzeszów in Southern Poland where it was made.

Stanislaus II became king in 1764, thanks to the influence of Catherine II of Russia whose lover he had

Right: *Bed from the Austrian Tyrol, inscribed with the owner's name and dated 1771. Gaily painted furniture of this kind – particularly bridal beds, cupboards and chests – were traditional products of peasant cultures in many European countries. What appear to be marble insets in the headboard are in fact simulated with paint.*

VRSVLA · ÖWERLIN · 177

Above: *Two Russian armchairs in the Neoclassical style, c.1770–90, the period of Catherine II. The arms, terminating in eagles' heads on the one and in eagles' claws on the other, derive from Roman ornament and are probably intended as imperial symbols.*
Left: *A group of late 18th century German furniture. The serpentine-fronted dwarf cabinet has supplanted the* bombé *commode as a fashionable item of furniture. The doors and end panels are decorated in parquetry to produce a three-dimensional effect. The chairs, with spade-shaped backs and turned, tapering legs with spiral fluting, show the influence of the French Louis XVI style.*

been. A romantic, well-meaning, if somewhat ineffective ruler, he was an enthusiastic art collector who encouraged fine craftsmanship. Warsaw became a major centre for furniture production and a number of workmen were brought from the Roentgen establishment at Neuwied, among them Andreas Simmler who founded a family firm which was later to become renowned. Warsaw produced two-drawer commodes of rather chunky form but elegance is present in more feminine pieces such as the *bonheur-du-jour* on tapering legs, the panels of the superstructure having painted flowers within rosewood crossbanding. Production during the years 1780–96 was considerable but the partitioning of the country in 1772, 1793 and 1795 between Austria, Prussia and Russia virtually eliminated Poland as a sovereign state.

Russia

During the long reign (1762–96) of Catherine II ('the Great'), French and English fashions were introduced both directly and indirectly into Russia. The French architect Vallin de Mothe was Director of Fine Arts in St Petersburg, while the Scot, Charles Cameron, designed palace interiors with Pompeiian décor in the manner of his countryman Robert Adam but also with personal knowledge of the classical world gained in Italy.

Catherine herself imported furniture from other Paris makers as well as the many pieces sold to her by David Roentgen. Many of these pieces were then copied by Russian craftsmen with varying fidelity to the originals. Sometimes the design, if too complex, was simplified; sometimes, if too austere for Russian taste, it was embellished with ornamentation that would have been thought excessive in whichever country the design had originated.

Commodes of serpentine shape, basically in the English manner, were raised on high legs, armoured with heavy bronze mounts and fitted with a superstructure in the form of a small cabinet derived from German models. As in Poland, a considerable quantity of furniture was produced on country estates. Ostankino near Moscow and Okhta near St Petersburg were two of the more important centres where furniture was made not only for the use of the landowner but also for sale. The majority of pieces made for middle-class homes were heavy in appearance, sporting various Neoclassical details of ornament but lacking any kind of grace.

Originally founded as a small-arms factory by Peter the Great, the Tula Ironworks in central Russia had in part been taken over, *c.*1725, for making steel furniture, fireplaces and ornaments. In Catherine's time, armchairs on X-shaped supports and occasional tables were among the items produced in cut steel with elaborate fretted patterns inlaid with copper, pewter and sometimes even silver.

England

By the mid-1760s the spirit of Neoclassicism – the disciplined antithesis to frolicsome Rococo – was stirring the interests of fashionable English cabinetmakers, and the new movement led to enormous changes in furniture styles during the next ten years. For several decades an élite minority had concerned themselves with the study of classical ornament, but it was not until the 1740s and 50s, with the excavations of Pompeii and Herculaneum, that a more general interest was stimulated.

In 1754 a young Edinburgh architect, Robert Adam, was sent on a grand tour which took him to Italy, at that time agog with interest in ancient Roman civilization. There he met Giovanni Battista Piranesi whose highly imaginative approach to archaeology was the chief influence on Adam. In 1758 he returned to the family architectural practice he shared with his brother James in London and soon began to enjoy the patronage of the wealthy and fashionable. One of his first commissions was for the interior of Kedleston Hall, Derbyshire, and this was followed by work for Harewood House (with Chippendale), Syon House, Osterley Park, Newby Hall, Kenwood and several others. For many of them Adam not only designed the decorations but also the furniture of the principal rooms. His concept of interior decoration as a total entity led him to design the smallest details like keyhole escutcheons for doors, and fireplace grates. Many of his ceiling decorations were complemented by carpets of his own design on the floors.

Adam's interpretation of the styles of ancient Greece and Rome involved decoration rather than form. Classical details such as rams' heads, urns, festoons, anthemion (honeysuckle), paterae (carved rosettes) and trophies were applied to shapes based on the rectangle, the square, the circle or the oval. It was a copying of the essence rather than individual examples of the antique. After the asymmetrical fantasies of the Rococo the elegant linearity of the Neoclassical 'Adam' style which swept England in the late 1760s and 1770s must have been refreshing indeed.

A good deal of Adam furniture is gilded, and the fashion for Neoclassical furniture which he began stimulated an increase in the number of carvers and gilders working in London and the provinces towards the end of the 18th century. Painted furniture also came into favour under his influence. The intricacy of his decoration on, for example, mirrors and girandoles led to the use of new materials such as composition on wire for tracery and filigree ornament.

Another of his innovations was the use of a sideboard table in conjunction with a flanking pair of urns and pedestals and with a wine cooler underneath. This imposing arrangement was at first found suitable for the grand interiors of Adam himself, but was later taken up by the cabinetmakers of the gentry. The urns or vases (a favourite classical form) were used for storing cutlery or as water cisterns, while the pedestals held cupboards for plates, bottles and sometimes a chamber pot.

Right: *A view of the Etruscan Room at Osterley Park, Isleworth. Designed by Robert Adam between 1761 and 1780, Osterley's interiors are some of the finest and most cohesive of the early Neoclassical period.*

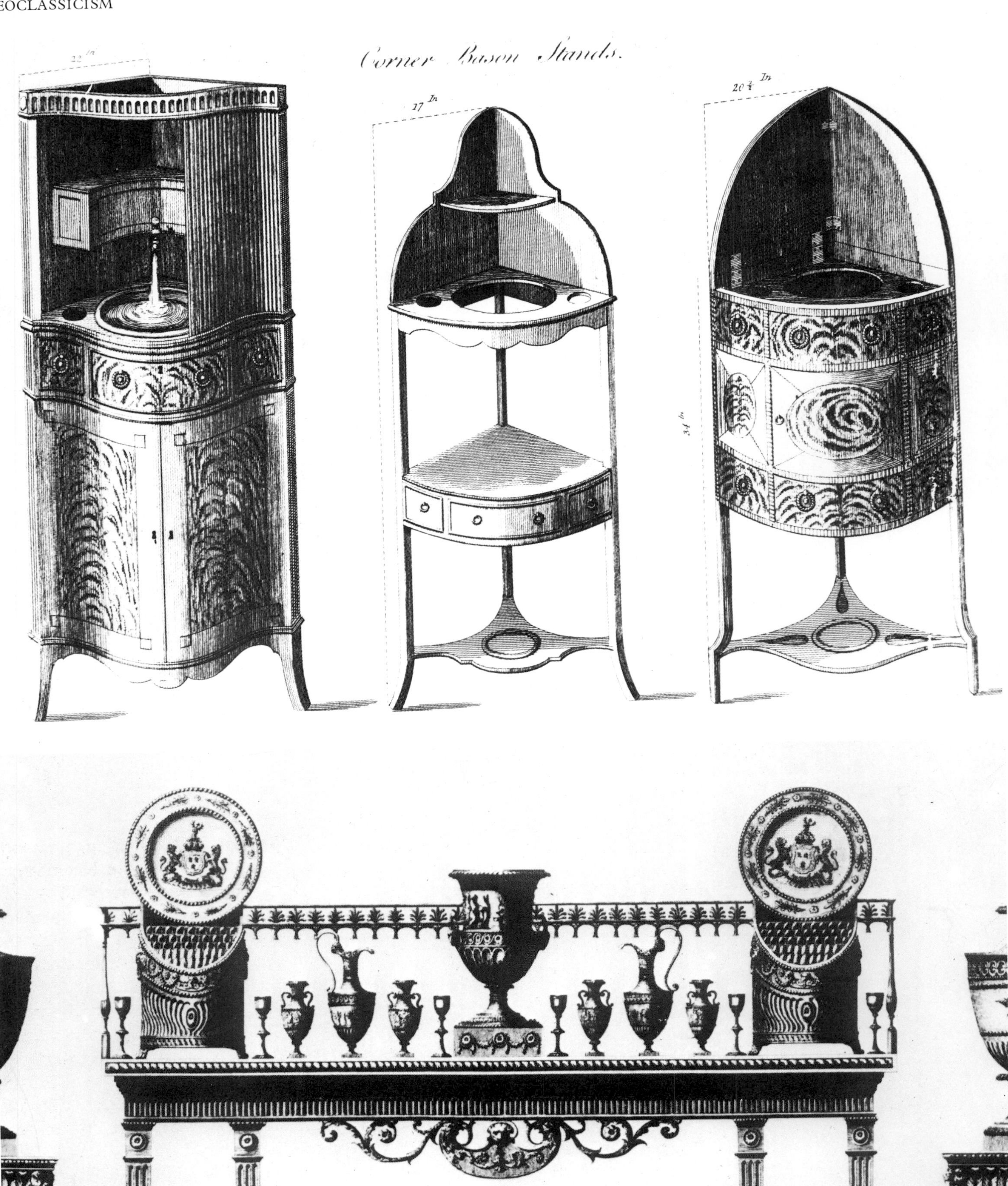
Corner Bason Stands.
22 In
17 In
20¼ In
34 In

Left: *An illustration from Sheraton's* Drawing Book *of three 'Corner Bason Stands'. The middle one shows a type of washstand especially popular in the closing years of the 18th century. As Sheraton himself suggested, 'The advantage of this kind of bason-stand is, that they may stand in a genteel room without giving offence to the eye, their appearance being somewhat like a cabinet.'*
Below left: *An illustration from Robert and James Adam's* Works in Architecture *of 1774, showing the sideboard table with its arrangement of plate- and knife-boxes, flanking urns and pedestals with a wine cooler beneath, originally designed for Kenwood House, Hampstead.*
Right: *A design for a chair from Hepplewhite's* Guide *in which the Neoclassical taste of Adam and his aristocratic clients was admirably distilled for the gentry.*

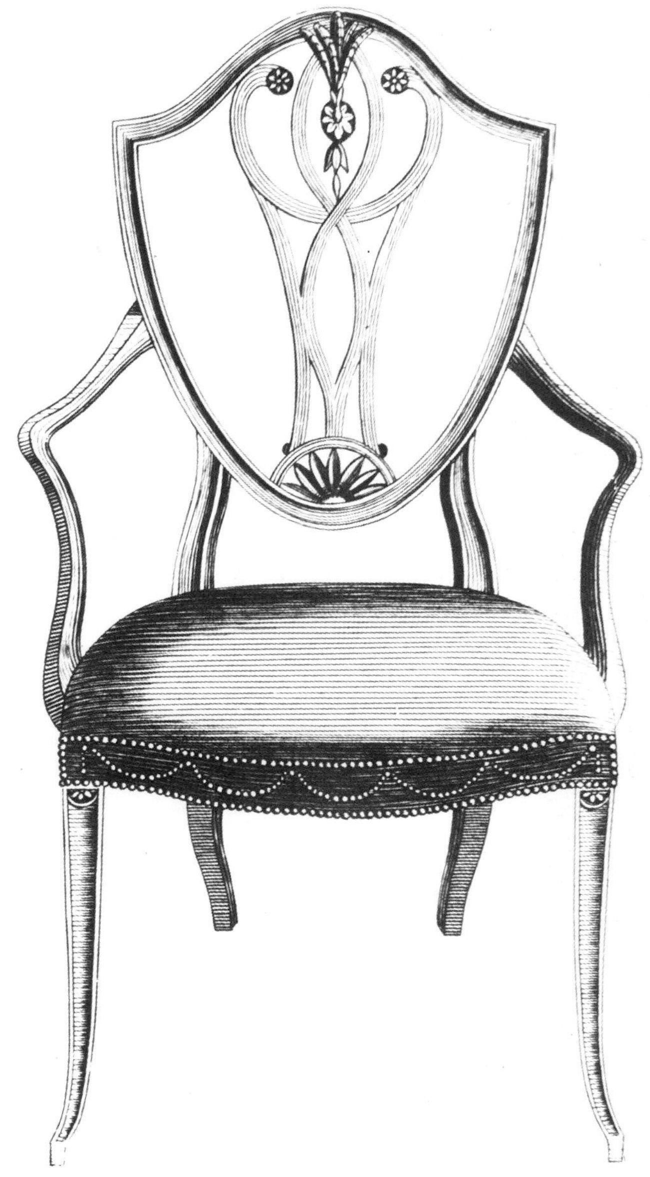

Under Adam's influence the bold mahogany carving of the 1740s and 50s gave way to inlaid decoration and besides mahogany, lighter woods such as golden-yellow satinwood made their appearance. Exotic timbers like the pinkish-hued tulipwood, kingwood and partridge wood were also used on occasions for furniture veneers, with marquetry decoration of Neoclassical designs or flowers in contrasting woods such as sycamore or harewood, holly, box or ebony.

Adam was employed almost exclusively by the rich and fashionable. It was left to cabinetmakers of less lofty aspirations, mostly working in the 1770s and 1780s, to translate his style into more practical terms for the middle classes. Several of them also published design books, and among these George Hepplewhite's *The Cabinet-Maker and Upholsterer's Guide* is the most famous. It was a posthumous work, Hepplewhite having died in 1786, and it was published by his wife Alice who apparently carried on his cabinetmaking business after his death. Not a single stick of furniture firmly attributable to Hepplewhite's workshop has ever been identifed, so it is indeed remarkable that this man should have lent his name to a whole period of furniture design. For the 'Hepplewhite style' sums up the range of furniture produced during the 1770s and 1780s. Restrained in its Neoclassicism and practical in its design, furniture of this period was, generally speaking, more graceful and refined than at any other time in the history of English cabinetmaking.

The preface to Hepplewhite's *Guide* reveals the publisher's aims – 'to unite elegance and utility, and blend the useful with the agreeable . . . to produce a work which shall be useful to the mechanic, and serviceable to the gentleman . . . and convey a just idea of English taste in furniture for houses'. This latter objective was an allusion to the popularity of English furniture abroad: by the late 1770s, a great deal was being exported, especially to the Netherlands.

The preface also mentions the country cabinetmaker 'whose distance from the metropolis makes even an imperfect knowledge of its improvements acquired with much trouble and expence'. This was a time when provincially made furniture was becoming less and less distinguishable from that made by London cabinetmakers, and many firms based in other cities produced up-to-date furniture of a high quality. Such design books as Hepplewhite's must have been extremely helpful in disseminating knowledge of the latest designs.

Chairs in the *Guide* are notably lighter in style than those of 30 years before. Their backs are vase-shaped, shield-shaped or squared, with decorated splats in Neoclassical mood, or Prince of Wales feathers. They have stuffed seats (and sometimes stuffed backs) with close nailing along the front edge, and legs are generally square or round and tapered. Although mahogany was still used a good deal for chairs and other furniture Hepplewhite mentions the 'new and very elegant fashion . . . of finishing them with painted or japanned work, which gives a rich and splendid appearance to the minuter parts of the ornaments, which are generally thrown in by the painter'. Indeed all kinds of furniture was by this time being decorated with painting. The backs of chairs, the friezes of tables, and the doors of round-fronted commodes were frequently embellished with flowers, arabesques, shells, Neoclassical motifs, or with figure subjects in the manner of Angelica Kauffmann.

Marquetry decoration was also used extensively, especially for furniture such as card and pier tables which had the minimum of wear and tear. Tea chests and caddies, dressing glasses and tea trays are among the smaller objects which were especially well suited to inlaid or painted decoration, and of tea trays Hepplewhite affirms 'this is an article where much taste and fancy may be shewn'. The gracefully curving serpentine form, for all its Rococo associations, was at its most popular at this time, and

Left: *A late 18th century kidney-shaped dressing table; the central section rises to reveal compartments for brushes, combs, bottles and other articles of the toilet. Fitted dressing tables of this type were a common feature of well appointed bedrooms in the late 18th century. Many took the form of chests of drawers with specially compartmented top sections. This kidney-shaped example is rare.*
Below left: *A serpentine-fronted mahogany chest of drawers in the Hepplewhite style, with fluted decoration on the corners and boxwood stringing to emphasize the lines of the drawers; the oval handles are typical of the late 18th century.*

appears in a number of Hepplewhite's designs.

Many of the tried and trusted forms of earlier decades are shown in the *Guide* but there are new developments too. Among the sofas, the confidante and the duchesse make their appearance; the sideboard with a central drawer flanked by deep drawers has developed from the much simpler sideboard table; the secretary or secretaire bookcase and the tambour writing table and bookcase are shown with the old favourite the bureau bookcase; dressing tables and shaving tables have acquired complicated arrangements of partitions and cubby holes 'for combs, powders, essences, pin-cushions, and other necessary equipage', but even these are overshadowed by 'Rudd's Table, or Reflecting Dressing Table . . . the most complete dressing table made, possessing every convenience which can be wanted, or mechanism and ingenuity supply'. Margaret Caroline Rudd [1745–99] was a courtesan with wealthy protectors, one of whom may have commissioned such a dressing table for her.

A good deal of the furniture in Hepplewhite's *Guide* – desks, bookcases, library tables, chests of drawers, dressing tables, shaving tables, night tables, wardrobes and so on – is extremely plain and obviously intended for usefulness rather than show. Yet the elegant proportions and the judicious use of veneers and accessories like brass handles give furniture in this style a most pleasing effect. Much has survived, and it is clear that Hepplewhite's *Guide* does indeed convey 'a knowledge of English taste in the various articles of household furniture'.

Hepplewhite is supposed to have contributed designs to another book of engravings published in 1788. This was Thomas Shearer's *The Cabinet-Maker's London Book of Prices, and Designs for Cabinet Work*. The book 'calculated for the Convenience of Cabinet-makers in General: Whereby the Price of executing any Piece of Work may be easily found', went into further editions in 1793, 1805 and 1823, and is especially interesting in showing how costs were calculated, but it never achieved the acclaim of Chippendale's, Hepplewhite's or, later, Sheraton's books. Of Shearer himself, practically nothing is known, and no records of the furniture he made, if any, have survived.

One of the most important cabinetmaking businesses of the later 18th century was not based in London at all. This was Gillows of Lancaster, established late in the 17th or early in the 18th century (the firm's records go back to 1731), and exceedingly prosperous by the 1760s. A showroom or warehouse was opened in London about 1760 but the main manufactory remained in Lancaster. Gillows were patronized by the gentry and aristocracy of the north, such as the Duke of Atholl and the Earls of Strafford and Derby, and they had a flourishing export business to the Baltic countries and the West Indies.

The greater part of their output, especially during the 1780s and 90s, consisted of well-made pieces at reasonable prices, and in following the fashionable styles of the period they exercised an elegant restraint. As an early 19th century writer put it, 'their work is good and solid, though not of the first class in inventiveness and style'. Gillows are perhaps best remembered now for their commodious clothes presses of the type known as a 'gentleman's wardrobe'. These had sliding trays in a cupboard section in the top half with a chest of drawers below.

More recently it has been suggested that Gillows originated many of the designs in Hepplewhite's *Guide*. A

JOHN BEST,

Cabinet-maker, Upholſterer, and Auctioneer,

St. COLUMB,

MAKES AND SELLS

The Following Articles,

In the neweſt Taſte, and on the moſt reaſonable Terms:

(Viz)

Mahogany, wainſcot, and other dining tables, either ſingle or in ſets, with octagon or circular ends
Ditto folding leaf, Pembroke, and card ditto
Ditto dreſſing, writing, and library ditto
Sideboards, with plain, ſerpentine, or circular fronts, with or without cellarets
Single and double cheſts of drawers
Wardrobes and bureaus
Secretories and book-caſes
Square, circular, and encloſed waſh-ſtands
Receptacles
Ladies' and Gentlemens' dreſſing ſtands
Mahogany framed and other chairs, with ſatin hair ſeats, looſe ſeats, or braſs nailed
A variety of painted and japan ditto
Dyed ditto with ruſh bottoms
Bed and eaſy ditto
Sofas and ſociables
Converſation and dreſſing ſtools
Bedſteads with mahogany or ſtained pillars
Field, bureau, and preſs ditto
Plain and circular bed and window curtain cornices, to match the furniture
A variety of chintz, printed calicoes, and other bed furnitures
Bed lace, cotton line and taſſels
Feather beds, mattreſſes, and London blankets
Quilts and counterpanes
Bed tick and ſackings
Oval, octagon, and round, mahogany tea trays and waiters
Ditto, ditto, japan ditto, with plain or gold borders
Tea urns and plate warmers
Bread baſkets and bottle ſtands
Plain, inlaid, and varniſhed, tea caddees
Pearled caddee ſhells
Oval and ſquare ſwing looking-glaſſes
Ditto fixed on dreſſing boxes
Mahogany framed ſconce glaſſes
Pier glaſſes in gilt frames, plain and ornamented
Mahogany or gilt frames put to old glaſſes
Mahogany portable deſks
Black tambour top Spaniſh ditto
Black ebony ditto, with ſilver topped ink, ſand, and wafer glaſſes
Gilt and black moulding for picture frames
A variety of faſhionable paper hangings for rooms, both plain and glazed, with an elegant aſſortment of wide and narrow fancy borders
Blue paper for rooms
Bruſſels and Kidderminſter carpets made to any Size
Terry, Scotch, and Venetian ſtair and bed-ſide carpeting
Hearth rugs
Painted canvas for paſſages
Dutch matting
Rope and Venetian door mats, of different ſizes
Regiſter, Bath, Pantheon, and Rumfordized ſtoves
Sham ditto with black bars
Plain and urn head fire irons
Plain and hollow iron fenders
Bath, bow, and circular poliſhed ſteel ditto
Green painted wire ditto, with plain or braſs tops
Green canvas for window blinds
Houſe bells and bell wire
Patent and plain bell cranks
Derbyſhire ſpar and other bell pulls
Enamelled and braſs cloak pins
A variety of curious braſs locks for drawers, deſks, and bureaus
Locks and hinges of all ſorts
Braſs handles and eſcutcheons for drawers
Oil and colours of all ſorts, &c. &c.

Patterns of Paper Hangings, Carpets, Bed Furnitures, &c. ſent to any Part of the County.

HOUSES FURNISHED ON SHORT NOTICE.

Furniture appraiſed and [illegible] on moderate Terms.

READY MONEY [illegible] FEATHERS.

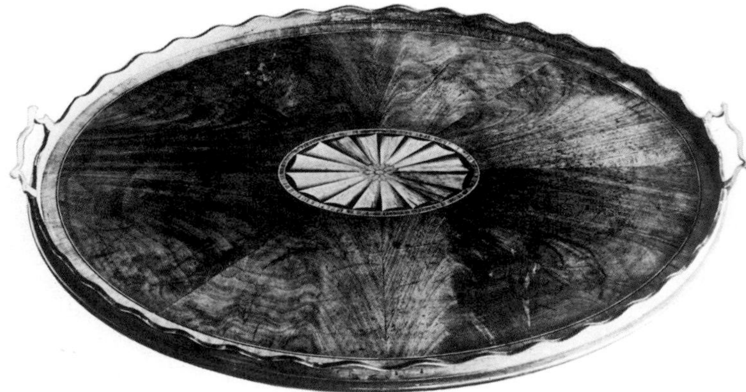

Above: *A mahogany tray of c.1770 decorated with an inlaid sunburst motif in kingwood and satinwood. Tea drinking had become a fashionable way to pass the time by the end of the 17th century, and the habit spawned an enormous array of equipment designed as much for show as usefulness, including fine porcelain and silver, tea-caddies, and by the late 18th century, trays such as this one.*

Left: *A provincial cabinetmaker's label from a work-table of c.1800, showing the wide-ranging nature of his business. It was usual for cabinetmakers in this period to include upholstery, auctioneering, wallpapering and floor covering among their skills, and to supply household furnishings of all kinds. Many also undertook funerals.*

number of pieces illustrated in the Gillow records (now in Westminster Public Library), among them the shield-back chair, have parallels among Hepplewhite's drawings, and according to one tradition Hepplewhite had been apprenticed to Gillow.

Gillows were among the few firms to adopt the French habit of stamping their furniture, and a good deal survives, marked – on the inside edge of a drawer or some other unobtrusive place – GILLOWS or GILLOWS LANCASTER. Stamped or labelled furniture is rare in England, but examples marked with the names of cabinetmakers from all over Britain do turn up from time to time, and they provide valuable pieces to add to the jig-saw of furniture history. Many of them also prove that a high proportion of good cabinetmakers were based outside the metropolis.

The best trade labels provide detailed information about the kind of work a firm was able to undertake. It was usual for cabinetmaking to be combined with upholstery, and many firms undertook funerals. Others specialized – in chairmaking, looking-glass manufacturing, carving and gilding or japanning. There were makers of particular items – among them Edward Beesly, maker of 'Cane and Stick Heads', John Folgham, 'Shagreen Case-Maker', 'Banks the cellaret maker', or Elizabeth Barton Stent, 'turner'. Women, incidentally, do appear from time to time in the annals of cabinetmaking, even in the unemancipated 18th century. Some, especially in the upholstery and similar branches of the trade, were in business on their own account but most, like Alice Hepplewhite and Elizabeth Stent, were successors to the firms of husbands or fathers.

One of the most extensive London firms in the later years of the 18th century was that of George Seddon, who was Master of the Joiners' Company in 1795. He set up premises in Aldersgate Street about 1750 and in spite of disastrous fires in 1768 and in 1783 his firm prospered and employed over 400 skilled men. It survived, under his sons George and Thomas, his son-in-law, Thomas Shackleton and several other generations of the family, until the mid-19th century. As early as 1768 George Seddon was described as 'one of the most eminent cabinet-makers in London' and his firm's output must have been enormous, yet few pieces attributable to him have been unearthed. Those that have turned up with their original bills or, very occasionally in the early 19th century stamped 'T&G Seddon', are of fine quality and workmanship and most are of satinwood.

Hepplewhite's reign was a short one: the 1790s were dominated by frenetic social upheavals and furniture was stylistically affected by the prevailing restlessness. The transitional style that closed the 18th century and at the same time heralded the cooler but still revolutionary period of the Regency, is known, for better or worse, as Sheraton.

Like Hepplewhite and Shearer, Thomas Sheraton is a somewhat shadowy figure who may never have had a workshop of his own. As his trade card of *c.*1795 suggested,

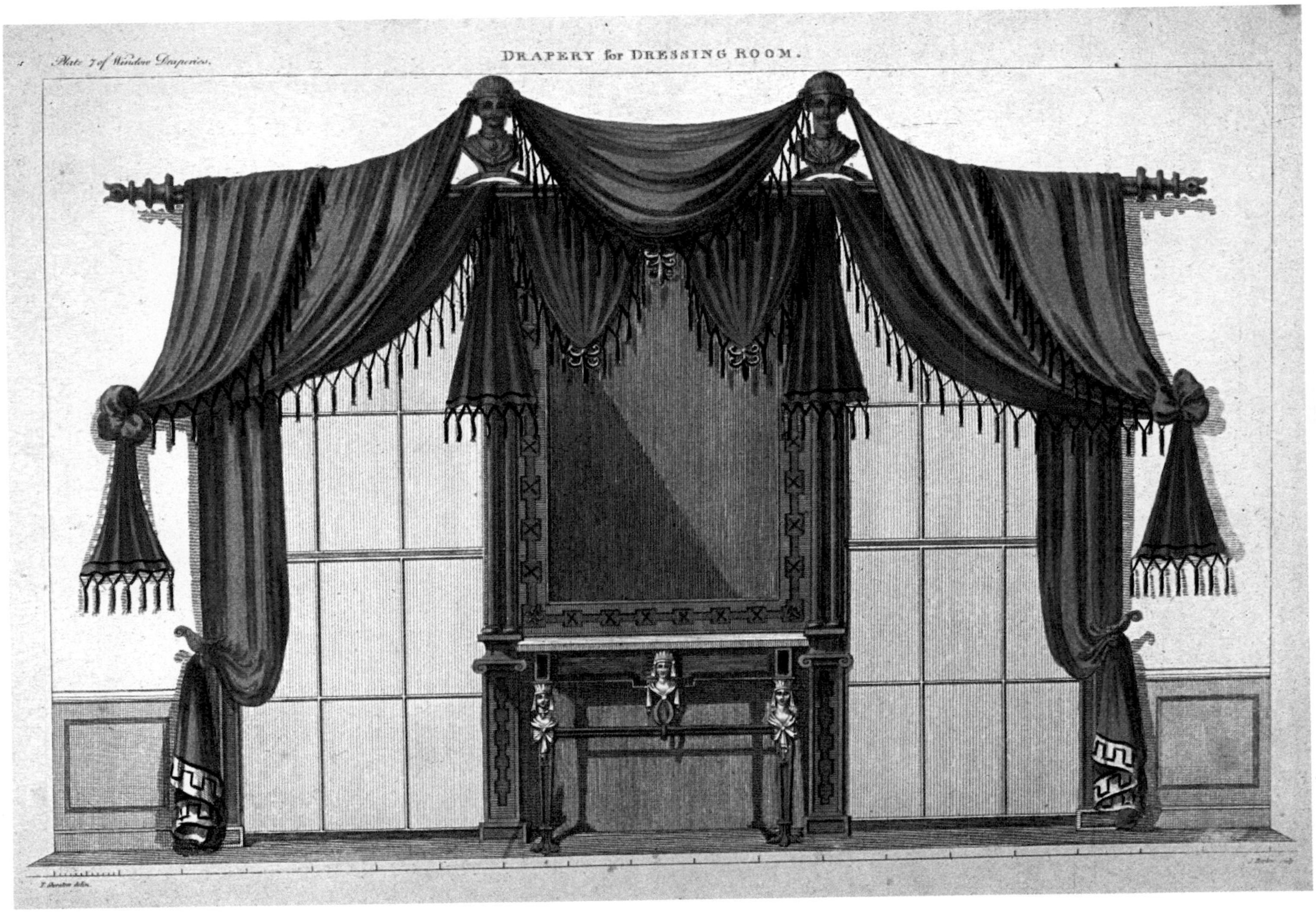

DRAPERY for DRESSING ROOM.

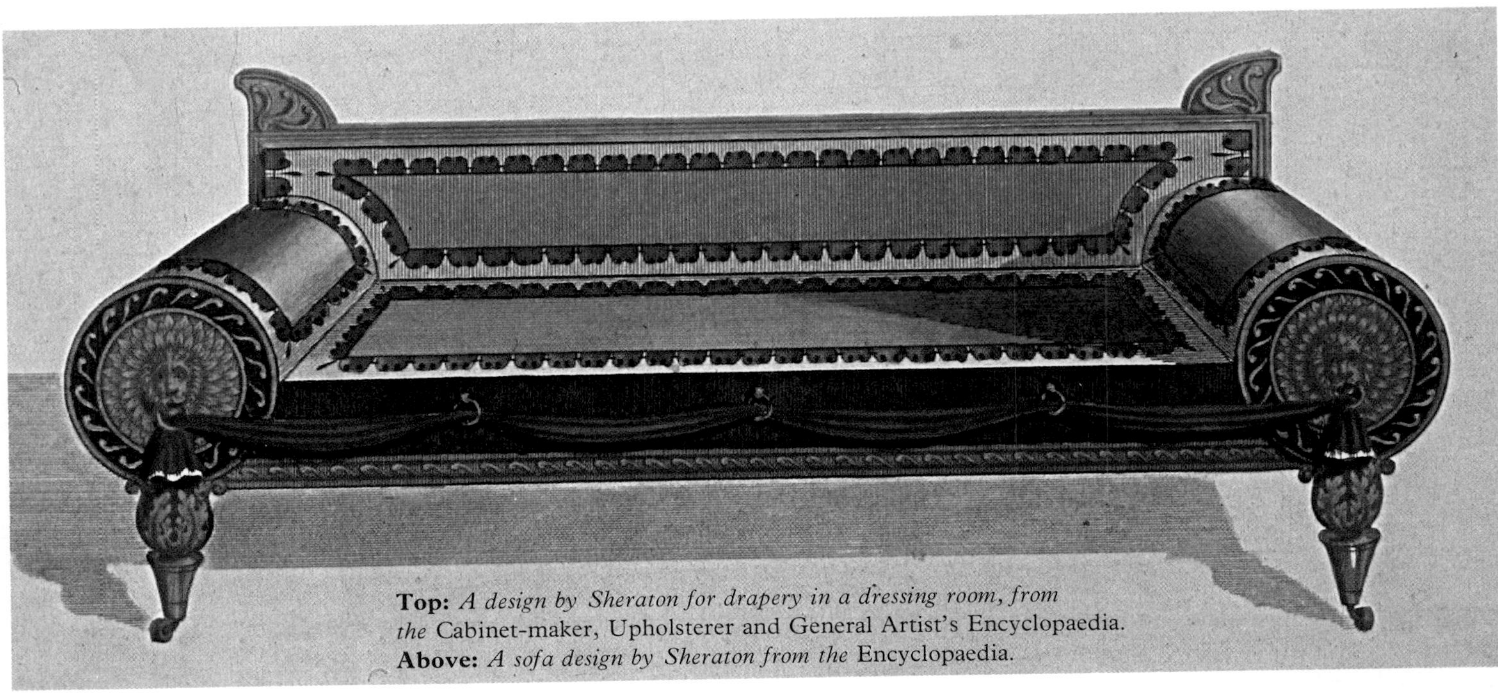

Top: *A design by Sheraton for drapery in a dressing room, from the* Cabinet-maker, Upholsterer and General Artist's Encyclopaedia.
Above: *A sofa design by Sheraton from the* Encyclopaedia.

he was a designer rather than a maker of furniture: 'T. Sheraton No. 106 Wardour Street, Soho Teaches Perspective, Architecture and Ornaments, makes Designs for Cabinet-makers, and sells all kinds of Drawing Books etc.' He also published a number of religious tracts.

His chief work, and the one which embodies what we call the Sheraton style, was the *Cabinet-Maker and Upholsterer's Drawing Book*, issued in four parts between 1791 and 1794. Its designs are full-bodied refinements of the Neoclassical, and at the same time give forward glimpses of the Regency and Victorian periods. Comfortably rounded forms appear with Neoclassical motifs and draped silk; turned, sometimes even bulbous legs replace the straighter shapes associated with the Hepplewhite period; there is an evident delight in mechanical artifice, and upholstery is given a new prominence. The natural beauty of wood is revered and while inlaid and painted decoration are favoured, gilding and japanning are kept to a minimum.

Sheraton was largely concerned with perspective and geometry and his book differs from its predecessors in its attention to these principles. He also provides 'accurate patterns at large for ornaments to enrich and embellish the various pieces of work which frequently occur in the cabinet branch'. The Sheraton style, which in actual furniture generally took a simpler form than most of the designs in the *Drawing Book*, was disseminated far and wide, and not just in the British Isles and her colonies. It spread to Russia, Germany, Scandinavia, Italy, Spain and of course America, and by the early 19th century had totally overshadowed Hepplewhite.

Sheraton followed the *Drawing Book* with the *Cabinet Dictionary* in 1803, another book of designs with practical guidance on cabinet- and chairmaking, and in 1805 came the first instalment of his most ambitious undertaking, the *Cabinet-Maker, Upholsterer and General Artist's Encyclopaedia* of which only about a quarter was completed before 1806 when Sheraton died, poverty-stricken, lonely and deranged, with no inkling of the influence his work was to have on succeeding generations of cabinetmakers.

Furniture of the late 18th and early 19th centuries had evolved as much in type and variety as in form from that being produced a couple of decades before. To begin with, dining rooms had become commonplace in the houses of the middle classes as well as in the stately homes of the aristocracy, and a whole range of furniture – generally of imposing dimensions – developed for them. The dining table itself was by now a large affair, fitted with extra leaves when company was expected; chairs were 'respectable and substantial' and the sideboard, sometimes with a cellaret or sarcophagus under its middle section, had become a commodious item with a central drawer flanked by two smaller drawers or cupboards in which cutlery, glass, silver and a chamber pot could be kept. Lead-lined compartments were sometimes fitted for warming plates or cooling wine.

'The drawing room', according to Sheraton writing in the *Cabinet Dictionary* in 1803, 'is to concentrate the elegance of the whole house, and is the highest display of richness of furniture.' Here, furnishings were formal and upholstery lavish, but it was in the ante-rooms and breakfast rooms that the greatest changes were seen. For in these smaller rooms the main occupations of the household took place. Bookcases and writing desks had developed new forms. The Carlton House writing table with a superstructure of small drawers surrounding three sides of the writing space was probably named after a piece designed for the Prince of Wales' residence, Carlton House, and the davenport, a much smaller, feminine item appeared about the same time, that is, during the 1790s. It is named after a Captain Davenport for whom Gillows probably made the first of its kind.

Flexible sliding tambour doors for cupboards and tops for writing and work tables, made from strips of wood glued to canvas, were one of the many innovations from France in the late 18th century. They were in widespread use in England by the 1780s, and were popular for several decades, although by 1803 Sheraton was complaining that they were unsatisfactory for furniture in constant use 'being both insecure, and very liable to injury'.

Above: *A late 18th century mahogany and satinwood china cabinet in the Sheraton style. Known as the 'Weeks' cabinet, as the clock inset in the pediment is inscribed 'Weeks's Museum', it was probably made by the firm of Seddons. There was formerly a barrel organ in the base. Thomas Weeks had a museum of 'musical curiosities' in the 1790s.*

Left: *A lady's mahogany work-table of* c.1800. *Made by John Best of St Columb, Cornwall, it is an example of good provincial workmanship.*
Below left: *A late 18th century figured mahogany breakfront wardrobe, with three rows of drawers beneath the cupboard part, probably made by Gillows of Lancaster.*
Right: *The State Bed at Osterley Park designed, with its special bed-carpet (a strip which does not extend under the bed) by Robert Adam in the most luxurious Neoclassical style. The posts are ornamented with fine stripes and rows of tiny bell-flowers, and the bed-head and tester are decorated with carved and gilt sphinxes and figures.*

Workboxes and tables, firescreens, and reading and music stands in umpteen shapes reflected other typical occupations among the leisured classes. Sets of three or four graduated small tables were known as trio or quartetto tables in the late 18th and early 19th century when they began to be made. Although somewhat flimsy in construction these nests of tables were invaluable for refreshments, needlework, cards and many other activities. At this period appeared a range of useful pieces of furniture combining several functions. There were needlework-cum-games tables, and reading, writing and needlework tables (often housed in the bedroom) all with appropriate fittings. Because it was an essentially feminine occupation, the furniture made for needlework was among the most daintily elegant of all. Specially fitted needlework tables and boxes were made in noticeable profusion from the early 19th century. They were usually lined with padded silk or satin, with compartments for thread, needles, scissors, knotting shuttles, crochet hooks, stilettos, and all the other paraphernalia of the worker. These accessories, of ivory, tortoiseshell or mother-of-pearl in the best examples, are now much collected.

Card playing was always a favourite pastime and for more than a century had given rise to special tables, generally with fold-over tops concealing a baize or needlework surface. Similarly shaped fold-over tables with polished wood inside surfaces were for tea. Some tables had three leaves, providing a baize surface and a plain one, to accommodate both card playing and tea drinking.

The elegant ritual of tea begat numerous other small tables including a variety supported by a pillar on a tripod base known as a teapoy. Later the name teapoy was given to a large tea caddy supported on one of these pillar and tripod bases. The sofa table – a rectangular form of the Pembroke – appeared at the end of the 18th century. Its central section, usually with a drawer or two in the frieze, sometimes slid open to reveal a chess board, or rose on brackets as a reading or writing stand. In the design of most small tables, a central column with splayed feet was replacing four legs by the closing years of the 18th century.

Developments in bedroom furniture, apart from the changing styles of beds, were most noticeable in washstands which, by the close of the 18th century, were well supplied with fittings and compartments for washing, shaving and other aspects of the toilet. The familiar and still useful corner washstand, with drawers and sometimes a cupboard below, was a popular and space-saving form. Night tables and cupboards often had tambour doors in their upper parts, while a lower section drew out on castors to reveal a close-stool, commode or, as 18th century parlance had it, 'convenience'.

The Empire Style

France

The French Revolution began in 1789 and the reign of Louis XVI ended with his execution in 1793. During the violence and upheaval, many aristocratic homes were sacked and much fine furniture was wantonly destroyed. The revolutionary government sold a great many pieces from the royal palaces, the agents of foreign powers being among the biggest buyers. Many craftsmen with known monarchist sympathies fled abroad to escape the Terror. Yet, two years before Louis and Marie Antoinette finally went to the guillotine, furniture was being officially commissioned for the *Convention Nationale* in a severe, no-nonsense style which was really a late version of Louis XVI, deprived of its trimmings. Known as the *style républicaine*, it was made for the government of the day by Georges Jacob, to designs by Charles Percier (1764–1838) and Pierre-François-Léonard Fontaine (1762–1853).

Having completed their first task for the *Convention*, they separated briefly, Fontaine going to London for a time and Percier becoming – significantly, as his future work demonstrated – a designer of scenery for the opera. In 1798 they joined up again in Paris, designing furniture to be made by Georges Jacob for the Council of Five Hundred (one of the two chambers in the government of the *Directoire*, 1795–99).

At that time, Napoleon Bonaparte (1769–1821) was establishing himself, having put down an insurrection in 1795 for which he was rewarded with the hand of Joséphine, and the command of the army of the Alps and of Italy. He had established his headquarters, in an almost royal style, at Mombello, near Milan. Here he assembled works of art which he sent home to Paris. In 1798 he conquered Egypt and the triumph was commemorated in a greatly increased use of Egyptian motifs on the furniture being made, furniture which was already beginning to shake off the short-lived austerity of the *style républicaine*.

France, ringed with enemies, made Napoleon 'First Consul' in 1799, and in the same year Fontaine and Percier were given an introduction to Joséphine, who commissioned them to redesign the Château Malmaison as her residence. Having thus demonstrated their talents, they were given the task by Napoleon himself of creating a suitable background for him in his capacity as military dictator of France. Furniture of the Consulate (1799–1804) displays an increasingly archaeological interest in ancient Greek, Roman and Etruscan forms, with a heavy admixture of Egyptian ornament. This is particularly noticeable in the more expensive, commissioned works, such as the chairs in the music room at Malmaison which have sabre legs *à la grecque*, topped with arm-supports in the form of winged sphinxes. For the bourgeoisie, a simpler rendering of the same ideas had to suffice, the legs often being square-tapered or turned types, and the sphinxes appearing as

Above: *Dressing table with swing mirror on marble top, with lyre-shaped supports in the Graeco-Roman manner, veneered in yew with bronze mounts. Made by Jacob-Desmalter in the early 19th century, when mirrors came generally to be made as integral parts of dressing tables.*

Left: *The Salon des Saisons, Hotel de Beauharnais, Paris. The chairs have distinctive turned legs at the front, while the uprights of the padded backs are shaped to balance the rake of the rear legs. These features were partly derived from paintings found on ancient Greek pottery, but in the hands of capable craftsmen they proved highly practical.*

Left: *Mahogany armchair of sabre legs inspired by Greek designs and with winged sphinxes derived from Egypt. It was probably made by the Jacob family* c.*1799–1804 to a design by C. Percier and P.-F.-L. Fontaine. It closely resembles the chairs they designed for the music room at Malmaison, particularly in the bold use of the sphinxes.*
Below left: *Circular table, French Empire* c.*1810, the marble top resting on a mahogany frame with four curved legs resting on a platform base – at that time a novel form of construction which was to become widely adopted. The paw feet and the mounts are in cast and gilded metal. The quality of the metal mounts declined during the Empire period.*

heads only, shorn of their wings. The style is recorded in the first edition of the designs of Fontaine and Percier, published in 1801 as *Recueil des décorations intérieurs* – the first known use of the term 'interior decoration'.

Their furniture, much of which was made by the Jacob family, was based on a close and rather pedantic study of actual pieces, or authentic representations of them, from the ancient world. The Greek chair of *klismos* form with sabre legs, the classical couch with scrolled end, the circular tripod stand of Roman times, the sarcophagus adapted as a wine-cooler, even the pyramid itself conceived as a support for a circular table-top – all these provided good basic shapes, as did the Roman *curule* (stool on X-shaped support) and the Egyptian throne-chair with its lion-legs. To these were added, in ever greater profusion, such imperial symbols as eagles, winged lions, bees, fasces of arms (from which fascism derived its name), not to mention Napoleon's cipher, the letter 'N' in a laurel wreath. An important medium for disseminating fashionable ornament, as well as simplified shapes, was La Mésangère's *Meubles et objets de goût*, first appearing in 1802 and then continuing in magazine form. It provided patterns for good, honest, bourgeois furniture.

The basic Neoclassicism of La Mésangère, Percier, Fontaine and others was well under way before the Revolution and the rise of Napoleon but the direction this movement took in Napoleonic France, influencing as it did the development of furniture throughout Europe, was the result of an entirely conscious attempt to create a stage setting for the Emperor, as he was styled 1804–14. As such it has a grandly theatrical air about it due, perhaps, in no small part to Percier's scenic work for the opera. For practical reasons, he and his partner often had to work as stage designers do when quick changes are called for; they could take their time over the throne-room at the Tuileries, but it was often necessary to run up something effective but temporary for one of the Emperor's lightning visits to an ill-prepared provincial city. For this kind of emergency, they made effective use of tent-like draperies in striped material, and so created a fashion for the decoration of rooms and particularly for hangings over beds.

The beds themselves lacked posts and were often elaborately shaped. The *lit bateau* was boat-shaped, with curving prow and stern. One side, rather than the head, was set against a wall and the drapes were suspended over it. In some examples, the ends of the bed were shaped to resemble swans. A simpler type, much favoured by the middle classes, was the *lit droit* with an architectural headboard of painted wood. The classical scroll-ended couch of Greek derivation became the immensely fashionable *chaise-longue* – David's famous portrait of Madame Récamier shows her reclining on one.

Another very popular item was the *psyché* – a free-standing mirror, originally circular, slung between upright supports, and soon to develop into the rectangular, full-length cheval looking-glass. The commode began to lose its importance as a status symbol and gradually became relegated to the bedroom. It was rectilinear but not break-fronted, with flush drawers veneered in the fashionable mahogany – for those who could afford it. The blockade of France made the importation of exotic woods difficult and expensive, and native woods such as oak, ash, elm, walnut and fruitwood were promoted from the sphere of regional

Above: *This bedroom in the Château d'Amboise is furnished with pieces which are typical of the French Empire style. The* lit bateau *(boat-shaped bed) has drapes suspended from a matching pelmet. The stool, with X-shaped supports terminating as swans' heads, is derived from an ancient Roman type.*

furniture to the more luxurious products of the capital.

Marquetry was little used, and the finely-tooled bronze mounts of the Louis XVI period were replaced with ones which, for all but the most expensive pieces, were cast and burnished but not chiselled by hand. They were applied sparingly, and followed the general trend towards rather austere Grecian motifs, such as the laurel wreath. A little further down the scale, bronze was too costly and stamped brass took its place, particularly for the capitals of columns used for flanking carcase pieces – commodes, secrétaires and chiffoniers. About 1800, the *chiffonière* or small chest-of-drawers underwent a change of sex and emerged as the *chiffonier*, a small cabinet with cupboard below, a drawer and a shelf with decorative supports above.

The guilds had been abolished in 1791, but the furniture industry was as active during the Napoleonic period as it had ever been. About 10,000 people were employed in it in Paris, one employer alone – Jacob-Desmalter – having 350 on his wage-bill. He was the son of Georges Jacob, who formally handed over the business to his sons in 1796. They traded as Jacob Frères until the death of Georges the younger in 1803. The father had come out of retirement in 1800, and worked in partnership with his son François, who called himself Jacob-Desmalter (de Desmalter being a Burgundian patronym). They were the most important makers of the age in France, executing the designs of Percier and Fontaine for the Emperor and manufacturing large quantities of good quality, distinctive furniture, much of it in mahogany, for less distinguished clients. Their work represents a continuation of the style adopted by Georges Jacob during the late Louis XVI period, rather than a revolutionary break with tradition.

Many other cabinetmakers survived the changing circumstances, notably some of the Germans, including Beneman and Weisweiler. Henri Jacob (1753–1824) – a cousin of Georges – imitated the celebrated family style and cashed in on the name, but his work is not as fine. P. Brion made some very grand furniture for Napoleon's apartments at Fontainebleau, while J. Louis produced large quantities of sabre-legged chairs and other more modest furniture for the middle-class market.

These simpler versions of Neoclassical types in the manner of Louis and La Mésangère did not end with the fall of Napoleon, but continued after the restoration of the monarchy when, in 1815, ten days after Waterloo, the House of Bourbon returned to the throne in the person of Louis XVIII, who was followed by his brother Charles X (reigned 1824–30). Fewer bronze mounts were used, and there was a preference for light-coloured woods (*bois clair*) such as maple for furniture in a style similar to that of Schinkel in Prussia, or to Austrian *Biedermeier*. The quality of bourgeois furniture gradually deteriorated with the ever-increasing use of steam-driven machinery and the commercialization of the furniture industry, which was encouraged by a series of exhibitions. That presented at the Louvre in 1819 marked, as decisively as any such event can, the end of an epoch. It may be some small consolation to know that the two great architects of the Empire style survived the downfall of their patron. Fontaine worked as an architect and Percier as a teacher. Their friendship survived, too, and they were buried in the same tomb.

Above: *This bed is part of the furnishings of the Château de Malmaison, designed by Percier and Fontaine during the consulate of Napoleon. It has Grecian motifs – swans and cornucopias – as symbols of majesty and plenty at the head and foot, and is draped with a tent-like awning – perhaps to remind the Empress, in the absence of the Emperor, that he was campaigning for the glory of France, and sleeping in a tent.*
Below: *Empire commode, early 19th century, by Jacob-Desmalter, with gilt bronze mounts – laurel wreaths, winged torches, anthemion – typical of the period. Sometimes known as a* bas armoire, *this type usually has drawers concealed behind the doors.*

Germany and Austria

The Empire style followed Napoleon and his armies across Europe. David Roentgen, endeavouring to save something from the wreck which the French Revolution had made of his business, adopted a simplified and dignified version of second-phase Neoclassicism for the palaces of Berlin. At Würzburg *c.*1808–12, Johann Valentin Raab produced numerous pieces in which swan-shaped supports played a vital part. This feature was adopted with enthusiasm in the Germanic countries, swans in triplicate forming the stands of circular tables resting on shaped plinths known as 'platform' bases, while swans in duplicate appear very frequently on the arms of armchairs and comfortably upholstered settees.

In Prussia, a distinctive version of the style was evolved by the architect Karl Friedrich Schinkel (1781–1841) who, after studying at the Berlin Academy, travelled in Italy and Austria, visiting Paris *en route* and returning to Berlin in 1805 to begin a career as a painter, but also as a designer of furniture and ultimately of buildings. The bedroom furniture he designed for the Charlottenburg Palace in 1809 succeeds in being original without sacrificing elegance to novelty – a trap into which so many designers of furniture have been prone to fall. The woods used were mainly beech and pear, carved to simulate the hanging folds of the bed linen. In 1817, he designed a set of chairs for Prince Friedrich of Prussia, in which the backs are composed of rounded pads connected to an outer frame with turned members. Many of his chairs are carefully thought out to provide maximum comfort and convenience. One model even includes a movable reading-stand for books, attached to the arm of the chair. In spite of this practicality, his work is imbued with the spirit of Romanticism which was, in the first decade of the 19th century, presenting Gothic Revival designs alongside the most pedantic of Neoclassical models. However, just as the first phase of Neoclassicism had borrowed heavily from the repertoire of antique ornament, without attempting to reproduce the shapes or forms of ancient furniture, so the early Romantic school was content to employ 'Gothic' motifs – pointed arches, crocketing and crenellated cornices – without trying to copy actual pieces of medieval furniture.

Typical pieces of furniture related to the Empire style in Germany are 'high-waisted' corner-cupboards (i.e. with the upper stage less than half the height of the whole); bookcases, their doors with glazing bars representing crossed arrows; bedside cupboards which splay outwards towards the base, like an obelisk with the top sawn off; the fall-front secretaire (*Klappsekretär*) which often had a third deck of small drawers placed on top of the carcase, making it rather heavily architectural; a type of three-drawer commode, the top drawer projecting forwards a little and appearing to be supported by herms with sphinx heads, and either fitted with brass handles of octagonal, oval or round pattern, or with no handles at all – a sacrifice in the cause of purity in design making for considerable inconvenience if the key happens to get lost.

Below: *A group of furniture at the Residence, Munich, belonging to the second phase of the Neoclassical style in Germany and showing the influence of the French Empire. The backs of the chairs are shaped to a bold curve. On the settee, this is extended down to floor level, thus dispensing with conventional legs and anticipating the fully upholstered settees of the mid-19th century.*

Above: *A Polish bedroom of* c.*1820–30, furnished in peasant style. The chair, with 'peg legs' driven into holes in the seat, and its back cut from a solid board, is of a type produced over a wide area from the 16th century onwards. The bridal chest, with painted decoration, belongs to a tradition which was continued well into the 20th century.*

In Vienna, Johann Haertl adapted the lyre shape, already widely popular for chair-backs, to carcase pieces, of which cabinets with fronts following a lyre-shaped profile are perhaps the most original. As often before, Austria found the secret of carrying a fashionable style to its logical conclusion in a way that should, according to all the laws of good design, have resulted in utter disaster, but instead proved charming if a little eccentric.

In 1804, Josef Danhauser opened a factory where furniture in the Empire style was made for such members of the nobility as the Duke Albert von Sachsen-Teschen and the Archduke Karl. Before his death in 1830, Danhauser had successfully developed large-scale production of a more functional, less costly range of post-Empire furniture for the middle classes. About 2,500 of his designs are preserved in the *Osterreichisches Museum für Angewandte Kunst* in Vienna. The style was emotionally linked to a school of literature and drama known – at first derisively – as *Biedermeier*, *bieder* being the German word for 'upright' or 'honourable'.

Poland

Having lost their independence at the end of the 18th century to Russia, Prussia and Austria, the Poles entertained high hopes of deliverance by Napoleon and followed him loyally even after the disaster of 1812, their leader Prince Poniatowski losing his life in covering the retreat from Leipzig. The partition being confirmed by the Congress of Vienna, only a small area – the 'Congress Kingdom' with the Russian Tsar as king – emerged with a national identity in 1815. Here, and in the Grand Duchy of Warsaw, the distinctive furnishing style known as 'Simmler' evolved, taking its name from a leading family of makers of whom Andreas Simmler had been the first to come to Poland from Germany. The Simmler style combines Neoclassical designs drawn from various sources – German, French and English. Many of the chairs and settees have an elegance which suggests familiarity with the designs of Thomas Sheraton, while others are nearer to those of the Jacob family in Paris. Andreas Simmler having originally worked for Roentgen at Neuwied, this influence was also handed down to the next generation.

After the Simmlers, the best-known makers in the Congress Kingdom were Friedrich and Johann Daniel Heurlich, whose style was nearer to the Austrian

Biedermeier school but rather more decorative, carving of a slightly old-fashioned kind being extensively employed.

Although Cracow was a free city republic, Austrian influence was dominant, and here the Biedermeier style was to develop in a way quite close to that of Vienna. A tradition continued there uninterruptedly until the early years of this century, however, which managed to ignore political upheavals and foreign influences. This was the making of bridal chests, painted by specialists some of whom are known by name. Even the poorest family tried to provide such a chest to hold their daughter's dowry, and these basic, ritualistic yet cheerful articles express better than any souvenir of Napoleonic grandeur the pride of place that a piece of furniture can occupy in the affections, as well the home, of its owners.

Sweden

Sweden had finally abandoned neutrality and fought with Russian and Prussian troops against Napoleon, but it was Jean Bernadotte, one of Napoleon's marshals, who became king of Sweden and reigned as Charles XIV John from 1818–44. Although in many ways similar to the style of Hetsch in Denmark, the Empire style in Sweden came nearer to the French original, especially in the hands of the court cabinetmaker in Stockholm, Lorentz Wilhelm Lundelius (1787–1859). In the more modest range, a peculiarity of Swedish furniture of this period is that drawer-fronts, when veneered on a pine foundation as they so often are, do not have the top edge masked with a veneer or a 'cock-beading', as is the case with the furniture of most other countries using an otherwise similar construction.

Marquetry was used more extensively during the Empire period than in France or Germany, especially during the earlier years, in place of bronze mounts. Later it was replaced with motifs carved in mahogany and glued to the surface. Less expensive decorations were made in moulds from a mixture of sawdust and glue – an early version of 'plastic wood' that may be seen as a symptom of declining standards.

Denmark and Norway

Early examples of archaeologically inspired, 'second-phase Neoclassical' furniture were designed in Denmark by Nikolai Abraham Abildgaard (1743–1809) who had it made for himself about 1800, finding his inspiration in the shapes depicted on Greek vases. In 1807 he produced a scheme, somewhat less academic, for Prince Christian Frederick.

The taste for English styles suffered a traumatic setback as a consequence of the Napoleonic wars, soon after the commencement of which a pact of armed neutrality between Russia, Sweden, Denmark and Norway led to a bombardment of Copenhagen by the British who were anxious that the Danish fleet should not fall into French

Right: *Carved and gilt pier table with looking glass above, in the early 19th century Swedish version of the Empire style, complete with eagle, dolphin supports and a panel between them depicting the wand of Aesculapius. A pier table and glass occupied the narrow wall or 'pier' between a pair of windows.*

Above: *Fall-front secretaire in Karelian birch (often mistaken for satinwood), in the severe Neoclassical style of the reign of Tsar Alexander I (1801–25).*
Right: *The Yellow Drawing Room at Ca' Rezzonico, Venice, furnished mainly with pieces in the late Neoclassical style, showing extensive use of twined and fluted legs. The very long settee is typically Venetian.*

hands. Norway and Denmark, which had been politically tied, were now separated by the British blockade.

There was, however, one piece of furniture of English type which was very popular in Denmark, in spite of politics. This was the sofa table, of rectangular shape and with a drop leaf supported on hinged brackets at each end. This occasionally stood on four tapered legs but much more often it rested on either a central column or on end supports of 'slab' or lyre form. Danish homes did not normally have rooms set aside for dining. The sofa table stood in front of the sofa and was used for meals, the china for which was kept in a pair of pedestal cupboards, one standing at each end of the sofa. The usual place for storing cutlery was the upper section of the *chatol*, a bureau-cabinet having a cylinder top to the bureau section and an upper stage of break-front form.

As in France, imported woods became scarce because of the war, and various native timbers took their place; birch, carefully selected and cut, was an excellent understudy for satinwood which came from the East and West Indies, and is often mistaken for it. A taste for using boldly contrasting woods was satisfied by employing burr alder in association with birch – a feature sometimes seen in geometrically designed commodes. The middle drawer in a bank of three is deeper than the other two, and has a lunette-shaped recess set in it, veneered in wood different from the rest. Metal mounts were seldom used and, as in Germany, even handles were commonly regarded as superfluous.

For construction, pine was the main material for carcases, but the better-class pieces were provided with oak drawer-linings. The continuing peasant tradition depended almost entirely on pine. In most countries, pine furniture has proved vulnerable to woodworm, but apart from a few areas, Norwegian pieces are remarkably free of the pest – probably because of the Norwegian practice of regularly scrubbing all the furniture with soap and water, and removing the eggs of the beetle in the process.

A post-Empire fashion for mahogany furniture gradually spread through Scandinavia, one of the principal designers being Gustav Friedrich Hetsch, professor at the Copenhagen Academy and later (1828–57) director of the Royal Porcelain Factory. He had worked with Percier in Paris and absorbed his scholarly but romantic approach to the late Neoclassical style.

Russia

The Empire period in Russia was covered by the reign of Alexander I (1801–25), at the commencement of which the *Directoire* style was adopted in St Petersburg for furniture of severe yet bold outline – especially noticeable in the somewhat exaggerated, mushroom-like profiles of chair-backs. Pale-coloured woods, particularly Karelian birch, were used extensively and perhaps rather earlier than in Austria, Germany and France, where they were later to become very fashionable under the general heading of *bois clair*.

After Napoleon's retreat in 1812, furniture was made in considerable quantities in Russia, and so much was imported that even Russian authorities find it difficult to decide what was truly Russian and which pieces were brought in from Central Europe. The situation is further complicated by the influence of foreign architects such as Thomas de Thomon from Switzerland – itself a meeting-place of many currents of fashion, leading to eclecticism – and Carlo Rossi from Italy, both of whom imposed their own brands of the second-phase Neoclassical style on the native product. There are, however, some strikingly handsome pieces which, for all their air of cosmopolitan sophistication, could hardly be mistaken for anything other than Russian. Most notable of these are centre-tables with circular tops of malachite reposing on central columns mounted in gilded bronze.

In the 1820s new types of furniture were designed by a group of architects led by Rossi and Vasily Stasov. A distinguished group of cabinetmakers, all working in St. Petersburg, included Vasily Bobkov, Franz Grosse, Johann Boumann, and Heinrich Gambs. The shapes of many pieces display originality and a wide range of woods was used, including mahogany, birch, poplar, walnut and Brazilian amaranth. Chairs and settees were often upholstered in silk or woollen cloth, both materials being embroidered with floral patterns.

Italy

Many important elements of the Empire style, such as a bold use of animal forms for supports, were adopted for

luxurious furniture in Italy before they had become fully accepted in France, and continued to be fashionable long after the fall of Napoleon. During the period of the French Empire proper, various members of his family on whom the Emperor had bestowed titles were busily redecorating their new, palatial homes in a manner that would do honour to their august relative. His sister Elisa Baciocchi had a workshop set up in Florence where, under the direction of a craftsman called Youff, brought for the purpose from Paris, furniture in the Empire style was produced by French cabinetmakers – much of it still to be seen in the Palazzo Pitti, along with that of the most distinguished native Italian cabinetmaker of the period, the Florentine Giovanni Socchi (*fl.*1805–1815), who was a protégé of Elisa's.

Symbolic of Napoleon's military triumphs is a set of marble-topped cylindrical cupboards designed to look like drums and resting on feet formed as pine cones. This drum-like conception occurs again, though less obviously, in a type of desk made by Socchi which, when closed, appears to be an oval table with six very deep drawers side by side, standing on six splayed legs spaced around the perimeter, and one vertical one at the centre. The whole construction stands on an oval plinth. All this opens up to form a writing table and chair, one of the false drawer-fronts being the outside of the chair-back which, when drawn out, reveals the seat resting on two of the splayed legs plus the vertical one. The top of the table divides, the two halves sliding sideways to reveal an extending writing-leaf and an inkstand that springs up into position. The entire piece of wizardry is veneered in contrasting dark and light woods and is mounted with lions' heads in gilt bronze. Socchi made and signed at least four of these ingenious novelties.

Pelagio Palagi (1775–1860), who was born in Bologna and trained there as a painter, went to Rome to work on the conversion of the Quirinal into a palace for Napoleon in 1806. Deeply imbued with the spirit of Neoclassicism but affected too by the Romantic movement, he was still designing furniture in the Empire style for the Palazzo Reale in Turin as late as 1836. This post-Empire manner, with an emphasis on carved and gilded lions and eagles rather than on the severe outlines and flush surfaces of the original style, became the official mode thought suitable for the furnishing of private palaces and public buildings in many parts of Italy during the first half of the 19th century.

Furniture for the middle classes displays some of the same liking for sculptural qualities in carved and applied decoration on tables and chairs especially, but tends more to the solemn manner of the Austrian Biedermeier style for commodes, wardrobes, cylinder-top bureaux and other carcase pieces.

Spain and Portugal

The Spanish version of the Empire style is known as *Fernandino*. Prince Ferdinand was arrested in 1807 for plotting to kill his father and mother. The scandal provided Napoleon with an excuse to increase the size of his army in Spain, put his brother on the throne and place Ferdinand under military guard for six years, during the War of Independence. By 1814, when Joseph had retired from the fray and Napoleon knew that his position in Spain was untenable, he had little choice but to release Ferdinand, who then reigned in a thoroughly reactionary way until 1833. This brief summary of events gives no idea of the suffering of the Spanish people during this period, but it may suggest the pattern of turmoil against which it is surprising that any furniture at all was made.

Before the Napoleonic invasion, furniture in the severe *Directoire* style was fashionable, but under Joseph Bonaparte this gave way to the full Empire treatment, in which an extensive repertoire of ornament derived from antiquity, in carved and gilt wood or gilded bronze, was exploited – sometimes with more enthusiasm than discretion. A desk made for the King in the royal palace, Madrid, has that favourite Empire device, a large swan in full relief, as a support at each of the four corners. As turned legs are employed in addition, the swans look as though they have arrived almost by accident.

Chairs have stuffed seats and padded backs, surmounted by carved and gilt cresting rails. Sofas, especially, are comfortable – in spite of rather forbidding, overstated sphinx supports to the arms. The style gradually gave way to the Gothic Revival about 1830.

In Portugal a heavy version of the French Empire style influenced the production of furniture from about 1805, surprisingly enough in view of the unpopularity of the French invaders who had marched through Spain. After the expulsion of Napoleon's army in 1811 there was a swing towards the late Georgian and Regency styles of the English liberators. After *c.*1820, German influence at court encouraged a preference for the Biedermeier style.

The Netherlands

Napoleon adopted the same policy in the Netherlands as elsewhere by installing, in 1805, a member of his family as king – in this case, his brother Louis, who took the job seriously, tried to protect the country's interests and was forced to abdicate in 1810. There was barely time for him to get the old Town Hall in Amsterdam refurbished in 1808–9 with large quantities of furniture in the Empire style, much of which is still on view there.

Some of it was made in Paris and taken to Holland, but most was produced locally and, although conforming in broad terms to the international Empire style, a distinct Dutch accent can be detected in the sturdiness of construction and the attention to detail of pieces made by Carel Breytspraak, who had become a master of the St Joseph's Guild in 1795. The commode he supplied for the apartments of the Crown Prince in 1809 has panelled ends and a moulding around the edges of the drawer-fronts – both features being a little reminiscent of traditional Netherlands furniture dating back to the 17th century. Breytspraak, who was of German descent, died the following year. A supplier of seat furniture for the Napoleonic royal family was Joseph Cuel. He is described as an upholsterer and may have ordered the frames from a number of joiners, as the quantity he had to supply in a short time was a large one.

After the Napoleonic era, the Empire style was continued during the reign of William I, for whom the Royal Palace at the Hague was largely refurnished in 1818. A local cabinetmaker, G. Nordanus, supplied a variety of pieces in mahogany. For the general public, many pieces were made at this time with severe carcase shapes in the Empire style, but lavishly decorated with the traditional floral marquetry. Tall chests of drawers flanked by columns, and with the top drawer projecting slightly, were especially popular. Sabre-legged chairs of simple shapes with flat rails to the backs, of the kind decorated with brass inlay in England, were often embellished with flower arrangements in contrasting woods.

Above: *Mahogany armchair in the Fernandino style – the Spanish equivalent of the French Empire. This is a relatively restrained example, but even so is a little exaggerated in the treatment of the arms, boldly curved to represent eagles but giving little support for elbows.*

Left: *Bronze dressing-table with winged sphinxes supporting the attached mirror, and front legs formed as monopodia with putti supporting the table-top. Dressing-tables with fixed mirrors first appeared early in the 19th century. Based on ancient Roman furniture found at Herculaneum and Pompeii, Italian adaptations continued long after the French Empire style had ceased to be fashionable elsewhere.*

England

The opening years of the 19th century saw a renewed enthusiasm among the English both for Neoclassicism and for the Gothic taste. Although the Neoclassical style introduced by Adam and other architects in the 1760s had never died out, it had become watered down and overlaid with non-classical influences, particularly from France. The new Greek revival was more strictly purist in its search for classical form and design and, again, the influence was chiefly French. The Prince of Wales, a supporter of the Whigs and a sympathizer with the revolutionary aspirations of the French, led the fashion for classicism and many of his commissions were carried out by Frenchmen.

By the opening years of the 19th century the classical designs of the French architects Fontaine and Percier were being widely circulated, but at the same time, a distinctly English version of the Greek revival style was emerging. Its chief influence was the architect Henry Holland who had been in charge of the refurbishing of Carlton House for

Left: *The Regency Room at the Geffrye Museum, London, showing the type of furniture that might have been found in a middle-class home in about 1815. The carved mahogany sofa is supported on sabre legs terminating in brass paw feet, and the armchair decorated with brass lions' masks is modelled on the ancient Greek form of* klismos *chair. The card table is of zebra wood inlaid with brass.*
Below: *A circular table with central pedestal designed by Thomas Hope for his house, The Deepdene, Surrey, in about 1810. It is made of mahogany and decorated with inlaid ebony and silver. The design appears in Hope's* Household Furniture *of 1807.*

Above: *A Gothic Windsor armchair of c.1800, with cabriole legs, a 'cow-horn' stretcher, and fine openwork Gothic splats at the back. The legs and back are of yew, and the seat, in common with most Windsors, of elm.*

Above: *A country chair of the type known as a Mendlesham, from the Suffolk village where many of them were made in the late 18th and early 19th centuries. The seat is of elm, the legs of birch and the back is of yew embellished with holly stringing.*

the Prince of Wales and who worked for many other eminent Whigs. He was the close friend of another Greek revivalist, Charles Heathcote Tatham, whose *Etchings of Ancient Ornamental Architecture*, published in 1799, proved invaluable to contemporary designers. In his furniture, Holland made use of darker woods, especially rosewood which began to replace satinwood for the best quality furniture. Ormolu (gilt bronze) mounts and brass inlays were also beginning to be used in preference to marquetry or painted decoration.

The most enthusiastic exponent of the Greek revival in England was the wealthy dilettante Thomas Hope, whose book, *Household Furniture and Interior Decoration*, was published in 1807, a year after Holland's death. This was mainly a record of Hope's London house in Duchess Street and the furniture he had designed specially for it to complement his remarkable collection of classical antiquities. It contained designs in the Egyptian style as well as the Grecian.

Napoleon's campaigns in Egypt in 1798 had stimulated interest in the antiquities there, and Egyptian motifs such as sphinxes, terms and hieroglyphic figures began to appear on furniture soon afterwards, often intermingled with classical ornament. An especially English brand of Egyptian taste, manifested in the occasional appearance of crocodile heads on furniture, was stimulated by Nelson's victory at the Nile in 1798, while the national nautical interest fostered by the Battle of Trafalgar in 1805 found expression in rope-back or Trafalgar chairs. Anchors and dolphins also appeared on furniture about this time as decorative features. Of these, the dolphin was the longer lasting and was used on chairs and table legs for the next two decades.

Hope was a collector of Egyptian as well as classical antiquities and at his country house, The Deepdene, in Surrey, he furnished an Egyptian room to show them off. But Hope's exoticism did not end there for he also incorporated decorations in Turkish, Chinese and 'Hindoo' styles – with hardly a vestige of comfort in any of them.

His Greek designs were of most lasting influence: anthemion motifs and Greek key patterns were used for decoration, and swans, griffins, caryatids or massive claw feet form supports, while rams' heads, lion masks and classical busts become terminals. Forms such as the X-stool and the *klismos* chair with sabre legs and often a tablet back were widely adopted and variations of it persisted into the Victorian period. Hope has been called 'the man of chairs and tables, the gentleman of sofas', and it was probably in these items of furniture that his influence was greatest. He made widespread use of gilded metal mounts as decoration for furniture, a habit adopted by many cabinetmakers of the time.

The ideas embodied in Hope's furniture were distilled by contemporary cabinetmakers into what has become known as the Regency style. Strictly speaking, the Regency period encompassed the years from 1811–20 when the Prince of Wales (the future George IV) acted as Regent during the illness of his father George III. It was associated with the flamboyant taste of the Prince Regent himself – epitomized by his extravagant pleasure dome, the Royal Pavilion, Brighton. However, the term Regency is now generally used to describe furniture of the first quarter of the 19th century, often much more restrained in design than anything associated with the Prince Regent and much less pedantic than the designs of Thomas Hope, but still influenced by both of them.

Brighton Pavilion was an oriental fantasy; its architecture was vaguely Indian and much of its interior decoration was Chinese. The furnishings included chairs, sofas and tables of bamboo, and this provoked a general fashion for bamboo furniture, much of it simulated (from stained or painted beechwood), which persisted for several decades.

One style which Hope avoided in *Household Furniture* but which found its way intermittently into all kinds of Regency furniture was the Gothic. Often mixed indiscriminately with the Neoclassical or the Oriental, the Gothic taste was associated with romanticism. Its most important champion in the early 19th century was William Beckford, a rich and reclusive eccentric whose Fonthill Abbey, a vast folly built at ruinous expense by the architect James Wyatt (and rebuilt several times when it fell down in the course of construction), towered above the Wiltshire countryside. People flocked to see this Gothic extravaganza, and artists like Turner painted it but, like the Gothic taste itself, it had insecure foundations, and it crashed magnificently to the ground only 25 years after it was built.

In furniture the Gothic taste was no less exciting than it had been in the mid-18th century. Chairs sported gothic tracery in their backs (even if they had sabre legs and were made of simulated bamboo); gothic arches and crenellations appeared on bookcases, and all kinds of furniture sprouted crockets and cusps, trefoils and quatrefoils, arches and columns. On the whole, Gothic was reserved for heavier furniture – for the hall, dining room or library – rather than elegant drawing room pieces. It was left to a later generation, the Victorians, to revive gothicism in a more conscientiously archaeological way.

Above: *A view of the Music Room at the Royal Pavilion, Brighton – the embodiment of Regency taste at its most exotic. It was designed by John Nash as part of the remodelling of the Pavilion carried out between 1815 and 1822. The circular carpet, 9.75 m (32 ft) in diameter, was woven at the Aubusson factory in France for Catherine the Great of Russia in about 1780.*

Below: *An X-framed stool of the revived Neoclassical type favoured by Thomas Hope; this one is of ebonized wood with decorative features of brass. Hope's most important legacy was probably his advocacy of good design principles applied to mass produced furniture. This stool with its simple shape and sparse ornament shows his influence in this respect.*

While Thomas Hope left the Gothic alone until late in his life (when it became one of his enthusiasms) another designer, this one a practical cabinetmaker, included many illustrations of Gothic furniture in his books. This was George Smith whose *Collection of Designs for Household Furniture and Interior Decoration* had first appeared in 1804 and 1805 but was issued in its most famous edition in 1808. Smith 'Upholsterer and Cabinet-maker to HRH Prince of Wales', and later 'Upholsterer and Furniture Draughtsman to His Majesty, and Principal of the Drawing Academy', was much influenced by Hope, but translated his ideas into more practical terms for the furniture-buying middle classes. His classicism was less disciplined but a great deal more comfortable than Hope's. His main claim to fame is said to have been his popularization in England of the circular dining table and the ottoman, but several other items of furniture he illustrated, notably the chiffonier and the convex mirror, were to become indelibly associated with the Regency style. Smith later published *A Collection of Ornamental Designs after the Antique* (1812) and *The Cabinet-makers' and Upholsterers' Guide* (1826), but his first work provided by far the freshest and most vivid portrayal of Regency furniture.

While chinoiserie continued to flower in the exotic interiors of the Prince Regent and at the hands of ladies pursuing their 'fancy works' (never at the forefront of changes in taste) it was, generally speaking, out of fashion

Right: *An early 19th century cane-seated chair in ebonized beech carved to simulate bamboo; its decoration combines the Gothic and the Chinese tastes of the Regency period. Although the revived Neoclassical style had a somewhat purifying effect on the design of much furniture in the Regency period, the exotic and fanciful still held its appeal, particularly for the Prince Regent whose Pavilion at Brighton set a fashion which was followed far down the social scale.*
Below: *A design for a sofa which was illustrated in an 1823 issue of Ackermann's* Repository of Arts, Literature, Commerce, Manufactures, Fashions and Politics – *a widely circulated magazine of the period.*

quite early in the 19th century. The Egyptian taste too had blown over by about 1810, much to the relief of critics like Rudolph Ackermann who wrote in his magazine *The Repository of Arts*, 'the barbarous Egyptian style, which a few years since prevailed, is succeeded by the classic elegance which characterized the most polished ages of Greece and Rome'.

'Classic elegance' did indeed prevail in the smartest interiors during this period, but a great deal of furniture was still made in styles deriving from the 18th century – gentle, convenient and very English.

As well as large two-tier bookcases with glazed doors above and cupboards below, there was now the smaller chiffonier, or sets of tiered bookshelves, sometimes circular and sometimes incorporating a drawer or two. Other bits and pieces – trinkets, needlework, sheet music, papers and so on – were accommodated on the invaluable whatnot or etagère which first appeared in the 1790s and enjoyed popularity for the whole of the 19th century. Occasional tables for all purposes proliferated, many of them of a more compact size than was popular in the 18th century but of heavier construction than before.

Indeed many items were made in conveniently small sizes by this time. The voluminous hooped skirts of the 18th century had given way to the straight flowing lines of the Empire style in ladies' dresses, and chairs in particular became correspondingly less capacious, with narrower seats and lighter construction. This lightness was sometimes enhanced by caning in the seats and backs.

The lofty overmantels and pier glasses which had dominated 18th century rooms were now superseded by oblong overmantels, often in three sections with gilt decoration in the Neoclassical manner, and by circular convex mirrors in gilt frames sometimes flanked by candle sconces. Upstairs the convenient cheval glass with its long adjustable mirror had arrived in the bedroom.

There were more decorative finishes in use at this period than ever before. Gilding was used a great deal for the showiest furniture, sometimes on its own and sometimes in conjunction with dark woods such as ebony, mahogany, rosewood or simulated versions of them. Indeed, simulated effects were very popular as a cheaper but still fashionable alternative to such expensive commodities as rosewood, bamboo or ivory inlaid furniture.

This latter type had been among the luxury items imported to Europe through the East India companies during the 18th century. Magnificent cabinets, desks, mirrors and other furniture made of ebony or coromandel wood were intricately decorated with all-over patterns of inlaid and incised ivory. They were, of course very costly, and besides, supply could never keep up with demand, so

Above right: *A giltwood convex mirror dating from the early 19th century. This type was very popular in the Regency period. Some, in emulation of Brighton Pavilion taste, had large and menacing birds (or even dragons) hovering over them and candle-sconces twirling beneath, while others were merely embellished with gilt balls round the frame (see page 152 for another example).*

Right: *The 'Barcelonette' – a child's cot draped in taffeta, illustrated in the* Literary and Fashionable Magazine *in 1807. Elaborate draperies were very fashionable during this period.*

the expedient of imitating the technique with black and white 'pen-painting' was hit upon. Predictably, most penwork designs – mainly on small pieces such as work boxes, tea caddies, chess tables, firescreens and miniature cabinets, but occasionally on quite large pieces of furniture – were of chinoiseries and oriental plant motifs, but Neoclassical scenes were also favoured. Penwork was taken up by lady amateurs often very skilfully, and was a popular pastime well into the Victorian period.

Simulated rosewood and bamboo furniture was generally made of beech and then painted and varnished appropriately. Japanning on furniture had by this time degenerated into a form of painting with varnish and chinoiserie was mostly superseded by painted flowers or Neoclassical motifs in a variety of colours. Japanned tin plate was used for some small pieces of furniture. The Pontypool factory produced dressing tables in this material, about 1805. This factory, which produced the best

Above: *A tripod chess table decorated with flowers and chinoiseries in penwork, c.1820–30. Penwork, originally a painted imitation of the ivory inlaid decoration on Indian furniture, was a popular pastime among ladies during the first half of the 19th century. This is an especially accomplished example and may have been the work of a professional.*

Left: *A Regency rosewood davenport with a sliding sloping upper part with fittings inside, and drawers opening sideways in the base. This is an early example of the davenport, which became bigger and was more often made of walnut in the Victorian period.*

japanned tin plate in Europe, closed in 1822, although many other factories, chiefly in Wolverhampton and Birmingham, flourished until the mid-19th century. The japanning done at Pontypool was a complex industrial process, with handpainted decoration burnt in. Rather similar decoration appears on examples of furniture made from various forms of papier-mâché, but this material reached its heyday in the early part of the Victorian period.

Brass inlay, as we have seen, was a favourite form of embellishment for the rosewood furniture of the Regency period. The technique was French in origin (it is known as boullework after André-Charles Boulle who first perfected it in the later years of the 17th century) and was practised in London to a large extent by emigré craftsmen from the

Above: *A rosewood cabinet with a marble top and glazed doors lined with pleated silk,* c.*1825. The brass inlaid decoration is typical of the period when it was still known as boullework, although by the 19th century it was somewhat less elaborate than the type perfected by André-Charles Boulle in the late 17th century.*

French Revolution. The most famous of these was Louis Le Gaigneur who set up his 'Buhl Manufactory' in Edgware Road in the second decade of the 19th century. Another expert in the field was John Bullock, some of whose pieces are recorded. He made a pair of cupboards inlaid with brass for Blair Castle, Perth, in 1817. Brass, sometimes backed with pleated silk, was also used in decorative trellis patterns on the doors of cupboards or for small ornamental grilles round the tops of cabinets and side tables. Indeed, one of the most pronounced characteristics of furniture of the Regency period was the use of metal for all sorts of decoration.

Although the Grecian style persisted for many years – even into the pages of J. C. Loudon's *Encyclopaedia of Cottage, Farm and Villa Architecture and Furniture*, a comprehensive record of vernacular furniture published in 1833 – the elegant lines of the Regency began to give way, after about 1820, to the international hotch-potch of ideas and styles that characterized the greater part of the 19th century. By then, improvements in communications, changes in class structure and, above all, the extraordinarily rapid development of mechanical technology, had begun to change furniture making for ever.

Victorian Furniture

Although the years immediately following the French Revolution saw drastic social changes in almost all European countries, it was not until the end of the Empire that the most important of these became fully apparent. While it is an obvious truism to state that furniture reflects social custom, the evident differences in the relative importance of the social classes and the alterations in manners had significant effects both on the design and use of furniture. Following each major war, changes have taken place in the general patterns of social behaviour at a significantly faster rate than usual. Prior to the Napoleonic Wars, life, especially among the upper classes, was a courtly minuet full of formal movements. This was reflected in the use of furniture, as well as its design; when not in use, furniture was arranged around the walls of the rooms, creating impressions of great formality, leaving large voids in the centres of rooms, which were only filled when the furniture was actually required. After the wars, this custom, even among the wealthy, ceased to be followed and the furniture was grouped naturally in the room ready for use.

It is also an almost inevitable concomitant of major wars that the centre of power shifts by an increase in the wealth and importance of the lower ends of the social strata with a corresponding and real reduction at the upper end. By the end of the Napoleonic Wars, the centre of political and economic power was shifting towards the middle classes. Logically, the history of furniture must, and indeed does reflect this trend. There were, of course, still incredibly rich and powerful families, who furnished their houses in flamboyant style, but it was no longer the case that the rich completely set the fashions for others to try to follow, perhaps because the experience of the French aristocracy suggested that conspicuous overconsumption was not a trait likely to be viewed with approval. Even in Britain at this time, revolution was daily expected. Further, the number of major individual clients available to the cabinet-makers, in relation to the increasingly powerful and numerous middle classes, became relatively insignificant.

Throughout Europe, the old ruling classes had become less sure in their control of events, while the middle classes, who had achieved some measure of power during the course of the revolutionary period, were reluctant to return to a subservient role. It is true that during the period 1830–48 the rulers of the German states reasserted their strength but the middle classes regained their position after the revolutions of 1848–49.

Left: *Queen Victoria was a frequent visitor to Hatfield House, home of the Marquis of Salisbury, and this bedroom, which was specially furnished, was kept for her personal use. While mainly in the 'Louis' style, some pieces are in the classical manner, and it demonstrates the clutter of personal belongings that became such an important feature of Victorian interiors of all social classes.*

Right: *The Biedermeier style depended mainly upon simple geometric forms for its inspiration. In this mahogany sewing table, the oval top is paired with a rectangular base. The lyre supports were a continuation from the Neoclassical style, and in keeping with the philosophy of simplicity of ornamentation, the use of decorative inlays is minimal.*

Above: *During the Biedermeier period, the sofa was one of the most important pieces of furniture in the house. This Austrian example, possibly by Josef Danhauser, is a fine example of the style. The simple curve of the back rail, which is of fruitwood, shows the restraint that was an essential element of the style, and the decoration, of ebony and gilt, is minimal in comparison with the preceding period.*

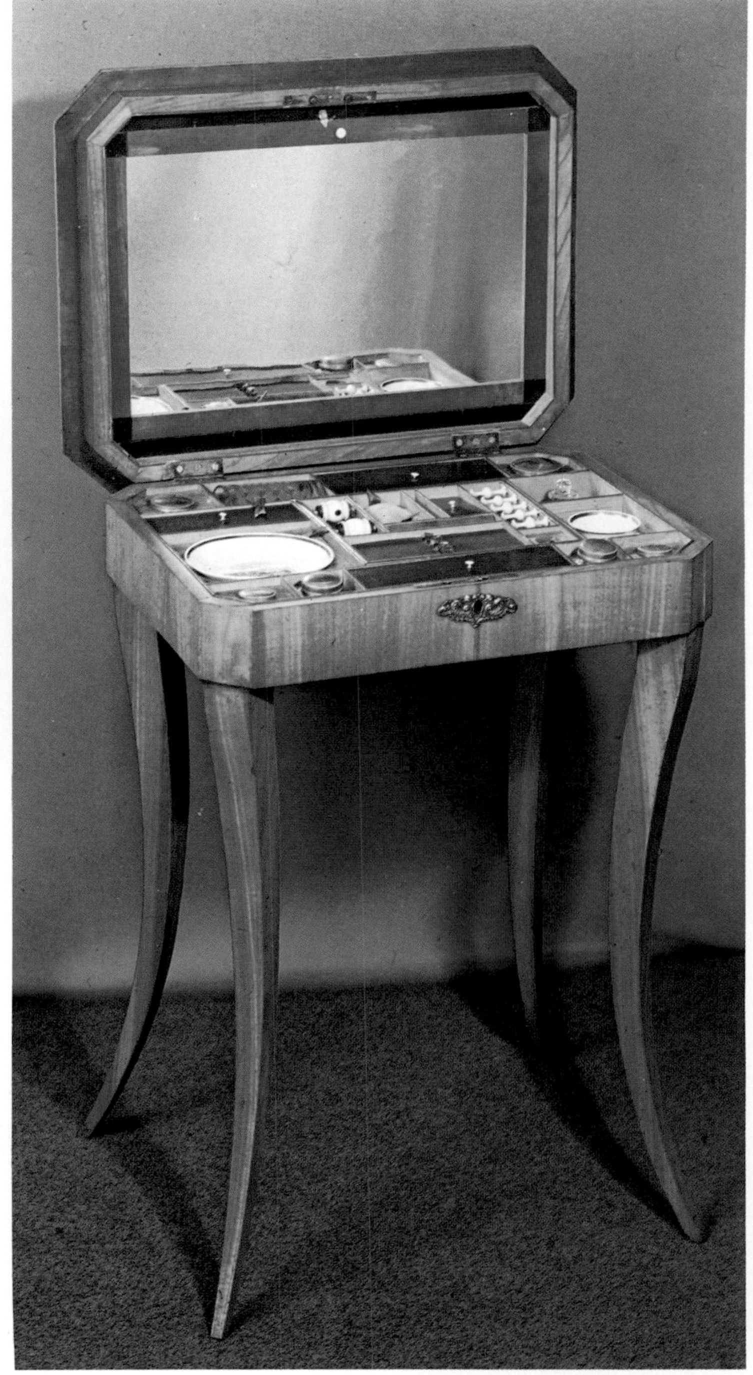

The Biedermeier style

This middle-class strength was perhaps the most important influence on furniture design during the period, for they were less sure in their taste than the former aristocracy, and in great measure sought the comfort of the familiar in design. Thus, style became largely retrospective or imitative and indeed ended in direct reproduction. This lack of sureness of place and taste was not to end until the next generation was established in the last third of the period and the beginnings of a truly innovatory design again appear.

Although there were outbursts of furnishing on a truly magnificent scale throughout the period which have some importance in the development of taste – such as the work undertaken for the Empress Eugénie or King Ludwig II of Bavaria – these are atypical, and it is among the bourgeoisie that the major influences are to be sought. Biedermeier, the name given to the styles found in Austria and Germany after the wars, is perhaps the best evidence of this.

The name Biedermeier derives from *bieder*, which is translated as plain or unpretentious, while 'Meier' is simply a common German surname. Academic argument has raged over the origins of the term Biedermeier but it was certainly in use with its present connotation by the 1890s. Loosely, the term approximates to the English 'Everyman', but a decidedly bourgeois Everyman. The style was a conscious revolt against the magnificence and ostentation of the Empire and its predecessors. Its beginnings lay in the Congress of Vienna, which created the Confederation of German States, and at which the citizens of Germany, exercising their new-found power, obtained for themselves rights that they had previously been denied. The formal end to the period is said to be in the years of revolution, 1848–9; however, from 1830, and coinciding with a period of repression from the German princes, the style degenerated and it is argued that the true end of the style should be put at this earlier date. While there were many Biedermeier craftsmen, none of them gained the total pre-eminence of, say, Chippendale or Boulle. Not surprisingly, in view of the fact that the Austrian Empire was still the most powerful of the Germanic States, it is the Viennese whose names are best known, and of these, Josef Danhauser was the most important. Aside from the brilliance of his designs, he was also responsible for another significant strand in the history of furniture-making: the beginning of factory techniques.

Danhauser was not a native of Austria, having left Wurttemburg where he had trained as a sculptor at the beginning of the century. When he arrived in Vienna, he at

Left: *The true Biedermeier style was of short duration, and had begun to deteriorate by the 1830s. This worktable, of about 1835, although elegant, clearly shows the decline. The top is not a simple rectangle, but has become an irregular octagon, and the legs do not conform to the early ideal of simple curves within a single plane. The piece is, however, especially interesting, as it retains its original fittings.*
Right: *This bedroom, in the Kasteel Duivenoorde in Holland, shows some evidence of the influence of the Biedermeier style, although the furniture has a great deal more surface ornamentation than would have been acceptable in the Germanic states. The chair and table, which are made of ash and amboyna, show this divergence quite clearly.*

first made carved ornaments for furniture but by 1804 he had opened his *Etablissement für alle Gegenstande des Ameublements* (Establishment for all Furnishing Requirements), and by 1808 he was employing 130 workmen, the largest number up to that date within the Austrian Empire. Everything he sold was made to his own designs and over 2,500 of these still exist, all of which exhibit the essential ingredients of Biedermeier, on which he was such a seminal influence.

In its outlook, the style had much in common with the Bauhaus philosophy; truth to materials and functionalism were of major importance to the Biedermeier designers. Thus wood, being the most significant element, was used in smooth flat sheets, and as architectural details lost their importance, they were replaced by shallow applied strips. No attempt was made to hide constructional methods, and on chairs for example, the joints of seat rails and legs are clearly displayed. The shapes used were invariably simple and geometrical and intended almost to be viewed only in two dimensions. Thus, curves were almost never serpentine or bombé, but rather curves within a single plane. Being geometric, the designs are derived from the square or the circle, extended logically in the third dimension as the cube or the sphere. These were, even more than in earlier periods the essentials of design, in that their line was normally pure and uncluttered by surface decoration. They were, of course, often linked together, most frequently by the use of concave curves.

One of the most unusual results of this simple geometric approach is a writing bureau, to be seen at the Museum für Kunsthandwerk, Dresden, which consists of a cubic two drawer base, on which stands the bureau section made up of three elements, the first of which is a rectangle with a height to width ratio of 2:1. Within this rectangle is a square which opens to reveal the writing surface. Described around this square and therefore in part falling outside the limits of the rectangle is a circle, the circumference of which is defined by an applied band of contrasting veneer. Surmounting this section is a smaller cube, linked to the base by concave curves. Borrowed from the classical are its decorative metalwork elements: lions' paw feet and winged griffins supporting the circle.

In its 'truth to materials', decoration was minimal, for it was the grain of the wood that was the most important element in the successful execution of Biedermeier design. Partly as a conscious rejection of the Empire and partly for economic reasons, mahogany fell into disuse and was replaced by walnut, pear and cherry, all of which were indigenous, although towards the end of the 1820s mahogany began to return to fashion.

The style, although peculiar to the Germanic states, was not without external influences, of which the most important were the Neoclassical style and English furniture design. Many of the Neoclassical motifs were used, such as the lyre, lions' paw feet and sphinx heads, while certain pieces designed by Sheraton found their way, barely changed, into the German design books. This glance towards England was an acknowledgment of her role in the overthrow of Napoleon as well as a deliberate disregard of the French Empire and Restoration styles.

The fact that Biedermeier was so pre-eminently a middle-class style perhaps forced its functionalism. A chair could not be simply a graceful object to look at, as was frequently the case in previous periods, but it also had to be functional: comfortable to sit on, in fact. During the period few armchairs were produced, however, the most popular form of seat furniture being the sofa. The fronts of these were often heavily decorated with carving, the exception to the flat sheets of wood rule, and the upholstery was deep and comfortable, often being supplemented by additional cushions. It was perhaps the most typical piece of the period, placed as it was normally behind a large round table, which was the other essential element in the living room, so that people could sit comfortably both for conversation and for eating. Sometimes the desire for a fully functional piece led to the inclusion of cupboards or drawers in the arms.

Chair shapes were simple, in the early part of the period normally standing on square tapered legs, straight at the front and with a curve at the back. The backrests were normally of simple curved shapes, seldom with decorative splats. Sometimes they have plain caned seats, but more frequently they were upholstered, as the primary consideration was comfort rather than appearance. The efforts of the upholsterer to create an interesting effect can, however, look strange to our eyes, as in a design by Danhauser,

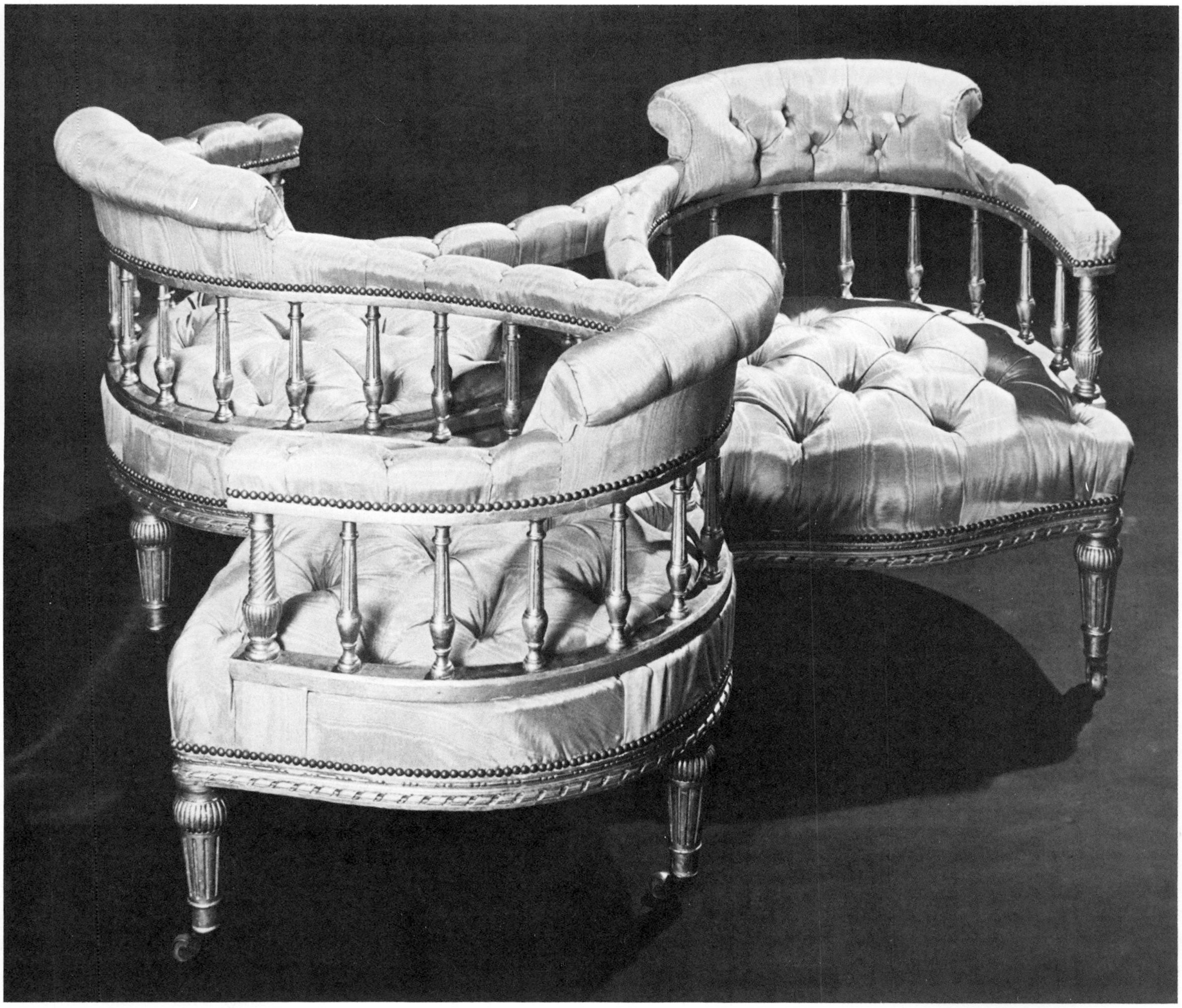

Above: *The Indiscret, otherwise known as a conversation sofa, was a piece of furniture that originated at the court of Napoleon III. In its simplest form, it consists of two or three chairs constructed in a linked manner. It is most commonly found in the 'Louis' styles, but this more unusual example is based on elements from the classical.*
Left: *That trends in interior design during the 19th century were almost universal can clearly be seen in this painting of the study of the Tsar Nicholas II of Russia in the Winter Palace, by Edward Gow. The vast array of family portraits and furniture creates an impression of clutter that would find its echoes in houses throughout Europe, becoming only muted in its opulence as one descended the social scale.*

where the fabric radiates in pleats from a central button, hanging like a shawl at the front and sides, with tassels at each of the corners. Upholstery was of major importance to the Biedermeier designers, who used it more imaginatively than had previous generations, and it was Georg Junigl, a Viennese, who is credited with the invention of the coil spring in 1822, which he claimed was '. . . so elastic that it is not inferior to horsehair.'

There were, of course, regional differences, which were mainly caused by the differences in political circumstances. North Germany, which both through trade and the connection of Hanover with the Crown of Britain had closer links than the south or Prussia, followed more closely the English styles, and at the same time favoured darker woods. Berlin, which was the centre of activity of Karl Friedrich Schinkel, followed the Neoclassical. Schinkel, an architect mainly concerned with public buildings, is in fact considered to be the creator of a peculiarly Prussian Neoclassical style. In Munich the Court architect was Leo von Klenze, who had worked for King Jerome of Westphalia under the Empire, but moved to Munich in 1816 at the invitation of Ludwig I. His main responsibility was a large public building programme, but he also designed interiors and furniture, mainly derived from the classical but which in contrast to the northern states was normally made in light coloured indigenous woods.

From 1830, the purity of the taste began to decline, simultaneously with the beginnings of political reaction, and after that, although a considerable number of pattern books survive, surprisingly little attributable furniture can be found. Whether this is a function of its impermanence or the inability of the makers to sell the new designs is, however, not clear. In common with the rest of Europe however, taste was becoming less certain in its direction and therefore began to split into differing retrospective styles, including Gothic and the coarsened neo-Rococo which is normally considered to be so typically Victorian.

Above: *With the decline of the Biedermeier style, neo-Rococo gained in favour. This mahogany work-table, made in Germany in about 1840, is the antithesis of all that had immediately preceded it. No curve is simple, and strength of design has vanished in favour of an impression of insubstantiality. Sewing tables have survived in great numbers.*

Neo-Rococo

Neo-Rococo continued to develop in most countries throughout the entire period. While the style is now most frequently called neo-Rococo when a name other than High Victorian is used, it in fact has very little in common with its alleged prototype, for asymmetrical designs were only infrequently produced. Indeed, during the period itself, the style was most commonly called 'Louis' or 'French'. Its most notable points of similarity with the original style are the use of flowing curves and cabriole legs, in contrast with the severe architectural manner of the Neoclassical. The coarsening of the style is evidenced in the amount of show-wood on chairs, which grew greater as the period progressed, as well as in the infilling of the arms and backs entirely with upholstery, which was at first relatively flat but thickened progressively and eventually became deep-buttoned at the later dates. In the decoration of furniture, the same lessening of restraint in design is evident. Partly, of course, this was due to the fact that the general standard of workmanship inevitably deteriorated, for the increased demand led to a relative decrease in the number of expert craftsmen, thus necessitating the use of mechanical techniques and of designs that were at the same time visually impressive while relatively simple to execute. That the demand was able to be filled was due to the application of techniques such as mechanical carving, which came into use in this period and which enabled the flowing lines as well as the detailed carving to be reproduced speedily and cheaply, an essential in terms of the rapidly expanding market.

Somewhat surprisingly, in view of the recent wars, England was the first country in which this revival and continuation of the French styles took root. Although when it first appeared, it was in work for George IV, it was essentially a style of popular appeal, never being taken up seriously by the more respected architects and designers. Although furniture in the style was available for all rooms, it was most commonly used in the drawing room where the influence and taste of women was most strongly felt. Aside from its obvious use in seat furniture, it was also used fairly extensively in carcase furniture, as well as for console tables and mirrors – uses that suit the style admirably.

Another piece most typically associated with the English Victorian owes nothing to neo-Rococo but everything to deep buttoning: the overstuffed armchair or chesterfield. Deep buttoning, which was first used on the balloon-back chairs, was itself largely dependent on the by-product of another technological development, for it required the use of short staple cotton and wool combings.

It is often mistakenly assumed by antique dealers that the progression of design was entirely logical and that as one style, for example the balloon-back chair with cabriole legs, became unfashionable, it was replaced by the same chair with turned legs. Although this may be true of design progression, it is not true of manufacturing, for even as late as 1900, it is possible to find in the current catalogues types that according to common lore had disappeared some 30 years previously. Neo-Rococo, therefore, had a currency of some 70 years in England, making it one of the most long-lasting of styles.

Left: *In this reconstruction of a Victorian boudoir in the Geffrye Museum in Shoreditch, London, an excellent impression is given of the mixture of styles, the heavy floral patterning and the profusion of ornaments that were so typical of middle class interiors of the period. Particularly interesting is the sofa, which has no back.*
Right: *The monopodium table is a particularly 19th century style, and this example is the more interesting as it seems to fall into a transition between the late Regency and the Gothic. Although elements derived from architecture are present, their use is restrained, and they are combined with acanthus leaf carving, which is more usually associated with the Rococo style.*

The style was only taken up in Germany from the 1840s, when the Biedermeier styles were dying out. Even on the level of the middle-class market, it attracted many excellent practitioners, most of whom also operated in the other fashionable styles. These included Karl Leistler, better known for his work in the Gothic idiom, and Michael Thonet, who made a great many pieces in the neo-Rococo style before his total involvement with bentwood furniture. The largest of the manufacturing centres in Germany was Mainz, which supplied both the home and the export markets. The most important of the makers there was Bembe, who began working in the style in the early 1840s and Wilhelm Kimbel, who included such pieces in a partwork design book that he published as early as 1835. Both of these continued manufacture in this and other currently fashionable styles throughout the century.

France did not revert to the taste until some five years after Britain, although still ahead of Germany. The real impact of the style was not, however, felt until the beginning of the Second Empire, when it and other Louis styles once more became popular, reflecting an upsurge of national pride and a belief that the great days of France were returning. Pieces of furniture that owed little to any of the Louis other than a passing resemblance began to appear everywhere in the profusion and clutter beloved of Victorians: occasional tables, stools, work-tables, whatnots and embroidery stands all took their place in rooms that became so crowded that it could be difficult to cross them without knocking something over.

These debased forms of the 'Louis' styles were made alongside more accurate representations of the originals, which never went totally out of fashion. Indeed, during the Second Empire, when the Empress Eugénie was refurnishing the Imperial palaces, not only did she have copies made but she also had new and original pieces constructed that blend in with the Louis XVI masterpieces.

Other monarchs, such as Ludwig II of Bavaria, whose nostalgia for a grandiose past was even greater than that of the French court, also had numerous pieces executed in the manner, his fairytale castles of Herrenchiemsee, Neuschwanstein and Schloss Linderhof being entirely furnished in the taste. This pure re-creation was however, mainly confined to the royal houses or those of the excessively rich, as indeed it had been during the original period. Thus, while the furniture fully exhibits the capabilities of the craftsmen, it is both less typical of its period and less relevant to the history of the development of furniture than the other, less expensive and more mass-produced styles, most of which were equally or even more retrospective.

Gothic and Elizabethan styles

Possibly the most retrospective of all these styles was the Gothic, which had seen a new flowering during the 18th century in England but which achieved its most popular heights, both in Europe and America during the 19th century. In the course of the 1820s, George IV was engaged on the renovation of Windsor Castle, and a great deal of the work was done in the Gothic style. Much of the furniture design was entrusted to Augustus Welby Northmore Pugin, who was only 15 when first commissioned. Pugin, as well as being a talented designer, was also an extremely able self-publicist, and above all it was this that enabled him to obtain such a commanding influence over his contemporaries.

Because of his extremely strong religious faith, he became convinced that Gothic was the 'only true style of architecture' and therefore by extension, of furniture design, but even he was never able satisfactorily to solve the difficult transition between ornament that was suitable for buildings and ornament that was suitable for tables and chairs. His designs, however, appealed strongly to the middle-class mass market, for it was a taste with which they were instantly familiar from their religious observances. While in his hands the style had some hold on everyday reality, in the hands of less restrained practitioners it could be positively dangerous and he himself commented on the danger of impalement on irrelevant crockets or of cracked shins on stray flying buttresses.

Above: *This design for a chaise longue appeared in the* Repository of the Arts, *which was published between 1809 and 1828. The Gothic taste was at that stage used rather tentatively, in comparison with the later excesses, and although the elements of the design would be more appropriate to a building than to a piece of furniture, it would be possible to sit on it without undue discomfort.*

Below: *Although Bruce Talbert was the author of* Gothic Forms applied to Furniture, *his designs were in fact more medieval in their sources. They also do not borrow so heavily from architectural forms, and this sideboard, designed by him in about 1870, although ornate and complex, is more functional than many of the truly Gothic pieces made in the previous period.*

Pugin was a compulsive worker, cramming more into his 40 years than most men could into 100. Perhaps the work for which he is best known is that undertaken for the rebuilding of the Palace of Westminster, where, aside from any involvement with the design of the building itself, the subject of acrimonious pamphleteering between the sons of Pugin and Sir Charles Barry, the official architect, he was certainly responsible for the design of most of the furniture. This reflects his conscientious and scholarly approach to Gothic, but was without the more excessive detail of his earlier work, for he himself publicly decried his own designs for Windsor Castle. He died in 1852, worn out it is said, by the work that he undertook for the Great Exhibition of 1851, when he was responsible for the Medieval Court. This was the type of work, involving committees and commissioners that he disliked most, being more accustomed and indeed better suited to working on his own.

Not surprisingly, in view of the English influence in Germany, especially on the northern states, the taste developed there as well, and in the international exhibitions so popular during the period, the German and English craftsmen vied with each other to produce the most extravagant colossi for the stupefaction of the juries. Scale in these special pieces seems to have become unimportant: surfaces that logically should be at waist level are not reached until eye level, giving a sense of having strayed into Brobdingnag. One of the foremost makers of this type was Karl Leistler of Vienna, who made a display cabinet in this style for presentation to Queen Victoria by the Austrian emperor, which was received with approbation at the Great Exhibition.

The improved communications throughout Europe naturally affected the universality of appeal of designs, and the Gothic taste even spread into Italy. This was surprising, for in all other countries where it took root, it was in fact a harking back to a previous native style, whereas in Italy the true medieval Gothic barely reached the northern frontiers. The style was spasmodically popular throughout the century and in most parts of the country, tending towards medievalism as the years advanced, although even as late as 1898 several Gothic items were shown at the Turin Exhibition when interest in the taste had almost entirely faded elsewhere.

After Pugin's death, the torch was taken up in England by Bruce Talbert, who published in 1867 his *Gothic Forms applied to Furniture* and by C.L. Eastlake in his *Hints on Household Taste*, which was published in the following year. These were however, the rearguard of the movement, and their designs were less extreme and tended more towards the medieval.

Talbert, in common with most of the other well known designers of the period, trained as an architect. A strong feature of many of his designs is the use of heavy ornamental ironwork, not surprisingly in view of the fact that he was responsible for the detailed drawings for the metalwork used on the Albert Memorial. He was one of the most famous of the 'exhibition designers', whose pieces were almost invariably greater than human scale. When one realizes that many of these pieces were more than 4.5m (15ft) tall, it is startling to think that they were actually used in normal households. His designs have more in common with the work of William Burges than Pugin,

Above: *This throne chair, one of a set of four, designed and made in Germany in 1851 by Hofmeister and Behrens, typifies the excesses that could be perpetrated in the name of Gothicism. The ornate carving looks as though it should have been used on the exterior of a building, and the Biedermeier concept of fitness for purpose has been completely lost.*

Above: *One of the most famous of the 'Exhibition' pieces is this Gothic bookcase, presented to Queen Victoria by the Emperor of Austria. Made of oak, it was designed by B. Bernardis and J. Kranner and was built by the firm of Leistler and Son of Vienna. In its vast scale and totally architectural quality, it is a gigantic overstatement of the use of Gothic forms when applied to the making of furniture.*

Right: *The architect Anthony Salvin, who designed this bed for Scotney Castle in the 1840s was one of the more important proponents of the style known as 'Elizabethan'. Most of the inspiration for such designs was in fact Jacobean, as can be seen from the massive bulbous carving of the bedposts, which, if based on Elizabethan originals would have been more delicate.*

being evolved from earlier styles. His influence on design from this first book was not as great as from the second, *Examples of Ancient and Modern Furniture, Tapestries and Decoration*, published some five years later, by which time his interest was moving away from Gothic towards the Jacobean, which was more to the popular taste.

Eastlake's influence was wider than Talbert's, as his book achieved wide acclaim on both sides of the Atlantic. His strictures on his contemporaries make amusing reading, and it must be conceded that his designs are in fact an improvement on the general standard of work at that time, for they are comparatively simple and logical. He was aiming at furniture that would be easy to construct, whose decoration would not be excessive and yet when made to high standards would not be expensive. In this, of course, he was echoing the ideals of the Morris group; even with all these favourable factors, however, very few of his designs seem actually to have been executed. He was extremely fond of the use of rounded arches and turned wood, frequently also using carved mottoes as a decorative element. His influence in America was so great that his name came to be used as a verb, a house being said to be 'Eastlaked' when it had been refurnished in accordance with his principles.

Simultaneously with the Gothic revival of the 1820s, there was another popular retrospective style, called at the time 'Elizabethan' which in fact owed little to the furniture of that period but was in fact relatively direct copying of Jacobean, certainly for seat furniture. Most of the furniture made in this style in the early years of the period was anonymous, and it only appears to have attracted Anthony Salvin and Henry Shaw among known designers. Shaw included several pieces in his design book *Specimens of Antique Furniture*, which was published in 1836, while Salvin designed pieces for Mamhead and Scotney Castle in the style.

Carcase furniture, when made in the idiom, was massive in the extreme, with almost overbearingly heavy carving. One of the best examples of this type of work is the sideboard in the dining room at Charlecote Park, Warwickshire; Sir Walter Scott, perhaps wishing to feel that he was living in the period of many of his novels, refurnished much of Abbotsford in the manner.

While significant as an early pointer to the trend towards historicism in England, the 'Elizabethan' style was never as all-embracingly popular as Gothic and certainly was of little direct influence on other parts of Europe.

Above: *Perhaps because he wished to feel that he lived in surroundings that approached those of the settings of many of his novels, Sir Walter Scott had his house, Abbotsford, decorated in the Elizabethan style. This view of the library shows the melée of derivations: the bookcases were Gothic, much of the furniture Jacobean, with only the ceiling apparently having much relation to Elizabethan originals.*

Neoclassicism continues

Classical sources continued to provide inspiration throughout the period, although when compared with the work of earlier craftsmen who followed the source material more closely, the line became more indistinct as the period advanced. Most of the great English designers worked in the idiom and many of the design books that appeared in such profusion include pieces in the style. It was however a rather debased form of classical, for the line changed from being relatively severe to being enriched by a considerable amount of ornamentation and having more flowing lines than the original. This evolution was of course in line with the desire of the middle class for furniture which was a visual statement, not merely of their affluence – which was in any case proved by their ability to purchase in the first place – but also of their permanence and status as settled and solid members of society. The style was most commonly used where a great display of opulence was not required, as in the rooms of the Reform Club, furnished by Holland and Sons in 1838. It continued to appear in catalogues throughout the century, but lost much of its popularity after the 1860s.

Since the style was a reflection of past glories, it was naturally revived in France during the Second Empire. The manner varied somewhat from the English, being rather more fussy, with a greater amount of surface ornamentation and the addition of motifs borrowed from the Louis styles. It was largely an anonymous, decorators' fashion, having little following among the more serious and noted designers.

One of the most spectacular of the Neoclassical rooms anywhere was executed in Italy. Designed by Pelagio Palagi for the Castello Reale di Raconigi, near Turin, it was based fairly closely on an Etruscan theme, with rich gilding, painted friezes and wall panels, a mosaic floor and exquisite marquetry furniture, and compares extremely well with the work of the earlier masters. Some pieces from the room were exhibited at the Great Exhibition, where they were received with overwhelming praise.

It was a style that travelled well, for it was popular on both sides of the Atlantic, many of the best known of the Victorian cabinetmakers in America working in the idiom. One of the reasons for its success may well have been that with its large flat surfaces and minimal carving it was possible to mechanize production to a large extent. The Americans made some idiosyncratic contributions to the vocabulary of the style, including a decorative process whereby the flat surfaces could be stencilled with gold, a practice that seems not to have been followed elsewhere.

Designers of the period were continually searching for new sources, whether in other times or in other cultures, and expressing, it may be thought, a dissatisfaction with their own. It was not uncommon to find in middle-class houses that individual rooms were furnished in totally differing styles. Indeed, certain conventions arose as to which styles were suitable for men and which for women. Neo-Rococo for example, with its gracefully fluid lines, was felt to be best suited to the use of ladies and was therefore found particularly in drawing rooms and boudoirs, where their influence was either strongest or total. Gothic, which was felt to be a masculine style would have been used for the library, while 'Elizabethan' which was neutral was considered appropriate for the dining room. Billiard rooms, smoking rooms and bathrooms, which were downright outlandish, might well be Moorish, but the bedrooms, which were again neutral, were commonly Neoclassical.

Above: *During the 19th century, retrospective styles were popular throughout Europe. The Etruscan Room in the Castello Reale di Raconigi was designed in 1834 as a dining room by Pelagio Palagi, and the chairs received special praise when they were shown at the Great Exhibition in 1851.*

Left: *Gillows were one of the more important commercial manufacturers of furniture during the Victorian period, and made pieces in every popular style. This cabinet, made for the 1867 Exhibition, is in the Neoclassical manner, and although more human in scale than most of the exhibition pieces, it shares with them an almost vulgarly over-ornamented appearance.*

The diversity of styles available to the 19th century customer is evidenced in the design books that appeared so frequently during the first half of the period and which present most strongly the confusion of taste. Gothic jostles 'Elizabethan' and Rococo, and indeed sometimes mingles in the designs of the less competent, all the time becoming heavier and more overpowering until the 1860s, when the revolt against the weighty styles began. During the middle years, however, the really spectacular pieces achieved a quality that was more akin to sculpture than furniture. One example is the bed, made by Speluzzi for Gian Giacomo Poldi-Pezzoli, now in the Poldi Museum in Milan, the legs of which rest on the backs of dwarfs with appropriately agonized faces. Another is the Kenilworth sideboard, which was shown at the Great Exhibition, on which every

Above: *Painted furniture was extremely popular with the Pre-Raphaelites, but this piano with scenes painted by Sir Edward Burne-Jones is unusual, in the sense that such instruments were seldom decorated in this way. It shows, however, how members of the movement would cover every possible surface with paintings, even where it was impractical, such as the back board by the pedals.*
Right: *Furniture made by associates of William Morris. The oak table was designed by Philip Webb, the framed panel of four tiles is by Morris and Co., the rush-seated, stained wood chairs are by Morris and the St George cabinet on the back wall was designed by Philip Webb and painted by Morris. All clearly show how dependent the group was on the medieval for its inspiration.*

visible vertical surface was covered with carvings representing scenes from Sir Walter Scott's novels, while the pilasters were replaced by figures carved fully in the round or by groups of bears.

Neo-medievalism – Morris and Burges

This excess, which affected most countries, was bound to suffer a reaction and that was not long in coming. The solution was a retrospective form, a reversion to what was felt to have been a simpler, more innocent and less rapacious lifestyle – neo-medievalism. The most prominent proponent of the manner was William Morris, who was born in Walthamstow, the son of wealthy parents. He was educated at Marlborough and Exeter College, Oxford, where he met a group of young men, including Edward Burne-Jones, who, like himself, wished to work for the betterment of social conditions. Originally intending to be ordained, he gave up the idea since it conflicted with his own view of the way that the improvement would come about. It was, admittedly, somewhat eccentric, depending as it did on the abandonment of industrialization and reverting to a craft-based society. For a while after he came down from university he trained as an architect but abandoned this career also, as he felt that the detailed designs prepared by his profession were stultifying to the craftsmen entrusted with carrying them out.

In 1861, in conjunction with Burne-Jones, Rossetti, Madox Brown and Philip Webb, he founded Morris, Marshall, Faulkner and Company. The firm was willing to undertake all kinds of work in relation to household interiors and churches and was formed because the group was appalled by what they felt to be the generally low standards of design and execution on the part of the commercial manufacturers. In addition, Morris hoped to encourage the artisan class to a greater appreciation of design and the use of colour, which he felt would lead to the betterment of their conditions and for which he was to strive continually. Further, he wished to try to revive the old spirit of fellowship which he believed had existed in the old days of the guilds. What, curiously, he did not allow for was the unsurprising fact that the only people who could afford to support the enterprise were the same leisured classes whose standards he so decried. He was however, forced to rely on their patronage to enable the company to continue to employ its craftsmen.

The furniture made by the company, whether cheap or

expensive, was all very soundly made of honest materials, for one of the major reasons behind the company's formation had been the conscious revolt against the shoddy commercial standards that were prevalent. Much of their work was based on 13th century architecture, which they felt expressed the spirit of the golden age, not recognizing the paradox that the days of the greatest importance of the guilds were from the 16th to the 18th centuries. As a result, their work fell into two distinct categories, the first being utilitarian and the second important display pieces which were elaborate in the extreme. It is the latter, of course, which are the best known, such as the sideboards and cabinets, every surface of which was enriched by carving or painting. In the early period, much of the furniture was designed by Philip Webb, while the painting was undertaken by artists such as Burne-Jones, Madox Brown, Rossetti or Morris himself. These were, of course the ultimate in prestige pieces and could only be purchased by the extremely wealthy. The forms, while derived from architecture, are in the main relatively simple and satisfactory, the richness of their effect being almost entirely dependent on the decoration.

The firm first exhibited its work at the International Exhibition held in London in 1862, showing amongst other pieces the 'King Renée Cabinet', which was designed by J.P. Seddon. The panels showed scenes which were based on characters from *Anna von Geierstein* by Sir Walter Scott, an author with whom Morris felt a particular sympathy, echoing as he did Morris's own view of an entirely romanticized past, and they were painted by a cooperative of almost all the practising artists associated with the company. It was not the first example of painted furniture made by the members, for as early as 1858, before the formal foundation of the company, Philip Webb had designed the Chaucer Cabinet, which was painted by Burne-Jones, as a wedding present for Morris. Inter-

Left: *The washstand designed by William Burges for his house, the Tower House, Melbury Road, Kensington, has a carcase of carved, painted and gilded oak, while the top, basin and soap dishes are of marble, and the tap of bronze. Burges claimed to find his sources for his designs in French illuminated manuscripts, and this piece, signed and dated 1880, has the invitation 'Venez Laver' inscribed upon it.* **Right:** *Much of Burges' furniture was derived from architectural sources, such as the carved and painted cabinets shown here. So richly are they decorated that they seem to be more art objects than pieces of furniture. Even the bed, although more obviously functional, still has the high degree of ornamentation that made his work very expensive.*

estingly, this was a trial piece in other ways, for it was, coincidentally, the first oil painting that Burne-Jones completed.

The work of the firm embraced all forms of furnishing, from wallpapers and fabrics to tapestries and metalwork. Morris himself, despite his short training as an architect, did not design any of the commercial furniture himself, concentrating instead mainly on fabrics and wallcoverings. All the so-called Morris furniture is, therefore, entirely the work of others, Webb, for example, having designed the 'Morris chairs', which were of turned wood with cane seats and based on Sussex originals.

The company was also the first to use coloured stains on its furniture commercially, although again the actual first example was made by one of the members before its establishment. In 1857, William Holman Hunt had made for his own use a simple oak table, upon which he applied a green stain. This idea was again taken up after 1861 and used on the simpler, more functional pieces, particularly those designed by Webb or Hunt himself. Indeed the stain was the only decoration of any sort that was used by Webb on his oak tables.

Throughout the period covered by this chapter, the company grew and expanded its activities, retaining by and large the relative purity of its ideals. By the 1880s however, Morris became less certain of the practicality of social change by reversion to the craft society and more committed to straightforward socialism. At the same time, perhaps slightly corrupted by its own success and its increasing take-over policy, the furniture produced by the firm became more commercial, even though the standards of construction remained high, until, by the time of his death, there would have been little to choose between his work and that of any other conscientious and high-priced manufacturer.

Painted furniture, although never a fully commercial proposition, was not exclusively the realm of Morris and Company in Britain. Indeed, perhaps its most startling practitioner was William Burges, who is mainly remembered for his creations at Cardiff Castle and Castell Coch. He also built and furnished for himself the Tower House, in Melbury Road, Kensington over which Mrs Haweis, the Victorian apostle of good taste, gushed her enthusiasm, and which he himself described as the model residence of the 15th century. Burges was, in most respects, a conscientious antiquary researching for the basis of his designs, for example in illuminated manuscripts, although this conscientiousness did not necessarily extend fully into his relationship with his clients. For example, when engaged on the rebuilding of Castell Coch, which the Marquess wished to be totally authentically British, Burges imported into the drawings conical roofed towers from French originals and wooden balconies or 'bretaches', which would have been much more at home in Nuremberg. Mrs Haweis commends Burges as a man who brought a sense of fun into architecture but which we are more likely to feel is the piling of whimsy upon whimsy, as in the case of a fireplace in Cardiff Castle, which is itself in the form of a castle. Completing the whimsy, the figure of a prisoner can be seen, forever gazing forlornly out of a window.

All of Burges' work has a brilliant, jewel-like quality, with rich ground colours and much use of gilding. Again the panels were often painted by artists well known in their own right. An example is the cabinet now in the Victoria and Albert Museum painted by E.J. Poynter, which was shown at the 1862 exhibition. The construction of the cabinets themselves was simple, to a large extent giving a feeling that they could really be based on genuine pieces, but a difficulty that Burges was never able to overcome without a result that gives rise to gasps of incredulity was the creation of a suitably 13th or 15th century washstand! For example, at Castell Coch in the Lady's Bedchamber, the washstand takes the form of a castle (again the small visual pun that he found so hard to resist) with small turrets on each side that act as cisterns, the whole being decorated in gold and cream. In fact this piece, although completely in the spirit of Burges, was created by J.S. Chapple, his assistant. At the Tower House, he solved the plumbing problem by having taps especially cast in the form of a tortoise.

Burges was in no sense a commercial designer, for all of his furniture was made for specific persons and places. His eccentric style necessitated a wealthy patron or the self-indulgence of a successful architect. While therefore his relevance to the generality of neo-medieval and neo-Renaissance work is strictly limited, his work is an excellent example of what could be achieved given access to almost unlimited funds.

It should not be thought, however, that these styles were a purely British foible. The third quarter of the 19th century was a time of intensely powerful national awareness throughout Europe, which in terms of source of

Left: *Many of the pieces created by Burges were decorated by artists who were well known in their own right, such as this cabinet, painted by E.J. Poynter. Although as flamboyant in effect as all of Burges' furniture, it gives a more definite impression of being based on an actual original, unlike his more architectural extravagances.*

Above: *This X-framed chair was obviously inspired by medieval forms. One of a set of four, it was designed in 1860 by G. Bertili and G. Speluzzi. The frame is of mahogany, richly inlaid with bands and fillets of ebony and ivory, while the seat, back and arms are upholstered in hand-embroidered yellow silk.*

design took the form of retrospection to the 'Golden Age' of the Renaissance. In contrast to the work in Britain, most of the furniture produced in the style was massive, dark and over-elaborated, although in France the pieces were occasionally lighter in appearance. Napoleon III began an intensive programme of building and restoration after coming to power as emperor, favouring in particular the styles of François I and Henri II. Fontainebleau, which was in fact a Renaissance palace, was refurnished in keeping with its period to designs by Ruprich-Robert and executed by Guillaume Grohé, who had previously made the cradle presented by the people of Paris on the occasion of the birth of the Prince Imperial. Naturally, the style was taken up by all levels of society, though it never entirely replaced the Louis idioms. The Franco-Prussian war, which resulted in the overthrow of the Empire led inevitably to a temporary disfavour, as it had been almost an official Imperial style, but after a few years it returned, although with less force and assurance than formerly.

Italy's approach was slightly different, favouring the Dantesque view of the past and coming to prominence at the time of the Risorgimento. The taste was almost entirely middle class in its appeal and there could have been few middle-class houses that did not boast at least one neo-Renaissance room. It relied heavily on X-framed chairs and stools and tables with very heavy carving for its effect, and in this respect the Italians were at variance with most of the rest of Europe, for their designs were often relatively accurate, being based on Renaissance paintings. The designs of the major pieces, such as sideboards and beds tended to be very heavy and overloaded with unrestrained carving, with detail piled upon detail. Andrea Boccetti, who worked in Florence in the 1860s was a typical exponent of the style and his work was always well received at the exhibitions.

At much the same time as the Risorgimento, the unification of Germany under Prussia was taking place, with the same upsurge of nationalism and the same interest in the neo-Renaissance. As in France it became an almost official style, being used in many public buildings but it was equally well accepted by the middle classes. Many of the well known names worked in the style, which continued almost unabated until the turn of the century, including Leistler in Vienna, Pallenberg in Cologne and Bembe in Mainz.

Neither should it be thought that the style was confined to the Western European countries. Work was carried out in the manner in places as distant as the castle of Peles in Rumania and the Winter Palace in St Petersburg, while in Scandinavia King Christian IX of Denmark had furniture made in the style while still Crown Prince.

Moorish and Japanese styles

There were of course many other styles that gained currency during the latter half of the period principally due to the increased ease of communications. The Moorish style, loosely based on Near Eastern originals, was one of the most popular, being derived mainly from architectural detail again rather that actual Arabic furniture. It was felt to be most suitable for rooms that either had a masculine or a totally foreign connotation, the smoking room being an example of the first and the bathroom, which was a comparatively recent innovation, of the second. The style attracted some interesting adherents, such as Lord Leighton, the President of the Royal Academy, and William de Morgan who provided panels of Persian-type tiles for interior decoration. Although the total effect of the rooms was almost unmistakably Arab, it was achieved with relatively few pieces of furniture, the most important being the overstuffed divan, which was used in conjunction with a plentiful supply of cushions, brightly coloured rugs or carpets, curtains and embroideries. It was a fashion that was to continue to hold some appeal even into the 20th century but it was not of such importance that it formed the basis of further development.

It was always the case that as new countries were opened to the west, they became the objects of intense curiosity. Thus, as trade with China increased during the 18th century, so chinoiserie became fashionable; when India was being conquered, there was some work in the 'Hindoo' style. During the 19th century, the only country which was virtually unknown in the west and which possessed an advanced civilization was Japan, which was not opened to

Above: *One of the most famous Victorian rooms is the Peacock Room, which was designed by Thomas Jeckyll and decorated by J.M. Whistler. Completed in 1877, it had a strongly Japanese appearance, although the original furniture was in fact based on the Neoclassical. At one time, the shelves around the walls held a collection of Japanese porcelain.*

trade until 1854. The effect on taste was by no means immediate for little Japanese art was available until the 1860s. An early and perhaps unlikely enthusiast was William Burges, who was buying Japanese prints as soon as 1862. He claimed to detect affinities between the art of Japan and his almost entirely fictionalized conception of 13th century Europe. A fellow architect, E.W. Godwin, who had previously worked in a conventional medieval manner, became obsessed with all things Japanese after buying some prints at a post-exhibition sale, possibly the same as that at which Burges acquired his. From that date, all of his work was heavily influenced by Japanese art, with an unfortunate effect for one of his clients, for whom he had designed a Gothic guildhall in 1861. This was then furnished in a very simple, plain, Japanese-influenced style which bore no relation at all to the original concept.

Godwin's first furniture designs date from 1867 and thereafter he produced a considerable quantity. Much was originally intended for his own use but was later manufactured commercially. Japanese art, to a greater extent than European, is dependent on the juxtaposition of solids and voids, and this was the avowed basis of Godwin's designs, using only Japanese leather paper or genuine Japanese carved wood panels as ornament. The most important showing of his work took place at the Paris Exhibition of 1878, and it was from that date that the Anglo-Japanese style really began to take a hold on public taste. The furniture was, on that occasion, decorated by James McNeill Whistler in shades of yellow, and included lightweight chairs, occasional tables, a sofa, a music case and the 'Butterfly Cabinet'. Possibly because the butterfly was a device used by Whistler as a signature on his paintings, it has been suggested that the cabinet was made for the artist's own use, but unfortunately there is no record of its eventual fate. Godwin favoured this approach of using just one colour in a decorative scheme, going so far as to design a room for Oscar Wilde in tones of white, a clear derivation from the Japanese.

Of all the Japanese rooms, the most famous is the Peacock Room, designed by Thomas Jeckyll and decorated by Whistler. Jeckyll's first commission in the Anglo-Japanese style was for the art collector Alexander Ionides' house at 1, Holland Park, where he created several rooms

Above: *This ornate papier mâché sofa, whose shape is derived from the Rococo, is black enamelled and decorated with gilding, flower paintings and inlays of mother-of-pearl. Although insubstantial in appearance, strength was given by the use of an armature of steel. The technique was, of course, a relatively cheap way of producing furniture of a good standard with a minimal use of craftsmen.*
Right: *A large number of tables were needed in the Victorian drawing room, especially for the taking of afternoon tea, and nests of tables, such as these of papier mâché were extremely popular. Most commonly found are those with floral decoration; these, with paintings of scenes and animals and a chess table, with the white squares formed of an inlay of mother-of-pearl, are more unusual.*

in the manner, together with most of the furniture. As a result of this, he was commissioned by F.R. Leyland in 1876 to redesign his dining room both for the display of his collection of porcelain and for Whistler's painting *Princesse du Pays de Porcelaine*. It was an outstandingly original room, with its inspiration taken both from English Tudor and Japanese sources. While the room itself survives, having been transported to the Freer Gallery in Washington, it is divorced of its original furniture, and can no longer be seen in all its former glory.

New materials – papier mâché, bentwood and cast iron

It should not be assumed that all furniture of the time was derived solely from retrospective or foreign sources. Some, particularly that which owes its existence to the technological advances of the age, have no directly apparent precursors. In particular, papier mâché was a material that came to its greatest heights during the period. Although the substance had been used commercially certainly since the middle of the 18th century, prior to the Victorian period its use was seldom for objects much larger

Above: *Papier mâché was used for making almost every type of furniture. Although often seen in catalogues of the period, complete bedroom suites such as this are rarely found, even though their basic construction was strong. While the ground colours of the painted surfaces are normally dark or black, the total effect is normally far from sombre, as the use of mother-of-pearl and the bright floral painting gave considerable brilliance.*
Right: *Side tables of papier mâché are seldom found, even though the material was perfectly adequate for the function. Decoration of such pieces as this table was normally with gilding and flower painting, although more popular today are objects painted with scenes.*

than tea trays. Papier mâché was used commercially for furniture making from the 1830s and everything from settees to pianos, tables and wardrobes was made from the material. Its advantage was that it required minimal skilled labour in construction once the moulds had been made, and was eminently suitable for the sinuous, fluid shapes so beloved of the Victorians, who even tried to make wood appear to have been moulded rather than carved. The finished pieces were japanned, most commonly black, often inlaid with mother-of-pearl, and then painted and gilded, sometimes with a scene, but more frequently with flowers.

Papier mâché, being a substance that is viscous in its early stages of manufacture, lends itself particularly well to shapes that are sculptural or exotic. Among the more exotic pieces shown at the Great Exhibition in papier mâché was a cot called the 'Victoria Regia' made by Jennens and Bettridge, who are probably the best known of the Victorian manufacturers, and designed by J. Bell who was a sculptor. The body consisted of a nautilus shell shape, japanned and painted with roses, poppies and nightshade, while the base was an S-scroll from which grew at unlikely angles the flowers of the eponymous Victoria Regia. From the head of the cot, a metal rod sprouted, curving over the body – again with a finial of the flower – from which the canopy was draped.

This was, of course, the ideal use for a material that was truly plastic. The lines flow smoothly and naturally in a manner that can only be successfully achieved by a moulded body. Had it been made of wood, it would have looked tortured; not that the manufacturers were above misusing papier mâché, for also shown was the 'Elizabethan Chair'. This was the normal misuse of the term, for the chair owed its design to a rather bizarre mixture of Jacobean and Gothic. One could, perhaps, imagine it constructed of wood but the only virtues that could be claimed for using papier mâché were lightness and exact repeatability. This did not deter the critics however, for it was noted that it was a 'favourable specimen of the success which may attend the manufacturer who fearlessly carries out his designs in any materials, however discouraging it may appear at the outset'. So much for the 'truth to materials' that had so tentatively reared its head during the days of the Biedermeier.

It has been said that the Victorians aimed at plasticity, even in woodworking. This was most notably achieved by Michael Thonet, who in 1842 moved from his native Boppard in Germany to Vienna, under the patronage of Prince Metternich, where initially he continued the experiments that he had begun some 12 years earlier with the lamination of veneers. Eventually he began working with the steaming of solid woods and by 1849 he had opened a factory in Vienna for the manufacture of bentwood furniture. The underlying theory, that when wood is saturated with steam it becomes pliable, had been known for many years and had been used with success in the application of veneers. What was new was the application of the process

to solid woods and the realization that light but extremely strong forms could be achieved. Thonet was able to attain effects that conventional woodworkers had only been able to appear to attain – continuous sweeping lines from the arms of chairs and over the backs without joints or interruption. It was also a method of construction that was ideally suited to mass production without involving a sacrifice of standards. Thonet's ability to use both long, elegant curves and relatively tight curls in his designs was to have an almost universal appeal, and by the end of the century his furniture could be seen in almost every country of the world, finding a ready acceptance by all classes of society. While the early catalogues issued by the firm show that some of their designs were rooted fairly loosely in conventional design, in their rocking chairs, which are perhaps the most famous of their products, the shapes owe almost nothing to the past but instead could easily belong to a much later period, having very strong affinities with Art Nouveau.

In total contrast to the lightness, both physical and actual, of Thonet's designs was the use of metal as a constructional material for furniture. Iron had occasionally been employed for garden furniture, but it was not until the 1840s that the practice of making cast iron furniture for indoor use became almost commonplace. Much of this was intended for places such as public houses, where it would have been subject to extremely heavy wear. Its durability, even under conditions as unsavoury as those which pertained in Victorian pubs, is attested to by the number of pieces that have survived the years unscathed. Indeed, a few years ago, when there was a vogue among decorators for the use of pub tables, the antique trade was able to buy and resell them at very low prices – an indication of how common they were. Probably the best known of the manufacturers was the Coalbrookdale ironworks, which produced, among other pieces, the attractive fern garden seat, which is frequently reproduced even today. As most of the iron furniture was unmarked, with the exception perhaps of the diamond shaped design registration symbol, attribution is normally impossible.

Left: *Michael Thonet of Vienna was the first to apply the technique of steam bending of wood to furniture making, which made the use of sinuous shapes, such as in these chairs, possible. Dating from about 1860, they are unusual in that there is additional decoration in the form of carving. Chairs of this type have been made almost continuously since 1851.*

Below: *One of Thonet's most forward looking designs was for his rocking chair. Made in the 1860s, it has little in common with design of previous periods or of his contemporaries, but rather foreshadows the lines of Art Nouveau, with its long sweeping curves and almost tendril-like twists. The method was well suited to mass production, as it required little use of skilled craftsmen.*

Not all of the cast iron furniture was intended for garden or public house use; the Victorians, ever eager to adapt their designs, even to the most unlikely functions, even succeeded in designing nursery furniture in the material. With hindsight, it could be argued that metal is ideally suited to a function where ease of sterilization is called for but this was unlikely to have been a major consideration at the time. While most were of the simple hanging basket type on a wrought iron base, at exhibition times the manufacturers' imagination was prone to run riot. For example, W. Winfield, a Birmingham manufacturer of metal bedsteads showed at the Great Exhibition the delightfully extravagant 'Angel Cot'. The body of the cot was boat-shaped with a scalloped edge, and from each of these scallops a panel with a raised perimeter curved obliquely to the keel and was decorated with painted flowers. The base was heavily Rococo, each of the legs

being formed of S-scrolls smothered with acanthus leaves, while the stretcher was a double S, joined centrally by a positive clump of greenery. The foot pillar was again an S, with leaves and foxgloves trailing everywhere, but it was on the head pillar that the real detail was applied. This was made of two C-scrolls, one on top of the other, joined by more acanthus leaves and foxgloves, the bells of which curl coyly in the curve of the upper C. Around the outer curve trailed the skirt of the robe of the angel which hovered over the cot with its wings slightly spread, holding in its outstretched arm a crown from which was draped the lace canopy. Whatever the rationalization of the design might have been, lightness would not have entered into it, for it appears that it would have needed a reinforced floor.

The same manufacturer, who was a specialist in the making of metal beds, showed other designs, ranging from the relatively simple four-posters with panels of ribbons and flowers on the head and foot boards to a rather more exotic neo-Renaissance example. This, in keeping with the norms of the style was extremely heavily decorated, each pillar having groups of figures prancing around its central section and surmounted by an anachronistically classical urn. The head and foot rails were mainly formed by trails of flowers and leaves but enlivened by the figure of a nude woman squatting rather uncomfortably at the top centre of the head board, while a nude man was encaged in a grille at the centre of the foot rail. Possibly because these reminded the spectator too forcibly of Adam and Eve and the origin of original sin, it aroused growls from the *Art Journal*, which complained that 'the figures on the head and foot rail are objectionable.'

Above: *Most typically, cast iron was used for the making of garden furniture, such as this seat which was shown at the Paris Exhibition of 1879. An advantage of the material was that it was possible to mass produce furniture, the design of which included a tremendous amount of closely packed detail. This example is of particular interest, as it has little in common with the more normal influences of the period, but in its use of linked concentric circles foreshadows the Art Deco styles.*
Right: *Cast iron furniture does not always give a visual impression of weightiness, and this washstand, whose design elements are mainly drawn from the Gothic, has a less substantial appearance than the material would perhaps be expected to imply. Although much cast iron furniture for interior use was made, few pieces have survived.*

Possibly the most important contribution of the period to the history of furniture is somewhat oblique. While in past ages there had been fashions for the assembling of curios and of paintings, it was only during the 19th century that the systematic collecting and therefore preservation of furniture began. Even cultivated people, such as the Ladies of Llangollen in the early years of the century, were happy vandals; they, for example collected early oak coffers, breaking them up and using the carved sections as wall panelling. Throughout Europe, however, during the 19th century there were individuals forming large and important collections, such as the Marquess of Hertford in England, several members of the various branches of the Rothschild family and, in her own way, the Empress Eugenie. Because of the impossibility of obtaining certain original pieces however, they were forced to have them made anew, giving birth to the reproduction industry.

This differs from our current understanding of the term, for frequently the manufacturers of the original pieces were still in existence, and were able to work to the original

designs and in the traditional manner. Because of this, even experts now have difficulties when faced with a piece made, say, in the 1870s by Gillows to conform to an 18th century original. The cost of some of these reproductions can even now seem startling. Lord Hertford, for instance, paid £3,600 to Pierre Dasson for a copy of the *bureau du roi*, which he placed with his collection of original 18th century pieces.

By the end of the period, taste had reverted, or perhaps caught up with the 18th century, as was inevitable, for during 60 years it ranged over many historical styles for its inspiration, and the masters of the 18th century were bound to come back into favour. Thus, many copies began to be made, some of good quality, but more frequently indifferent. It was, however to prove to be one of the most long lasting of the trends in furniture-making, for all countries still have thriving reproduction businesses. This, like most of the retrospective styles, can be seen as an expression by a middle class, conscious of its relative newness, attempting to show its faith in its ownership of objects that at least appeared to have withstood the test of time. Although the first tentative steps towards Art Nouveau had been made which were to bear fruit in the following period, little that was truly innovative appeared, for it is only those who are sure of their status and position that dare to be thought eccentric. It was not until the end of the century that the middle classes were sufficiently established to be sure that their roots would not be shaken.

The Arts and Crafts Movement and Art Nouveau

The design consciousness of a public that was becoming increasingly interested in interior decoration had received much of its inspiration from the writings of men such as William Morris and John Ruskin who had preached the creed of artistic integrity in the crafts. No longer was ornament simply considered as an incidental detail but was accorded its own importance and had to be completely integrated into the structure of the furniture for which it was intended. As fashionable interiors were regarded with the seriousness of works of art, designers and craftsmen were also culturally elevated and their work eagerly studied.

A particular feature of the period was the fact that so many craftsmen, architects and painters were prepared to write about their conception of good design and explain their personal philosophy in a way that even the less well educated could understand for most of the progressives shared the socialist ideals regarding the cultural education of the masses. Theorists in Europe such as Henry van de Velde extended Ruskin's ideas in statements that were to have a significant effect on the development of late 19th century German furniture such as 'The relationship between the structural and dynamographic ornamentation and the forms or the surfaces should appear so intimate that the ornamentation seems to have determined the form'. This preoccupation with the complete interrelation of ornament and form was the greatest and most lasting contribution of this period to the general development of European furniture.

A spate of advisory books and articles manifested the new preoccupation with personal surroundings and even magazines intended purely for young girls frequently included ideas on how to decorate a room in one of the fashionable styles, from Moorish to Japanese. In most of this popular writing there is a basic assumption that the artistic arrangement of books, hangings and furniture was essential both for emotional security and for social acceptance as a person of impeccable taste. At times, this self-conscious preoccupation became almost unhealthy, as in some of the advice liberally handed out by men such as Oscar Wilde who, with great aplomb but little originality, carried the torch of European aestheticism to the United States.

In general, however, the new design consciousness was helpful to the furniture trade, as it encouraged the more fashionable young people to abandon the traditional idiom and buy progressive, exotic or novelty pieces which they

Left: *This impressive dining room, created by Eugène Vallin (1856–1922), perfectly illustrates the manner in which designers of the period saw it necessary to lavish their attention on even the smallest items of furniture in order to create a completely integrated composition. Included in this setting are some of his greatest works such as the magnificent bronze and glass chandelier. The room was designed for the house of M. Masson between 1903–1905.*
Right: *A highly decorated cabinet with metal mounts designed by W.A.S. Benson and made by Morris and Company c.1899. This piece, of rosewood inlaid with purplewood, tulipwood and ebony is one of the more fanciful products of a group that usually relied on simplicity.*

were prepared to replace as styles changed. This new awareness of the transitory nature of design gave great impetus to the furniture industry and although the bulk of production was still traditional, the more adventurous spirit is obvious in contemporary advertisements and trade catalogues which, though aimed at the middle classes had some effect on poorer homes.

The activities of enthusiastic artistic socialists who had talked about furniture and good design to groups of workmen from the middle years of the century were also beginning to have some effect and a whole section of the public that had previously been concerned with basic survival was for the first time beginning to show an interest in the adornment of their small homes.

Middle-class women with sufficient help and little in the way of household duties were frequently bored and derived some entertainment from following some of the daring schemes suggested by the art periodicals. The boredom of cosseted middle-class life was enlivened by a Moorish smoking room or an Egyptian dining room and a touch of adventure was added by strange pieces created from parts of exotic animals such as the ubiquitous elephant foot umbrella stands.

New designs and ideas shown at an exhibition in France could be fully explained to the world within a few weeks in the art journals which were published in some number, over 100 for instance appearing for the first time in the 1890s. Increasing prosperity, better housing and education conditions were all combining to create a climate where furniture-makers at all levels could find a market for their wares: never before had there been a time in which so much rubbish was constructed alongside items upon which very sincere artistic talent was expended. The late 19th century is a period of such complete contrasts that the various styles which made many furniture emporiums resemble vast jumble sales, have to be separately examined in order to gain some understanding of how such great disharmony was created.

Above: *This interior with its painted panels and stained glass windows was commissioned by Sir Henry Cole in 1866. It was created by William Morris assisted by Philip Webb. The complex frieze was inspired by the ornament on the font of Norwich Cathedral.*
Right: *Philip Webb (1831–1915) was one of the leading designers in the William Morris group, being particularly remembered as the originator of the simple rush-seated 'Morris Chair'. This open shelved sideboard shows Webb in a more extravagant mood, creating a piece that was to provide a centre of interest. In drawing rooms of the period several cabinets were often needed for the display of the blue and white china collected so avidly by those of an artistic disposition.*

The Eastlake style

Although William Morris was one of the greatest influences on British taste, the writings and designs of Charles Locke Eastlake appear to have made the widest impact. As his books were eagerly read in several countries both by manufacturers and the public in general, his effect upon taste generally and American taste in particular was very considerable. His popular *Hints on Household Taste*, first appeared in 1868 but reached its maximum importance in the 1880s, augmented by several other books, the last of which appeared in 1895.

Eastlake's creed lay in a romantic simplicity of style such that a dining table for instance, should be assembled using the medieval joined construction method without glue or nails; it should be finished simply by oiling or polishing, as he disliked the contemporary love of heavy stains and thick, obscuring varnishes. The method of construction was, in itself, noble and should be perfectly obvious in the completed item. There should be no covering up of basic and necessary design with superficial applied ornament and the wood should be developed with delicacy, to reveal the fine natural grain and colour.

Eastlake's beliefs were similar in many respects to those of Ruskin but he appealed to a much wider readership that was thirsty for education. He believed implicitly that good taste and an awareness of design could be taught and preacher-like, he castigated the masses who were continuing to buy poorly made, retrospective furniture that exhibited their complete lack of education in design. He

Left: *The east has exerted its influence very strongly on the design of European furniture, but for relatively short periods, in the 18th, 19th and 20th centuries. This cabinet, designed by G. Viardot* c.*1880 and made in France, is typical of the adaptation of the period in which Oriental motifs are used to create an atmosphere rather than to provide a direct copy.*

Right: *While designers such as Eugene Vallin, inspired by high-flown artistic motivation, created sumptuous and expensive settings, the middle classes were supplied with basic yet co-ordinated interiors such as this bedroom offered by Heals in 1884. The basic elements are in complete accord with mass-produced furniture of the period but artistic touches are provided by the draped canopy of the bed and the hanging cupboard.*

chastised his readers with statements of great vehemence:

> The character, situation and extent of ornament should depend on the nature of the material employed, as well as on the use of the article itself. On the acceptance of these two leading principles – now universally recognized in the field of decorative art – must always depend the achievement of good design. To the partial and often direct violation of these principles, we may attribute the vulgarity and bad taste of most modern work.

Eastlake was particularly annoyed at the large output of reproduction furniture and warned his readers about the Wardour Street 'antique dealers', who sold pieces that were not only fakes but quite improbable.

> A fragment of Jacobean woodcarving or a single linen fold panel is frequently considered sufficient authority for the construction of a massive sideboard that bears no more relationship to the genuine work of the middle ages than the diaphanous paper of recent invention does to the stained glass of old cathedrals.

This bitter reference to stained glass was a reminder of that unfortunate late 19th century fashion for glueing transparent coloured papers to glass cupboard doors and fanlights – a type of sham decorative technique that particularly angered all the progressives.

Despite his apparent dislike of the general public who were 'giddy seekers after novelty' and his love of the medieval form he was also completely aware that design, to be viable, had to be united to new technology. He also emphasized the fact that the comforts and advances of the late 19th century could not be sacrificed to simplicity of style. Every piece of furniture should proclaim its purpose at first glance and his aim was to make even the meanest aware that a hall table or a chair constructed to resemble part of a church or a piece of sculpture, was ridiculous.

Strangely, no completely authenticated specimens of Eastlake's work remain, though some items can be identified through his drawings and a number made by the firm of Jackson & Graham are obviously to his design.

This 'Eastlake' furniture reveals a curious mixture of late Victorian simplicity and medieval detail and is characterized by his affection for antique-style iron locks and handles. Some of his designs, such as a hall stand with turned legs and carved side supports are almost completely in the Morris idiom but others, such as a new method of extending a dining table, show Eastlake as an inventive as well as an imitative worker. One of his sideboards, with massive metal hinges, arched central shelf and rows of subsidiary ledges underlines his debt to Morris, especially as he also carved mottoes and quotations along the frieze.

These designs, published in books that were readily available even to the individual small carpenter, were eagerly copied and adapted so that a whole group of late 19th century furniture found both in Britain and America is termed Eastlake style. Harriett Prescott Spofford, an American writer, commented in 1878 that New York upholsterers were already busy copying designs from his books and described the derived styles as 'of solid wood, unvarnished and usually without veneer, made in the simplest manner that conforms to the purpose of the article, with plain uprights and transverses, slightly chamfered at the corners.'

Eastlake's disapproval of the manufacture of fake anti-

ques was shared by many other progressives but it must be remembered that the mass of furniture sold from the huge shopping emporiums that were becoming such a feature of European and American towns were made in this despised retrospective idiom. Massive furniture with showy veneering, generous amounts of machined carving and an obvious air of ostentation fitted well into the 19th century concept of stability and respectability. Huge furniture proclaimed a man's status to the world and gave an air of permanence to his home. Allied to these social needs there was also a genuine interest in the collecting of antique furniture.

Neo-Renaissance styles in Europe

The manufacture of 'antique' furniture is thought to have begun on a significant scale after neo-Renaissance pieces were shown at an exhibition in France in 1839. This style, with its concentration on massive rectangular shapes based on 16th and 17th century furnishings, quickly spread to Italy and Germany where it remained highly popular until the early 20th century. This heavy furniture with more affinity to designs for stone rather than wood, its heavy carving and inlay and its dark staining, was for many years almost unsaleable in the antique trade but has now regained some popularity in Europe. It is interesting historically as it is so typical of the period when the growth of European nationalism fostered the development of what were considered traditional pieces even though many were an amalgam of north Italian, French, Flemish and German styles. The unification of Germany had resulted in a particularly idealistic type of nationalism and there was even a substantial manufacture of peasant type furniture mainly of Bavarian origin, a taste that has survived to the present in its more colourful forms.

The late 19th century German interior was characterized by an air of dark oppressiveness which was to continue for some years after Britain and France were moving towards lighter styles. Firms such as George Scholte of Stuttgart, Franz Michel of Vienna and Ziegler & Weber of Karlsruhe all produced pieces in this traditional manner which was believed to proclaim the stability of family life and encourage a man to take pride in his home and his possessions.

This massive, impressive style was also considered particularly suitable for public buildings (a parallel being the British use of Gothic in this context) and the Reichstag in Berlin, designed by Paul Wallot in 1884 was a complete exercise in the manner with the designs executed by Possenbacher of Munich. This interior was much copied but, as the century ended, there was, even in traditionalist Germany, some production of antique-type furniture in lighter woods and styles. In general, however, the mid-European taste remained firmly in favour of the heavy neo-Renaissance styles and it was not until the upheaval of a major war that the furniture industry changed significantly.

Left: *The concern for an interior co-ordinated not only in basic design but in style and atmosphere is realized in this scheme that was designed by W.W. Davidson. This simplified adaptation of the work of the more progressive was termed an 'Old English Scheme' by the* Decorative Arts Journal *in 1911. The sketch suggested ways in which less affluent people could adapt the greatest work more economically.*
Below left: *Ernest Gimson (1864–1919), was a founder member of the small firm of Kenton & Co. He was originally an architect and had an architect's appreciation of strong line. The simplicity of this oak dresser with simple gouged decoration and chamfers is typical of his affection for unadorned wood with its potential realized only by wax or polish.*

Although Gothic had enjoyed some popularity in late 18th- and 19th-century Britain it did not become the taste of the middle classes as neo-Renaissance did in Germany. In Britain, as in America, popular taste for traditional styles was for items made in the 18th century manner, some of which were almost perfect copies. Several firms had been in existence since the original, much admired, items were made and their cabinetmakers, working to old specifications, recreated such good copies that the general antique dealer is frequently misled into thinking he has a genuine early piece.

The progressive designers treated with contempt rooms fitted with reproduction Chippendale, Louis XVI, Hepplewhite or Sheraton furniture, though some were made to the very highest specifications such as Chippendale chinoiserie-style cabinets and fine bureau bookcases that sometimes surpass 18th century examples in finish. Those made for the cheaper market were frequently dreadful: shoddy veneering, poor basic construction and gold paint instead of ormolu fully deserved the castigation of men such as Morris and his Arts and Crafts followers.

Among some of the firms who manufactured pieces of the highest quality was Hindley & Wilkinson who claimed to make accurate copies of pieces in French museums, and Edwards and Roberts of Wardour Street, who also specialized in French styles and whose work still commands substantial prices in the salerooms.

Art Furniture

While the *avant-garde* furnished in the Morris style and the masses purchased traditional pieces, a completely different trend, inspired by the Aesthetic Movement of the 1870s was developing, which involved the use of lightweight furniture placed in rooms with pale carpets and pastel painted walls. The term 'art furniture' embraces a whole variety of styles but it is frequently characterized by dark or black painted wood, a generous use of turned detail on legs, chair backs and shelf supports and a love of line carving usually representing leaves or flowers, used on cupboard doors and chair rails. When these light chairs with spindly legs and rush seats were set amongst whatnots and sideboards of similar construction and augmented with Japanese pots, fringed shawls, tall vases holding a single flower or a group of carefully selected feathers, the typical 'art' interior, so admired by the journals of the period was created.

Art furniture had made its first appearance in the 1850s and was originally more retrospective than progressive though its followers were of some interest as evidence of how an awareness of design and the philosophy of fitness of purpose was gaining ground. Many of the pieces produced by the art furniture shops owed their inspiration to the basic designs of the William Morris group, in particular the use of slender, turned legs for chairs and small tables and the liking for dark stained or painted woods but while Morris kept strictly to his 'medieval' inspiration the Arts and Crafts furniture-makers pursued their own curious, whimsical idiom. Despite the difference of aim, the products of both were frequently mixed in fashionable interiors. The Cosy Corner (corner settles) and rush-seated chairs produced in large numbers by Morris, Marshall, Faulkner & Co. were to be found in many homes by the 1890s and, in fact, were well complemented by the Japanese vases, the colourful tiles, fabrics and art pot stands that contributed towards the desired effect.

The term 'art furniture' is generally believed to have been coined by Eastlake though he would have blanched at the excesses of the makers who mass-produced furniture in the style. Its charm however lay in its great adaptability as it could be used to embrace a large number of styles which

Above: *The firm of Liberty & Co., founded in 1875, was in the forefront of British advances in interior decoration and was particularly alive to the importance of interiors that showed a conscious attention to detail. In settings such as this the firm undertook all the decoration from cornices and pelmets to lampshades and fire irons.*

could all command respect with readers of the popular art magazines, if deified by the title 'artistic'. Variously, this type of furniture was produced in Queen Anne, Jacobean, Tudor, neo-Renaissance, Japanese and Moorish styles, the only unifying feature being the black or ebonized bay wood that was so popular, black walnut, basswood (American lime) and unpolished oak also being to the taste of the movement. A company producing art furniture was formed as early as 1867, though the nature of its work is not known, so that the taste is usually associated with the 1880s when it was most popular. Many of the cabinets, distinguished by slender, turned columns linking small niches, shelves or cupboards, rely heavily on traditional Japanese designs, and grass paper panels and oriental motifs are frequently incorporated.

Japan had begun to export furniture to Europe in the 1850s but the great popularity of this novelty style meant that the imports were insufficient to meet demand and by the 1880s there was also considerable European manufacture of pieces in the style. Sometimes genuine bamboo was specially imported for the furniture-makers who also used the widely available grass paper to create Anglo-Japanese pieces that are often almost indistinguishable from the genuine items. As the same manufacturers were also frequently creating art furniture, it was inevitable that the two should be combined as in many of the pieces produced by Collinson & Lock.

Another great influence on the form of art furniture was Bruce Talbert's *Gothic Forms Applied to Furniture* published in 1867, that showed a light, almost ethereal use of the usually rather heavy Gothic, combined with a lavish use of turned columns and fretted borders – a type of ornamentation that was to appear on many cheap parlour cabinets for the next 30 years.

The art furniture warehouses soon became a feature of every town and the vast sales they enjoyed is evidenced by the number of pieces in the characteristic spindly style that still appear in auction sales.

The best known exponent of the style was William Godwin (1833–86), much of whose work was characterized by a lavish use of Japanese leather paper. Godwin was a progressive designer and much of his furniture, created in the 1860s, was most appreciated and imitated a decade later. He designed not only furniture but wallcoverings and textiles for the houses he created, even going as far as to personally supervise the mixing of paints – a type of involvement that characterized the work of the best 18th-century architect designers. It was Godwin who in 1884 designed Oscar Wilde's famous aesthetic room in shades of white and he combined his talents with those of the artist Whistler, to create furniture in shades of yellow and pretentiously described as 'Harmony in Yellow and Gold'.

These three men were the leaders of the Aesthetic Movement, a purely British phenomenon that also greatly popularized furniture in the Japanese taste. Like many other artist craftsmen of the period Godwin established his own art furniture warehouse as he too believed in the mission of artists to educate the taste of the general public. The Aesthetic Movement with its well known and colourful leaders was of some lasting importance as it helped direct popular thought towards 'good taste' and set new standards in the use of light colours and appropriate ornament which the younger furniture buyers eagerly

welcomed as an escape from the oppressive, heavy interiors of their parents. The term 'aesthetic' was widely used in books on decoration, magazine and newspaper articles and by the popular lecturers who talked persuasively to groups at all levels of society.

The greatest popular influence was not the elegant lecturers and designers but a shopkeeper, Arthur Lasenby Liberty, who opened his first establishment in Regent Street in 1875 in an attempt to satisfy the demand of the more artistic for unusual pieces, mainly in the Japanese taste. Like so many of the art furniture enthusiasts Liberty combined his business acumen with a genuine desire to educate the public and was personally involved in exhibitions organized by the Arts and Crafts Society. His customers included Burne-Jones, Ruskin, Shaw, Godwin and the Rossettis who, together with their eager imitators bought oriental lacquered furniture and, within a few years, pieces of a more general kind.

The shop was soon imitated both in Britain and in other European towns and a complete decorative idiom was eventually termed 'Liberty style'. The Regent Street shop soon expanded and sold, in particular, furniture in the Moorish style, epitomized in the arrangement of Sir Frederick Leighton's house in Holland Park Road, London.

As well as pieces in Japanese taste, which for some years remained the most popular, the company also produced a wide assortment of 'Arab' sideboards, wardrobes and writing tables, all constructed in a heavily ornamented style. At first the Moorish pieces were imported from Cairo but soon the Furnishing and Decoration Studio was established and, after careful study of the originals, skilful British copies were mainly sold. Smoking rooms, fully decorated and furnished in this style could be ordered from Liberty and such schemes were soon a feature of most fashionable homes.

Arts and Crafts furniture, though popular with the more excitable progressive buyers had many critics, including some of the employees of Liberty himself, who considered the attempt to create Japanese and Arab furniture from pieces of floor matting and lengths of bamboo pathetic; to a great extent posterity has echoed this viewpoint, as examples of the style, except when created by a known designer, are today very lightly considered. In the development of European furniture, its contemporary importance lay in the use that was made by its exponents of the machines that were widely available. They, for the first time, used turning, fret cutting and carving in a new and imaginative manner that was a complete break from the imitative work of the traditional cabinetmakers. The Arts

Above left: *Public interest in ancient Egypt was fostered in the late 19th century by several exhibitions of objects from the tomb excavations. In 1884 Liberty & Co. offered a simple 'Thebes' stool that stood on three legs and was made of oak or mahogany, but at the same time this much finer piece was also offered under the same name. It is made of mahogany with leather seat and was designed by L.F. Wyburd.*

Left: *Despite its very basic general construction, this chest, sold by Ambrose Heal* c.1900, *is of great interest as it points the way to the extreme simplicity of furniture that was to be seen in the mid-20th century. Though this structure is fairly basic the designer has used wood creatively, so that the grain itself provided all the decoration.*

Above: *Sidney Barnsley (1865–1926) was a founder member of Kenton & Co. and was mainly concerned with architecture. His furniture was described by the* Cabinet Maker *as being of the 'Butter tub and carpenter's bench style' because of his affection for conscious and exposed structure. He was particularly fond of the squared effect seen on the base of this cabinet, designed in 1910.*

Above: *Ernest Gimson designed a number of extremely mannered cabinets, some of which included a lavish amount of bone inlay. This example, with marquetry of palm, ebony and orangewood was constructed by Kenton & Co. in 1891. The stand is made of ebony and the interior, fitted with twelve drawers, is finished in holly. The silver handles are hallmarked 1891.*

and Crafts movement also attracted buyers who had to some extent received some design education either from lectures or articles and were therefore creating furniture as a direct answer to their demand for more artistic interiors. Some pieces, such as a 'Combination Buffet and Cabinet', designed by Robert Edis, that appeared in *Healthy Furniture and Decoration*, published in 1884, pointed the way towards the fitted furniture that was to become such a feature of the 20th century.

Fashionable homes also became refreshingly lighter in atmosphere as a result of the taste and, though the matchstick-legged cabinets and chairs were later to be scorned they marked a very positive trend away from the massive sideboards and wardrobes, towards a much more functional approach. This charming, fresh lightness was reflected even in less fashionable homes by the 1890s and cream paintwork and much paler carpets and furnishing fabrics fitted in well with the odd pieces in Anglo-Japanese style that, by this time, graced even seaside boarding houses. Another decorative motif that owed its popularity to the Japanese influence was the sunflower whose head, carved, painted, printed or moulded appears on a whole range of furniture. This device was particularly liked by Bruce Talbert who designed furniture for several leading cabinetmakers of the period and created, in particular, small enamel panels that were used as insets for chair backs and cabinets.

The very strong reaction of the more adventurous designers against the pretentious neo-Renaissance type of furniture was almost inevitable, as popular style changed with ponderous slowness in the 19th century. In the 1880s the *Furniture Trade Catalogue* was still mainly advertising the cabriole-legged, button-backed chairs, chaise-longues and matching footstools normally associated with the 1850s and 60s. Beautifully inlaid loo tables, chiffoniers and writing desks, all which are now dated by antique dealers to the middle years of the century were, in fact still generally manufactured to satisfy popular taste. The heavy continental neo-Renaissance pieces that had gained some popularity in Britain and America had added to the atmosphere of extreme retrospection, so that the work of the Aesthetic and Arts and Crafts movements came as a complete contrast and prepared the way for the even greater changes that were to come.

Above: *Arthur Heygate Mackmurdo (1851–1942) was a founder member of the Century Guild and his early furniture is very much in the William Morris idiom. This satinwood cabinet was made by E. Goodall & Co. of Manchester, probably for Pownhall Hall, Manchester. The lower section has drawers under the ledge.*

The Century Guild

One of the most interesting but short-lived artistic brotherhoods was the Century Guild that was founded in 1882 and whose influence was to extend to both France and Germany. The work of the Guild, formed as a reaction against the shoddy appearance of mass-produced furniture, is of great interest as it reveals the progression of a group of designers away from the retrospection of the Morris group and towards the style often referred to as English Proto Art Nouveau. Many of the pieces made by the group have survived and in their construction we can see the way in which designers of great artistic integrity strove to coordinate the fashionable influences in their work though the result was frequently a compromise.

The Guild's great driving force was Arthur Heygate Mackmurdo (1851–1942), who, as a young man had come under the influence of Ruskin. While working in the office of the architect James Brook, Mackmurdo was made very aware of the difficulties a conscientious designer like his employer encountered in obtaining furnishings that would create a harmonious whole. Brook was unusual among architects of the period as he retained a completely personal control over every ornament and object that went into the decoration of his buildings and a great deal of time was spent simply in locating artists prepared to supply items exactly to his taste. Mackmurdo saw, as the solution to the problem, the concept of a group of craftsmen, with common aims and ideals, who could, collectively, supply such demands.

In Mackmurdo's unpublished memoirs he refers to the powerful forces of the period which led 'those workers to band together who dearly love their art, not as a means of living but as a fulfilment of life'. This was very much in the idealistic vein of the other art brotherhoods of the closing years of the century but the Century Guild was to produce from this idealism some of the finest and most important furniture of the period. Like the Morris group, the members favoured cabinets and settles decorated with painted or carved inscriptions but they arranged them in much lighter interiors. In true brotherhood style the members lived, studied and worked together and were expected to become reasonably competent in several crafts so that they could for instance, decorate a cabinet with panels of brass they had worked themselves or complement the structure of a chair with fabric they had personally designed.

Among the craftsmen associated with the group were Selwyn Image, Heywood Symner and Herbert Horne but their work was augmented by that of other workers whose products were approved of by the Guild such as William de Morgan and the Morris group of craftsmen. Great publicity was given to the furniture produced by the Guild at the fashionable trade exhibitions that had become such a feature of 19th-century business both in Europe and America. A complete music room was created by the members for the London Health Exhibition of 1884, a room that was most effectively dominated by the painted glass windows of Selwyn Image.

The Guild's most successful furniture designer was Mackmurdo who, in company with many other artist-craftsmen of the period, worked at his drawing board in a rustic peasant's smock. His furniture, at this early period, was something of a mixture of neo-Renaissance and aesthetic form and frequently in a single piece the opposing elements fall into real discord. His decorative work was almost invariably based on Owen Jones' theory of 1856 that was later to motivate those working in the pure Art Nouveau style: 'Beauty of form is produced by lines going out one from the other in gradual undulations – in surface all line should flow out of a parent stem.' Mackmurdo frequently set fretted panels created in this almost purely Art Nouveau manner into very stolid pieces of furniture that seem almost out of accord with the decoration. At other times his furniture is constructed in the medieval style, embellished with painted panels and inscriptions and obviously heavily influenced by William Morris.

One of Mackmurdo's most impressive pieces in this manner is a satinwood cabinet constructed by E. Goodall & Co. of Manchester in 1886. This massive cabinet has three cupboards in the upper section with the inscription 'Nor heed nor see what things they be, but of these create he can, forms more real than living man'. This piece is without the colourful painted panels that characterized so much work in the medieval idiom but performs its function as a piece of furniture more honestly as the designer relies on the use of the wood itself to create a rich effect.

Above: *Mackmurdo's work shows the development of English design away from the medievalism of William Morris towards Art Nouveau. This writing desk, made in 1886 and constructed of oak is one of his most important pieces as the design was of revolutionary simplicity. The brass knobs form the only additional decoration.*

In complete contrast and of much greater importance in the development of European furniture are Mackmurdo's simplified designs which fit perfectly into this pre-Art Nouveau period, when form was becoming much more severe and controlled. His oak writing desk without any form of decoration, designed in 1886, would appear to many people of today as a progressive item as the whole design of the piece was completely based upon the function of the object.

Equally interesting, as a foretaste of the development of French Art Nouveau, was a chair with a fretted back which he designed in 1882. The chairback depends completely on the Owen Jones theory of line, as a group of swirling leaves and stems swirl restlessly out from one point. Incorporated into this highly adventurous design were the initials 'CG', for the Century Guild. This symbol was placed unobtrusively on both furniture and decorative pieces designed by members and was intended in the nature of a secret sign

Above: *This chair, made in 1882, is one of the most photographed items of 19th century English furniture as it illustrates the early beginnings of European Art Nouveau. The chair is astonishingly progressive as the swirling fretted back forms a forecast of the later idiom. It was designed for the Century Guild by Mackmurdo and made by Collinson and Lock. There is painted decoration on the back and the letters 'CG' for Century Guild can be seen in the left hand corner.*

familiar only to the initiated. Although the back panel of Mackmurdo's chair is startlingly progressive for a designer in the early 1880s, the remainder of the design, in mahogany with tapered very traditional legs and substantial seat, is completely in the conventional manner of the period. This example of Mackmurdo's work can be seen at the William Morris Gallery, London and is of considerable importance in the development of European furniture as it is regarded as the first real three-dimensional evidence of the Art Nouveau taste.

Mackmurdo's belief that a designer's work depended very heavily on natural forms for inspiration was completely in accord with French thinking, especially that of the School of Nancy. In an essay on art education, written in 1882 he commented that the love of nature that had made the English landscape school so successful was a characteristic feature of the best in 19th-century design 'leading to the personal observation of facts and consequent independence of thought that was first to be discerned in the work of Wordsworth, Burns and Shelley and afterwards in the arts of the Pre-Raphaelites'.

Many of his textiles and designs for decorative panels were based on this belief and these sections were incorporated into the chairs, screens and settles that were designed by members of the Guild. Another ideal that lay behind much of Mackmurdo's work was his aim 'to make ornamental the things of familiar use'. Some of the furniture that he designed in strict adherence to this principle is, to modern eyes, strange, such as a jewel cabinet in mahogany with a removable front that he made for the Rowlands Club. The painted decoration is of a surprisingly low standard and represents straggling flowers that incorporate the words 'Here are jewels rich and rare'. When standing upside down, the viewer can also read 'But what gem with her compare'. Shortcomings such as this in basic design, were almost inevitable in the experimental period, especially among a group like the Guild whose motivation was based upon precepts such as those of Selwyn Image, to the effect that he could forgive almost any shortcomings as long as the design was sufficiently interesting.

A great deal of the work produced by the Century Guild is typical of that made by other, less idealistic, cabinet-makers though basic tables and cabinets were sometimes given the unmistakable Guild touch by some small decorative detail such as inlaid panels designed in particular by Selwyn Image. Other members applied a medieval style of ornament in copper, brass or textiles to furniture that was almost Morris in inspiration. Frequently the ornament and the structure of the piece are in discord, as in a clock face, probably designed by Herbert Horne, at the William Morris Gallery. The painted Roman numerals and signs of the zodiac compete with one another in complete disarray and threaten to obscure the clock's function.

In 1887 the Century Guild Inventions Exhibition was held in London and at this, a room almost in the Arts and Crafts manner with a high plate shelf for blue and white china and furniture in almost neo-Renaissance style, was created. Electric light stands, oil lamp bases and huge candlesticks were made of the brass and copper that always characterized the Guild interiors and were the work of Kellock Brown and George Esling.

The tremendous idealism that lay behind the formation of the brotherhood became overwhelming for many of the members and they gradually left to establish their own workshops. In 1889, Mackmurdo and Horne, the main organizers, set up their own company which promised to 'design complete interiors to the highest ideals and yet with reasonable economy', but even this concern was not to hold the idealists' interests for long and eventually all the leaders were to become more interested in education and writing rather than in furniture design. Like the Morris brotherhood, the Century Guild was virtually predestined for failure, as it aimed at making the common man appreciate beautiful and completely modern objects in his home. The individually designed furniture was however necessarily expensive and suited the pockets of the wealthy

Above: *The staining of wood in green was a particular feature of the work of the Morris group and is believed to have been first used by Holman Hunt. The carved decoration of this table made by Farago c.1900 is cleverly emphasized by this light finish that exposes the grain of the wood while providing a surface shade.*

artistic intellectuals who also enjoyed a flirtation with the socialism preached by the Guild.

Despite the fact that, in general, the population remained almost untouched by the influence of the artistic socialists, the effect of the Century Guild's work in furniture design extended well into the 20th century and also brought British designers more into accord with the European progressives. Other Arts and Crafts brotherhoods on the lines of the Guild were established in Europe and they produced adventurous, free designs for many items of furniture though in such small quantity that their commercial viability was doubtful.

In Britain, one of the more interesting was the Guild of Handicrafts that was established by Ashbee in the East End of London but moved to Chipping Camden in Gloucestershire in 1902. Most of the furniture was designed by Ashbee himself and made under the supervision of the chief cabinetmaker, J.W. Pyment. The basic shapes were usually strong and rectangular but decorated with veneers, panels and other devices often in a rather controlled Art Nouveau style. The brotherhood ideal again lay behind the establishment of the group and to further this aim one piece of furniture often involved the co-operation of several members. The most important commission obtained by the Guild of Handicrafts was for the Palace of the Grand Duke of Hesse at Darmstadt. This furniture, designed by Baillie Scott and made by members of the Guild, was of considerable importance in the mainstream European development of Art Nouveau.

Small, idealistic groups in some number attempted to follow in the Guild manner but most were very short-lived as the marketing of their work remained a considerable problem. Lewis F. Day (1845–1910) was a Master of the Art Workers Guild and, like most of his friends designed not only furniture but wallpapers and textiles. He avoided the problems of commercial viability by concentrating on the creation of large pieces of furniture made purely for display at the popular exhibitions. To most general collectors of antiques today he is remembered for his mantelpiece clocks with a sunflower motif. These clocks, with ceramic faces painted in bright blues and with the cases usually of ebonized wood, were manufactured by Howell & James.

Art Nouveau in France

With the gradual demise of the mainly British inspired Arts and Crafts movements, abounding in idealism but too often descending into historicism, the sphere of interest moved away from England and centred itself in France and Germany. The continental furniture-makers based their activity on a much more logical premise: as the development and supply of good pieces for the masses depended upon the use of machinery, artists should familiarize themselves with the new possibilities. As a result shoddy work, aimed at imitating traditional hand-made pieces, would supposedly disappear with artist designers in control of the machines. New designs, ideally suited for factory assembly, would herald a completely new idiom. This vivid concept was alive with the excitement of the period and much of the Art Nouveau furniture, with its restless, sinuous, twisting lines and tall, slender forms suggests this upward reaching search for a perfect artistic solution to the problem.

Although now generally grouped together under the title Art Nouveau, the movement developed quite separately in several countries and it is virtually impossible to trace exactly the progression of the style as so much of the activity happened simultaneously. Furniture-makers who were eager to be in the forefront of European fashion visited exhibitions in other countries and studied the many photographs of exhibits that were almost instantly available, not only for admiration but imitation. In Britain the followers of the Arts and Crafts movement had revealed many elements of the style in their work. In Germany the emphasis was much more upon functional forms allied to artistic designs which resulted in work that looked forward to the 20th century. In France the movement was largely organic in inspiration with great reliance on the whiplash tendril and other plant forms as design inspiration. In France the style was termed Art Nouveau, in Germany it was Jugendstil, in Austria Sezessionstil and in Italy, Il Stile Liberty.

The French Art Nouveau gained its title from the name of a shop owned by Siegfried Bing that opened in 1895. Here, alongside the Japanese furnishings that the fashionable artists of Paris loved, Bing exhibited the progressive work of his acquaintances and friends in the various media. The impression is frequently given that the new style suddenly appeared, for the first time, in the new shop but in fact, a revival of tendril-like decoration, based mainly on plant forms, had been much in evidence at the 1889 Exposition Universelle. As Bing was familiar with so many of the creators of work in the new style he felt it

Above right: *This desk c.1900, attributed to Hector Guimard, is made of rosewood and embellished with brass mounts. His work is cleverly stylized and in items such as this table there is no compromise, as is so often seen in British work.*

Right: *A somewhat stolid beech armchair designed by Otto Eckmann (1865–1902) for Siegfried Bing between 1891 and 1900. Eckmann was one of the leading Jugendstil artists of the Munich group and his finest work is in book illustration as he was originally a painter. This attention to surface decoration is seen clearly in this chair where the interest lies completely in the flat areas used to display his designs.*

Above: *In this interior we see a more cautious interpretation of Art Nouveau that contrasts well with the explosive power of furniture made for instance by Guimard. This suite is precise and almost formalized and exhibits little of the French flair. It was designed by Louis Bigaux who was mainly an architect but who became associated with Bing.*

necessary to promote the more interesting pieces. In his own words, the term Art Nouveau 'was simply the name of an establishment opened as a rallying point for youth keen to show their modern approach'.

His first exhibition showed work by all the leading exponents of the new style including Tiffany, Lalique, Eugène Gaillard, Georges de Feure and Henry van de Velde. The new approach to the design of interiors aroused great controversy and this very dissension among the fashionable helped promote the taste. Like the members of the Arts and Crafts movements, the artist designers believed that completely unified decorative schemes should be the main aim and it is fortunate that several complete interiors have survived, such as that by Eugène Vallin. The furniture in the new style was characterized by a lavish use of rich visual effects, such as generous inlays of mother of pearl or pewter and a lively appreciation of both the colours and the refractive possibilities of veneers of different woods.

French Art Nouveau was itself internally divided between the group who worked with and drew their inspiration from Bing in Paris and another group working around Gallé at Nancy. Possibly Bing's most important associate, especially with regard to the theory of Art Nouveau, was Henry van de Velde, who was among the

Above: *In this walnut and leather chair designed by Eugène Gaillard (1862–1939) there is again a very visible concentration on design that is linked to integral form. Despite its apparent simplicity the basic structure of this chair is one of great precision. This piece was designed for Bing's establishment, where Gaillard often showed work.*

best known of the early designers and acknowledged the influence of British designers such as Mackmurdo. Van de Velde designed four complete rooms for Bing's shop and must therefore have established much of the exhibition's atmosphere. The other Parisian workers were much more romantic in their design approach than van de Velde, though still heavily symbolist, in contrast to the exuberant natural freedom that inspired the Nancy workers.

Among Bing's associates were Georges Hoentschel, Eugène Colonna and Georges de Feure. Colonna and de Feure were particularly fond of gilt furniture that was made even more sumptuous in effect by the carefully designed silk upholstery which, despite a traditional basis, was very much in the new idiom. De Feure's work is very much in the French Empire mood but this distinguished draughtsman adapted the frames of chairs and sofas to the Art Nouveau style by arranging leaf and tendril shapes in unified rhythm to enclose and embrace the complete object. This aspect of his work is best seen in a gilded and upholstered sofa now housed at the Danske Kunstindustrimuseum, Copenhagen. The gilded wood that he favoured was frequently combined with upholstery in pale grey or soft pastel colours, while both painted and embroidered silk were sometimes combined in a single piece. At the Paris Exhibition of 1900 Bing's firm was represented by six completely decorated rooms of which the dressing room and boudoir were the work of de Feure.

In complete contrast to the light, almost traditional French style of de Feure is the very dark mahogany that was favoured by Hector Guimard and Rupert Carabin, the latter being the more visually exciting as he often twisted his furniture into and around the nude form, carving elongated shapes with the most perfectly mannered assurance. Guimard was the leading French architect in the new style which in fact was sometimes described as 'Style Guimard' or, derisively as 'Style Metro' because of the complex ironwork he designed for the entrances to the Paris underground system. The impressive metro ironwork exemplifies the complex designs that he favoured, frequently in combination with glass, though in general his furniture is more restrained and relies for its effect upon a unifying main cursive line that sometimes encloses a fundamentally asymmetrical construction.

Like Guimard, Georges Hoentschel was basically an architect though his most productive work was as a potter. Like most of the other Art Nouveau designers, he also created furniture on which he used almost sculptural ornament. His work is perhaps best remembered in the reconstruction at the Musée des Arts Decoratifs, Paris of a room he designed in 1900 to display the work of several designers. The room, in almost traditional French taste, was displayed at the Paris Exhibition and perfectly describes the strange mixture of conservatism and exploration that characterizes the work of the Bing group. Eugène Gaillard was also typical as he was fond of the cursive, Art Nouveau line to enclose, and make more interesting, furniture that was basically traditional. He worked mainly on furniture, though, like other idealists of the period, he was also a writer. It was possibly his great interest in jewellery design that encouraged his lavish use of bronze or brass detail on furniture.

The School of Nancy, which developed under the guidance and inspiration of Emile Gallé, was, in comparison with the Paris group, almost quicksilver in atmosphere. Many of the designs were based on the Japanese style of drawing that moved so easily into the organic linear inspiration of Art Nouveau. The Nancy craftsmen were also much more imaginative in their approach to structural problems and favoured romantic themes and a more adventurous use of materials. The best known of Gallé's followers include Eugène Vallin, Jacques Gruber and Louis Majorelle. The Nancy school first began to develop around its central figure in the early 1890s and in 1901

Left: *A particularly elegant carved ash marquetry work-table designed by Emile Gallé and bearing the inscription 'Travail est Joie' – 'Work is Pleasure'. This piece is important as it shows how so many French designers simply added panels in Art Nouveau style to fairly basic and conventional structures. Gallé designed very little furniture and his few pieces reflect a fusing of 18th century form with his advanced decorative ideas best seen in the glass he designed.*

Below left: *This massive sideboard was designed by Eugène Vallin in 1901. Vallin worked with the School of Nancy and concentrated on the integral design of new pieces rather than working in an adaptive genre similar to that of Gallé. Furniture by Vallin and Majorelle is often compared as both liked impressively proportioned objects with a perfectly controlled line.*

L'Ecole de Nancy, Alliance Provinciale des Industries d'Art was established, which aimed at a provincial renaissance of the arts and crafts. The furniture created by the Alliance is noticeable for the lavish use of marquetry, mainly based on themes from nature and often used on items made from the local fruitwoods.

Gallé himself produced a relatively small amount of furniture, as glass remained his main interest. When he worked in wood it was with such an artist's flair for decoration that he invariably completed the piece with his signature. Like Bing's followers, his furniture is basically French Empire in form and it is in the decorative detail that his progressive touch is seen, as in the writing desk with fruitwood marquetry that he made for the 1900 Exhibition. He decorated the lid with part of a poem by Baudelaire, a type of device of which he was particularly fond as he also created a very mannered work-table with the inscription 'Travail est Joie'. A great deal of the furniture produced by Gallé's followers was almost completely imitative and was decorated with the marquetry panels that were the speciality of Victor Prouve and Jacques Gruber.

One of the best known interiors created by the group's main furniture designers can be seen at the Musée de l'École de Nancy and is the work of Eugène Vallin. It was constructed around 1905 and its most impressive single piece is a large dresser, basically derived from a double arch from which other, secondary shapes develop and themselves enclose shelves, cupboards and drawers. Handles, decoration and door panels all carefully echo the basic shape which is given great presence by the designer's skill in developing the colour and refractive effect of the basic wood.

Louis Majorelle, undoubtedly the most important furniture designer of the group, worked mainly in mahogany. His background was in the fine arts as he had trained as a painter under Millet but was attracted by the revival of crafts as an art form. His early furniture was made in an almost traditional manner but around 1898 he began to produce pieces in a pure Art Nouveau manner and established his own studio, Maison Majorelle, which was in existence until the 1930s. The Bethnal Green Museum, London has an interesting cabinet that incorporates a Louis Majorelle plant with stylized roots forming the base and a central stem that separates to reveal a decorative scene. This cabinet, bought at the Paris exhibition, was concealed for several decades, as its design was thought to be both immoral and corrupting. It is now among the most important pieces of the collection.

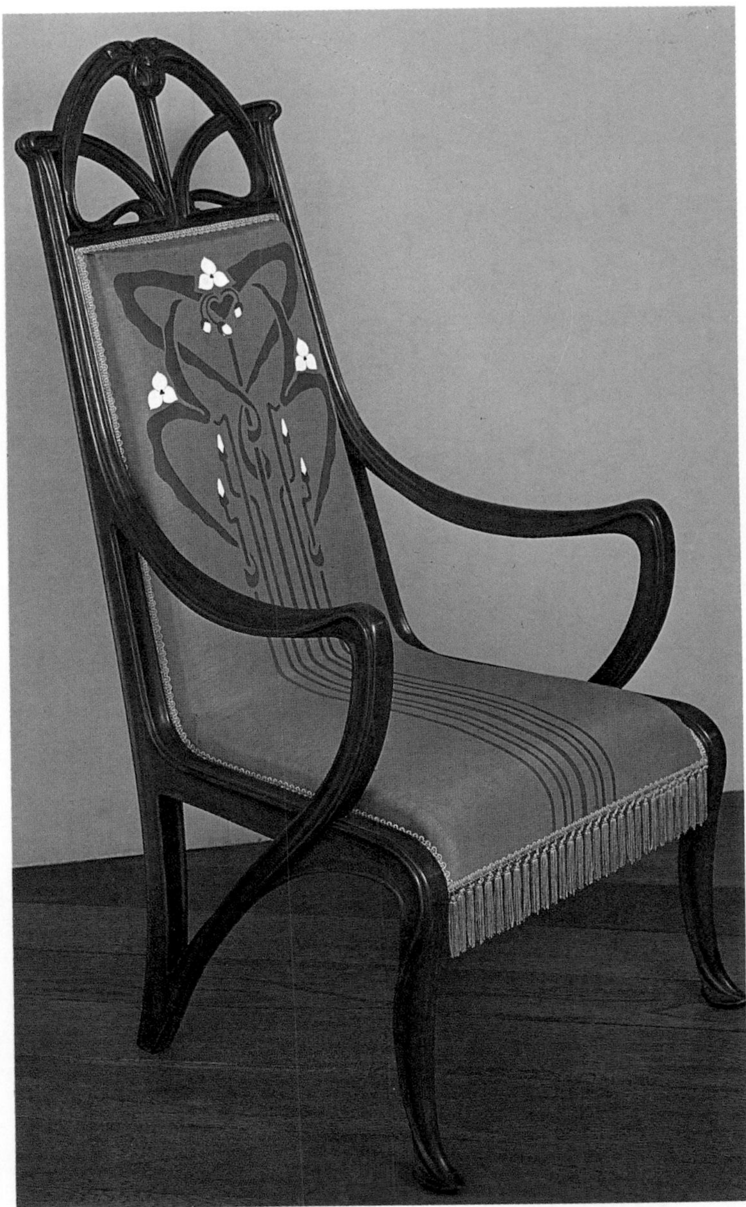

Above: *In this armchair that was first displayed at the Paris Exhibition of 1900 we see Majorelle in a restrained mood but working with an even greater assurance than in the more expensively produced cabinet (left) that was inlaid with several woods. In order to achieve a perfect composition it was necessary to print the upholstery fabric specially with a design that echoes the wooden construction.*

Left: *This cabinet, designed by Majorelle* c.*1900 is one of the most inventively created objects in the Art Nouveau style. It was also first shown at the 1900 Paris Exhibition. An aquatic plant grows upwards from the base to form a thick stem terminating in fronds that surround a lakeside scene.*

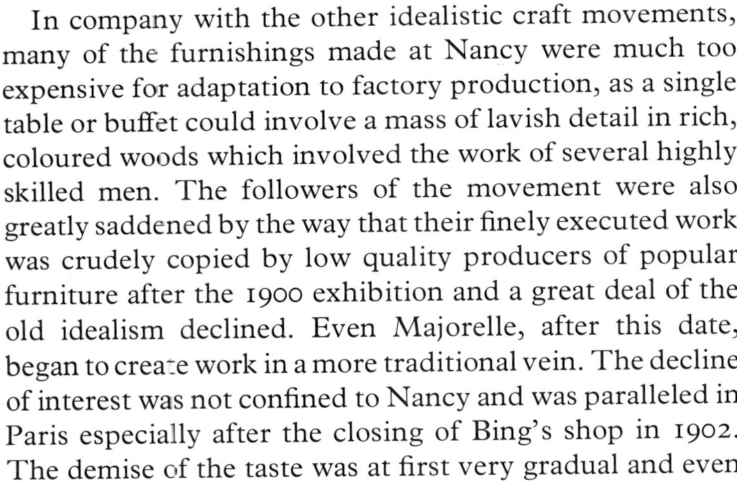

In company with the other idealistic craft movements, many of the furnishings made at Nancy were much too expensive for adaptation to factory production, as a single table or buffet could involve a mass of lavish detail in rich, coloured woods which involved the work of several highly skilled men. The followers of the movement were also greatly saddened by the way that their finely executed work was crudely copied by low quality producers of popular furniture after the 1900 exhibition and a great deal of the old idealism declined. Even Majorelle, after this date, began to create work in a more traditional vein. The decline of interest was not confined to Nancy and was paralleled in Paris especially after the closing of Bing's shop in 1902. The demise of the taste was at first very gradual and even after Gallé's death in 1904 some fine interiors were created.

The French furniture designers had found in Art Nouveau yet another solution to the problem that concerned all thinking artist craftsmen of the 19th century – how to create a unified interior from items obtained from several sources. The new style was completely adaptable and could be used as a distinguishing feature on almost any

Right: *This formal French interior, a reconstruction of a room shown at the 1900 Paris Exhibition, shows Majorelle in a heavier and almost historical mood. The complete setting was designed by Georges Hoentschel to exhibit the skill of Bing's followers. The furniture was the work of Majorelle. The painting,* L'Isle Heureuse, *is by Albert Besnard. The piano with its lively use of strongly patterned wood is among the most impressive items and is typical of the work of Majorelle who liked highly polished surfaces.*

item, from a small music stool or stand to large pieces of fitted furniture. Provided that harmonious colours were selected, an impressive coordinated effect could result from the products of several workshops and studios. This was the problem that the Arts and Crafts brotherhoods had attempted to solve with their communal working but it was effected much more logically by Art Nouveau. This latter movement was better suited to the age of mechanization, as it gave even the owners of small factories a design idiom within which they could work. The allure of French Art Nouveau also lies in its complete freshness, as the designers were no longer copying the traditional pieces but were forcing their own way into completely new areas of design. The awakened French interest in interior decoration was manifested by the publication in 1898 of *L'Art Decoratif*, a magazine that was of equal importance to *The Studio* that had appeared in England in 1893.

Belgium, the Netherlands and Italy

Inevitably, French Art Nouveau spread to the Low Countries where a few groups were already imitating the British craft brotherhoods. In 1884 a group known as 'Les Vingts' was formed in Brussels and the 1890s saw the establishment of several associations fostering a superior standard of artistic furniture. One of the finest interiors of Dutch origin to have survived complete is now at the Gemeente Museum at the Hague. It was created by Gerrit W. Dijsselhof (1866–1924), and is a perfect example of one man's complete immersion in a project. He designed not only the cabinets and a rather throne-like chair but also the flamingo hangings and lamps. In doing so he created a unified synthesis which was less flamboyantly progressive than the French style but illustrated how its basic linear form could be adapted with sobriety as well as passion. The room and furniture rely for effect on the play of light on the shapes and patterns of the wood and on the texture of the hangings which are the only additional decoration.

Above: *This almost austere room setting was designed by Gerrit W. Dijsselhof between 1890 and 1895, though some items are believed to have been added in 1896. The proportions of the woodwork and the decorative panels are perfectly controlled and the designer was responsible for each detail, including the flamingo hangings.*

One of the great theorists of the movement, Henry van de Velde (1863–1957), originally worked in Belgium and in 1894 published his *Le Deblaiement d'Art (Cleansing of Art)* which had considerable influence, not only on the Bing group with which he was associated but, later, on the development of German design. Van de Velde's work was given prominence as early as the opening of Bing's shop, for which he designed four of the rooms. His work was soon influenced by the British designer Mackintosh and like him, he favoured white-painted furniture. Another Dutch furniture maker who derived much of his inspiration from the British artist craftsmen was H.P. Berlage, though in general most of the pieces in the taste depended more on French inspiration and a considerable amount was purely imitative. Victor Horta (1861–1946) was one of the few really original producers of high quality work and was very much in sympathy with the leaders of the movement, being an architect who found it absolutely essential to design the furniture for use in his buildings, favouring his native Belgian woods.

A handful of Italian designers adapted their style to conform with the French, though few of them developed unmistakable characteristics: an exception is the furniture of Carlo Bugatti whose rather eccentric style was achieved by very individual basic shapes made opulent by decoration in coloured woods, ivory and vellum. The universal attempt on the part of the better architects to create complete unity in their interiors was supported in Italy by the furniture of Pietro Fenoglio. At the Turin Exhibition of 1902, the last important event where the new style took precedence, the new furniture came to the attention of the wealthier section of the public and consequently very fine pieces can be found in the museums and richer homes even though the taste never attained any real importance in a country that loved more historical pieces.

British styles

The British involvement, though very strong in the formative period when the work of the Century Guild was so important, never became commercially productive, though Ambrose Heal and Liberty made some cheaper work in the style. The output of two-dimensional designs, such as the drawings of Walter Crane or the textiles sold by Liberty, was substantial, but the British public, like that of Italy and the Netherlands, had little appreciation of furniture executed in the taste.

Above: *A renewed interest in objects and designs of historical content inspired many large pieces of furniture often less functional than historical in spirit, such as this painted pine armchair designed by G.E. Christensen of Norway* c.*1900. The decorative devices and basic structure rely heavily on early Norwegian art and result in a chair curiously out of line with progressive work in France and Germany.*
Left: *Carlo Bugatti (1855–1940) is one of the curious designers whose work does not fit readily into any school. He designed several chairs that exhibit a Middle Eastern influence and utilized the device of a metal disc suspended by cords that contained parchment panels. His work exhibits his fondness for copper and brass inlays and silk tassels.*

C.F.A. Voysey (1857–1941), one of the founder members of the Art Workers Guild, did much to promote progressive English furniture though in essence his designs have only slight affinity with the lively French style. Like so many of his contemporaries in the art movements, Voysey was basically an architect who sought, through the creation of furniture of the highest craftsmanship, to engender in his interiors the spirit of repose that he found so necessary. He lavished great care on the smallest details so that the finished effect was perfection but in a very controlled and English manner. One of the characteristics of his work is the complex detail that he put into huge ornamental hinges, frequently the most arresting feature.

Above: *M.H. Baillie Scott (1865–1945), in collaboration with Broadwoods, designed several pianos of the upright type known as 'Manxman pianos'. The cases were usually of oak, decorated with steel and brass fittings. This example has an unusually high degree of decoration. He also designed very stylized music cabinets.*
Left: *This oak writing desk, designed by C.F.A. Voysey between 1896 and 1900 is a typical example of the striving towards a simple construction enlivened with only minimal decoration, in this case the spectacular and specially designed brass hinges, a regular feature of Voysey's work. This desk was constructed by W.H. Tingey.*
Below: *This room shows a lavish use of exposed timbers, popular with the Arts and Crafts movement. It was designed by Baillie Scott in 1902 and formed the Music Room from a set of plans that were never executed. It was entered for a competition, Hauseines Kunstfreundes, in 1902. Rugs, piano, shutters and chair backs are all contrived to achieve a design much lighter in tone than the designs of William Morris.*

Voysey's furniture, mainly of oak, was most admired and was to have its greatest influence in America where its structural simplicity was liked. Though his furniture is frequently included in books and lectures on Art Nouveau he never considered himself part of the movement, feeling that the conditions that had made the French style possible were doubtful and that their manifestation was 'distinctly unhealthy and revolting'. His furniture is refreshingly simple in basic structure and, like that of Mackmurdo, points the way to 20th-century functionalism whereas the French style, though beautiful, was transitory.

Above: *The basic design of this chair was particularly adventurous as it used a main strut running from back to front leg. It was designed in 1899 by Richard Riemerschmid, one of the most adaptable of the Jugendstil artists who was originally highly influenced by the work of the Arts and Crafts movement. His interest in it was fairly short-lived as his style developed quickly and by 1902–3 he had abandoned the Jugendstil.*

Left: *This high-backed cream painted chair with a stencilled canvas back by C.R. Mackintosh was first shown at the 1902 Turin Exhibition. It is made of oak and has a rose motif on the back.*

Another contributor to the restrained British movement was M.H. Baillie Scott who worked mainly in oak and mahogany often inlaid with coloured woods, pewter, ivory or brass. His furniture was constructed by J.P. White of the Pygtle Works, Bedford. Baillie Scott created completely unified interiors which frequently exude an almost Pre-Raphaelite atmosphere with painted furniture of medieval inspiration that was echoed in the colourful painting of ceiling beams. His work, like that of Voysey, can be only loosely associated with the European, though his commission for the New Palace at Darmstadt established his continental reputation.

The development of European design was considerably affected by the work of a group of Scottish designers usually referred to as the Glasgow School led by Charles Rennie Mackintosh (1868–1928). The unforgettable interiors for the Willow Tea Rooms in Glasgow were created by Mackintosh who, like Voysey, was an architect. The tall, high-backed white-painted chairs that he supplied between 1897 and 1904 for the three tea rooms epitomize his

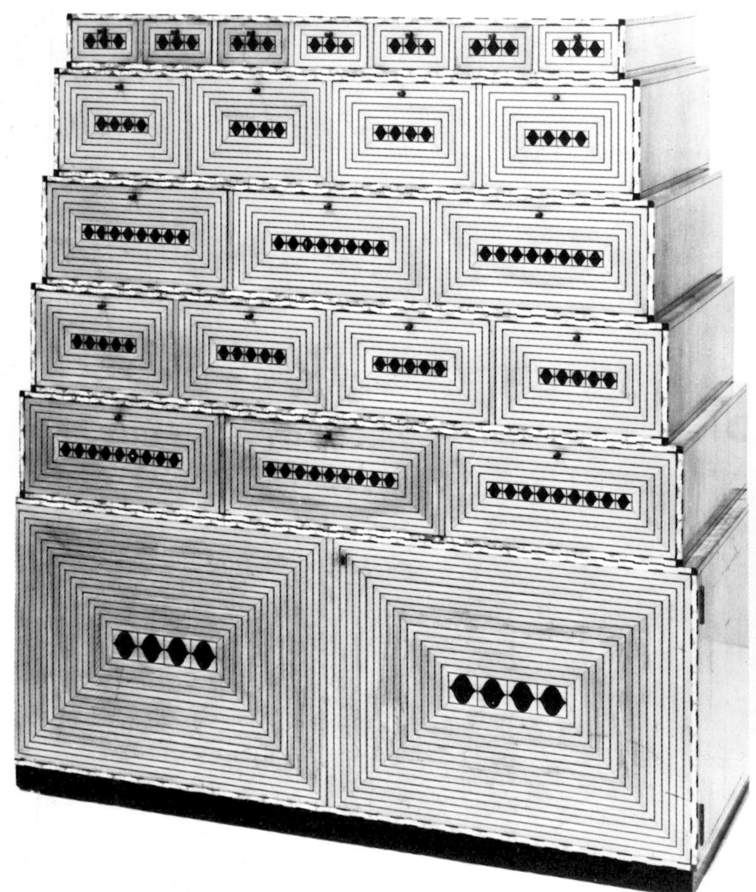

Above: *A pinewood cabinet veneered with boxwood, mother-of-pearl and ebony, designed by Joseph Hoffmann between 1910 and 1911. Hoffmann trained as a painter and was consequently most interested in the surface ornamentation of furniture. By 1898 he was making such extensive use of the square as a motif that he became known as 'Quadratl' Hoffmann – 'Square' Hoffmann.*

Above: *One of the most distinctive features of Hoffmann's work was the lavish use of mother-of-pearl inlay, seen to advantage in this cabinet, the second of this pair. The furniture he created was hand finished and obviously very expensive but was greatly respected even during his lifetime. This cabinet shows the use of his favourite device, a continuous repetition of a basic elemental shape.*

style for many people. That the chairs are elegant and perfectly suited to the interiors while being less than comfortable, is typical of the man. All secondary considerations were laid aside in the creation of a visually perfect interior and he seems to have regarded a piece of furniture almost as a sculptural addition to a work of art, seeing the space between objects nearly as important as the pieces themselves. He was particularly fond of inset panels of stained glass or enamel in the very tall cabinets and screens that characterize several of his interiors; he also frequently used inlaid mother-of-pearl. Most of his furniture is painted in soft colours and often decorated with a linear, stylized, tightly-furled rose that was his hallmark. His ability to work in a much more conventional and progressive manner is seen, for instance, in bedroom designs where he made use of fitted furniture, again often decorated with his rose.

Developments in Germany and Austria

Traditional, heavy furniture was so much a part of the German scene that the new attitudes were at first distrusted and retarded what was eventually to become a particularly vigorous movement towards functionalism. The Munich review *Jugent*, first published in 1896 was part of the general awakening and 'Jugendstil' became its popular title. Although a secondary group, incorporating the Artists Colony, worked in Darmstadt from 1899, Munich was to remain the centre of Jugendstil. The German furniture had much more in common with British rather than French Art Nouveau because it was the basic form rather than ornament that remained the foundation of virtually all the work produced. It was mainly from this Northern offshoot that the severe style which dominated fashionable European interiors in the 1920s developed, the Bauhaus later evolving from the Weimar School.

The German artists were greatly influenced by the British craft brotherhoods and a number of similar groups were established in the last few years of the century, frequently based on socialist ideals. The theoretical side of the German movement gained from the contribution of Van de Velde who worked mainly in Germany after 1899, though his furniture is often disappointing as it too often reveals how he was struggling to combine the basic Art Nouveau cursive shapes with the almost austere use of materials that he knew was essential.

The Munich designer August Endell created furniture that was even more functional and is of particular interest as several pieces were made of steel. In some of his furniture, often made of elm, there is fairly obvious French influence though the general tone is fairly severe with some relief given by his clever use of the grain of the wood. Similarly restrained but much more delicate work came from Hermann Obrist who combined a great interest in decorative embroidery with his furniture-making. Richard Riemerschmid who created the 'Room for an Art Lover' at the Paris Exhibition of 1900 also made some furniture in the manner. Few of the Munich designers concentrated long on Jugendstil, as for many it was simply a youthful experiment, though in fact its influence was to extend into the middle years of the 20th century.

Austrian designers began to work with a really adventurous spirit in the closing years of the century, and in 1897 the Wiener Secession, which, among its other activities, exhibited the work of designers such as Van de Velde, came into existence. In imitation of craft brotherhoods, the Wiener Werkstatte aimed at the manufacture of works of art for the people and was founded in 1903. This interest in the marketing as well as the creation of work is a characteristic of both the German and Austrian movements and is also evidenced by a more economical range of furniture that was made by the Deutsche Werkstatte, Dresden. The leading force behind the Secession was Josef Hoffmann, nicknamed 'Square' Hoffman for his love of black and white squares as decoration. This effect was often achieved by ebony and mother-of-pearl inlays.

The Werkstatte's most famous work was the Palais Stoclet in Brussels where geometric design and lavish ornamentation were combined in an interior for which every item from china to basic fittings was specifically created. This complete unity of concept is exemplified in the work of Koloman Moser, whose furniture is rather stark but decorated with veneers and inlays. The last important designer of the Secession was Joseph Olbrich who designed the houses for the artists' colony at Darmstadt and again favoured geometric shapes but whereas Hoffman liked the square, Olbrich was to concentrate on the circle in his almost unadorned Austrian style. The development of the Austrian school is interesting as it reflects the mood of designers in several countries at the end of the century, when much harsher colours and geometric shapes were fashionable and the excesses of Art Nouveau were already derided.

The general public reacted against Art Nouveau furniture with a return to traditional styles rather than by a movement towards cubism and the pre-First World War period is therefore something of a watershed in the development of interiors. Antique pieces once again became highly popular and to meet this demand the makers of reproductions created vast quantities. The Japanese style that had been so popular in the 1870s and 80s also enjoyed a short revival and the Queen Anne, Chippendale and Hepplewhite suites that had never completely gone out of favour with the middle classes were, for a while, bought even by the fashionable.

In these years Liberty style furniture and textiles became famous all over Europe and the firm obtained many contracts to furnish complete houses in their idiosyncratic manner, which they advertised as 'English Domestic'. This baronial style was liked at this time in countries as far apart as South Africa and India and the linenfold panelling and massive carved historical furniture still found in colonial homes shows the unmistakable Liberty touch. Many interiors of this period are characterized by the use of cane and wicker furniture often in combination with cabinets and chairs in pale painted wood.

Above: *This adventurously styled cabinet by Koloman Moser shows the development of progressive design away from the light atmosphere of French styles towards a use of bolder, firmly controlled shapes. This piece, designed in 1907, is veneered in lemonwood and is part of a suite made by Niedermoser of Vienna. His fascination with surface ornamentation is manifested in this instance by the decorative panels of the upper doors.*

Mediocrity ended for the fashionable with the production of the ballet *Scheherazade* whose brilliantly coloured settings engendered a passion for strong effects. Things Persian suddenly became the rage and conventional furniture was sometimes abandoned for large Persian cushions. The designer Paul Poiret was largely instrumental in the revival of painted furniture and in fact produced a range in 1910 known as Martine furniture and designed by Pierre Fauconnet. In general the French furniture-makers developed a form reminiscent of the simple style of the 1820s, whose oval shape predicted the Art Deco style that developed after the First World War.

The important furniture that was made at this time of transition towards factory production on a huge scale was that created by the artist craftsmen, and it is these attributable pieces that now command very high prices as they mark the most positive influences in the development of design throughout this period.

American Furniture

By 1620 European settlement of the Eastern seaboard of America was under way and by the end of the century there were settlements all along the coast from Maine to South Carolina. Land was under the control of powerful trading companies who took their authority direct from the throne, such as the London Company in New England or the Dutch West India Company around the Hudson River and Manhattan Island. The first settlers, for example the English who arrived in Plymouth, Massachusetts, via Holland to escape religious persecution, came with few possessions and their first energies were devoted to material survival and defence. It was only with the later arrivals that any attempt at organization in townships could properly be made.

Between 1629 and 1640, 26,000 Puritans emigrated from England during Charles I's attempts to rule without Parliament. They settled in New England and brought with them the beginnings of prosperity. Similarly, the first settlers on the Hudson River were adventurers who exploited the rich fur market and it was not until the Dutch West India Company began to encourage land settlement in 1639 that more prosperous families set out from Europe. In the south, the first permanent English settlement was at Jamestown in 1607 and there, in the rich tobacco lands of Virginia, settlements quickly prospered, keeping in closer contact with their motherlands through trade than the northern colonies usually did. Under Cromwell in England, the Cavalier supporters emigrated in great numbers to Virginia.

By 1650, then, life in the colonies had begun to take on a security and permanence that the first settlers had lacked. The different classes who had originally emigrated once more found their levels in a new society and were able to move into new areas; Pennsylvania was colonized in 1682. But although towns were growing and better houses being built, furniture was still a valuable commodity. To begin with, the only furniture would have been absolute necessities, such as beds, tables and chests, which were brought from England, and often there were items more vital than furniture when it came to filling space in the ships from Europe. Even where skilled craftsmen were present in a colony, they might lack the necessary tools to achieve the sophisticated finish found in their homelands. Although there was a growing demand for furniture produced in America, few customers would have felt the need, or indeed had sufficient prosperity, to commission elaborate or luxurious pieces.

Left: *Early Federal period breakfront bookcase. The top and bottom are in separate pieces, both decorated with contrasting veneers and fine inlaid lines. The shape of the base is a softer version of the earlier bombé line and the top is adorned with a carved swag, also derived from the earlier finials found on highboys. The piece is typical of the English inspired styles of Charleston, South Carolina.*

American colonization began during the reign of James I when England was not a great manufacturing country, and the English at this time derived many of their furniture styles from the Dutch who were then trading with Spain, Portugal, Italy and the East Indies. The continued use of the great Dutch built-in bed in the New York area is proof of the strength of their influence on furniture in the New World. This Anglo-Flemish style concerned itself with massive oak pieces, rectangular in form and relying on surface carving often based on Renaissance marble motifs, for decoration. In houses where oak panelling prevailed, with the fireplace as the centre of decoration, there was little furniture, perhaps only a trestle table, chests and stools; even chairs were rare. Furniture-makers were themselves joiners or carpenters, not cabinetmakers, and would have been as concerned with the making of doors or window frames as with individual pieces of furniture.

The 17th century

Furniture-making began in America around 1640. The construction of this early furniture was around a basic rectangular frame inset with panels, the frame being joined with mortise and tenon and secured with square carved pins driven into rounded holes. Oak was used for the frame and pine, because of its width, was generally employed for the panels, whether sides, lids or seats. Using this model, the similarity of construction of the trestle table, the chest and the 'great' or 'Wainscot' chair is clear, as is the origin of the concept in architectural principles. Where most houses used simple joint stools or benches for seating, the chair became a symbol of authority, adequately demonstrated by the monumental dimensions of the Wainscot chair, with its high back, usually ornately carved, solid oak seat and heavy frame and arms. The name Wainscot is derived from a Dutch word, *wagonschot*, meaning a fine grade of oak planking or board.

Many Wainscot chairs of American origin are known, some large but plain, with little or no carving. One maker who worked in New England was English born and trained Thomas Dennis, who was working in Portsmouth in the

Above: *An early New England Brewster chair, 1650–1690, made of ash, maple and pine. The model for the Brewster chair was supposedly brought to America on the* Mayflower *and it was named after one of the early settlers in Plymouth, William Brewster. It is one of the many variations of turned or stickback chairs made at the time.*

1660s and in Ipswich, Massachusetts from 1668 until his death in 1706. He was a joiner by trade and his chairs are elaborately carved, as are oak chests attributed to him, some of which are painted. Plainer Wainscot chairs dating from 1640–80 are known in Saybrook, Connecticut. Like the trestle tables dating from this time, the legs are turned often with the large bulb turnings favoured by the Anglo-Flemish style. Less treasured pieces of furniture in the same manner, built to protect from draughts, are oak settles which are plainly panelled without carving.

The earliest native-produced type of furniture, however, is the chest. They were made entirely of oak in rectangular form, the legs being extensions of the stiles (the sides of the frame) generally with three front panels. The decorative motifs were at first architectural, with the semblance of arches or square or lozenge geometric patterns. The carving is in low relief, unlike European prototypes, the edges of the frame around the panels are chamfered and the edges of the lid finished with thumbnail moulding. Oak panels quickly gave way to pine and in Pennsylvania the native walnut or tulip wood was used instead of oak for the frame itself. There are as many types of chest as there were makers, but certain common decorative elements are found, such as the architectural or geometric designs or carvings with conventionalized rosettes, palm leaves, scrolls, fleur-de-lys and most commonly the tulip and the sunflower motif.

Various groups of chests which employed distinctive motifs are known. These include the Hadley chests which date from about 1690. They were made in Hadley, Massachusetts, and were decorated with a pattern of crudely-carved palm leaves, tulips and scrolls all over the front. The Hadley chests also had one or two drawers fitted beneath the panels, hung on runners fitting into grooves on the side frames. Another group of chests which incorporate the sunflower motif comes from Hartford County, Connecticut, and this motif is also known as the 'Connecticut' pattern.

Gradually the chest acquired sophistication; the square leg gave way to a ball foot, drawers were added and the carving became richer and more varied, the all-over flower patterns being replaced with firm geometric designs of crosses, diamonds, octagons, wheels within diamonds and a variety of square-based motifs. The bottom rail was often scrolled, or a carved skirt was added. The most obvious later development is the addition of applied spindles, usually in tulip wood but sometimes maple or birch; these half-turned spindles were always painted black. This applied decoration took different forms, from long shapes known as banisters or balusters, to round bosses, mounted slant-wise, known as turtle-back bosses.

Most of the early furniture was painted or stained, using either natural stains found locally or pigments for paint imported from England. By 1680 there were specialized workmen, such as Thomas Child, a painter-stainer, who came to Boston from England about 1688. He would not only refine his oils, grind his colours and make his own brushes, but would also be employed to stain woodwork and furniture, to paint houses and to draw his own figures and landscapes. The remnants of his stone trough and ball, used for grinding pigments, are still in Boston today. The first colours used were black, blue and red – two reds known as 'Indian red' and 'Spanish brown' were imported from the East Indies and Spain – followed by yellow and later green. As the geometric designs replaced floral patterns, the colours were used to highlight the relief and by 1700 painting had in many areas completely replaced carving. In both the Hadley area and in Connecticut polychrome painting on white tulip wood chests and other items were common. Painted furniture continued, especially in rural areas, as a distinctively American feature, although obviously the style of painting changed with other fashions; around 1820 painted landscapes, figures or swags of flowers were popular on mirror frames and clock

Above: *An ash Carver chair from New England, 1660–1680. The Carver chair, also named after one of the early settlers, John Carver, the first governor of Plymouth Colony, is a simpler version of the Brewster chair. The vertical supports, spindles and finials all show the variety that can be obtained by the art of turning and several American innovations can be traced to this type of chair.*

cases even in sophisticated homes.

Between 1640 and the turn of the century craftsmen had begun to establish themselves and European prototypes were swiftly developed and changed. Chairmaking was considered a separate craft from the production of other furniture, although in the early days, as has been said, there was little opportunity for complete specialization. The chairmaker was still a joiner by trade, but gradually the turner's art came to the fore. There are two types of American turned chair, both named after chairs supposedly brought over on the *Mayflower*, one the Brewster chair, named after William Brewster the Elder of Plymouth (1567–1644), and the other the Carver chair, named after John Carver (*d.*1621), the first governor of Plymouth Colony.

The Brewster chair tends to look fussy and cluttered with its mass of turned spindles running vertically to the cross-stretchers on the back, arms and runners. The seat was usually rushed. The Carver chair, in comparison, is simpler, with fewer connecting spindles and the turned frame itself is generally thinner. Both chairs are entirely perpendicular, the front legs rising to become the arm supports, finished with either a small urn shape or ball. In some cases, examples of these chairs show a distinctly American innovation in the shape of the turning, known as 'sausage' turning – a more elongated version of the bobbin turn. The turner usually preferred the softer grained maple to oak, and ash or hickory were also used, sometimes with juniper spindles.

The same woods were used in a slightly later type of chair, the slat back, which was common between 1670 and 1700. In construction the slat back chair is like the Carver or Brewster, but taller and without the connecting spindles. The back is formed from curved, winged slats fitted into the side supports, the curve taking the strain. The vertical supports have heavy ring turnings and the backs are topped with finials. The handrests often take the form of another solely American feature – wide flat 'mushroom' shapes – and the chairs have ball feet. The slat back chair is found throughout the East coast – although the mushroom handrests denote a New England origin – and continued in use, becoming thinner and more elegant, until the beginning of the 18th century.

A further variation of this construction is the banister chair, made between 1690 and 1720. Here the back is formed by vertical struts known as banisters or balusters which were half turned. This was done by glueing two blocks of wood together, turning both on a lathe and then separating them again so that they each had a flat edge. The banisters were placed, flat side toward the seat, between a rush seat and a crest rail which was often elaborately carved. Some also have ram's horn terminals on the arms. Around 1740 this technique was still in use, with a Spanish foot and narrow, grooved slats.

The last type of chair in use at this time was the Cromwell chair which was a heavy square-framed construction, usually in maple but also in oak or red oak, with no arms and turned bobbin front stretchers. The seats and backs were covered with leather or Turkey work. A variety of turnings is found on these chairs, such as the spiral 'barley twist' known as 'Crosswicks' from the area near Philadelphia where this turning, with a combination of turned and block members, is found. Crosswicks and the neighbouring Burlington were founded before Philadelphia itself and at least two English trained carpenters, Robert Rhea, of Freehold, New Jersey, and Matthew Robinson, were known to have worked in the vicinity.

The early 18th century

By the beginning of the 18th century it is possible not only to have a more complete picture of the kind of environment in which the first colonists lived but also of

their activities. By 1690 Boston had a population of 7,000 and was a thriving port. In the northern towns of Boston, New York, Newport and Philadelphia trade was more important than agriculture and the manufactures of the town defined its prosperity. The northern towns traded with the south, exchanging their goods for rum, molasses, sugar and slaves, while Virginia grew rich from its tobacco plantations and South Carolina from its rice. The main New England industries were fishing, fur trapping and lumbering and Boston traders began to ship furniture south, as the joiners and carvers who worked on the ships made furniture as well; local merchants had a new purchasing power and most craftsmen worked on a basis of exchange and barter. In Boston, certainly, this meant that the market was conservative and it was difficult for an unknown newcomer to gain trust and credit.

Between 1725 and 1760 there were approximately 127 joiners and cabinetmakers working in Boston, as well as 38 chairmakers, 23 upholsterers, 16 carvers, 11 turners and 9 japanners; proportionately more craftsmen than any other city at that time. A new arrival, however, such as the English trained cabinetmaker Charles Warham who ar-

Above: *Room from the Samuel Wentworth House, Portsmouth, New Hampshire. It was built in 1671, but the panelling dates from c.1710. The furniture is typical of the turn of the century – the circular gate-leg table, Dutch-inspired William and Mary chair (against the wall), six-legged high-chest and upholstered high-backed armchairs on wooden frames with carved feet – and shows the beginnings of sophisticated details in the turning and carving.*

Right: *Chest of drawers made for John and Margaret Staniford in 1678 and probably made by Thomas Dennis of Massachusetts for their first home. The chest is brightly painted and decorated with black half-turned spindles and Elizabethan strap-work carving.*

rived in Boston about 1723, could not break into the market. After numerous court cases for non-payment of bills, he sold up and went to Charleston in South Carolina, where, on his death in 1779, he left a substantial estate to his heirs. Boston-born Nathaniel Holmes, however, who conveniently married the daughter of a lumber dealer, ran a large and successful cabinetmaker's workshop making both functional and elaborate inlaid pieces, but eventually retired from furniture-making in favour of full-time trade by sea whereby he amassed a fortune.

Boston's two wealthiest upholsterers were Thomas Fitch (*b.*1669) and Samuel Grant (*b.*1705). Their experience in mixing trades shows how trade determined both sophistication in American homes and the development of an independent American style. Fitch had friends in England to whom he frequently wrote asking for new designs, samples and stuffs for upholstery and he also had many goods he could exchange, space for space, in a trading vessel, such as furs, whalebone, sugar, tar and lumber. His one-time apprentice, Grant, however, had only beeswax which he could exchange for European materials, and so the chairs which he produced, mainly in the 1730s, were covered only with leather or local coarse worsteds such as cheyney or harrateen.

In trading with the southern colonies, Boston styles became the most fashionable and sought-after. Philadelphia imported furniture from Boston and by 1725 the local craftsmen were copying Boston styles. Plunkett Fleeson (*b.*1712), Philadelphia's leading upholsterer, stocked 'Boston' chairs which were made in his shop, not imported, and soon afterwards was advertising 'compass bottom' chairs – a Philadelphia version of the Boston chair – at least one of which was brought by Anthony Palmer, the acting governor of the province. Other craftsmen, such as the joiner Thomas Stapleton (*d.*1739) trained in Boston to acquire the fashionable techniques but returned to Philadelphia to work. There was also greater diversity among the specializations of the craftsmen, as can be seen from the list of furniture-makers working in Boston, and as veneering or japanning became popular, men such as Charles Plumley (*d.*1708) who became known for his paper-thin veneered surfaces, would be patronized by other shops. Plunkett Fleeson traded 'At the Sign of the Easy Chair' and was probably personally responsible for promoting the easy chair form in Philadelphia.

The growth of a new landowning and merchant class also added to the local demand for new forms and new styles in furniture to replace the once basic essentials of the preceding century of settlement. William Penn who, with his daughter Letitia, patronized the ship's joiner Edward

Above: *An early high-chest in black walnut, yellow pine and cedar, made in Philadelphia c.1725. The stand is enhanced by the use of the small cyma curve skirt typical of Queen Anne furniture, with trumpet-turned legs and shaped connecting bottom rail, while the top remains simple and unadorned. It marks the transition from early methods of construction to the more complex furniture of the mid-18th century.* **Right:** *Early 18th century Queen Anne drop-leaf table with cabriole leg and claw and ball feet. This is an example of the important innovations in form taking place as the colonies became settled and prosperous. The exuberance of the knee carving demonstrates the varieties practised by the American furniture makers in their adaptation of English forms.*

Evans (1679–1754), built his house Pennsbury, near Philadelphia. In 1685 he wrote:

> Do not much hiring of carpenters and joiners. That I sent will do . . . There comes also a Dutchman, a joiner and carpenter that is to work one hundred and fifty days . . . Let him wainscot and make tables and stands; But chiefly keep on the out houses because we shall bring much furniture . . . Get some wooden chairs of walnut with long backs and two or three eating tables for twelve, eight and five persons with falling leaves to them. (Quoted in *Early American Furniture* by Charles O. Cornelius, New York 1926 *p*.89).

Walnut was the most frequently used wood in Philadelphia. It began to replace maple, which was extensively used in the north and which, as a hard wood, was difficult to work but could take a high shine with a good grain, such as the curled or 'tiger stripe' grain. The chairs with high backs ordered by Penn could well have been the new William and Mary style chairs with long backs, no arms and cane seats. Originally a Dutch innovation, the William and Mary chair had a long narrow back, usually caned, or, as in the spoon back or Boston chair, upholstered in leather. It would generally carry elaborate carving with Flemish scrolls.

The Boston chair had a 'square' form of cabriole leg, with sharp-edged knees and a squared 'paintbrush' or Spanish foot. The Spanish foot had arrived via England from Portugal and was more easily carved than a scrolled form from the square profile of the original block. The walnut 'compass chairs' which were sold in sets in Philadelphia were a more exuberantly curved version with a rounded seat. The versatile day bed which also developed at this time varied from following the simple slat or banister back chair to showing the more rounded lines of the later chairs.

By 1720 the solid rectangular, architectural forms had given way completely to the new, more delicate fashion based upon the cyma curve, a flattened S-stroke joined end to end symmetrically. This new style was very largely the result of the introduction of new woods, first walnut and then mahogany, which could be carved and shaped in a way that oak could never be, and thus effected a revolution in furniture technology. The new style was introduced in Europe at the court of William of Orange who was joined in England not only by his Flemish countrymen but also, following the Revocation of the Edict of Nantes, by many French craftsmen who fled religious persecution.

One important designer who joined the new court was the Huguenot Daniel Marot who had been Louis XIV's

chief designer. With the introduction of the cyma curve a new breed of craftsmen came into being; the joiner began to be irrevocably replaced by the cabinetmaker.

As the letter from William Penn shows, drop-leaved tables replaced the trestle construction and, in all furniture forms, shape became more important than surface decoration. The chest was raised on a frame and drawers replaced the drop cavity. The frame was constructed with six legs, four at the front, connected and braced with flattened perpendicular or diagonal stretchers. The legs were turned, often using the bulbous trumpet turn. Gradually the two central front legs were omitted and turned drops substituted as vestigial remains; the stretchers disappeared and the legs lost their turnings, becoming bandy-shaped with a pad or Spanish foot. To fulfil the need for a flat functional surface, the high chests often had matching dressing tables or chests of drawers, where, again, the ball foot gave way to a small cabriole leg. The new chests had skirts carved in the cyma curve.

The Queen Anne style

Bandy legs, japanning, the use of more pronounced, pointed cyma curve skirts – the demand for a more sophisticated rendering of the new curved forms soon resulted in a totally new design vocabulary. Between 1720 and 1750 the Queen Anne style was introduced and from the rich variety of forms produced in furniture between these years the demand for a style betokening a new prosperity and cultural independence can be clearly seen.

The first change was the addition of the scroll top to the highboy raised chest which gave the appearance of balancing the curving skirts and legs. Later variations added rosettes to the ends of the scrolls and finials at the outside edges or in the centre. A uniquely American variation, the bonnet top, appeared where the scroll is continued backwards as a solid piece of wood rather than as a decorative front-piece. The bandy leg gave way to the more pronounced curve of the cabriole leg with claw and ball foot. It is generally thought that this foot was adapted from Oriental carvings showing a dragon's claw clasping a pearl, a motif brought back by the merchants of the East India Company. The leg itself acquired carving at the knee, often in the form of acanthus leaves. The skirt began to lose the points and undulations of the cyma curve and became instead a plainer, more elegant quarter circle and line shape which in turn enhanced the new applied carving. The decorative brass hardware also became more ornate.

The new softer woods, walnut and then mahogany, allowed for more delicate relief surface carving and the popular motifs were all circular in shape – the fan, the shell, the rising sun – simply carved on the highboy between narrowed top drawers and on the base above the skirt. On matching dressing tables it was placed again above the skirt. Japanning, an imitation of Oriental lacquerwork, also became extremely popular as a form of surface decoration. Many japanned pieces were imported by the early Philadelphians and by 1720 *A Treatise of Japaning and Varnishing*, published in Oxford in 1688 by John Stalker and George A. Parker, was well known in America.

Above: *A fine example of the Philadelphia armchair,* c.*1775, showing the wide balloon seat, richly carved shell motif on the top rail and knees, solid urn-shaped back-splat, claw and ball foot and stumped back legs. The importance of the opulently curved shape demonstrates the development of the curve of the cabriole leg into a coherent style.*

The shell or fan motif also appeared on the crest rail or front seat frame of Queen Anne chairs. Regional differences can be seen most clearly in the chair. The area producing chairs nearest to the original English models was New York, where the rule of Holland under Peter Stuyvesant and the Dutch West India Company had been replaced by that of the Duke of York in 1664. The Queen Anne chair is distinguished by its carved vertical back stretcher. In the New York chairs, the back splat is generally broader, often a 'ginger jar' shape but more enriched, often with veneering or a 'Cupid's Bow' at the base of the splat. The seats are larger as well as lower. The shell motif is often found on the knees or crest rail and the claw and ball foot, or sometimes the pad foot was used. Chairs without stretchers are often found usually made in walnut but also in cherry, maple or imported mahogany.

Above: *Richly decorated highboy made for Commodore Joshua Loring c.1740–1750 by John Pimm of Boston. The japanning, imitating oriental lacquer, was probably the work of Thomas Johnson, and was a Boston speciality. The bonnet top and urn finials balance the ornate drops, which were all that remained of the original fifth and sixth legs.*

Above: *Secretary desk c.1750 with bonnet top and ogee feet. A relatively plain piece of furniture with elegant top finials and an unusual circular motif in place of the characteristic carved shell or fan. The drawers are ornamented with decorative handles and lock mounts common to the period.*

The Philadelphia chair was also close to the English model, with a 'stumped' back leg and balloon or horseshoe-shaped seat (not angular as elsewhere) which enabled the arm support to join the side of the seat by a separate upright rather than directly above the knee. There are generally no stretchers. They have a richly carved top rail and a variety of feet – slipper and drake (both narrow, pointed, outward-facing feet), trifid, stocking and web (a variety of carved forms of the ball foot) and claw and ball. Philadelphia chairs can be recognized by a distinctive type of construction, the 'bare-faced tenon', where the side rail tenon is placed through a mortise cut into the rear leg and then secured on the outside edge of the back leg by pegs, which remain 'bare'.

Most New England chairs retained the use of block and ball stretchers with front and side rails mortised into the

Above: *Parlour built for Captain Perley, leader of the Boxford Minute Men, in Massachusetts, 1763. The panelling is painted in imitation of grained cedar with marbled pilasters. Note the ubiquitous plain cabriole leg, the early plain highboy with vestigial foot, cyma curve skirt to the tea table and the typically Bostonian stretchers on the chair and stool.*

legs. The New Englanders were late in using the claw and ball foot and most chairs have either a pad or cushioned pad foot. Stretchers also remained in upholstered chairs, for which there was now a great demand. New England armchairs can be distinguished from Philadelphia upholstered chairs by the vertical scrolled arms in preference to the Philadelphian C-scrolls and by the absence of stretchers.

In Newport, Rhode Island, the chair-making industry was carried on by two Quaker families – the uncle and nephew Job and John Townsend (1699–1765 and 1732–1809) and John Goddard (1723–85), Job's son-in-law, who were probably all engaged in 'venture' cargo – the habit of sending goods to the captains of ships for sale in the south in exchange for other commodities. These two families made chairs with broad splats, relief shell carving on the crest rails and C-scrolls and carvings on the knees, with broad, shallow disc-shaped feet and stretchers. There is enormous variety, also, even within distinct areas, in the shape of the back splat, from conservative narrow-shouldered curves, to sharp pointed ends or to the more effusive vase or ginger jar curves.

Above: *Blockfront kneehole desk with ogee feet c.1775. The carved shell decoration is particularly associated with the Townsend and Goddard families of Newport, Rhode Island, as was the blockfront technique. The kneehole desk, with the secretary desk, was a new form of furniture, often replacing the popular highboy and lowboy set.*

The influence of Chippendale

In 1754 the publication in England of Thomas Chippendale's *The Gentleman and Cabinet-Maker's Director* (with subsequent editions in 1755 and 1762) firmly established the precedence of the cabinetmaker over the joiner, carver or chairmaker. The success of the *Director* led to a flood of pattern books such as Abraham Swan's *A Builder's Treasury of Staircases*, Thomas Johnson's *One Hundred and Fifty New Designs* (1758 and 1761) or Ince and Mayhew's *The Universal System of Household Furniture* (c.1762). What all these books had in common was the new element of the Rococo or 'rock and shell work' which led to a new flourish in carving and decoration. The Chippendale style was quickly seized upon in America and indeed, stayed in fashion for longer than it did in England due to the disturbances of the War of

Independence, 1774–83, and the preceding troubles over trade with Europe.

Chippendale had not, in his book, advocated one rigid style with specific forms for each type of piece; it was a pattern book and gave themes or examples which could be copied and adapted in a variety of ways. It included not only Rococo but also Chinese and Gothic motifs. The most obvious immediate effect was pierced carving for decoration on chairs or highboys, instead of solid central splats or scrolls. In chairs, the central splat was now opened and widened and made into various forms of foliation, bows or fretwork. On cabinets, the top scrollwork turned into fretwork or lattice work, often mirrored on the skirt. The relief carving became more detailed and elaborate, the now familiar fan or shell being surrounded by naturalistic leaves or flowers, or forgotten altogether in favour of a panel of rich carving. The finials surmounting the tops of cabinets were also enriched, giving way to urns or busts, or sometimes an eagle, a popular English motif.

Once again, regional differences became clear. Philadelphia combined Chippendale's patterns with the ornate scrollwork of the 'New French Style' and in most forms Philadelphia examples are seen to be more ornate and deeply carved than northern parallels. In Boston, where the tea-table originated, the long, plain cabriole leg with pad foot was retained with a tray top with rounded corners. Generally in walnut, cherry or mahogany, the New England model relied on plain surfaces and purity of line. By 1770 in Philadelphia the tea-table had reached its most ornate form in the 'pillar and claw' table – a circular top nesting on a birdcage which allowed the top to be moved to a vertical position, supported by a pillar and tripod. In New York, the card table had achieved a new sophistication with a serpentine frame on cabriole legs, frequently enhanced by veneering or carving.

Individual cabinetmakers also came to the fore in this period. In Philadelphia Thomas Affleck (1740–95) and the carvers John Pollard (1740–87) and Hercules Courtenay (*c.*1744–84), who both worked in Benjamin Randolph's workshops, dominated the cabinetmakers, and Plunkett Fleeson and Daniel Trotter were the major upholsterer and chairmaker respectively. Affleck, born in Aberdeen, had been apprenticed in Edinburgh where he would have worked from the *Director* and arrived in Philadelphia around 1760. He is known to have paid the waterfront businessman Levi Hollingsworth for his purchases of rum with mahogany furniture and, between 1763–6, to have made a sofa and chairs for Governor Penn using the straight 'Marlborough' leg. This straight, carved leg, often ending with a supporting plinth, was recommended by Chippendale as an alternative to the cabriole, and Affleck is known for his use of bold ornament. Pollard and Courtenay started work in 1766 as journeymen carvers for Benjamin Randolph, perhaps to pay off their travel debts, and enlarged Randolph's house-joinery business to include cabinetmaking. Courtenay is known to have executed carved interiors. Pollard later traded under 'The Sign of the Chinese Shield', a reference to the Chinese motifs advocated by Chippendale. With the Non-Importation Agreement signed by Philadelphia in 1765 these craftsmen would have been in great demand to keep up with prevailing European fashions. Other Philadelphia craftsmen who executed mahogany pieces using the scrolled and pierced forms which characterized the French Rococo style were William Savery, Jonathan Shoemaker and James Gillingham.

Left: *Highboy made by the Philadelphia cabinetmaker Thomas Affleck (1740–95). Affleck's style strongly reflects the absorption of Chippendale's designs with finer, more elaborate carving, especially on the knees and scroll tops. The openwork carving which surmounts the highboy certainly shows the influence of Chippendale's more intricate designs for woodwork.*

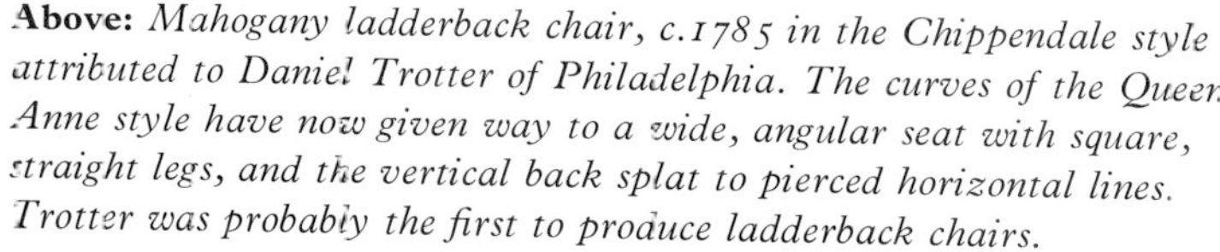

Above: *Mahogany ladderback chair, c.1785 in the Chippendale style attributed to Daniel Trotter of Philadelphia. The curves of the Queen Anne style have now given way to a wide, angular seat with square, straight legs, and the vertical back splat to pierced horizontal lines. Trotter was probably the first to produce ladderback chairs.*

Above: *Mahogany dining chair with heart-shaped back in the Hepplewhite style, made in Baltimore, c.1790. The cabriole leg has now been abandoned completely and the square leg refined to a tapering finish which complements the delicacy and prettiness of the shaped back. The legs and back are reeded and shaped to draw attention to the lines.*

Two other new forms which demonstrate regional affiliations are the serpentine or sweep front chest of drawers, with the ogee bracket foot, which was popular in Philadelphia, and the block front type of desk, secretary or chest of drawers which was a speciality of the Townsend and Goddard families of Newport and of Boston cabinet-makers such as John Cogswell, who was working in Boston around 1769. The block front secretary took over from the highboy, with a knee-hole chest of drawers replacing the lowboy, usually made of mahogany on a pine frame. The blocking followed a reverse curve along three front drawers, the weight of the outward curve being counter-balanced by reverse blocking on the inside of the drawer or fall-front. In the Newport models, the blocking is decorated with rich carving, usually, again, the shell motif, and the use of the ogee bracket foot is customary. The Boston model uses plainer relief carving, if any at all, as in New England chairs, where extremely low relief carving was used, and keeps the claw and ball foot. Similarly on the Boston speciality, the bombé chest of drawers, the claw and ball foot was still employed in preference to the ogee bracket. In almost all forms, it can be seen that Philadelphia was the most advanced in using new patterns, for in New York, for example, the chair retains the old form of rounded seat while in Boston the chair seat is upholstered over the frame instead of having a slip-in seat with elaborate carving over the frame and down the knees.

Hepplewhite and Sheraton styles

It is to Philadelphia, therefore, that we must look to see other changes as the century progressed. Due to the disturbances of the War of Independence (when both Pollard and Courtenay downed tools and went to fight),

Above: *Sideboard probably made in Baltimore, 1790–1800, with mahogany veneer and decorative inlay of Grecian urns, based on a Hepplewhite design. Oval inlaid bands highlight the new oval design of the handles and also trace the delicate tapering legs, showing that applied surface decoration is now an integral part of the overall shape.*
Right: *One of 24 side-chairs made in Philadelphia, c.1796 for Elias Hasket Derby of Salem, Massachusetts, made of maple and painted black, decorated with colours. The ribbon and plume decoration of the oval back is derived from Hepplewhite. That a wealthy merchant should order his chairs from another city shows the importance of possessing fashionable furnishings.*

new English styles such as Sheraton and Hepplewhite were slow to be absorbed into the decorative idiom, and by the time that the Americans had become familiar with these innovations they were to be absorbed into the Federal style. In 1788 George Hepplewhite's wife published *The Cabinet-Maker and Upholsterer's Guide* posthumously and between 1791–4 Thomas Sheraton published his four-part *Cabinet-Maker and Upholsterer's Drawing Book*, both of which had an immediate impact on English design.

Chippendale's later edition of the *Director* had already introduced new forms, such as the adoption, following the architect Robert Adam, of Neoclassical motifs such as pendant husks, draperies, sheaves of wheat and Doric pilasters. The pattern-book also included Gothic and Chinese designs which led to square forms for chairs with more geometric piercing on the central splats. They were often surmounted by a pagoda crest, or even by carving in imitation of bamboo. The serpentine, kettle or bombé forms for chests of drawers, with a preference for veneering, beading and inlay over carving, led not only to the gradual outmoding of the highboy but also left room for the secretary, or *scrutoire*, the desk and the sideboard. *Aesop's*

Fables also became a favourite source for carved decoration and in 1777 three separate editions were published by Philadelphia printers, resulting in the common use of themes such as the 'Fox and Grapes' – a theme which was to recur in the 19th century Eastlake style.

Between 1770–80 the ladderback chair was introduced as an alternative to the pierced slat back; its introduction is often credited to Daniel Trotter of Philadelphia. The slat was replaced by four horizontal members, either plain, pierced or with a central rosette, plume or scroll and leaf designs known as the 'honeysuckle' pattern. The horizontals were curved in a serpentine bow and Daniel Trotter advertised 'pretzel-back' and 'ribbon-back' as well as 'pierced ladder-back' chairs. The legs were square, the front tapered and carved on two sides, and the back canted with box stretchers. Ladderback chairs are also attributed to Ephraim Haines of Philadelphia.

The Hepplewhite style is best seen in the chair and the sideboard. In the chair, the curved frame with slats gave way to a shield, heart or lyre-shaped back supported by reeded members at each side of the seat. At the base of the back would be a small carved swag or rosette. The legs were square, tapered and reeded. This inlaid, tapered leg appears again on the sideboard with a curved front whose entire elegance rests upon the shape. Finished with veneered and beaded drawers and side cupboards, it gives a slim and elongated effect. This was also achieved in the long couches, with upholstered seats but narrow, reeded supports and arms which were an important Hepplewhite innovation.

This more delicate, finished furniture was matched at this time by the upholsterer with the Martha Washington or 'lolling' chair – a high-backed upholstered chair with plain open arms and legs and extremely popular because of its comfort and elegance.

The Sheraton style once more outmoded the lines of the Hepplewhite curved back chair in favour of a slim square outline with raised central back rail. The central splats no longer ran into the seat but were contained by a horizontal bar, framing the elongated shell or scroll between the vertical members. All members were fluted in the form of columns, with bracket or turned feet and less elaborate skirting. Sheraton also favoured the swell front chest of drawers, and oval handles now enhanced the curved lines instead of the more elaborate Rococo styled hardware of earlier in the century. However, as has been said, both these styles were quickly absorbed into the new spirit of independence which showed in the furniture of the Federal period in America.

The Federal period

The Federal Constitution was signed on 17 September 1787 and Philadelphia became the seat of government while the city of Washington was under construction by the architect Pierre Charles L'Enfant. Thomas Jefferson in fact had written the Declaration of Independence in 1776 upon a small writing box decorated with fine line inlay (now in the Smithsonian Institution, Washington) made in the workshops of Benjamin Randolph in Philadelphia; this

Above: *An American speciality, the tambour desk, c.1790, veneered in contrasting satinwood and golden mahogany. A central cupboard in the upper half is flanked by sliding reeded sections which conceal the secretaire compartments, and the fall front provides a writing surface.*

was a harbinger of the new taste which was to become known as the Federal style. By wanting the Virginia Capitol to be built in the style of a Roman temple in 1789, Jefferson initiated the later popularity of classically inspired designs. The move towards Classicism still came more from elements inherent in the pattern books of Thomas Shearer, Hepplewhite and Sheraton rather than from their master, Robert Adam, but by 1810 the new Federal nation had a style which reflected a new-found wish for a grandeur of its own.

At the end of the Revolution the most important cities were Philadelphia, Newport, Boston, Baltimore and Salem but some rural areas, such as the Connecticut River Valley and the back country of Pennsylvania and New Jersey, were growing in organization. Different woods were used in different areas, although mahogany – from Honduras, San Domingo, Cuba and Jamaica – remained the most popular. Cherry and walnut were occasionally used, either painted or japanned, and in New England birch and maple were stained to look like mahogany; in the southern states buttonwood (American plane) and tulip wood were also fairly widely used.

The new style was encouraged by the publication of standardizing pattern books such as the *Philadelphia Journeyman Cabinet and Chairmakers' Book of Prices* (1794 and 1795) which set standards of quality and value, even if fixed prices did tend to discourage more individual

workmanship. The new style demanded different techniques with specialized knowledge of the idiosyncrasies of exotic woods for use in marquetry and veneering and most pieces were the result of teamwork carried out in large shops. As inlay was substituted for carving, projecting mouldings and pilasters were replaced by shallow patterns of wood grain and stringing, while rectilinear forms replaced the build up of three-dimensional curved forms. The woods most commonly used for veneering were crotch mahogany from Cuba, a honey-coloured figured birch, curled or birds-eye maple, satinwood, ebony or rosewood. It required work of the greatest precision to cut the fine layers necessary, although in the mid-19th century a circular saw was introduced which simplified the cutting process.

Veneering was done using a thin layer of grained wood, warmed, wetted and glued and either hammered onto the surface or screwed down with a caul, having been cut to shape and oiled and greased. Banding and stringing was done using the same process, there being three types of banding: straight, which runs along the grain, cross-banding, going against the grain, and feather-banding, at a

Left: *A bedroom in Samuel McIntire's Pingree House in Salem, Massachusetts, 1804. The furniture shows that the severity of Hepplewhite designs is already giving way to more decoration – the turned legs of the dressing table, the curled mirror supports and the robust pillars of the bed. The open backed armchairs show the legacy of the early Chinese inspired Chippendale style.*

diagonal angle to the grain. Stringing was generally done with holly, which is naturally white, and stained black to look like ebony, although in some cities satinwood, boxwood or ebony itself were used, as well as brass and some silver; in rural areas maple and birch were also used. Pieces made by these elaborate techniques would generally be for use in the drawing room, simpler furniture being bought for bedrooms and even for the dining room.

Among the regional centres producing Federal style furniture, the newer urban areas gradually began to rival the former supremacy of Boston and Philadelphia. In Baltimore, Maryland, particularly, a distinctive style arose, especially in the use of *verre eglomisé*, a technique of painting on the reverse side of oval or lozenge-shaped glass panels with gold and black paint. The painting generally represents allegorical figures. Baltimore furniture also has more marquetry than the northern cities, made by craftsmen such as John Shaw (1745–1829), a Glasgow emigré who worked in the Hepplewhite style. A favourite motif for marquetry panels was that of vines rising from an urn. Baltimore also became a centre for the production and export of 'fancy' chairs painted with figures or landscape scenes, such as the Hudson River with one of the first steamboats.

In Connecticut one finds the greatest variety of forms for chests of drawers, except for the bombé shape which remained a Boston speciality. At this period there were many types of desk, from the narrow tambour to the large gentleman's secretary, and from the lady's slim cabinet and writing table to the greater *escritoire* or *scrutoire*. In Boston the slender forms were retained with the use of contrasting veneers, painted decoration and reeded colonnettes. The major craftsmen were John Seymour (*c.*1738–1818) who arrived in Boston with his son Thomas in 1794 and Samuel McIntire (1757–1811).

Boston, however, had competition from its northern neighbour, Salem, which became rich from the China trade towards the close of the Revolution. The wealthy merchants there are known to have ordered furniture after designs by McIntire as well as a set of 24 white and gilt oval backed Hepplewhite chairs from Philadelphia, the backs decorated with knots of carved ribbon surmounted by either ostrich plumes or peacock feathers in pink and green. But Salem had its own craftsmen, such as Nehemiah Adams, Edward Johnson, William Hook, William Lemmon and Elijah and Jacob Sanderson. The 'Salem Secretary' became well known – a combination of a glass front bookcase and cabinet with thin bands of inlay, inlaid swags of flowers and oval inlaid panels.

Philadelphia became a social and cultural centre at the end of the war and its younger citizens were busy building in the Federal style. Many Philadelphia craftsmen in fact migrated south to Baltimore and Charleston, but numerous workers remained to make the most of the new style.

John Aitken (working *c.*1790–1840), a Scottish immigrant, received three orders from President Washington for furniture for Mount Vernon. In 1790, in an advertisement in the *Federal Gazette*, he showed a Hepplewhite-style heart back chair, while other furniture known to be by him uses cross-band inlay, veneering and fluted urn pediments. Other cabinetmakers were Samuel Claphamson, Jacob Wayne, John Douglass and Henry Ingle, while Daniel Trotter's apprentice, Ephraim Haines (1775–1837) and Henry Connelly (1770–1826) continued to make Sheraton-style ebony chairs with turned and ornamented

Above: *Piano made by Geib & Son in New York, 1830–40. The mahogany and satinwood case was designed by Duncan Phyfe in the Greek Revival style with inlaid decoration and applied raised lion heads. The reverse curve structure of the leg support is typical of Phyfe's Neoclassical furniture.*
Left: *Mahogany breakfront secretaire, probably made in Salem, 1780–1805, and decorated with contrasting veneer panels, boxwood border fillets and inlaid bell flowers. The wedge-shaped legs are a distinctively American innovation on what is otherwise a very typical English design.*

thin tapered legs and vertical fluted back members.

In 1789 George Washington began his first term as President in New York and between then and 1850 there was a period of extremely rapid growth in the city. In a sense, New York becomes a special case in comparison with other centres of manufacture, for it was in New York that Duncan Phyfe (1768–1854) worked and his work not only represents perhaps the finest and most individual of the Federal style but also the transition from the Sheraton and Hepplewhite styles of the 18th century to the Neoclassical designs of the early 19th century.

Duncan Phyfe was born near Inverness in Scotland and settled in Albany in 1783 or 1784; by 1792 he was listed in the New York City Directory and by 1794 had changed the original 'Fife-joiner' to 'Duncan Phyfe, cabinetmaker'. Even before 1800 he had wealthy New York customers and had probably established himself as a prominent New York cabinetmaker. His Fulton Street furniture shop and warehouse soon had orders from Philadelphia, Albany, New Jersey and the Hudson River Valley and would undertake to furnish an entire house, including the kitchen and servants' bedrooms, as well as to repair furniture. Before he retired in 1847 he employed more than 100 journeymen cabinetmakers, turners and carvers. Although trained himself in Chippendale's styles, he quickly absorbed the new French Directoire designs and later Empire styles, although his work in this fashion was not so good. He was certainly instrumental in introducing Greek and Roman styles to New York between 1805 and 1825 and probably took his first designs from *The London Chairmakers' and Carvers' Book of Prices for Workmanship*, first published in 1802 with a supplement in 1808. This book gave additional costs for added motifs, such as paw feet. On the whole the designs required strong, fine-grained mahoganies.

Phyfe's furniture is recognized for its structural integrity and economy of construction, using the narrowest possible vertical supports with necessarily heavier horizontal members, often with very slight curves. The reverse curves used in chair and table legs give an impression of strength despite their elegance. He designed three types of chair, the Sheraton, the Directoire and, later, the Empire style and also made a variety of tables for use as

Left: *Inlaid candle stand with a tip top on a tripod base, c.1800. Attributed to John and Thomas Seymour of Boston, who were known for their delicate inlay work and use of slender reeded uprights.*

card, console, library, dining, serving, sewing, dressing or candle tables supported either at the ends with reverse curve supports or in the centre with a central pedestal and curving legs.

He used much carving as well as turning, reeding, veneering and inlay, later using brass, often in a narrowly-edged rectangle. In carved panels he used such motifs as cornucopiae, laurel or oak leaves, drapery swags, caught at the centre with tasselled cords, ears of wheat, thunderbolts, trumpets or the then popular Prince of Wales feathers. Surface carving took the form of acanthus leaves, usually combined with reeding on legs and outer edges, the dog's foot on the front legs of chairs and tables, the water leaf, again combined with reeding on turned vertical members, the palm leaf, leaf and dart, rosettes, fluting and the lion's foot and eagle's wing and lion mask, sometimes in brass on table bases. Phyfe was also known for his flamboyant designs for mirrors, which spanned the Chippendale Rococo motifs, the ornate Adam-inspired flowers and swags, and the heavier frames of the Empire style, generally gilt or painted. Especially popular were matching pier tables and glasses which gradually became more intricate as the century progressed.

French influences

From 1803–19 Phyfe was joined in New York by the French emigré Charles Honoré Lannuier who supplied some healthy competition in the French Directoire style. In 1805 the scroll back chair was introduced with a cross, or lattice, back or ogee scroll back or a lyre or harp motif combined with Grecian front and rear legs, and, from 1810, brass lion paw feet. A host of new pattern books were full of Grecian and Roman designs, such as Rudolph Ackermann's *Repository of the Arts* (1817), Robert Adam's *Designs for Vases and Foliage, Composed from the Antique* (1821) or J. C. Loudon's *Encyclopaedia of Cottage, Farm and Villa Architecture* (1839). A new generation of cabinet-makers grew up, working in the new French 'Antique' and Empire styles. Among them were Joseph Meeks and Sons of New York, Charles H. White, who introduced the pineapple and leaf pedestal to Philadelphia, and Joseph B. Barry and Sons. Barry visited Europe from Philadelphia in 1811–12 and returned with many new designs including Egyptian and Gothic. Others included Michel Bouvier of Philadelphia and, perhaps the finest of the new Philadelphia cabinetmakers, Paris-born Anthony G. Quervelle (1789–1856) who arrived in Philadelphia in 1817: Quervelle supplied President Andrew Jackson with pier tables for the East Room of the White House.

Left: *One of a set of Empire style chairs, attributed to John and Hugh Findlay of Baltimore, c.1820. Made of maplewood with cane seats, each in the set was individually painted. The design is based on the Roman version of the Greek* klismos *chair and was extremely popular in the first half of the 19th century. The architect Benjamin Latrobe designed a similar set for the White House for America's fourth President, James Madison.*

Above: *Upholstered sofa with mahogany frame made in New York in 1815. The design of the leg supports is typical of the Empire style, and the whole is decorated with carved drapes and rosettes and carved seats. The sofa is handsomely proportioned and is one of the more elegant forms of the period.*

Below: *Mahogany 'Duchesse' dressing table with white marble top c.1850 designed by Prudence Mallard who came to New Orleans from Paris during the 1830s. The cabriole leg has returned along with ornate carving, showing the beginnings of the 19th century liking for an appearance of solidity and weight.*

During the 1812 war between England and America the French influence gradually became as strong in America as the English and although most architecture was still strongly English in conception, interiors in the French style were favoured. As the Federal style began to wane in favour of the gilt, ormolu and brass of the Empire style, coherence in American design was lost until the regulating influence of the 1876 Philadelphia Centennial Exposition. The 1820s saw the wide introduction of Empire motifs, such as the eagle's head, urns, columns, caryatids, swags, griffins, swans, bees, wreaths and cornucopiae. The transition happened gradually; Samuel McIntire's Sheraton style chairs had used bowls of fruit, rosettes, grapes and vine leaf carving. The square card table had given way to the serpentine front, or to the curved drop-leaf Pembroke table with inlaid tapered legs and thence to the pedestal table. Around 1805 the pier table and glass had become popular; the sofa gave way to the couch, daybed and chaise longue and, around 1825, to the excesses of the Grecian Dolphin design window seat with thick scrollwork. The *klismos* chair, more favoured in Philadelphia than New York, was introduced with an elaborately shaped and carved wide back support. The use of pedestal supports gave the excuse for elaborate carving with the central pillar in the form of pineapples or lyres supported on four curving lion's paw feet, all very richly carved. What had begun with the careful elegance of the Federal style had, within thirty years, given way to a confusion and search for novelty that was to continue through the 19th century in the many revival styles then fashionable, both in America and across the Atlantic.

Above: *Carved rosewood love seat made in New York c.1855. Once again the curves of the cabriole leg appear with a reliance on fulsome surface carving and exaggerated rounded shapes which also typified European furniture at this time. The love seat was extremely popular in the Southern states during this period.*

Below: *Desk in walnut, white pine and poplar designed by the Philadelphia architect Frank Furness. Furness was influenced by the eclectic designs of Owen Jones and Dr. Christopher Dresser and this desk shows a variety of influences, from the Moorish arch of the kneehole and the Moorish-inspired carving of the cupboard doors to the classical female figures which surmount the frame.*

By 1830–40 the elaborate scrollwork of the earlier period had given way to the late classical style, which retained the same shapes as the *klismos* chair and the pedestal table, pier table and scroll couch, but now employed good plain woods and neglected the surface decoration. This style, known as 'pillar and scroll' furniture, was the first to be mass-produced, using veneered pine. At this time however, a new element was being imported from England.

19th century revivals

During the 1840s the architect and designer Alexander Jackson Davis built Lyndhurst, a house by the Hudson River, for William Paulding, the mayor of New York. The house itself was in the Gothic style and Davis also designed furniture, made by Burns and Trainque of New York City, in oak in the Gothic style. As in England, Gothic was liked as a style befitting national enterprises and in 1847 James Renwick Jr designed some Gothic chairs for use in the Smithsonian Institution Building in Washington and in 1846–7 Joseph Meeks and Sons of New York made a set of twelve Gothic chairs for the White House which were later used by Abraham Lincoln in his Cabinet Room. As a decorative style however, Gothic was never entirely popular and most designers tended to combine Gothic elements with Rococo.

Anthony G. Quervelle made furniture in the Gothic and Rococo style, as did George J. Henkels (1819–83) of Philadelphia and John Jelliff (1813–93) of Newark, New Jersey. The Gothic style has survived however, in a great variety of forms, from couches, chairs, stools, tables, beds, desks and sideboards to bookcases, mirrors, hall stands, clocks and lamps. In Philadelphia Crawford Riddell (*d.*1849) used the Gothic style in rosewood chairs with a Gothic arch back and turned tapered front legs. George J. Henkels, who employed over 80 workmen in his shops, made turned, quasi-bobbin Gothic chairs as well as Renaissance revival dolphin-backed chairs. His furniture, described in his *Catalogue of Furniture in Every Style* and *Essay on Household Furniture* (1850) was admired by Samuel Sloan, one of the architects of the Second Masonic Hall in Chestnut Street, Philadelphia, built in 1853, where the Grand Lodge Room was entirely in the Gothic ecclesiastical style.

Also in 1853, at the New York Crystal Palace Exhibition, classical styles were described as 'frigid monstrosities' and were popularly replaced by a Rococo revival. Once again, a profusion of scrolls and carving prevailed, best known in the work of John Henry Belter (1804–63), a German trained cabinetmaker who opened the J. H. Belter and Company Cabinet Factory on 3rd Avenue in New York in 1858. In 1856 he had patented a laminating process using from 3 to 16 thin layers of rosewood, glued together using cross-graining for strength. After being pressed and steamed, the laminate was carved in the Rococo style and

Right: *Walnut bookcase designed by Isaac E. Scott for J. J. Glessners in 1875. This bookcase is typical of the Gothic style used by English architect-designers such as Bruce Talbert and popularized in America by Charles Eastlake, especially in the use of champfering and the trefoil motif. The Gothic style was based upon architectural principles.*

Left: *Side chair in oak designed by the Chicago architect George Grant Elmslie c.1910. Elmslie was an associate of both Louis Sullivan and Frank Lloyd Wright and was influenced by their work. The tall back and the continuation of the central back splat to the bottom rail is seen also in Wright's designs.*

proved immensely popular. The technique and the style were copied by Charles A. Baudouine of New York. John Jelliff of Newark used rosewood and walnut in the Rococo style, sometimes painted white and gold, and made many balloon-back chairs.

President James Buchanan purchased a Rococo parlour suite for the White House from Gottlieb Vollmer of Philadelphia. Vollmer also worked in the Louis XIV revival style with a profusion of C and S scrolls. In 1815 Joseph Bonaparte, Napoleon's brother and the ex-King of Spain arrived in America and his house, Point Breeze in New Jersey, was visited and described by the public. By the 1850s more American families were visiting Europe on grand tours and returning fired with enthusiasm for the French 'antique' tastes they saw there. French revival furniture was also featured at the International Trade Exhibitions held in Paris and London and it is said that a Louis XVI style suite won a first prize at the 1876 Philadelphia Centennial.

By the 1840s, although still outnumbered by Germans, there were many French cabinetmakers working in America and much French furniture was imported both by wealthy families and by cabinetmakers specifically to copy from, as for example by the Lejambre family in Philadelphia who imported *chaises volantes*. Between 1845–60 the Louis XIV Renaissance style predominated with ornate carving on massive forms. From 1860–76 the Rococo Louis XV–XVI style came to the fore with lighter forms and a greater use of asymmetrical ornament. New forms, too, were imported, such as the *chaise confortable*, a rounded stuffed 'cup' body and spring seat either in the rounded 'bergère' form or square 'fauteuil' shape, or the conversation or 'tête-a-tête' chair. The French revival also included Second Empire and Louis XV styles as well as the 'Marie Antoinette' style – gilded and painted furniture upholstered in tapestry, and was dominated in New York by French craftsmen such as Baudouine, Roux, Marcotte, Dessoir and Ringuet Le Prince.

Other popular revivals, all of which were attractive to an affluent and romantically-inclined public, were the Elizabethan, the Renaissance and the Egyptian. The Elizabethan revival began in the 1840s and meant a return to turnings, especially the spiral twist or corkscrew turning, in ebonized bobbin or ball-turned chairs, or corkscrew turnings, with tapestry upholstery. By 1860 this also included delicate painted 'cottage' style chairs. The Renaissance revival, which was immensely popular and was heavily represented at the 1876 Philadelphia Centennial, caused a return to trumpet-turned legs, massive carving, panelled medallions and inlay and incised decoration. In the 1880s Egyptian forms and motifs were adopted after the erection of the Cleopatra's Needle obelisk in Central Park, New York and Sphinx heads, medallions, scarabs and lotus capitals abounded. In fact, the use of Egyptian motifs dated back, sporadically, to Thomas Hope's *Household Furniture and Interior Decoration* (1807) but the prevailing mood of enjoying full-blown revival or 'antique' pieces led to complete reproductions of so-called ancient forms, including also Roman and Turkish. New inventions were also pleasant to a rising wealthy manufacturing class and spring chairs, iron rocking chairs, swivel chairs and the like were not only used in America but constituted the main American contribution to the 1851 London Great Exhibition. Thonet bentwood furniture was also on sale in New York during the 1870s.

America's first international fair had been held at the newly constructed Crystal Palace in New York in 1853. Most of the furniture exhibited was by European manufacturers and the American contribution was in the

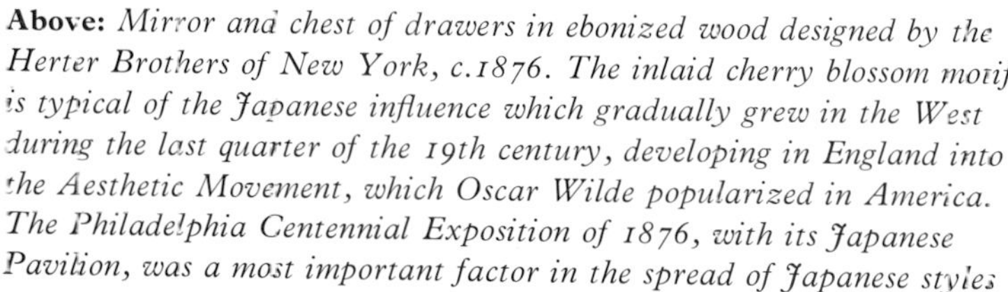

Above: *Mirror and chest of drawers in ebonized wood designed by the Herter Brothers of New York, c.1876. The inlaid cherry blossom motif is typical of the Japanese influence which gradually grew in the West during the last quarter of the 19th century, developing in England into the Aesthetic Movement, which Oscar Wilde popularized in America. The Philadelphia Centennial Exposition of 1876, with its Japanese Pavilion, was a most important factor in the spread of Japanese styles*

Above: *Early 19th century Windsor elbow chair with 'bamboo' turnings, the whole painted red. A vast variety of Windsor chairs were produced in America, with curved or square forms and differing arrangements of turned slats. 'Bamboo' turnings were quite popular during the early 19th century. The many types of Windsor chair produced in America demonstrate how a fairly basic European design could be interpreted across the Atlantic in scores of different ways.*

Renaissance revival style in massive oak and walnut. By the time of the 1876 Centennial Exposition, the Americans were trying to muster pride in their own artistic sense and despite stands devoted to European artefacts the Exposition remains as a watershed between the slavish copies and fearful imitations of the first three-quarters of the century and the following attempt to define some home-grown aesthetic criteria. This reassessment was largely helped, yet again, by English prototypes, from styles and theories resulting from the British criticism of their own muddled design seen at the 1851 Great Exhibition. Two important stands at the 1876 Exposition helped in this; one was the Japanese Pavilion showing Japanese artefacts which were swiftly adapted first by Kimbel and Cabus of New York and, later, by Nimura and Sato of Brooklyn. These helped lead American designers, such as Herter Brothers of New York, into an understanding of the Aesthetic Movement, so magnificently propagandized by Oscar Wilde's 1882 lecture tour of America. The other was the 'Colonial Kitchen' which sparked off a vogue not only for a colonial revival but also for the collection and preservation of early Chippendale-style furniture. Ferdinand Keller of Philadelphia began to copy American furniture of the 18th century.

An important contributor at the Centennial Exposition was the German born Philadelphia craftsman Daniel Pabst (1827–1910). Up until 1876 he made masterpieces in the Rococo and Renaissance revival styles with elaborate and massive carving, generally in walnut. The English designer Dr Christopher Dresser visited Philadelphia for the Centennial and his lectures on design motivated Pabst to adopt his aesthetic of severe rectilinear conventionalized design based upon the work of Owen Jones and the reinterpretations of the Gothic revival in England. Another Philadelphia architect who designed furniture in a slightly more flamboyant Gothic style was Frank Furness (1839–1912) who was also a customer of Pabst. Yet another architect, Wilson Eyre Jr (1858–1944), copied the

Left: *Shaker slat-back rocking chair – a design produced by the Shaker sect from the late 18th century until well into the 19th. Two types were made, the lighter 'Sister's' rocking chair and the sturdier 'Brother's' which often had 'mushroom' tops to the posts.*
Right: *Tailoress' counter from Watervliet, New York, 1820–30, made by the Shakers. The frame is of ungrained maple with pine panels and drawer faces of curly maple. There is an expandable flap at the back for cutting out the cloth. Although made for a specific purpose, the whole has been carefully considered, for example in the fine moulding on the drawers and the proportions of the tapered legs.*

furniture designs of the English Gothic architect A. W. N. Pugin and had scrapbooks containing photographs, drawings and newspaper cuttings of furniture by C. F. A. Voysey and C. R. Mackintosh, two prominent Arts and Crafts architect-designers. Eyre's style used fine applied ornament and stressed the craftsmanship of a piece, revealing the construction in bare mortise and tenon.

The Aesthetic Movement and Arts and Crafts

This fine and disciplined adoption of English styles was principally summed up in the so-called Eastlake style, based upon Charles L. Eastlake's influential book *Hints on Household Taste* which despised 'shaping', that is, curved forms, and advocated a return to the turner's art with rectilinear forms and applied surface decoration. Eastlake's influence however, is claimed for a great variety of types of furniture, few of which in fact have much in common with the original book, first published in London in 1868. Eastlake took his designs from a range of styles from 'medieval', 'modern Gothic' and 'Tudor' to 'Queen Anne' and they are not dissimilar to B. J. Talbert's *Gothic Forms Applied to Furniture, Metalwork and Decoration* (1867) republished in Boston in 1873. Kimbel and Cabus of New York and Mitchell and Rammelsburg of Cincinatti both showed 'Eastlake' furniture at the 1876 Centennial Exposition.

Eastlake furniture was essentially Art Furniture and combined the elements of the Japanese and Queen Anne which were the basis of Aesthetic Movement design. The use of low relief carved motifs of cranes, rushes, butterflies, cherry blossom, fans and chrysanthemums or inlay combined with elaborate Gothic style hinges were the staple of this idiom. The carving, dovetailing, shaping, moulding, fretcutting and spindlework of Eastlake furniture lent it to easy reproduction by new machinery developed in Williamsport, Jamestown, Cincinnati, Grand Rapids and Muscatine and also made it a link between the expensive hand-crafted ethic of William Morris and his followers and the cheaper end of the design conscious market. The style was also copied by the finest craftsmen, such as the Herter Brothers of New York who made an ebonized cherry desk with light wood inlay for the millionaire Jay Gould. Herter Brothers' delicate inlay designs are perhaps the finest of the American contribution to the Aesthetic style.

Before discussing the influence of William Morris upon American designers, it is necessary to point out that America did have its own indigenous tradition of craftsman furniture. The steady popularity of the many versions of the Windsor chair with its rounded shape and spindle turned vertical supports testifies to the continuation of local traditions which were also capable of absorbing new trends, such as the 'bamboo-turned' Windsor chairs. The most important local tradition, however, was that of the various religious craft sects, not least the Shakers, or the United Society of Believers in Christ's Second Appearing. By 1800 the original sect founded by Mother Ann Lee was firmly established but by 1900 there were only 1,000 members left. The Shakers based their design criteria upon their religious beliefs and stressed cleanliness, order, simplicity, regularity and harmony. The Shaker writings are full of the following sort of advice:

> Believers may not in any case, manufacture for sale, any article or articles, which are superfluously wrought, and which would have a tendency to feed the pride and

vanity of man, or such as would not be admissable to use among themselves, on account of their superfluity . . . Beadings, mouldings and cornices, which are merely for fancy may not be made by Believers . . . Beauty rests on utility. (Quoted in *Shaker Furniture* by E. D. and F. Andrews, Yale 1937.)

Some of the Shaker artefacts are among the finest and purest designs ever produced and do indeed reflect Mother Ann Lee's sayings 'Put your hands to work, and your hearts to God . . . Do your work as though you had a thousand years to live, and as if you were to die tomorrow' (*ibid*). Mainly made of pine, although maple, birch, black cherry, beech and walnut were also used, the functional chairs, chests and candle stands have a sparseness and elegance brought about solely by the regularity of the proportions with no applied decoration of any kind. During the 1860s Shaker furniture from the New York State communities became fashionable on the East Coast.

During the 1890s the ideas of the Arts and Crafts Movement had been absorbed in America and various individuals began their own craft communities based on William Morris' ideas. One was the Roycroft Community begun by an ex-soap salesman, Elbert Hubbard, at East Aurora in 1895 which opened a furniture workship in 1901 producing plain oak pieces. A similar, if less successful, venture called the Rose Valley Community was begun by the Philadelphia architect William L. Price in 1901. Others were the Byrdcliffe colony founded by an Englishman at Woodstock and the Elverhoj Colony near Washington. All these craft ventures followed Morris' socialistic aims and tried to return to a pre-industrial work pattern, priding themselves on the 'honest' simplicity of their hand-made furniture. The most successful venture was that of the stonemason Gustav Stickley who founded *The Craftsman* magazine in 1901 after a visit to Europe; the first two issues were devoted to John Ruskin and William Morris. His Craftsman Workshops made plain tables, settles, and 'Morris' reclining armchairs and his magazine devoted itself to articles on socialism and furniture design, propagating the ideas of the Arts and Crafts Movement throughout America. Most of the furniture was oak, of simple rectilinear construction and again stressed the 'honesty' of

Above: *Oak side chairs with leather seats designed by the Philadelphia architect William L. Price, 1901, for sale by the Rose Valley Community. The sturdy frame and lack of finely detailed decoration are typical of the American interpretation of the English Arts and Crafts Movement.*

Below: *Teak dining room buffet designed by Charles Sumner Greene for the Blacker House in Pasadena, which he and his brother designed in 1909. Both were influenced by Japanese architecture and the plain use of wood, displaying the grain, enlivened by applied silver decoration, is typical of their style.*

Top: *Bench seat by Gustav Stickley, 1909. Made in Syracuse, New York for his 'Craftsman' workshop, this is typical of his absolutely plain use of oak and leather. Stickley's furniture was conceived as being in keeping with his socialist principles, plain, 'honest' and unpretentious, and was extremely popular.*
Above: *Oak library table with leather top cover from the Syracuse 'Craftsman' workshops c.1909. This table shows clearly the exposed joints which were a principle of Craftsman furniture, stressing the 'honesty' of the production and its inspiration drawn from contemporary architecture.*
Left: *Stickley's version of William Morris' design for a reclining armchair, in plain oak and leather. Stickley's designs for furniture were published in the Craftsman magazine and through this means provided inspiration for many local furniture-makers. His work had a strong influence on many other tiny arts and crafts communities at the turn of the century.*

Left: *Chest designed by Lucia and Arthur Mathews and made for The Furniture Shop in San Francisco, 1906–1920. The inlay, painted and stained, is brightly coloured and was inspired by the California landscape and flora. The top and bottom drawers are embellished with handles in the form of scarabs. The jar and candlesticks are also from The Furniture Shop and the portrait is by Arthur Mathews, of his wife Lucia.*

production by revealing the mortise joints and pegs. This style of furniture also became known later as 'Mission' furniture.

Not all the designers who admired Arts and Crafts English designers felt the need to withdraw into cranky isolation. The idioms were adopted by men such as Charles Sumner Greene in California who designed furniture for the houses he designed in and around Pasadena with his brother Henry, and the artist and muralist Arthur F. Mathews and his wife Lucia who opened The Furniture Shop in San Francisco after the 1906 earthquake. Greene's furniture also followed Japanese tenets of construction. It was made usually in teak or walnut and was often decorated with inlaid silver, semi-precious stones, ebony and fruitwood, or with small amounts of carving. The Mathews' furniture was carved and painted, using the local colourful flora as their central motifs. Frank Lloyd Wright also reflected the ideals of the Arts and Crafts Movement in his early furniture with its subordination of form to principles of architectural design.

Art Nouveau was never a strong influence upon American design although after some was exhibited at the St Louis Exposition of 1904 in the French Pavilion the designs were copied by Karpen Brothers of Chicago. The poster designer Will H. Bradley also contributed designs for furniture which reflected English Art Nouveau motifs to the *Ladies' Home Journal* in 1901 and 1902. One individual craftsman who worked in the Art Nouveau idiom was Charles Rohlfs who worked independently on commission from his own workshop in Buffalo. Mainly in oak, his pieces have elaborate, swirling carving in the sinuous, plant-like style of the French designers. The more delicate work, usually fine carving and marquetry inlay, was carried out by one of his craftsmen, the carver George Thiele. His work was of very high quality and received a good deal of attention outside the United States. Rohlfs showed several pieces of furniture at the Turin Exhibition of 1902, and was later commissioned to make some pieces for Buckingham Palace.

The Mission style furniture produced between 1890 and 1920 was most influential, not in its immediate popularity, which was never very great, but in its theoretical influence on later designers and architects. This was especially strong in Chicago where Mission furniture served as a prototype for Prairie School design. The mainstream of American furniture continued much in the way it had during the 19th century and fads such as that for Turkish and Moorish interiors, following the Turkish padded-frame furniture with coil springs seen at the St Louis Exposition, enjoyed more popularity in many wealthy gentlemen's smoking rooms or studies. America continued in the main to follow the designs of Europe, its craftsmen often European immigrants, right up until men such as Louis Sullivan or Frank Lloyd Wright, who both worked in Chicago, began to forge a uniquely American style of interior which was to influence even European designs well into the 20th century.

Above: *Carved oak chair by Charles Rohlfs* c.*1898. Rohlfs was one of the few American designers to be influenced by Art Nouveau, as the sinuous, intertwining curves of this chair demonstrate, although the decadent appearance of French Art Nouveau is lacking.*

Upholstery from 1660 to 1900

It is not generally realized just how important a part the upholstery of chairs and beds played in the history of furniture from the late 16th until the late 19th century. The reason for this neglect is easy to find. Textiles are particularly vulnerable to the destructive effects of light, dirt and wear and have not survived, whereas the wooden framework of the chairs has. Many 17th and 18th century chairs were re-upholstered later using 19th century techniques which altered the original appearance. Fortunately, some examples of upholstery have survived and these, together with paintings and drawings of the period and contemporary descriptions in bills and inventories, allow us to form a picture of how a 17th century chair might have looked. It must be stressed at this point that for a long time upholstery was a luxury and thus the furniture described here was strictly for the very rich. Most people had to make do with bare wooden seats until well into this century.

Throughout much of history textiles, both in dress and furnishing, have been considered a status symbol. In the medieval period, rich damasks and brocades were hung on walls and behind the chairs of important people. These hangings were movable and could be taken down and re-erected in another room or house, a necessary feature at a time when courts regularly moved from palace to palace. Embroidered cushions made wooden seats more comfortable but upholstered chairs, by which is meant chairs on which some form of stuffing was fixed to the frame, first appear in any quantity in the 16th century. The reasons for their introduction were twofold. First, with the more settled way of life that existed at home under the Tudors, the aristocracy began to build vast country houses which they then proceeded to furnish in lavish style, paying more attention than they had previously to comfort and luxury. A second, more intriguing reason given by a contemporary writer is that changes in fashion which did away with the massive padded breeches worn by Tudor gentlemen made them more conscious of the disadvantages of wooden seats and opened the way for upholstered chairs.

Left: *The State Bed at Houghton Hall, Norfolk, designed by the architect William Kent c.1730. This is one of the finest state beds of the 18th century. It stands 4.5 m (15 ft) high and is dominated by the huge shell headboard. The moulded details on the headboard and the cornice are picked out in gold braid of several designs while a broader braid edges the curtains. A superb gold fringe trims the valances. The cost of the trimmings alone was over £1,200.*

Right: *Farthingale chair at Aston Hall, Birmingham; walnut frame, mid-17th century. The seat and back are lightly padded and covered with Turkey work, a knotted wool pile fabric made in England, probably around Norwich, in imitation of Oriental carpets. Turkey work was popular in the 17th and early 18th centuries and the designs usually feature stylized floral motifs. The clustered nailing on the back is a typical 17th century arrangement.*

The 17th century

The first upholstered chair was the X-frame type in use until the second quarter of the 17th century. Based on earlier folding chairs, it was completely covered with fabric nailed tightly to the frame. The seat sometimes had a thin layer of padding but this was usually supplemented by a

Above: *Sleeping chair at Ham House, London; carved and gilt frame, c.1678. This is one of a pair of chairs described in a contemporary inventory as 'sleeping chayres' since the backs are adjustable. The chairs retain their original upholstery of crimson silk brocaded with silver thread and trimmed with a plain silver fringe.*

cushion filled with down. Such chairs had the status of throne chairs and appear in portraits of Mary Tudor and James I. During the first half of the 17th century, the so-called 'farthingale' chair became popular and remained in use for much of the century. It had a stuffed seat and the back was usually similarly padded. This type of chair sometimes had leather coverings which were certainly favoured during the Commonwealth period, and for institutional use, for example, in colleges. Examples also survive covered in needlework or Turkey work.

Turkey work, or set work, occurs in considerable quantities in inventories of the 17th century and was still being supplied during the first quarter of the 18th century. It took its name from the Turkish carpets which it was intended to imitate. Oriental knotted carpets had been known in Europe since the Crusades. They were expensive items and were more often to be found on tables and cupboards than on the floor. Turkey work is formed by knotting the wool around the warp threads during the weaving process. The designs are usually floral and sometimes incorporate coats of arms. A high degree of stylization is common, with stiff flower heads arranged in uncomfortable rows, although some later designs were less formal. Turkey work was particularly hard-wearing and was used for table carpets as well as chair coverings. Towards the end of the 17th century, a petition to Parliament complaining about the widespread use of caned chairs claimed that previously more than 'five thousand dozen' chairs covered in Turkey work had been produced annually. Even allowing for possible exaggeration, this is proof of their popularity.

The leather used to cover 17th century chairs was generally plain, but embossed and gilded leather was sometimes to be found on grander types of chair.

The Restoration of the monarchy in 1660 heralded a new phase in upholstered furniture, as in other branches of the decorative arts. Charles II and his court had spent several years in exile in France and Holland where, particularly in France, there was no shortage of comfortable furniture and rich silk fabrics. On their return to England the aristocracy set about importing such luxuries and this trend was strengthened some years later when Louis XIV's measures against Protestants caused an influx of Huguenot craftsmen into England. It is no coincidence that the leading upholsterers of the time in this country, among them Casbert, Poitevin and Guibert, were of French origin. Caning was introduced as a cheap way of making chairs more resilient and therefore more comfortable, although it was usual for caned chairs to have a thin 'squab' or cushion on the seat. Woollen cloth was a common upholstery fabric, but for the wealthiest homes there were now chairs fully upholstered in rich silks.

At Ham House, which the Duke and Duchess of Lauderdale were refurbishing in the 1670s, there are two particularly fine examples of 17th century upholstery. A suite of chairs with carved and gilded frames in the form of dolphins is still covered with the original, though restored, brocaded silk, as are two 'sleeping chayres' with adjustable backs. These latter are covered in a crimson silk brocaded with metal thread. Such a combination might not seem ideal as a seat covering but this was by no means an isolated instance. Similar upholstery can be seen at Knole in Kent, which contains the finest collection of 17th century upholstery in the country. Particularly worthy of mention are the two sets of chairs accompanying the two Royal beds and dating from the 1680s. One set is covered with gold and silver tissue, the other with a green and oyster-coloured cut velvet with a pink fringe. Slightly later in date are the sofa and daybed originally made for the Duke of Leeds around 1700 and now at Temple Newsam House, Leeds. They are covered with a rich silk Genoa cut velvet in green, red and gold on an oyster-coloured ground. The two pieces are amply provided with cushions and clearly represent the ultimate in contemporary luxury.

Above right: *The Spangle Bedroom at Knole, Kent. The bed dates from c.1620 and is hung with crimson satin; the cornices, valances, headcloth and headboard, counterpane and bases are richly appliquéd with a strapwork pattern cut out of white silk and edged with couched cord. The bed takes its name from the small sequins or 'spangles' sewn into the strapwork. The valances and bases have silver fringe.*

Right: *Sofa from the Duke of Leeds suite now at Temple Newsam House, Leeds; carved, painted and gilt frame, c.1700. This sofa and its accompanying daybed (p.246) were made for the Duke of Leeds' house, Kiveton Park, Yorkshire. They are covered in a silk Genoa velvet in the usual colouring of green, red and gold pile on an oyster ground.*

Above: *Walnut settee, c.1660. It is now upholstered in velvet but is more likely to have been covered originally in leather or Turkey work. With plain fabrics such as silk velvets which have changed little over the centuries, it is often difficult to judge whether the upholstery is original or not; a fabric will 'age' convincingly in less than 40 years.*

Below: *Daybed from the Duke of Leeds suite, c.1700. This is upholstered* en suite *with the sofa (p.245). Although the velvet and fringe on both pieces are the original, they were rearranged early in this century, perhaps to conceal worn or faded areas. The piping is modern. The bolsters on the sofa were fringed and supported two more cushions.*

A feature of 17th century upholstery which is in evidence on all the above examples, is the lavish use of trimmings. Chairs are invariably fringed. The 'dolphin' suite has a plain fringe of striped silk and the sleeping chairs a fringe of gold thread. Perhaps more typical of the period are the tasselled fringes on the velvet-covered chairs at Knole and Temple Newsam where each hanging thread ends in a small tassel of silk threads. On the Duke of Leeds' pieces, two lengths of fringe were used, and in some cases the fringe even concealed parts of the carved chair frame. Another type of trimming found particularly on beds took the form of an elaborate band of interwoven wire bound with silk and ornamented with parchment strips or rosettes similarly bound. Such expensive embellishments were brought from France which always led the way in items of this kind.

The silks used in furnishings were not English but were imported mainly from Italy and France. The trade in silks from the Orient had been largely conducted through Italy and the Italians soon learned how to produce damasks and velvets which could compete with those from the East. Venice, Florence, Lucca and Genoa were all noted for the high quality of their silks and although the products of the French silk weavers led the field in the 18th century, Italian furnishing velvets were rarely surpassed. The silks most frequently used for upholstery were damask (usually a one-coloured fabric in which the pattern is created by alternating the weaves; the pattern is therefore seen in reverse on the back), brocade (a fabric into which are woven small areas of pattern, originally in gold or silver thread, but later in coloured silks), and velvet.

The impact of chairs at this date was due to their rich silk trimmings but beneath the expensive cover the actual stuffing was still somewhat primitive. The usual stuffing was curled horsehair although mixed and adulterated stuffings were undoubtedly used. To support the weight of the person sitting on the chair, narrow strips of webbing were interlaced across the seat frame. The hair was heaped onto a piece of linen tacked above the webbing and a second square of linen was fastened over the hair to keep it in place. This was the basis of all traditional upholstery but a number of refinements were adopted in the 18th century. At first little attempt was made to shape the stuffing and this explains the domed appearance of a large number of 17th century chair seats.

The full effect of damasks and velvets is best seen on the beds of the period since the pattern repeats might be as long as 1 m (3 ft). The habit of surrounding a bed with curtains had begun as a purely practical measure. The canopy, or tester, protected the occupants from falling insects and the curtains provided both privacy and protection from cold draughts. While 'best' beds were always expensively hung, beds in daily use were furnished with less sumptuous but more effective plain woollen materials. The years between 1670 and 1720 are noted for the great state beds supplied to a number of country houses. They were intended for the use of visiting royalty and were distinguished both by their height and by the richness of their hangings. A state bed was a treasured possession and for this reason a surprising number have survived. That made for the Earl of Melville around 1690, and now in the Victoria and Albert Museum, is hung with fringed crimson velvet lined with oyster-coloured silk. The carved headboard bearing the Earl's cipher is covered with silk and profusely trimmed with fringe and braid. The state bed ordered for Dyrham Park, Avon, around 1705 and still in the house has curtains of red velvet panelled with yellow. The scrolled and shaped valances which conceal the curtain rail are trimmed with braid and thickly fringed and the carving at the head of the bed is covered with a sprigged satin. In both these examples no woodwork is visible; even the foot posts which are hidden by the curtains are covered with fabric. State beds were still being commissioned in the second half of the 18th century but the last great example of this earlier period is the green velvet bed designed by William Kent for Houghton Hall, Norfolk, around 1730.

The desire for comfort in the late 17th century led to the adoption of new types of furniture such as the fully

Above: *Design for a bed by Daniel Marot, c.1690. This example is of the type known as an 'Angel' bed; the canopy is suspended from the ceiling and there are, therefore, no foot posts. The valances and bases are draped and ornamented with 'bells' and bows. The protective 'case curtain' is pulled back but could be drawn around the rod at the top.*

upholstered sofa and daybed. Another innovation was the winged easy chair which appeared around 1680 and gained popularity during the reign of Queen Anne. A recently discovered wing chair, now in the Victoria and Albert Museum, retains fragments of its original silk brocade covering in crimson, blue and gold. The design of the brocade is of the type known as 'bizarre' from the strange semi-abstract motifs which were in vogue during the first decade of the 18th century. As a rule, it is not easy to date furnishing silks accurately since fashions in furnishing did not change so swiftly as those in costume, and a particular pattern might remain popular over many years. The wing chair referred to above had two stripes of plain crimson silk down the back and seat; the juxtaposing of different fabrics or colours is typical of the early 18th century. The 'paning' on the Dyrham bed is another example and is repeated on the covers of the chairs that accompany the bed. A feature of these covers is that they are removable. When in place they are fastened by ties or hooks and eyes but they can be slipped off, revealing the plain linen beneath. Such covers were expensive and presumably when not in use they were removed and stored in a safe place.

The 18th century

The early years of the century saw the development of the English silk-weaving industry which was centred on Spitalfields and which employed many Huguenot weavers who had been driven from France. The greater part of their production consisted of dress silks but some furnishing fabrics were made; the crimson and gold cut velvet on a bed of 1714 at Hampton Court Palace is thought to be of English manufacture.

A number of winged easy chairs are covered with needlework. The use of needlework in furnishings has a long history and several ladies are famous for their prolific output, among them Bess of Hardwick and Mrs Delany. The inventory of Hardwick Hall, drawn up in 1601, contains numerous references to embroidered hangings, bed furnishings, cushion and seat covers. Many ladies did produce worked chair covers but, except in a few instances, the larger sets were probably the work of professional needlewomen.

Those covers worked in the first 30 years of the 18th century were of a distinctive type. In the centre of the back and seat was a pictorial scene, often taken from a published engraving and worked in fine detail in tent stitch with wools and silks. Around this was a border of flowers worked with wool in tent or cross stitch. It is not always easy to decide whether a piece of needlework is the original covering since needlework had a certain sentimental value and was sometimes re-used. In certain cases there can be no doubt because the outline of the design exactly follows the shape of the seat and back. As well as the pictorial needlework, there are surviving examples of chairs upholstered in geometric patterns. A winged easy chair dated 1730, at Aston Hall, Birmingham, is covered with Florentine stitch in a pattern of triangles.

Knotting was another favourite pastime of ladies. It was worked with a small shuttle similar to that used in tatting and produced a length of knotted thread. On a set of chair covers at Ham House the scrolled design is made up of knotted red wool couched down onto yellow satin.

By the middle of the 18th century needlework was no longer the sole occupation of young ladies and its use in furnishing slowly declined. The detailed pictorial scenes had gone out of fashion with the arrival of Rococo taste and were replaced by all-over floral designs worked in large cross stitch. The finest example of such work covers the Long Gallery suite of furniture at Temple Newsam House. The chairs, four settees and one daybed were ordered for the Long Gallery in the early 1740s and the

Left: *Two winged easy chairs upholstered in needlework; that in the foreground c.1730, that in the background c.1760. Needlework was a popular covering for winged easy chairs. Some early ones had intricate figure scenes taken from engravings but by the 1730s designs were usually completely floral and bolder, being worked in coloured wools on the canvas base. The screen with needlework panel dates from 1760.*
Right: *Detail of a sofa seat, c.1730. This is a good example of the use of engraved sources as inspiration for the needlewoman. The sofa seat and six accompanying chair seats depict scenes taken from William Kent's illustrations to John Gay's* Fables *(1727). As was usual, the scene is set within the floral border, here worked quite finely. The design is executed mainly in wool but details are done in silk.*

Above: *Chair of painted beech, c.1715; upholstered in contemporary English tapestry from the Soho manufactory. In the early 18th century the main English tapestry manufactory was that of the Great Wardrobe in Great Queen Street, Soho, run, until 1727, by John Vanderbank. This is particularly famous for the large hangings depicting subjects after Teniers or 'chinoiseries', but also produced tapestry chair covers.*

Above: *Rosewood armchair inlaid with brass, in the style of John Channon, c.1740. The drop-in seat is covered with contemporary needlework. Large numbers of chair seats were upholstered in needlework since it was no hard task for the ladies of a household to produce six or eight relatively modest-sized canvases quite quickly.*
Below: *Detail of needlework on a wing chair, c.1760. The most commonly used stitches were tent- and cross-stitch. In tent-stitch the thread is laid diagonally, usually from right to left, forming small slanting stitches all sloping in the same direction. Unless the canvas is held taut in a frame, the stitches tend to pull the work out of shape. Cross-stitch consists of two opposing diagonal stitches worked one above the other.*

covers, worked in coloured wools on a gold ground, are surely the work of professional needlewomen.

During the first half of the 18th century, silk damask was the usual choice for state rooms. The heavy carved and gilt furniture designed by William Kent to go into his architectural interiors looked best against strong colours such as red, blue and green. Silk damask, however, was expensive at around 14s 6d a yard and various cheaper substitutes were available. Mixed damasks of silk and wool, at around 6s a yard, and all-wool damasks at 4s, were used for wall and bed hangings, window curtains and chair covers. Silk velvets were less fashionable than they had been, although a Genoa velvet was used at Holkham Hall, Norfolk, as late as the 1750s. Woollen velvets, or plush, were obviously considered worthy substitutes and were used in the saloons at both Houghton and Holkham Halls. A cut woollen velvet called 'caffoy' was used in the saloon at Erddig, Denbighshire, in 1726. That woollen velvets were intended to simulate silk velvets is shown by the green, red and gold colouring of the cut wool velvet covering a set of chairs of *c.*1760 at Ham House, which clearly derives from the colours of Genoa velvets.

A step below the wool velvets were the other woollen fabrics much used in the early part of the century. Few have survived since they have suffered much damage from moths but inventories list amongst others, harrateen, moreen, camlet, cheney, calimanco, darnix, linsey-woolsey, tammy and paragon. Of these, tammy occurs mainly as a lining, and cheney, darnix, linsey and paragon were more suited to bed hangings than seat furniture. Camlet, which was generally of silk and wool, was used extensively in the furnishing of houses for window curtains, wall and bed hangings and cushion covers. Accounts show that scarlet camlet at 4s a yard cost 6d more than the green. This difference in price was usual in the 17th and 18th centuries as red dyes were more expensive than other colours. Harrateen and moreen were favourite furnishing fabrics, being used particularly for beds but also on seat furniture. The prevalence of woollen furnishing fabrics in the first half of the 18th century cannot be stressed too much. Certainly the modern practice of covering all 18th century chairs in damask or velvet is at variance with contemporary documentary evidence.

A new type of bed, called an 'Angel' bed, became fashionable at the beginning of the 18th century. The tester, instead of being supported on four posts, was suspended by chains from the ceiling. The most famous Angel bed is probably the state bed at Erddig which dates from 1720 and is hung with Chinese embroidered silk. Four-poster beds remained in fashion, but towards the middle of the century the woodwork became more important and carved mahogany foot posts and pierced cornices are typical of the period. Fringes were less in evidence but braid was used to outline and emphasize the scrolling line of the valances.

Right: *The state bed at Erddig, Clwyd, c.1720; the upholstery work probably by Philip Hunt of St Paul's Church Yard, London. Of the 'Angel' bed type, the bed retains its original upholstery of embroidered Chinese white satin. Rather unusually, the furnishings have been cut from several coverlets, with the borders forming the valances.*

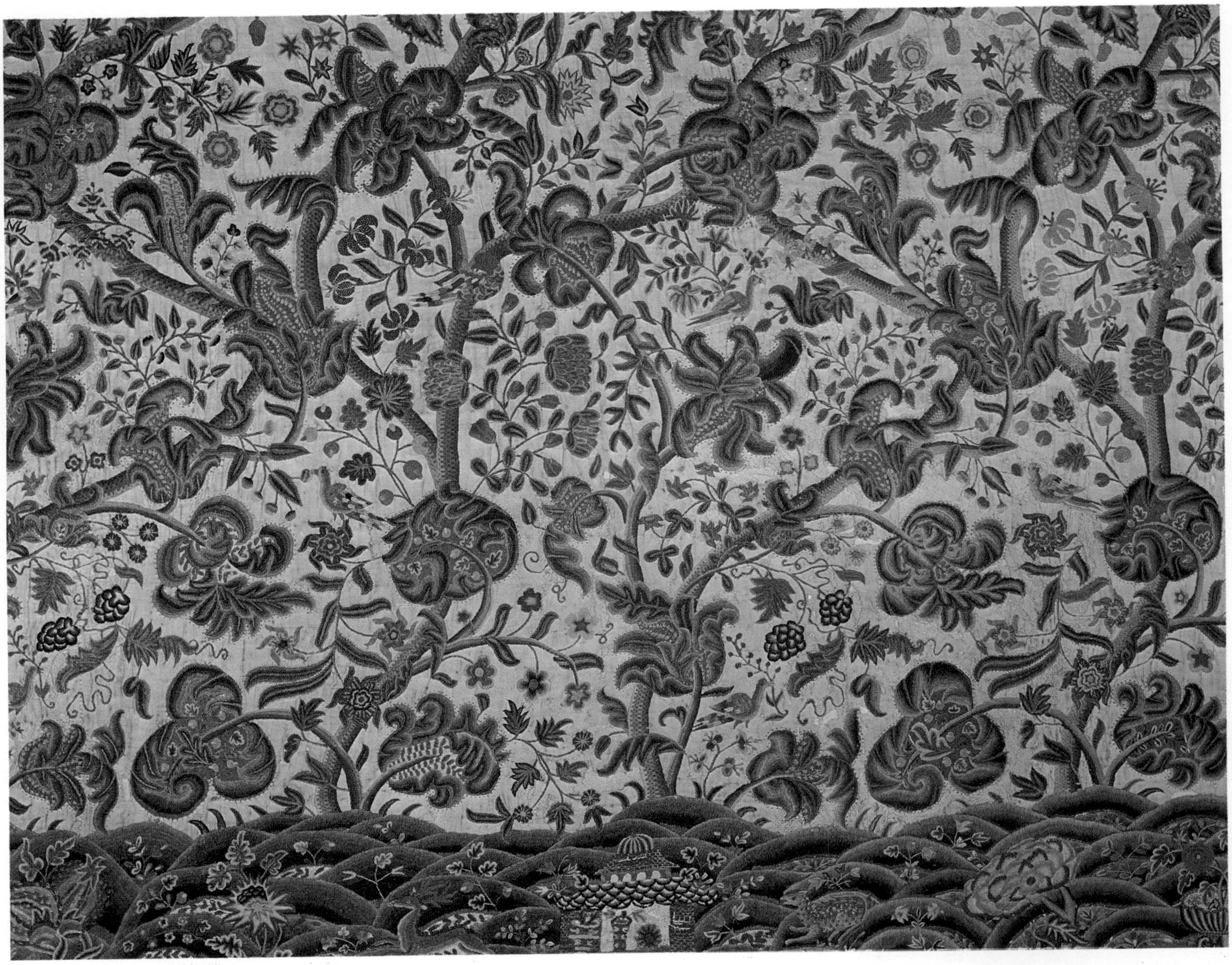

Above: *Crewelwork bed hanging,* c.*1680. Crewelwork bed furnishings survive in some quantity since they were worked on a strong linen and cotton fabric. They were not grand enough for State beds but probably adorned the 'best' beds of the merchant classes. Although the colours have often faded, the original brilliance of the dyes is usually still apparent on the back of the work.*
Right: *Design for a French chair by Thomas Chippendale, 1762. Chippendale achieved fame through the publication of his book of designs for furniture,* The Gentleman and Cabinet Maker's Director. *Although upholstery work accounted for a large proportion of his firm's business, the* Director *makes only general remarks on upholstery.*

Embroidered hangings occur on state beds at the turn of the 17th and 18th centuries, either in conjunction with other fabrics, or alone as at Clandon Park, Surrey. More humble were the crewel-work hangings which are found between 1660 and the second quarter of the 18th century. These were worked in thin worsted threads on a distinctive linen and cotton twill fabric. Early examples were worked in monochrome in an all-over scroll pattern that continued the coiled designs of Elizabethan needlework. More typical, however, is the slightly later tree design in which sinuous stems supporting scrolling leafy branches rise from hummocks; birds and animals are often included. This design has obvious affinities with the Oriental 'Tree of Life' motif but there is also a clear link with Elizabethan blackwork, particularly in the use of numerous filling stitches. Greens and blues are the predominant colours but some of the later examples also include quite brilliant reds and yellows.

From around 1750 a number of changes are apparent in upholstery. Techniques had been considerably improved since the 17th century. Although the basic components – webbing, linen, curled hair and linen – had not changed, it was now usual to give some shape to the stuffing. The front edge of the seat, which is the first area to wear thin, was strengthened by an extra roll of stuffing which was tightly stitched to form a firm edge. The loose hair in the centre of the seat or back was also stitched into place with long stitches. This could be done invisibly under the covering fabric or visibly, by bringing the thread through the fabric and finishing the end with a small tuft of silk. 'Tufting' was the forerunner of later buttoning and, by arranging the tufts in alternate rows, it could be used to achieve a decorative effect. Not all seat upholstery was fixed to the chair frame; many chairs had loose, or 'drop-in', seats which were upholstered on a separate frame and dropped into a rabbet or groove.

The design books of the late 18th century were, on the whole, not particularly concerned with upholstery. They were intended principally as aids to cabinetmakers and the texts make only passing mention of upholstery. Thomas Chippendale does suggest that his French chairs should be covered with Spanish leather, damask, tapestry or needlework, and his designs have patterns drawn on the backs and seats which do indicate needlework or tapestry. In fact, both these coverings were out of fashion and the chairs actually supplied by Chippendale's firm and by his contemporaries were more likely to be covered with leather, damask or haircloth. Haircloth, or horsehair, which was woven with a horsehair weft, was introduced around 1750. It was very hard-wearing and, presumably because of this, soon became immensely popular among all ranks of wealthier society, being used in royal palaces and middle-class homes. Black was the most frequently mentioned colour but red and green haircloth also occur and as well as plain weaves there were striped and checked varieties.

The choice of fabric for upholstery was largely governed by the room for which it was intended. Damask and needlework were to be found in saloons and drawing rooms, whereas haircloth and leather were more suited to libraries and dining parlours. Fabric was not considered suitable for dining rooms as it was believed that it would absorb and retain the smell of food.

Carved ornament was a feature of seat rails during the second quarter of the 18th century and this made fringes inappropriate. As a result they had largely fallen from favour and in their place the edges of upholstery were finished with either a single or a double row of brass-headed nails which followed the line of the frame. This provided a neat edge which instead of concealing the rail actually drew attention to it. In a few cases, a strip of brass was fixed over the edge of the fabric. Chippendale himself remarked that seats look best when they 'have a Brass Border neatly chased; but are most commonly done with brass Nails, in one or two Rows'.

In the third quarter of the 18th century cotton became increasingly popular as a furnishing fabric. Indian chintzes had been imported into this country in the 17th century but in 1700–1 their import was prohibited in an attempt to safeguard the English textile trade. This did not prevent a certain amount being brought in by devious means and even so eminent a person as the actor David Garrick had a set of chintz bed hangings impounded by the customs. (They were later released and graced Garrick's bed which is now in the Victoria and Albert Museum.) Cottons printed by the wood-block technique were produced in England from the late 17th century, but, in the 1750s, a new technique was developed in Ireland. This involved printing by means of engraved copper plates which were capable of reproducing fine detail. Although it was possible to add extra colours, the majority of copper-plate printed cottons were in monochrome. After a few years, the process was transferred to the south of England and for a time, the cotton printing industry flourished around London until the rise of the Lancashire firms.

Designs were either taken from engraved sources or were specially commissioned. The earliest surviving dated

Above: *Bed supplied by Chippendale for the 'Chinese Bedroom' of David Garrick's villa on the Thames at Hampton, c.1775; now in the Victoria and Albert Museum. The bed now has new hangings. The original furniture was to have been made up from Indian chintz given to Mrs Garrick.*

Left: *Armchair from a suite of 6 chairs and 2 settees made by William Ince and John Mayhew for the Tapestry Room at Croome Court, Worcestershire, 1769–71; carved and gilt frame upholstered in Gobelins tapestry. The suite is now in the Metropolitan Museum, New York. The floral-patterned seat covers were designed by Maurice Jacques and Louis Tessier and all the tapestry was woven at the workshop of Jacques Neilson at the Gobelins manufactory.*
Right: *French sofa (*canapé*), attributed to Georges Jacob,* c.*1780; carved and gilt frame, the upholstery of Beauvais tapestry illustrating scenes from La Fontaine's* Fables.

cotton of this type includes amid the pattern the inscription 'Robert Jones Old Ford 1761'. It is printed in red with pastoral scenes taken from three different engravings. These cottons, finely printed in one or more colours on a white ground, are sometimes known as 'toiles de Jouy' after a French manufactory at Jouy, near Versailles, although the English cottons pre-date those of Jouy. In addition to pastoral scenes, chinoiseries and flower prints were produced.

Printed cottons were particularly suited to window and bed hangings, but they were also used extensively for chair covers. Since the major advantage of cotton over silk and wool was that it could be washed, an old form of upholstery was revived to obtain the full benefit of the cotton. The slip-on covers of the years around 1700 have already been mentioned. This type now became far more popular. The chair was stuffed as usual and finished in a plain linen, and the loose cotton covers were tied or hooked into place. In most cases, they must have looked rather baggy, although some were specifically designated 'tight' covers.

It was usual to supply two sets of identical cases so that one was always in use while the other was being cleaned. Later generations did not consider these cotton covers to be of the same worth as silks or needlework, and so few have survived. One that did, and which is now in the Henry Francis du Pont Winterthur Museum in the USA, is a seat cover for a parlour chair. It is made from the 1761 Robert Jones cotton referred to above, but the deep frill around the lower edge concealing the top half of the legs indicates that it was made in America since frilled covers were not common in England. Not all cottons had such elaborate patterns; stripes, spots and sprigs were fashionable, as were combinations such as striped and flowered. It is clear from documentary sources that cotton was being used extensively for furnishings from 1760 onwards, superseding the woollen fabrics of earlier years, and that they were to be found not only in bedrooms and dressing rooms, but in drawing rooms, too.

Silk damask remained the favourite material for state rooms, although the whole concept of state rooms was losing currency. A crimson silk damask was used for the hangings, curtains and upholstery of the Picture Gallery at Corsham Court, Wiltshire, in 1769. However, lighter silks such as sarsenet, satin and tabby, were considered more suitable for the elegant interiors of Robert Adam. In place of the large Baroque patterns found on damasks, these silks were either plain or had small repetitive designs. Riband-and-flower designs, such as that on the Spitalfields silk used in the Red Drawing Room at Syon House, near London, are typical of the middle years of the century. Slightly later, distinctive Neoclassical motifs, such as urns and festoons, occur.

As chair frames took on a new linear appearance in keeping with the Neoclassical interiors for which they were designed, so their upholstery was similarly affected. Chairs were now 'square-stuffed', that is, the edges of the seat were built up and tightly stitched so that the top and sides met at a sharp right angle which was emphasized by a line of piping. The same technique could be used on the back, although squared seats do occur in conjunction with rounded backs. Brass nailing was still practised but braid came back into fashion. A narrow gimp was used around the edges of the upholstery while wider braids were sewn onto the back and seat a small distance inside the piping.

Tapestry, which had been out of fashion for some years, enjoyed a brief revival in the late 1760s when a number of English gentlemen ordered sets of French tapestries from the Gobelins manufactory. *En suite* with the wall-hangings were specially woven chair covers and panels for fire-screens. The design consisted of a central cartouche containing a scene with figures after François Boucher, on a ground woven to simulate damask. As the hangings were designed to fit the particular room and were hung edge to edge, thus covering the entire wall space above the dado, an illusion of pictures hanging on damask-lined walls was created. Indeed, mock gilded frames were even woven around the 'paintings'. The upholstery panels differed

slightly; some sets had cartouches on the backs, others simply had bouquets of flowers. The damask grounds were woven in pink, beige or yellow. Sets of these tapestries were ordered for Osterley Park House, near London, and Newby Hall, Yorkshire (both still in situ), Croome Court (suite now in the Metropolitan Museum, New York), and Moor Park (suite split up; part in the Philadelphia Museum of Art, part at Temple Newsam House). Further sets were given by the French king to visiting monarchs but, these apart, tapestry rooms of this type were a peculiarly English, and short-lived, phenomenon. Even in France, where the various tapestry manufactories were producing upholstery panels, tapestry was not so common a chair covering as it would now appear from the large number of 18th-century chairs sporting tapestry covers. Many of these were re-upholstered in tapestry in the 19th century.

Of the main design books published in the 18th century, George Hepplewhite's *The Cabinet-Maker and Upholsterer's Guide* of 1787 is the only one that claims to be of use to upholsterers. The seats of mahogany parlour chairs, he maintains, should be covered with 'horsehair, plain, striped, chequered, &c. at pleasure', or be caned and provided with loose cushions covered to match the curtains. Fully upholstered chairs and sofas, he suggests, look well in red or blue leather with silk tufts. His actual designs show several interesting details. Some seats are still rounded and have brass nails. On one example the nails are arranged in a festoon pattern. In the early 1760s Ince and Mayhew published similar fancy nailing patterns but there is little evidence that these were ever adopted on any significant scale in England, although festoon nailing is to be seen in some American paintings. Hepplewhite's square-stuffed seats have printed borders and one has a central printed or painted medallion. Painted silk might not be considered particularly suitable for upholstery, but nevertheless there are a few references to chair covers of painted silk and velvet.

Towards the end of the 18th century, the cotton printers produced specially shaped prints for various uses. Borders with Greek fret or chintz patterns were made in several widths suitable for hangings and upholstery. A complete suite of bordered furnishings, ordered from France in the 1790s and now in the Rijksmuseum, Amsterdam, has hangings and curtains of plain blue silk, edged with a broad brocaded border. A narrower border trims the chair covers. This set of silk furnishings was probably quite unusual, but cotton borders were certainly used in large quantities. In addition to the printed medallions mentioned by Hepplewhite, which were sewn onto upholstery, shaped chair-seat covers were printed in one piece, incorporating borders and leaving plain those areas which would have to be cut out when fitting the cover to accommodate the back supports.

In both seat furniture and beds, the second half of the 18th century saw a proliferation of new types, almost all imported from France. Many had Eastern origins, or at least Eastern names, such as 'turquoise' and 'ottomane', both forms of sofa. Of the many new French beds, the 'polonaise' bed was the most popular in this country. It was distinguished by a small canopy supported centrally over the bed on four S-shaped iron posts. The original purpose of the curtains was no longer relevant. They ceased to be functional and became, instead, decorative. Several of Chippendale's bed designs are shown with curtains 'to draw up in Drapery'. The curtains are drawn up towards the corners of the tester by a series of cords and pulleys and the ends hang down in a swag. Despite the decline in the use of state beds, both Chippendale and Sheraton produced over-elaborate designs for state beds which were hardly likely to be executed.

Whereas previously beds had stood out into the room with the head against the wall, 'French', or 'couch' beds, which were placed lengthwise against the wall, became fashionable. 'Field' and 'camp' beds were small, plain beds with a folding and one-piece canopy and curtains which could be easily taken down. They were particularly useful for officers on military campaigns, but were also convenient for other travellers who did not wish to risk sleeping in the beds provided by inns. Printed cottons were particularly suitable for bed hangings since they were more hygienic than woollen stuffs. So, too, was dimity, a twilled cotton fabric used occasionally for chair covers but mostly for bed furniture. As it was usually white, upholsterers were able to exercise all their ingenuity in dressing it up with printed chintz borders or coloured trimmings.

Above: *Design for a State Bed in the Gothic style by George Smith, 1808. This design is unusual for its date in that the upholstery element is minimal; the bed is more of a carver's masterpiece.*
Left: *Design for a Chinese bed by Thomas Chippendale, 1762. He produced a number of designs in this taste but the 'chinoiserie' influence only extends as far as the woodwork; the bed hangings are the same as those on his other beds. The valances are festooned to suit the line of the cornice and the curtains are raised and lowered by cords and pulleys.*

The few state beds that were made during this period were on a smaller scale than earlier ones, but still tended to be hung with silk. Damask was used on the state bed at Harewood House, Yorkshire, while Adam's bed for Osterley had green velvet curtains and drapery. The more fashionable light silks were also used; the state bed at Audley End, Essex, was hung with pale blue silk.

That any original 17th and 18th century upholstery has survived is, perhaps, surprising. State furniture was used only rarely and so had little wear, and needlework, which is comparatively tough anyway, was often treasured for sentimental reasons. However, the main explanation for the survival of these fabrics is to be found in the almost universal use of protective loose covers. Early covers were fairly substantial, being made of leather or tough woollen fabrics, such as serge, and in 17th century France they were even ornamented. Washable materials were of course more suitable, and from the second quarter of the 18th century linen and cotton covers appear. These relatively cheap covers tended to be either striped or checked and, more

Above: *French bed, probably by Monbro Fils, Paris,* c.*1860: carved and gilt frame upholstered in a silk brocade. By the mid-19th century those beds that were still hung tended to have short, often semi-circular domed canopies suspended from the wall and ceiling. The hangings, which were no longer functional, were generally plain, but deep swagged valances trimmed with thick fringes and tassels were common.*

often than not, were green and white. Most simply covered the back and seat and were tied under the seat, but towards the end of the century there was a fashion for floor-length cases. Not surprisingly, such items have not generally survived and are known to us only from inventories and paintings; it was not unusual for chairs to be left covered when an interior featured in a painting. Upholsterers did not only supply cases for upholstery. Tubes of cloth, called 'stockings', safeguarded the gilding on chair legs and bed posts, and thick leather covers lined with flannel protected the tops of tables and commodes from fading and accidental knocks. The expensive hangings of beds were preserved from the effects of both light and dirt by 'case curtains', usually of a cheap woollen fabric, which could be drawn to enclose the bed completely.

As a rule, housekeeping techniques in the 18th and 19th centuries were more thorough than today. Care was taken to see that direct sunlight never fell onto furniture or textiles and housemaids were issued with detailed instructions on how to look after upholstery. In many large houses the use of loose covers was continued until the Second World War when a shortage of domestic staff led to many of the traditional housekeeping methods being abandoned. This has proved particularly unfortunate with regard to textiles which have suffered irreversible fading but, happily, the advantages of loose covers have been recognized once again and their use is being revived.

The 19th century

During the Regency period chair frames lost the delicacy so apparent in the late 18th century, and the darker woods and heavy ormolu mounts demanded stronger colours and fabrics. George Smith, writing in 1808, suggested leather for parlour and library chairs, and mentioned the practice of printing borders onto leather. For drawing rooms, silks, painted satin and velvet, woollens or chintz were used.

This was a period when drapery reigned supreme. Walls were swathed in festoons of fabric, and curtain valances consisted of yards of material looped over poles or other ornaments. During these years fashion was led by the Prince of Wales who had been furnishing and re-furnishing Carlton House since the 1780s. A series of drawings of the rooms there, published by W. H. Pyne in 1819, show the walls dressed with elaborate fringed draperies. Drapery was best suited to hangings but it appeared on chairs in the form of festoons across the backs of sofas or under seat rails, and as 'mantles' which were lengths of fabric loosely hung over the back or arm of a chair in a 'Grecian' manner. Stuffing was still mainly square-edged, but fringes now swept back into fashion. They were no longer the neat fringes of the 18th century but had deep open-work headings and long hangers, and sometimes extended from the seat rail to the floor. Occasionally hangers were even ornamented with small wooden beads wound with silk.

Bed-types scarcely changed; the four poster and the 'French' bed remained the basic forms. The curtains had reverted to the simple hang-down type but were tied to the posts or looped over ornaments. It was in the valances that contemporary fashion asserted itself. They were festooned in layers, gathered or draped around mock spears and similar trophies. All were fringed and trimmed with tassels.

The amount of fabric required to create these draperies was considerable and it is no coincidence that improvements in weaving at the beginning of the 19th century were enabling larger quantities of material to be produced. The introduction to Lancashire of the power loom led to the mass production of plain cotton and woollen cloths, such as calico and moreen, at a reduced cost, and the adoption of the Jacquard loom in the 1820s made it possible to weave patterned stuffs more cheaply. As a result, woollen, or Norwich, damasks were in plentiful supply. Less expensive still were stamped fabrics on which the pattern was impressed by machine. Printing, too, underwent various technical changes. At the start of the century the delicate copper-plate prints had been largely supplanted by more rumbustious chintz patterns printed in polychrome by means of wood-blocks. Typical of the patterns found at this time were large floral and leaf designs printed in 'drab' colours, that is browns, yellows and greens. By 1820, brighter colours had returned and architectural motifs such as pillars begin to appear. In the 1820s roller printing of textiles was developed. The pattern repeat was engraved onto a copper roller and printing became a continuous process. Extra colours were added firstly by wood-blocks and later by additional rollers. The so-called 'Regency stripe' has little basis in fact since striped patterns do not

Above: *The Queen's Room, Penrhyn Castle, Gwynedd, mid-19th century. The canopy above the brass bedstead shows how the elaborate hangings of earlier days had been considerably streamlined by the mid-19th century. Chairs, however, continued to be thickly stuffed and richly upholstered. The deep buttoning on the chair and chaise longue are particularly associated with Victorian upholstery.*
Below: *Lamp mat, Berlin woolwork,* c.*1850. The Victorians developed a taste for furnishing accessories such as mats, antimacassars and valances around mantelpieces, often worked by the ladies of the house.*

appear in any noticeable quantity until the 1820s.

At the beginning of the period woolwork was out of favour, but delicate embroidery in coloured silks on a silk ground was to be seen on upholstery, bed valances and screen panels. Thirty years later, a revival in wool embroidery swept the country. Berlin woolwork, so called because the wools and patterns were originally imported

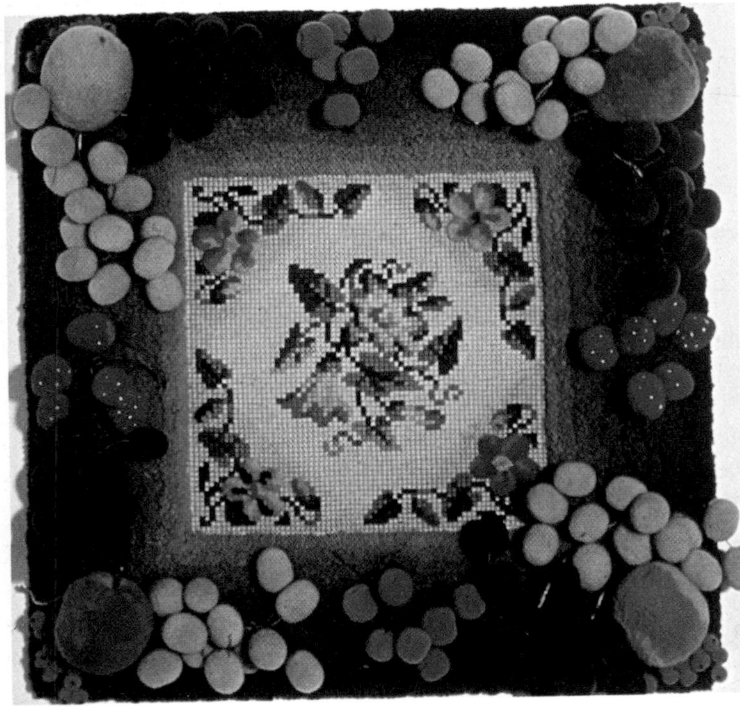

from that city, was first encountered in this country early in the century but it did not become widely popular until the 1830s. The designs were worked on canvas from squared paper patterns which were available commercially, and since large cross or tent stitches were used, it was relatively quick to execute. The earlier examples have subdued colouring, contrasting sharply with the garish hues found later.

The 1830s marked a decisive turning point in the history of upholstered furniture with the adoption of the first significant innovation in technique since the 17th century. In 1828, a patent was taken out for the use of coiled wire springs in stuffings. Five years later John Claudius Loudon, in his *Cottage, Farm and Villa Architecture*, described their use in upholstery. The chair frame was webbed as before but onto the webbing were placed the double-cone springs which were all tied down to the same height. A piece of canvas was laid over them and a layer of horsehair on top of this cushioned the sitter from the uncomfortable effects of sitting directly on the springs. The introduction of sprung upholstery made a radical difference to the appearance of chairs since the seat, in order to accommodate the springs, had to be considerably deeper. At the same time, there was a movement away from square-stuffing to rounded edges and a combination of these two facts gave rise to the description 'overstuffed', so often applied to Victorian upholstery.

Another technique associated with Victorian upholstery is buttoning. That this was no new idea has already been shown, but around 1820 the silk tufts of the 18th century were replaced by buttons covered to match the upholstery. For the next 30 years, the buttoning, which was arranged in alternate rows so that a diamond pattern was produced, remained fairly shallow. It was not until the middle of the century that deep buttoning became fashionable. To achieve this effect, springs were inserted between the buttons and the excess fabric was taken into pleats.

In the 1830s and 1840s, completely upholstered chairs

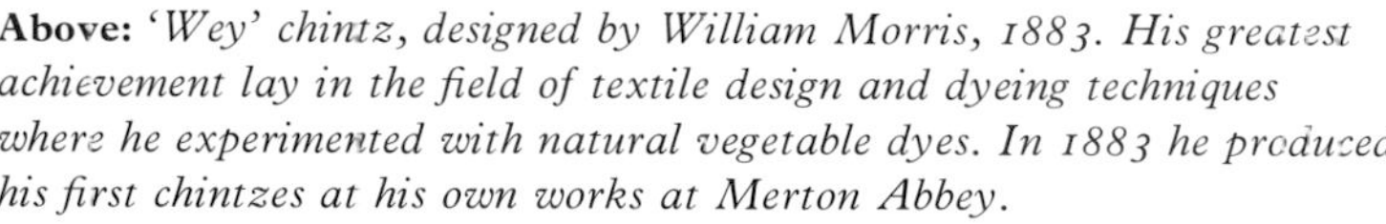

Above: *'Wey' chintz, designed by William Morris, 1883. His greatest achievement lay in the field of textile design and dyeing techniques where he experimented with natural vegetable dyes. In 1883 he produced his first chintzes at his own works at Merton Abbey.*

Above right: *'Wandle' chintz, designed by William Morris, 1884. Morris' designs for textiles and wallpapers are taken from nature and cover the entire surface. The layout of his patterns owes much to the influence of early Italian silks and velvets which Morris had studied in the South Kensington Museum (now the Victoria and Albert Museum). This design was block printed.*

Below: *'Artichoke' embroidery, designed by William Morris c.1880 and executed in wool on linen by Mrs Godman for Smeaton Manor, Northallerton, Yorkshire. Morris' early designs for embroidery were executed by members of his family but from the 1870s he designed for other needlewomen and for the Royal School of Needlework.*

and sofas with little, if any, wood showing, brought the upholsterer into prominence, but from the late 1840s the polished wood frame was again visible. There was another increase in types of upholstered furniture, particularly in variations of the sofa and ottoman which were given cosy names, such as 'sociable' and 'tête-à-tête'. The introduction of 'comfortable' furniture indicated a significant change in social habits; from the middle of the century it was permissible for men to 'lounge', although for most women, still rigidly corseted, the benefits of the new furniture cannot have been immediately noticeable.

The spread of the Jacquard loom led to an increasing use of figured stuffs. For wealthy households there were silk damasks, both English and French, velvets and new weaves, such as tabaret which had a striped effect, but more common were woollen and cotton damasks and velvets, or plain woollen stuffs. The *Workwoman's Guide*, published in 1840, lists damask, merino, stuff and haircloth as suitable for upholstery, and suggests washable cases of Holland linen, chintz or calico.

The quality of printing declined slightly as roller-printing increased production but fine block-printed textiles were still available. Although floral patterns remained popular, the various historical styles which dominated the decorative arts in the 1840s were evident in printed and woven fabrics; Elizabethan strapwork, Moorish arabesques, Rococo scrolls and Gothic arches all occur. By 1850, the styles had become confused and were used more or less indiscriminately, and the light colours, crimson, yellow and pale green, were giving way to the darker greens and clarets associated with the Victorians. A major influence on all textiles was the discovery of chemical dyes, in particular aniline dyes, which produced harsh, bright colours.

These dyes were also used for Berlin wools. By 1850, Berlin woolwork had become immensely popular. Worked in garish colours, usually on a black ground, bouquets of full-blown roses, parrots and other pets, and historical scenes appeared on slippers, purses, screen panels and chairs in almost every home. In some examples, a three-dimensional effect was achieved by working areas of the designs, such as flower petals or a bird's plumage, in a loop stitch which was cut and carefully sheared to form a pile. It

Left: *The 'Saville' armchair, designed by George Jack; mahogany, c.1890. Jack had trained as an architect and worked for Philip Webb. In 1890 he became the chief furniture designer of Morris and Co. The chair is upholstered in Morris' 'Strawberry Thief' chintz.*
Right: *Armchair with adjustable back; turned ebonized wood, c.1866. Although commonly known as the 'Morris Chair', the design was, in fact, adapted by Philip Webb from a traditional Sussex chair. William Morris worked primarily on two-dimensional designs and apart from a few early pieces made for his own use, most of the furniture attributed to Morris was designed by Webb. The upholstery is in one of Morris' woven designs, the 'Bird' pattern wool tapestry, first produced in 1878.*

is, perhaps, fanciful to suggest that the *prie-dieu* type of chair was specially designed to display woolwork to its best advantage, but at least one book of designs for furniture particularly suitable for being covered in Berlin woolwork was published.

The main change in beds during the Victorian era was brought by a new awareness of hygiene. Loudon showed designs for iron beds which did not harbour vermin and stressed the importance of using washable fabrics such as dimity and printed cotton for the hangings, but this idea was still in its infancy. Woollen hangings remained popular and the bed designs illustrated in the *Workwoman's Guide* showed little change from the designs of the beginning of the century; draped valances, the perfect nesting place for bed-bugs, were still very much in evidence.

The Great Exhibition of 1851 brought about a fundamental change of ideas. The general consensus of opinion was that in most fields British design had reached lamentable depths. The wide range of misused and over-commercialized historical styles and the lack of any new ideas struck the more enlightened visitors and led to an outburst of criticism. As early as 1841, the architect A. W. N. Pugin, in *The True Principles of Pointed or Christian Architecture*, had fulminated against contemporary upholstery which he described as 'a surprising vehicle for bad and paltry taste'. In particular he disliked 'the modern plans of suspending enormous folds of stuff over poles, as if for the purpose of sale or of being dried', and the use of wooden beads on fringes. The essential function of the object – to conceal the curtain rail in the case of the valance and to prevent threads unravelling in that of the fringe – had been forgotten. Another critic was Charles Locke Eastlake in his *Hints on Household Taste*, first published in 1868. He agreed with Pugin on the matter of fringes and had some scathing remarks to make about upholsterers, comparing their creations to 'the gimcrack decorations of a wedding cake', and describing the typical highly padded Victorian sofa as an 'eccentric combination of bad carpentry and bloated pillows'.

In the face of such criticism, the role of the upholsterer was bound to be affected by the rise of the various movements reacting against the status quo. The most influential of these was led by William Morris who wanted to revive the medieval concept of the craftsman. Although Morris did not actually design any chairs, he was instrumental in the popularization of traditional chair types, such as the 'Sussex' chair. The one ideal common to most of these movements was that of 'honest construction'. Their furniture was simply put together and no attempt was made to conceal the method of construction. Above all it was functional. Caned and rush seats were particularly suited to this concept and upholstery, where it was present, was of the traditional form with horsehair or flock (wool waste) stuffing.

If upholstery was no longer so important, the design of furnishing textiles was the subject of much thought. One result of the Great Exhibition was that people had begun to question the practice of reproducing nature exactly on textiles. Morris' designs, although based on nature, were formalized into flowing patterns which covered the entire surface of the fabric. He experimented with vegetable dyes and, from the 1870s, produced both printed chintzes and woven fabrics. His designs continued to be produced after his death and enjoyed considerable popularity, firstly among the more enlightened but later among a wider public. Other textile designers, such as Christopher Dresser, Lewis Day, A. H. Mackmurdo and C. F. A. Voysey, followed Morris' lead, although they were not constrained by his preoccupation with medieval society. Thus they were open to influence from the taste for the exotic, particularly for 'japonisme', and their flowers and birds have an elongated, sinuous appearance which clearly foreshadows the restless, curving Art Nouveau patterns of the turn of the century.

Such avant-garde designs and ideas were, of course, confined to a small group of art-conscious modern thinkers. In the majority of middle-class homes, thickly-upholstered seats continued in favour. In 1881, Robert W. Edis could still lament in his book, *The Decoration and Furniture of Town Houses*, that 'the designing of furniture is, as a rule, handed over to the upholsterer', and it was not

until 1897 that the periodical *Furniture and Decoration and the Furniture Gazette* was able to report that thin stuffing was coming back into fashion.

The ideal of functionalism finally brought about the demise of the four poster bed, although it lingered on through the third quarter of the century. Even Eastlake, with his forward-looking ideas, was happy to recommend bed hangings of white dimity, cretonne (plain or printed cotton), chintz or damask. However, by the end of the century the simple bedstead of either wood or metal had largely replaced the creations of former years.

The last 40 years of the 19th century witnessed a slow decline in the importance of the upholsterer. For the first time since the medieval period textiles ceased to dictate the appearance of a room. Even in the late 18th century, an age not particularly noted for drapery, it had not been uncommon for the hangings of a bed to cost twice as much as the woodwork. Of course, comfortable upholstered furniture had not disappeared for ever, but henceforth the status of the upholsterer was to be that of a mere tradesman, rather than an instigator of fashions, a role that was taken over by a new phenomenon, the interior designer.

Oriental Furniture

Oriental furniture is the complete antithesis of furniture from the West. Its functionality and simplicity, sometimes to the point of austerity, contrasts with the indulgent tastes of Europe and America, not only because of obvious cultural differences but also because in the East, architecture and social habits that were alien to the West dictated shapes and usages which were, in many cases, unique. These differences are not only reflected in the styles and designs of furniture but also in the method of manufacture and in the varieties of woods and techniques of decoration commonly used.

In the Far East, furniture is essentially functional, a fact which is reflected in the combination of superb craftsmanship and design which express the maker's deep knowledge and feeling for wood. It demonstrates Eastern ingenuity in applying art and technology to produce furniture totally in keeping with the demands of Oriental civilization. The indigenous furniture of the Orient perfectly reflects the social conditions and surroundings in which it was meant to be used. Thus, it is not surprising that apart from short periods in Europe when Western tastes for chinoiserie flourished, Oriental furniture has not been popular with collectors, furnishers, or interior decorators.

With changes in Western fashion and the introduction of more simple tastes to match contemporary trends in architecture however, Oriental furniture is increasingly finding a place in European and American homes. This acceptance has made antique Oriental furniture more collectable and pieces from China, Korea and Japan are now highly sought-after and international interior decorators often make a point of including Oriental furniture in their designs.

While it is easy to generalize on the differences between Oriental and European furniture, it is very difficult to be specific because the furniture of the Orient is not itself homogeneous. There are major differences between the furniture of Japan and China, while Korean furniture is different again, and that from India, Burma and Tibet is almost from a different world. These differences lie not only in the form and shape of the furniture but also in the technique of manufacture. In the case of China and Japan, one obvious reason for differences is that Chinese and Japanese houses are architecturally different from each other, due to reasons of climate and geography, as well as social behaviour. The Chinese, for instance, built substantial buildings with permanent internal divisions, while the Japanese, perhaps out of the necessity of dealing with earth tremors and other climatic hazards, designed buildings of more modest materials, without permanent internal divisions, that could either withstand tremors or prevent major loss of life should the buildings collapse.

China

A major reason for the differences between Chinese and Japanese furniture is that while the Chinese originally lived at floor level, sitting on mats and so on, and only later designed furniture to enable them to perform household activities above this level, the Japanese style of living remained more or less at floor level. In north China however, the two modes of living and hence the furniture continued alongside each other. Much everyday activity, as well as sleeping, took place on a platform called a *k'ang*. This structure, which was heated from underneath by hot

Left: *The studio or study of a Wen Jen, a scholar-poet-artist of China, typifies the conservative attitude of Chinese society. The rustic freedom of nature was introduced through wide doors, opening onto a verandah. The pavilion-like feeling was underlined by the sparseness of furniture, creating an air of spaciousness which was thought conducive to literary and artistic achievement. This studio, although photographed in Hanoi in Vietnam, embodies the formal elements of the Chinese interior.*
Right: *Chinese hardwood hua-li ch'uang of the 18th century. The ch'uang is a combination of chair and small couch, much favoured as a sort of throne by mandarins and court dignitaries. The simplicity of line and sparsity of carving is accentuated by the choice of hua-mu panels.*

Above: *Large t'iao-an, formal side table, sometimes also called an altar table. These tables were placed in the centre of the rear wall in the main reception room of the house. They were made in the traditional hardwoods for most domestic applications, as well as lacquered, usually for temple or palace use. This 17th century lacquered example follows a classic design popular over a number of centuries.*

Left: *Fine Chinese hardwood armchair, inlaid with mother-of-pearl, dating to the first half of the 19th century. Chairs with marble seats were intended for use in summer, but, with the addition of cushions, might also have been used in winter. The Chinese, however, were most particular in the use of the correct furniture for specific seasons.*

air extended along the whole of one side of a room and on it, one could recline, smoke, drink tea and conduct all manner of business. Special furniture designed for use on the *k'ang* consisted of a low central table – a style much used today in the West for coffee tables – a low cupboard in which were kept objects used on the *k'ang*, and of course a quilt for use at night. In south China, while it was the custom to sit on mats in open pavilions during the summer, all other activities were conducted at raised levels.

Chinese furniture can be both simple and baroque. To the European eye it can look alien, or extremely familiar. This latter characteristic is due to the fact that European interest in China during the 17th and 18th centuries generated the style called 'chinoiserie', which was taken up by master European furniture makers and designers like Chippendale, who took elements of Chinese furniture and expressed them in his 'Chinese' pieces. In many cases the Chinese characteristics were accentuated almost to the point of caricature.

The quality of Chinese furniture is variable. At its best, it is superb, with each piece of wood slotting perfectly into the next (the Chinese craftsman did not use nails or screws). On the other hand, Chinese furniture can be very badly made. In fact, in the 18th century, the quality of furniture which the Chinese exported to Europe was generally so bad that patrons and lovers of coromandel lacquered furniture preferred to send European furniture to China to be lacquered, taking the risk of the piece being damaged in transit and often waiting years for its return, rather than accept the frequently shoddy workmanship which the coromandel lacquer hid and which the Chinese merchants chose to export to the European market.

The art of furniture-making developed very early in China, and it is probable that many of the traditional Chinese shapes had already evolved by the time of the Chou dynasty (1122–255 BC). By the Han dynasty (206 BC–AD 220) we know that tables, stools and a wooden *k'ang*, which was used for reclining or sleeping, were being made. Brick *k'angs* were built as part of the structure of the house. The chair is not thought to have made its appearance until the end of the dynasty.

Few examples of very early Chinese furniture survive, and nearly all our knowledge is derived from archaeological remains or from ancient Chinese illustrated books. Our knowledge of the early period is however still very scanty and leaves a great deal to be desired.

Chinese historians paid little attention to furniture styles; even the major and multi-volume Chinese encyclopedias do not help, illustrating only a few random examples in crude woodcuts. In Chinese society, the carpenter and cabinetmaker occupied a very lowly position and, unlike the painter and calligrapher, who were highly esteemed, remained anonymous. As far as documented pieces are concerned, even these are few and far between as much has disappeared in China's almost perpetual wars and crises. Very little furniture earlier than the Sung dynasty (960–1279) has survived and even here there are very few pieces. Exceptions to this are the few small pieces of the T'ang dynasty (618–906 AD) which are preserved in the temple storehouses like the Shosho-in, in Nara, Japan. The majority of surviving examples date from the Ch'ing dynasty (1644–1912), and many of these have been restored in some way or other; precise dating is almost impossible. Western observers have not added to our knowledge for they were rarely given the opportunity of entering Chinese homes. Even dated paintings are of little use for reference, as artists tended to use archaic forms. Woodcut illustrations in early books are on the whole more reliable but suffer from lack of detail.

By the T'ang dynasty most furniture forms were already well developed. These forms continued in use with stylistic variations until the end of the Ch'ing dynasty in 1912.

The majority of Chinese furniture in museums and art collections, or offered for sale in antique shops, was made between the late Ming dynasty (1368–1644) and the late Ch'ing dynasty. The finest pieces date from between the 15th and 18th centuries.

The Chinese are conservative by nature, a fact which is clearly reflected in both their philosophy and their art. This conservatism is also reflected in their furniture. Thus, designs that were popular in the Ming and Ch'ing dynasties had their origin many centuries earlier.

Above: *This richly ornamented Chinese chair was never intended for comfort. Chairs were considered status symbols – women rarely used them, being mainly confined to stools. Fine chairs such as this were seats of honour. The superb scroll-like carving which forms the back and sides symbolizes clouds.*

Chinese furniture can be divided into two categories: indigenous furniture made according to Chinese taste and designed to be accommodated in Chinese buildings, and furniture made for export which combined Occidental and Oriental styles but was specifically designed for use in Western homes.

The first category can be subdivided into furniture made for use in the imperial household and for the nobility, which is generally sumptuous and ornate, and that made for use in ordinary households, which is basically utilitarian, but often very simple and elegant.

Indigenous domestic furniture may also be further divided into formal (upper-class) furniture influenced by Confucian philosophies; rustic or natural furniture, influenced by the expression of the *Tao*; and over-ornate, carved and painted furniture, which were cheap reproductions of the imperial taste adopted by the nouveau riche or merchant class as status symbols.

Above: *19th-century painting of Kuan-ti, god of war. The type of marble-topped table on which he rests his arm continued to be made over a long period of time, right until the end of the 19th century. He is shown sitting on a 'lohan' curved back armchair.*

Above: *Detail of the leg and foot and cross-member joint of an 18th century Chinese hardwood ch'uang. Chinese craftsmen did not use nails or screws, relying on the skilful use of glue with mortise and tenon joints and the occasional use of dovetailing.*

The difference between the Confucian formality and the naturalism of the Taoist-influenced forms may, in fact, account for the unsatisfactory results that have been achieved in previous attempts to allocate differences of style to the regions of China. For instance the north has been equated with the formal and sedate, while the south has been accredited with the production of less formal and more natural styles. As the distribution of these styles, as far as we can tell, appears to be fairly uniform, the continuing presence in Chinese society of furniture over-ornamented with carving, painting and gilding, may be explained purely as a difference in the taste of the merchant classes. The preference for a degree of ornamentation also began to take hold after the assimilation of the Manchu into Chinese society during the Ch'ing dynasty. The emperor Ch'ien Lung was particularly fond of decoration. In addition the further north or west one goes in China, the closer one gets to the influences of the ornate art of Tibet and Mongolia.

An interesting distinction was made by Chinese curio dealers between southern and northern furniture. Contrary to what one would normally expect, fine furniture was labelled *Kuang tso*, i.e. made in Kuangtung, a southern province, while pieces of lesser quality were *ching tso* or made in the capital, Peking. Apparently furniture was not traditionally associated with the capital but was made in workshops elsewhere. Whether it was made in Kuangtung is debatable, and this may represent simply an attempt at general labels to distinguish the two types of furniture. The finer and rarer timber used for some pieces was imported from countries to the south of China, so it would not be surprising if, rather than transporting the timber to workshops in the north, some was converted into furniture in southern workshops.

The construction of Chinese furniture is radically different from that of Europe. Nails and screws were not used, while dowels too, with few exceptions, were completely absent. Chinese craftsmen created furniture using only mortise and tenon joints, with a limited use of glue and occasionally the use of dovetailing. The use of dowels generally indicates that a repair has been made at some time. The technique of constructing furniture in this way made it possible for pieces to be easily dismantled for transport if required. It was also extremely practical in that it protected the furniture from the acute changes in temperature and humidity that occurred in some parts of China. If the furniture had been rigidly constructed, changes in humidity would have caused either an expansion or shrinkage in the wood and stress on the joints, resulting in the wood splitting or the joints parting, or both. Thus, the use of mortise and tenon was in fact the only practical method open to the Chinese carpenter.

Joints were cleverly positioned so that the interlocking

Above: *Early 19th century Chinese hardwood k'ang table, with carved openwork 'cloud' railings. These small low tables were placed in the middle of the large brick or wooden k'ang, so that two people could be seated sharing the table between them. K'ang tables are normally rectangular rather than square, as is this piece.*

points would generally not be visible and thereby would not interfere with the line and balance of the piece. Most of the intricate parts were carved from single pieces of wood as were large carved pieces, although it was perfectly possible for the latter to be joined as, indeed, they sometimes are. Where joints in large curved pieces were present, they were not hidden but were cleverly designed to merge with the overall contours of form.

Chinese furniture can be both angular and curved. One of its attractions is the superb use of convex edges, which, when bevelled edges or beading is present, both accentuates and complements the lines. Chinese craftsmen never resorted to turning wooden members on a lathe; instead all rounded pieces were shaped entirely by hand.

The Chinese were great connoisseurs of wood, and the attention to choice of wood has given Chinese furniture an enormous appeal. Some of these types of wood have now disappeared through extensive deforestation and exact identification of the true species can prove almost impossible. Hardwoods were more popular than softwoods as they withstood termites.

The finest furniture was more often than not made in *hua-li*, popularly known as rosewood (*Pterocarpus indicus*). Though not identical to European rosewoods, it is not dissimilar. Though the tree is native to south China, it also grows in India, Burma, South-East Asia and the Philippines, from which countries supplies were also imported. Old *hua-li* has a lovely satin-soft surface with superb colour and tone of almost translucent quality – in colour it can range from a rich deep hue of brown (not red) to quite light. It has a fine grain in some ways similar to mahogany. When dark, it resembles another Chinese hardwood, *hung-mu*, popularly known as redwood – a wood much used in the 19th and early 20th century, and often elaborately carved.

Fine classical furniture of the conservative 'Confucian' school was not usually made in either of the above woods but instead in *tzu-t'an*, or blackwood (*Pterocarpus santalinus*). It is extremely dense and heavy, and to the Chinese its rich dark colour gives it a quality of great dignity. *Tzu-t'an* grows mainly in Kuangsi province, and much of it was imported from southern India or Annam.

A number of unusual woods were used, among which may be mentioned 'Chickenwing wood', *Cassia siamea*, and *Ormosia*, which the Chinese called *Chi-Ch'ih mu*. This lovely wood, which was very popular for less formal furniture, is dark coffee in colour, with a well-marked,

Left: *An 18th century black lacquered wardrobe, probably made for the Chinese Imperial court. This fine piece of furniture, made in the late K'ang Hsi period, is richly decorated with dragons in gold lacquer on a black lacquer background. The top section separates from the lower cupboard. Wardrobes such as this were normally made in pairs.*
Right: *Large Chinese six-fold screen, decorated in black and gold lacquer. Large screens were generally six- or twelve-fold, while smaller screens tended to be three-fold. Both sides of the screens were decorated, one more elaborately than the other. This piece dates to the 18th century, the 'golden age' of Chinese lacquerwork.*

slightly coarse grain. When fresh, it is a shade of greyish brown and it is extremely strong and durable. *Hua-mu* or burl was also greatly cherished by the Chinese and used especially for inlay or panels. *Wu-mu* or ebony is occasionally found, as is *nan-mu*, a variety of cedar, which was greatly favoured when furniture of a lighter colour than usual was desired.

Of the softwoods, *hsiang sha-mu* or 'fragrant pine' was favoured. *Chang-mu* or camphorwood was extensively used for making chests.

Where forms of European furniture were parallelled in China, their shape generally differs, influenced by Chinese conventions of formal interiors. Unlike Western rooms, rooms in Chinese houses were generally not cluttered with furniture. Almost without exception, Chinese furniture was designed to be arranged at right-angles to a wall – the intention being for all the furniture to be arranged symmetrically both horizontally and vertically. Even when the arrangement appeared to be asymmetrical, especially in the case of large halls, a companion arrangement would more than likely be seen at the opposite end of the room. Tables were arranged between pairs of chairs, an arrangement that could be repeated, forming groups of six, and so on. The tables so arranged were used either for holding refreshments or for displaying works of art.

Chairs were made both with and without arms, those with arms being principally reserved for the use of men. The chair was a place of honour and position only being offered to honoured guests or to elderly people, while everyone else usually used stools. Chairs without arms were used by women. All chairs were normally fairly high and extremely formal, with seats being perfectly horizontal and backs and arm supports perfectly vertical. Decoration, too, was extremely formal and sedate and could take the form of simple carving, combinations of different woods or occasionally inlays of stone slabs. This latter practice was employed either on the back or on the seat or on both. Very occasionally, the seat was inset with cane matting.

Generally speaking, the Chinese did not have dining rooms. Instead, tables and chairs were set up in whatever room was chosen for the occasion. Tables were not too large as it was essential for all the diners to be able to serve themselves from the food which was arranged in the centre of the table. If the number of guests exceeded that which could attend a Chinese dinner party without actually was quite in order for further tables to be set up in the room to handle the overflow. It was quite conceivable that one could attend a Chinese dinner party, without actually sitting down to eat with the host. In addition to dining tables and the low tables employed in wall arrangements in the formal reception room, there were also very low, square tables with stools (sometimes of ceramic) which were placed in pavilions or on the courtyard terrace. There was also another kind of table, a small side table which was long and low in shape, about 15–20 cm (6–8 in) high and intended for use on the *k'ang*.

The study or library was one of the less formal rooms of a Chinese house, and was extremely private and personal. The furniture was arranged in a manner which was aesthetically pleasing but which could also be informal. Amongst the furnishings would be a writing table and a chair which was not of the formal type but was more comfortable and for use at the desk. There would also be a bookshelf, an open affair often made of hardwood or, in southern China, of bamboo. It was also often made in hardwood simulating knotted branches of bamboo and occasionally lacquered. It was designed to accommodate both books and scroll paintings, as well as writing materials. Also in the room would be perhaps a small single-panelled screen and a chair for receiving scholar friends, as well as perhaps a hardwood plant stand. This natural and rustic atmosphere was essentially for the *Wen-jen* or literati. It was also symbolic of the *Tao*. Every gentleman or scholar would follow the pursuits of painting, poetry

and prose, and thus the library or study was designed to be aesthetically pleasing while at the same time academically and artistically inspiring.

The informal rooms of the house included the bedroom, which housed a rather elaborate box-like bed with curtains or a brick *k'ang*. By the Ming dynasty the bed had become similar in some respects to the European bedstead, except that it was surrounded by a railing which had an opening in the middle of one side. As well as curtains, it was fitted with a canopy. During the day the curtains were pulled back and the upper and lower quilts folded in large pleats and placed along one side. These were replaced by a pad and the bed then doubled as a couch. In some cases the bed was so large that it became a built-in elevated box complete with ante-chamber!

Also in the bedroom would be simple travelling boxes, in which the clothes were folded and stored, or more elaborate two-tiered wardrobes. The latter were constructed with a large cupboard-like area at the bottom and the *ting kuei*, a similar chest-like arrangement with front-opening doors or hinged lid, which fitted on the top. The top section could become a travelling wardrobe when the occupant of the house went visiting. There were normally four cupboards – two large on the floor, and two small *ting kuei* on top. Clothes were always folded and stored flat. Heavy fur-lined garments were kept in chests – *t'ang hsiang*.

Each season had its own costumes, marked by different colours, which would be rotated within the wardrobe. Wardrobes could be of any scale and most were fitted with a removable central bar in the front that slotted into place, onto which the two doors would close allowing the metal loops in the bar to fit through ornamental brass plates on the doors; a Chinese horizontal padlock was threaded through the loops. This system kept the doors tightly shut – the Chinese did not use any form of inner clasp to keep doors in place.

Some of these wardrobes are extremely beautiful and are great works of art, the best being made between the 15th and 18th century. They were made either of hardwood, lacquer, lacquer decorated with paint and mother-of-pearl inlay, cinnabar lacquer, or coromandel lacquer. The decoration, often in gilt or colours, is extremely beautiful in contrast to the severity of the furniture of the formal reception rooms. The most ornate examples were made for the imperial apartments in Peking. Each piece was enhanced by fine brass clasps and hinges, mounted on the front and made into decorative features. The unit placed on the top of the wardrobe normally had brass carrying handles.

Screens, either small with two or three panels, or large with as many as six very tall panels, were present throughout the house. The larger examples were in permanent use in the large formal reception room. Another piece of furniture that could be placed in the study or even in the reception room was the couch or *ch'uang*, a kind of double wooden seat resembling a throne. These were popular in the 17th and 18th centuries.

In most households there was a small room set aside for worship of the family ancestors, the household deity or, if the occupants were Buddhist, for housing a figure of the Buddha or a Bodhisattva. In this room there would be a tall, long, narrow table used as an altar-table. This would sometimes have storage room underneath. Among the

Right: *Detail of a late 17th century Chinese large twelve-fold coromandel screen. Beautifully worked in many colours, the screen is decorated with a large central scene, depicting a view of a large palace building with numerous interconnecting courtyards, surrounded by a wide border of flowers, birds and mythological animals.*

Left: *The magnificent carved and engraved red lacquer throne of the emperor Ch'ien Lung. The throne, originally in the Summer Palace at Peking, was removed about 1900 and is now in the Victoria and Albert Museum, London. The extremely fine and rich lacquer is a masterpiece of 18th century Chinese craftsmanship.*
Right: *The lower half of a Chinese coromandel twelve-fold screen of the late 17th century. The screen is decorated with a mythological scene, depicting a chi-lin (an animal of good fortune) running on turbulent water. Beneath the main scene are symbols of good fortune. The screen has a black lacquer base, incised with polychrome decoration.*

household accessories would be a number of circular tables and plant-stands, both of which are popular today and used for a similar purpose in Western homes. Some of these tables are intricately carved, with pierced friezes around the skirt and the tops inset with marble.

Ordinary domestic furniture of the 17th to 19th centuries in north and central China tended to be of simple form, relying on the grain of the mature wood for effect, cabinets and similar pieces occasionally being highlighted with yellow brass fittings. In contrast to this, in south China, which is much warmer, expendable furniture such as that made from bamboo, which could also be used outside the house, was much favoured. Lacquer furniture was also more popular in the south of China than in the north. The reason for this may lie in the fact that it had a greater resistance to insect attack, an important fact in the warmer climes of south China. Lacquer was thought to afford even greater protection than the use of hardwood.

While most Chinese furniture tended to be made in hardwood, lacquer-coated furniture was particularly favoured for more elaborate pieces. The shapes were very much the same as those employed on hardwood examples but, unlike the latter, red lacquer was ornately decorated with carving and gilding, while at times it was painted, inlaid or overlaid with hardstones or mother-of-pearl. One of the most famous examples of red lacquer furniture is the magnificent carved lacquered throne of the Emperor Ch'ien Lung, now in the Victoria and Albert Museum.

Red lacquer furniture was popular during the Ming period and parts of the Ch'ing period, especially during the reign of Ch'ien Lung (1736–95). In the Ming dynasty, by the beginning of the 15th century, lacquer was produced on a large scale, although furniture accounted for only a small proportion of the total output of the lacquer workshops. Chinese lacquer of the Ming dynasty is nearly always red and cleanly carved with deep incisions. Floral motifs are the most common though some pieces with figure carving are also known. Their colour was originally deep vermilion but as lacquer is apt to fade when exposed to light, particularly strong sunlight, much of the original brilliance and tone has disappeared. The surface is normally covered with minute hair cracks. One of the finest surviving examples of Ming lacquer furniture is a table made for imperial use during the Hsüan Tê period (1426–35) now in the Low-Beer collection, New York. The entire surface is covered with intricately carved designs.

It is often difficult to distinguish between the lacquer of the Ming dynasty and that produced in the early Ch'ing dynasty. However, by the time of Ch'ien Lung a true Ch'ing style had blossomed. Ch'ing designs tended to be more detached and fussy, with the artist concentrating on minute details, almost to the detriment of the artistic quality of the piece. The boldness so characteristic of Ming designs disappeared and in its place there was an extreme delicacy and fineness. The colour of Ch'ing lacquer was more brilliant than that of the Ming.

Towards the end of the 18th century, some specimens of inferior quality red lacquer furniture were exported to Europe. Other much finer specimens found their way to Europe and America after the sack of the Summer Palace during the Boxer Rebellion.

Lacquer is made from the sap of the tree *Rhus vernicifera*, which grows in certain parts of China. When about 8–10 years old, an incision is made in the trunk of the tree, and the sap collected. This is then purified by boiling, skimming and straining and stored in vessels protected from the light. Lacquer is coloured by the addition of pigments such as cinnabar, a red ore of mercury. The technique of using lacquer was both complicated and lengthy. Sometimes hundreds of coats had to be applied to a piece of furniture to build up a sufficiently thick surface to allow it to be carved. Only a thin coat of lacquer could be applied at a time, and after drying it had to be rubbed down before the next coat could be applied. Care had to be taken that the lacquer dried slowly and in a humid environment.

In addition to red lacquer, the Chinese also produced another kind of lacquered furniture which is known in Europe and America as coromandel lacquer. Although the name is derived from a town in southern India, it has no connection with India, other than perhaps passing through that country in transit to Europe. The idea that coromandel lacquer originated in India is pure myth. No such

Above: *A late 18th century ukiyo-e kakemono painting, showing women in a large Japanese room. At the far end can be seen the tokonoma with its hanging kakemono, while to one side is a small recess with table. The tatami mats and the sliding shoji screen can be clearly seen. The absence of furniture is noticeable.*

Above: *The sparseness of the Japanese interior is again clearly shown in this 19th century woodcut print of the tea ceremony. In one corner is the tokonoma, an alcove with a kakemono, a work of calligraphy or a cloth-mounted painting, and a simple flower arrangement on a low platform.*

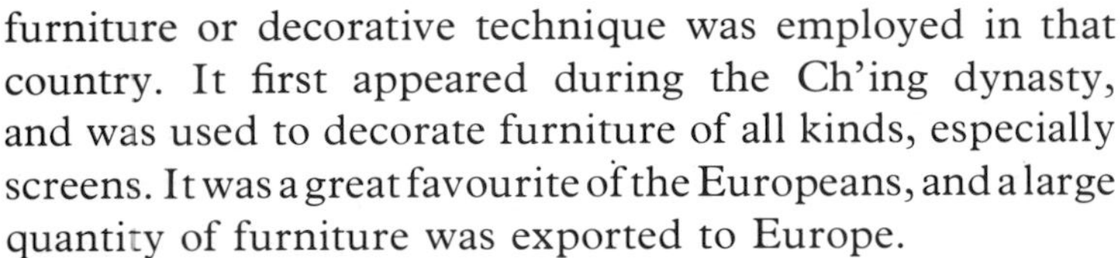

furniture or decorative technique was employed in that country. It first appeared during the Ch'ing dynasty, and was used to decorate furniture of all kinds, especially screens. It was a great favourite of the Europeans, and a large quantity of furniture was exported to Europe.

The technique was different from that employed for making red lacquer furniture. The lacquer was often applied not to solid wood but to a base made of a ply, formed from cloth sandwiched between thin layers of pinewood. This was then covered with a coating of finely-powdered slate mixed with vegetable glue, which was then left to dry thoroughly before being levelled and smoothed with ash until a high sheen was obtained. The lacquer was carefully applied to this until the correct thickness was achieved, usually about an eighth of an inch. The design was traced on the surface, and then carved in shallow relief, care being taken to ensure that the chisel did not cut too deeply, lest the wood and cloth be revealed. The relief design was then coloured with tempera (paint in which egg yolk is used as a medium) and sometimes gilded and inlaid.

One of the most popular forms of coromandel lacquer furniture was the screen, either large six- or twelve-fold pieces or smaller three-fold screens, or any variation of the two. They were formed by coromandel panels fixed into lacquered wooden frames (as was all coromandel furniture). The screens were worked differently on both sides. On one side the design would be cut in relief and coloured, while the other side would have a simple painted design. The finest and oldest of the screens date to the K'ang Hsi period (1662–1722). Later works have pieces of mother-of-pearl, jade and other hard stones carved and applied to the lacquer surface. Although lacquer furniture is still produced today, lacquer as a vibrant and original art form continued in China until only the mid-19th century. Thereafter it became mass-produced, losing much of its artistic appeal.

In Britain and Europe, coromandel screens were often cut up and used as decorative panels in cupboards or other furniture. With the ever-increasing trade with India and the Orient in the 18th century, interest in China ran high and chinoiserie became the vogue. Every opportunity was seized to decorate some form of furniture or other interior decoration with Chinese motifs. In furniture, this fashion was best expressed by Thomas Chippendale. The taste for Oriental designs had in fact begun in the Restoration court. The East India Company, which had been granted a Royal Charter, helped create enormous interest in, and demand for, objects with Oriental overtones. It imported vast amounts of Oriental works of art, including coromandel lacquer. However, supply could not keep up with demand, especially for good quality lacquer furniture, so coromandel lacquer was copied in England and Europe, although both the technique and the materials used were quite different from those of the Chinese originals. The designs were taken from Chinese sources, sometimes copied, sometimes modifed and sometimes even 'invented'.

Lacquer with designs in relief was also very popular and red was a favourite colour for the ground. Because of its Oriental origin, this technique of lacquering was called 'Japanning'. A book on the subject entitled *A Treatise of Japaning and Varnishing* by John Stalker and George Parker, published in 1688, had a great influence on its popularity during the 18th century.

At the end of the 19th century, Western influence had penetrated China to such an extent that Chinese furniture with Western characteristics was being made. This furniture, designed with European interiors in mind, was made chiefly for export and for sale to rich tourists making the Grand Tour. Much of it is extremely elaborate with only faint echoes of true Chinese style. In many cases it is very heavy, cumbersome, badly made, and decorated in poor taste (when compared with the Chinese originals). It is often ornately and very deeply carved, often to the point of making recognition of the design difficult or even impossible. Painted decoration is frequently gaudy and overdone with coloured overlay. Shapes are European and include glass-fronted cupboards, bulbous and heavy palm stands, heavily and ornately carved dining room suites, occasional chairs, bookcases, standard lamps, gong-stands, sideboards and rocking chairs. Some of this furniture is not made from the traditional Chinese woods but from teak.

Japan

The traditional Japanese house is based on entirely different principles from those of the Chinese, and is made of wood rather than stone. It consists principally of a wooden skeleton into which are fitted moveable panels. The dividing panels of the rooms, the *fusuma*, are simple wooden frames covered in paper which slide along shallow grooves in the wood floor and are held above by the *kamoi*, or lintel. By opening or closing the *fusuma* different interior spaces can be created. The traditional furniture that evolved for use in Japanese homes was therefore equally portable or changeable. Having said this, there is an area which, although used for various purposes, is the principal room and is called the *zashiki*. Within this room is the *tokonoma*, an alcove with a low platform on which is placed a decorative object or *ikebana* (flower) display, and beside or behind this hangs a *kakemono*, a cloth-mounted hanging painting or a work of calligraphy. Next to the *tokonoma* there is often a smaller recess called a *chigai-dana*, an area which contains shelves and a cabinet used for storing objects displayed in the *tokonoma*.

What furniture there is in a Japanese house is either small and low in form or hidden from view. Chairs are non-existent – one simply sits on the floor, on a *tatami* or thick straw mat, or on a *zabuton*, or a small cushion. A wooden *kyosoku* or arm rest may be used to support the body for lounging. These arm rests can be very beautifully made out of polished hardwood or lacquer. In form they resemble extremely small stools or large head rests. For

Below: *Most of the furniture in the Japanese house, like this hibachi in a black lacquered case, was small and portable, reflecting the Japanese way of life. Unlike the Chinese, the Japanese lived close to the floor in a changeable internal environment. It was therefore necessary for furniture to be shaped and sized to serve the purpose.*

Above: *Most Japanese furniture was intended to be small and portable. This miniature late 18th century black and gold lacquered tansu or chest of drawers was not, however, made for household use. Measuring only 22.9cm (9in) high, it was made for the Girls' Festival.*
Left: *The Butsudan or household shrine is one of the larger pieces of Japanese furniture. It was not intended to be portable and occupied a permanent position within the house. This particularly fine example, which dates to the late 18th or very early 19th century, was originally made for the castle of a regional lord.*

eating, part of the *tatami* may be removed to reveal a small sunken area over which a low rectangular table is positioned. This recess can accommodate a charcoal fire, *hibachi*, to provide heat. A wooden *kyosoku* or arm rest may be placed beside the small cushion on the floor to make eating more comfortable.

It is obvious that not all furniture could be small and moveable, and certain types of large pieces were made. In this category falls the *tansu* or chest. This is in many respects similar to the Chinese wardrobe or travelling chest, but may be found with a smaller chest on the base and a larger piece above. It may be extremely simple in form and decoration, using Japanese pine, or elaborately decorated with lacquer. Under the storage cabinet is the *bukhe*. This is a cabinet with sliding doors, similar to the type of cabinet that was used in the Chinese library.

An important item of furniture in the Japanese house is the screen, which performs a number of functions and can itself take a number of forms. Basically there are two types, the *tsuitati* and the *byobu*. The latter is a moveable folding screen which can be large and six-panelled, used to subdivide a room, or a two-panelled screen used to divide areas for privacy or even to stop a draught. A small *byobu* could also be used to screen the diners from draughts while eating. In this case it is not full but may only be between 45 cm (18 in) to 90 cm (3 ft) from the floor. When not in use, the *byobu* is kept in the corner of the room where its decoration may be admired by visitors and residents alike. Even large *byobu* are reasonably light, being constructed of paper or *shoji* over a wooden framework. The *shoji* itself could be extremely beautiful, covered in decorative fabrics or gold paper, with each central panel being covered with a painting, each a section of a complete picture.

The other form of screen, the *tsuitati*, is a portable single-panelled screen which was placed at the entrance of the room, providing a degree of privacy. Visitors entering could thus not see directly into the room and would have to make their way round the screen. The *tsuitati* could also be

Above: *A fine Japanese lacquered cabinet, containing an assembly of drawers of various sizes. The cabinet, which dates to the late 17th century, is decorated, both inside and out, with designs in gold lacquer on a black ground. It stands on a European 17th century carved giltwood table. Originally it would have stood directly on the floor.*

Below: *Japanese lacquered miniature tansu on stand. The highly ornate decoration in gold, silver and black and red lacquer, depicting trees and foliage, is typical of the lacquerwork of the late Tokugawa period, the golden age of Japanese lacquer. This piece was probably made between 1850 and 1865.*

used to place food and dishes behind, while they were between kitchen and table. As with the *byobu*, it was decorated either with a painting or with decorated material on both sides. Unlike the *byobu* however, the framework was more substantial being only single-panelled and made from pine, hardwood, or lacquered.

Perhaps the commonest and most utilitarian piece of furniture in the Japanese house is the storage chest. Unlike the decorative *tansu*, it is made in a variety of sizes and styles but is not intended to be seen and admired, and so little attention is directed towards decoration.

Much antique traditional furniture was finely and exquisitely decorated, usually in lacquer. Amongst the larger pieces may be mentioned the kimono rack. A simple structure, it consisted of two vertical poles on stands, connected by three horizontal bars – one at the bottom between the two stands, one at the top which was usually longer and protruded each side of the vertical poles, and one in the middle, equidistant from top and bottom. Although simple in form, kimono racks were quite often exquisitely decorated with enamelled lacquer designs and metal fittings. The rack was used simply by draping the kimono across the top bar. A much smaller version without the central horizontal bar was made for hanging towels.

The remainder of Japanese furniture was, as a rule, small and portable and usually superbly made and finely decorated in lacquerwork. The chronicles of Japan record that the first master of lacquer was Mitsumi-no-Sukune, a

member of the court of the emperor Kaon-Tenno, at the end of the 4th century BC. While this perhaps may be legend, there is a much later record which mentions lacquer in the 7th century AD. In this account, the emperor Mommo-Tenno makes an order instructing the landowners with extensive estates to allocate a part of the land for the cultivation of lac trees. Historians are not sure whether the tree grew naturally in Japan or whether it was introduced from China. Whatever the case, it is obvious from the document recording emperor Mommo-Tenno's edict that lacquer was in short supply, which may indicate that the tree was foreign to Japan. Although the Chinese claim to have originated the use of lacquer the Japanese can justly claim to have developed the decorative art of lacquer-work to perfection.

The first truly historical document in the imperial archives relating to lacquer is one from the reign of the emperor Kotoku-Tenno (645–754), recording details of taxes which were imposed on lacquer production. Another document of the 10th century, also in the imperial archives, describes a method of decorating lacquer with pieces of mother-of-pearl.

The use of lacquer for furniture was restricted to the coating of wooden cores. The different sections of the wood were shaped and joined together with pegs. It was then sometimes covered with cloth and gesso (a plaster composition), or gesso alone. This layer was then smoothed and coated with lacquer. On really fine furniture, as many as two to three hundred coats were applied. Each coat, which was extremely thin, was allowed to dry thoroughly before being rubbed down with charcoal. The process was very tricky, as care had to be taken to ensure that the lacquer dried slowly and did not flake off. If the atmosphere was not humid enough, the lacquer became extremely brittle and cracked. In an effort to overcome these problems, the Japanese made their lacquerware in naturally humid environments such as beside rivers.

Many clever techniques were invented for decorating lacquer, including the use of gold, silver and, as mentioned above, mother-of-pearl. These materials were used to great effect; the application of mother-of-pearl is known as *raden*, while the use of gold and silver dust sprinkled over the surface after the design has been drawn, is known as *maki-e*. There were numerous variations of this technique.

The golden age of Japanese lacquer may be said to be the Tokugawa period (1615–1868). During this period, really fine lacquer and lacquer furniture was created by some of the great artists of Japan. The material is extremely hard-wearing, being resistant to heat, acid and alcohol. This, and the customarily respectful treatment given to lacquerware in Japan, have ensured that a number of early examples have survived to the present day.

Because much of the furniture in the Japanese house was small and portable, it is rarely regarded by collectors as

Above: *This finely worked reading stand, decorated in gold maki-e lacquer, illustrates the ingenuity and artistry of the Japanese craftsmen in tackling the problem of living at floor level. The stand, which dates to the 18th century, contains a small drawer in which could be stored the book of the moment.*

Below: *This Japanese wood-cut print by Utamaro shows a lady at her toilet, using a cosmetic box. The box, which contains various drawers and compartments and holds bowls and jars, also houses a bronze mirror, which can be adjusted to various heights and angles. The whole assembly folds into an unobtrusive box.*

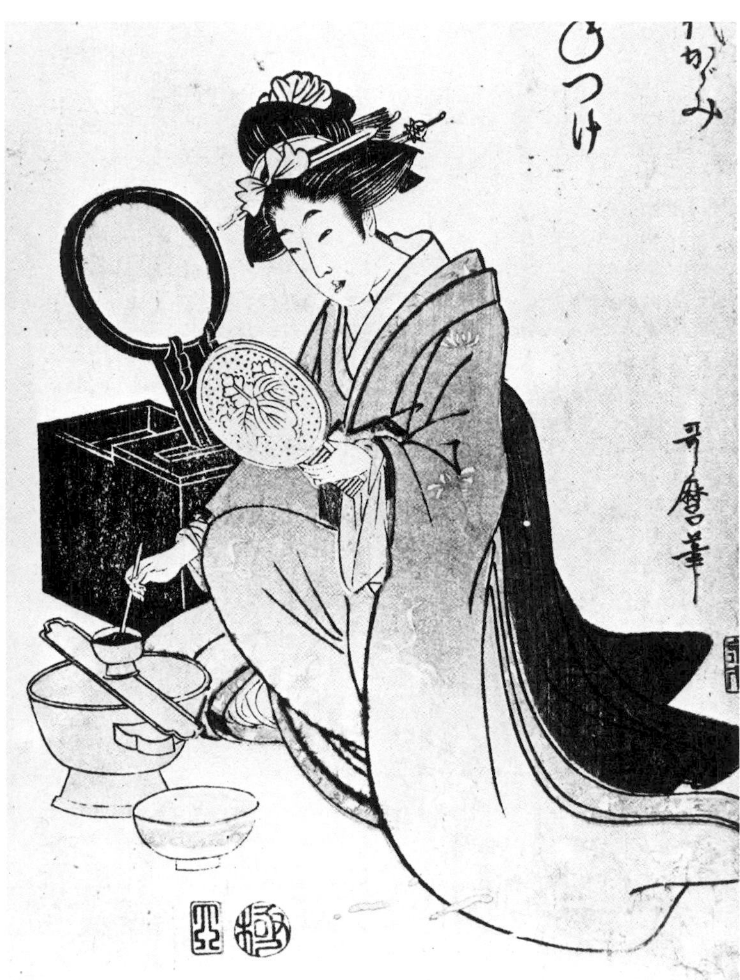

Top: *19th century Japanese black and gold lacquered tobacco bon, or smoker's companion. The silver smoker's utensils were used to contain tobacco, not opium. Tobacco was brought to Japan by the Portuguese.*
Above: *Early 18th century Japanese cabinet, decorated in black and gold lacquer. These cabinets were used to hold books and small items.*

Above: *A highly ornate 18th or 19th century Japanese cabinet, with drawers decorated with gold lacquer lattice designs and applied Imari porcelain plaques. The cabinet has had additional decorative motifs of European style applied to its base rail, to blend in with its European base.*

furniture at all, but furniture it is. Into this category fall items such as reading stands – little chests with a lectern-like structure; reading boxes for storage of books; miniature chests of drawers for books of poems; cosmetic boxes with mirror stands and the *tobacco bon*, the Japanese smokers' companion. These and many other miniature and portable chattels were the standard items of furniture in the Japanese house.

Unlike Chinese furniture, Japanese lacquer furniture, screens, and so on, are greatly sought-after by collectors and prices are generally high. They are, however, well worth collecting, for their size is ideal for modern homes.

During the third quarter of the 19th century, Japanese craftsmen strove to meet the demand created by the steady stream of rich foreign tourists. The result was horrifying to Japanese taste, for the foreigners wanted everything they had seen in Japan – lacquer, carvings, ivory, paintings and so on – all rolled into one, and made in sizes and shapes to suit the vogue in Europe and America. The results of this mixture do, however, include a few happy accidents which are exquisite works of art, as well as quite a number of monstrous failures.

Today, both are collected, the former because they are the final expression of ancient Japanese craftsmanship, and the latter because they are extraordinary enough to have sometimes caught the attention of fashionable interior designers. In no way however, can either be regarded as a true expression of Japanese culture.

Some of the most common items of this period are the ornately carved hardwood screens, containing lacquered panels which are decorated on both sides with designs executed in overlay with ivory, mother-of-pearl, hardstones and tortoiseshell. Further decoration was added by highlighting certain areas with gilding. Popular designs for panels included foliage and birds, usually peacocks or birds of prey, while the hardwood surrounds and lower panels were most commonly carved with dragon and rolling cloud motifs. Single-panel screens, *tsuitati*, were also made, but were not as common.

The other popular item of Japanese furniture for the European home was the display cabinet, made in hardwood or beechwood with asymmetrical and symmetrical arrangements of shelves and niches with drawers and cupboards with sliding doors. The surrounding framework was often ornamented with open-work fret-carving, while the panels at the back of the niches and drawers and door fronts were usually lacquered and decorated with *shibayama* (carved ivory overlay, itself inlaid and overlaid with mother-of-pearl and hardstones), mother-of-pearl, tortoiseshell and so on.

Designs were drawn from Japanese mythology, and from the tales of samurai folk heroes. Occasionally the background of lacquered inlaid panels has what is known as a 'grained' effect, simulating the grain of the wood. This is all artificial, a clever illusion created by the lacquer worker. Japanese furniture was also made in bamboo, lacquer and parquetry. Sometimes furniture was signed by the craftsman and artist, contrasting with the Chinese practice of complete anonymity. Names like Matsu, Ken Goku and Midzu occur fairly often.

Below: *Four panels of a Japanese six-panelled painted screen, showing a bird's-eye view of the streets of Kyoto. The screen, which is painted with colour on gold-leafed paper, is one of a pair which were made in the early 17th century, and belongs to the late Momoyama, early Tokugawa period. These byobu screens were used to sub-divide rooms. Although they can be quite large they are light in weight.*

Korea

Korea, lying as it does between China and Japan, received and passed on influences from both countries. Not surprisingly, Korean furniture, although it has a number of distinctive features, combines artistic elements from both China and Japan, mixing them in its own peculiar manner. Techniques of manufacture and decoration tend to be Chinese with a preference for hardwoods. Decoration is subdued and again predominantly Chinese in inspiration. It would be a mistake, however, to say that it was possible to identify Korean furniture simply by the presence of styles of these two countries, for it is sometimes difficult to attribute pieces with certainty. In fact, even less

Above: *A plain wooden marriage chest, with simple metal mounts. The chest is in two parts, with a cupboard above and drawers beneath. Although made in Korea in the 18th century, it shows very strong Japanese influence, reflecting as it does the simplicity of classical Japanese taste.*

is known about Korean furniture than is known either about Chinese or Japanese furniture. It is a field, however, that promises some exciting discoveries as more certain identifications are made.

India and Burma

India is very different indeed from China and Japan. Its climate, philosophy and social conditions dictated that its furniture followed forms and designs which were in many cases unique. Because of the vulnerability of wood to rapacious termites and other wood devouring insects, few specimens of early Indian furniture have survived. The ever-present danger of destruction by insects led the Indian craftsmen to design furniture in other materials, and so some of the finest antique furniture is actually not made on wood at all but in relatively indestructible materials like marble, ivory and silver. Ivory was used in the solid, or applied as a veneer – in which case a good hardwood was used as the base. When forced by cost to use wood, craftsmen chose teak, one of the hardest and relatively termite-resistant timbers available. Other timbers also occasionally used were mahogany, rosewood, sandalwood and mango-wood, but the majority of these varieties were vulnerable to termites.

Because India has an extremely hot climate, materials such as marble were very popular for their cooling qualities. Likewise the ready availability of materials such as ivory made possible the use of this material, which in other countries would have proved far too expensive for widespread use.

Furniture in India never became formalized as it did in China and Japan. Life tended to be lived at a relatively low level, i.e. on the floor, but unlike Japan everything was informal and sometimes a little chaotic. There were no rigid rules for internal arrangements and furniture, except of course in the palaces of the ruling princes. Even here, furniture was almost entirely absent, with the exception of a throne-dais in the formal reception hall. These thrones are not thrones in the European sense but are more like low tables, lotus-form or octagonal in shape. The incumbent sat on them cross-legged on cushions and rugs. All the visitors would sit on mats or rugs on the floor. In Indian homes, food was also taken on the floor. Beds were simple mattresses, or in some cases, raised on a heavy bed frame which sometimes had a canopy. They tended to be extremely large and were generally not ornate, with the possible exception of those made of carved wood or ivory, and were only possessed by the rich. The great majority of examples have remained in India.

Personal possessions, objects, clothes and so on, were

Above right: *An elaborate 19th century Indian armchair in silver. The chair, which has silver tigers for arms, is also covered with tiger skin. It combines British Regency lines with an Indian indigenous taste. Chairs in India were made from a variety of unusual materials, such as silver, marble and even horn.*

Right: *An extremely finely worked revolving armchair of unusual form, having six legs connected to each other with cross bars. The chair, which was made in India in the late 17th or early 18th century, is made of wood with an incised veneer of ivory. It is a curious mixture of European and Indian styles.*

Left: *This exquisite, small wooden Indian cabinet is finely inlaid with various woods and bone. Basically of European design, the cabinet, which shows a mixture of Mughal and European influences, was made in Sind in the early 17th century. Furniture combining European and Indian styles was made in various parts of India.*

stored in chests. The only other piece of furniture with any similarity to European forms was a swinging chair or settee which was usually placed on open terraces, in pavilions, or in the women's quarters or *zenana*. When wood was employed, the timber usually came from the teak forests of Burma. In southern India especially, much use was made of wood, and it was deeply and elaborately carved. Subjects tended to be drawn from India's rich mythology and consisted mainly of elephants, mounted warriors, gods and goddesses, all intricately carved in the manner of Indian stone sculpture. Door lintels and other household fittings would be constructed and decorated in this manner.

Left: *The normal custom of seating in India was on the floor, but dignitaries were always seated on thrones. These low, platform-like structures of rectangular or octagonal form were covered with rugs and cushions and the incumbents sat on them cross-legged. This fine, early Mughal miniature painting shows the three founder emperors of the Mughal dynasty sitting on typical thrones.*

In Kashmir in the 19th century, the Europeans discovered that the local craftsmen were expert in the carving of Indian walnut wood and in the decoration of wood and papier-mâché objects with painted lacquer. They seized upon the opportunity and ordered vast quantities of European-style furniture to be made, for use both in India and in Europe. Much of this walnut wood furniture is beautifully constructed and decorated with relief carvings, inspired by the rich vegetation of the Kashmir valley. Decorative subjects include the deodar leaf, which is very much like a maple leaf, the lotus, which grows in abundance on the lakes of the valley, and roses, tulips, lilies and other flowers. Wood carving is still carried on in Kashmir, the skill being passed from father to son. It is not unusual for a child to be introduced to the art of wood carving as early as the age of six.

Shapes include most of the European forms with slight Indian modifications, drawn from the fashionable catalogues of Europe. Thus, it would be fairly normal to find a European Regency-style dining suite in walnut, carved with Kashmiri designs. Indian shapes were also employed, in particular folding tables, which were very popular with Europeans in India.

Kashmir was not the only part of India where craftsmen were expert in the art of furniture-making. Europeans have been in India since the 16th century and have endeavoured to furnish their houses according to their own customs. The French, Dutch, Portuguese and English all taught the local craftsmen their own designs. Thus fashionable trends in Europe tended to be echoed in India, sometimes with amusing results when peculiarities were introduced through misinterpretation of the original design or purpose of the piece. Rational explanations can therefore be found for many of the 'rarities' of Regency, Chippendale, Sheraton and Hepplewhite furniture that turn up occasionally in antique shops; the peculiarity of the wood is due not to some eccentric patron in Britain, Europe or America, but due to local availability of timber in India. Close examination would of course reveal other differences, for although the Indian *mistris* (a name applied to local craftsmen) were craftsmen in the traditional sense, their methods were different and anyone used to handling good furniture would never confuse an Indian with a European or American specimen. But there are many inexperienced buyers who readily make this error. Some Hindi names for various pieces of furniture have been taken from the European word for the object from which they were first copied. For instance, the word for wardrobe in Hindi is *almirah* which comes from the Portuguese.

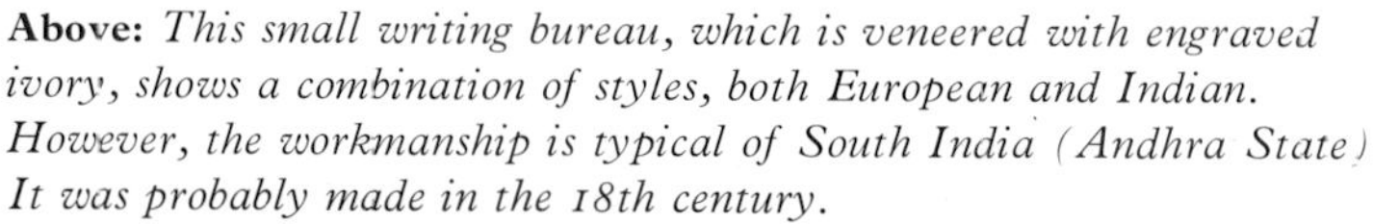

Above: *This small writing bureau, which is veneered with engraved ivory, shows a combination of styles, both European and Indian. However, the workmanship is typical of South India (Andhra State). It was probably made in the 18th century.*

Below: *Early Indian miniature ivory chest of drawers, decorated with gold, silver and pearls. Made in the late 17th century, the design has strong Indian overtones but is still tempered by European influence.*

Above: *19th century Burmese ornately carved teak armchair with upholstered back and seat. Elaborate chairs and other pieces of furniture were intricately carved with designs of dragons and other mythical beasts to suit European taste. The motifs were inspired from indigenous models and the shapes from European designs. This particular piece is a fairly restrained example – the effect of this type of elaborate decoration can sometimes be very heavy.*

Some of the finest Indian furniture was made for the great houses of Europe. This was no mere imitation of European furniture, but a true Indian interpretation of European shapes, using the best possible materials and craftsmen available at the time. In this category fall the superb ivory chairs and tables that occasionally turn up outside India. Many of these fine objects are still in the original house for which they were made. A particularly fine chair of sandalwood and ivory, part of a large set, is in the Royal Collection at Buckingham Palace. Other specimens of 'European' Indian furniture may be found at the Brighton Pavilion. Of these may be mentioned an elaborate suite of furniture made in Madras about 1770 especially for the Governor of Fort St George. It was acquired by George III and then later installed in Brighton Pavilion by George IV.

Burma, the home of good teak, produced a considerable amount of furniture purely for Western taste during the 19th century which at that time was influenced by the excesses of the late Victorian period. Thus, although the craftsmanship is superb, especially the carving, the overall effect of some of the furniture, in particular the occasional chairs, dining room suites and gong-stands, is a trifle too heavy for most modern taste. Another peculiarity of Burma is the decoration of some items of furniture with pieces of coloured and mirror glass. This was used to great effect on the frames of large mirrors made for the halls of great houses and palaces. Painted lacquered furniture, typically Burmese, was also made in profusion and includes items ranging from bedsteads to small storage boxes and tables.

Above: *Detail of an Indian teak wood travelling cabinet, decorated with inlaid woods and ivory. Made in Jatta, Sind, in the late 17th century, the decoration is typically Indian. Floral and tree motifs, such as those employed on this box, were also used on carpets and textiles and in pietre dure stone inlay on buildings.*

Nepal and Tibet

The furniture of Nepal and Tibet must, through their close geographical proximity, be considered together, although they are in fact quite separate. While Tibet was influenced culturally and artistically by China, Nepal was influenced by India and Tibet, and thus only indirectly by China.

While there are similarities of approach and design, there are also marked differences. Much of the furniture of Tibet was small and intended to be collapsible and portable, while that from Nepal was designed and produced for urban use, notably in Patan, Bhadgoan, and Katmandu, the main 'kingdoms' of Nepal. The designs of Nepalese furniture were principally religious in inspiration and were drawn both from Hindu and Buddhist sources. This is due to the fact that both religions exist side by side with the followers of both religions worshipping in each other's temples. Thus, the artistic motifs can present a very puzzling mixture.

Like India, Nepal does not have a wide variety of formal furniture. What furniture there was tended to be utilitarian and not of interest to the connoisseur and collector. There is however, an important exception, and that is the range of religious furniture and accoutrements made very much in the Tibetan style. This includes items such as small altar-tables and image cabinets. They are rather crudely made but are enhanced by painted decoration, which can create a somewhat gaudy appearance. Small areas of carving may also be included.

Quite separate from the Tibetan style pieces (identification and separation of the Nepalese and the Tibetan can sometimes be difficult) is a rather rare class of carved furniture made by the wood carvers who specialized in decorating the lintels, eaves and balustrades of the traditional Nepalese house. They also produced the most fabulous carved and pierced wooden windows so formed to let the air and the light in while still affording some measure of protection from the elements. Perhaps the most famous of these carved wooden windows is the 'peacock window' of Bhadgoan.

Dating all Oriental furniture is extremely difficult and in the case of Nepalese furniture almost impossible, as the same styles and designs have been made for centuries. Freshness of paint or colour is no indication of its date, as furniture was periodically repainted.

The Tibetans are racially akin to the Mongolians and like the latter the greater part of the population at one time lived a nomadic life, the only settled existence being in small villages, towns and in the monasteries. Before the building of the great permanent monasteries, even the ecclesiastical establishments were nomadic. Everything needed for religious services was specially designed to be portable.

This applied not only to the accoutrements of services but even to frescoes, *thangkas* (rolled paintings on cloth) and furniture. Size was determined by ease of portability, as well as by the necessity of fitting the furniture into tents. These tents, made of yak hair, were not haphazardly designed or erected, but had an interior arrangement into which the pieces of furniture including storage chests, altars, yak-hide bags, tables and boxes could be fitted. This was a normal part of the organization necessary for a nomadic existence.

Religion was paramount in Tibet and thus every family had its own altar (*chösham*) on which stood a bowl of holy water, butter-lamps and an image. The altar was enclosed and a lower part was used as a chest for religious furnishings. These altars were of simple construction, the work of village craftsmen, and are thus not great works of carpentry. However, their design and decoration is most attractive and has a unique charm.

Another essential item for the tent was a small, low table (*jogtse*), designed to fold in sections into a separate table-top. There were also storage boxes and chests (*nyindrog* and *tobo*). The decoration is principally carved, or painted in bright colours and gold and the motifs are drawn from the rich symbolism of Tibetan religion.

It will be clear by now that Oriental furniture is far from homogeneous, coming as it does from vastly different backgrounds and making use of numerous kinds of materials. Like Western furniture, however, it requires to be treated and looked after with care, for if it is not given such respect, it will deteriorate rapidly, and lose much of its attraction. In particular lacquer suffers from sunlight and low humidity. In China, the majority of furniture was made from carefully chosen timber that was normally well seasoned, but because of the method of construction drastic variations in temperature and humidity can make themselves felt by a visible change in the joints. This is particularly noticeable in furniture that is subjected to central heating. Chinese and Japanese inlaid decoration is also extremely vulnerable to being placed in centrally heated environments and often shows its disapproval by disintegrating rapidly. Ivory too is vulnerable. The only kind of furniture that is completely indifferent to central heating is that made of marble. Thus, if one is lucky enough to have fine pieces of Oriental furniture, care should be taken to display and look after it correctly, for only then will it last and become a valuable investment for the future.

Below: *Tibetan portable altar table made of beaten brass with repoussé decoration and copper repoussé plaques, enhanced with blue glass overlay. Folding altar tables such as this were also made in wood and were brightly painted in many colours. They have their origin many centuries ago, when many of the ecclesiastical establishments were nomadic. This piece dates to the 19th century.*

Twentieth Century Furniture

The story of the development of furniture in the 20th century is hard to tell, partly because it is highly complex, and partly because it is difficult to view it with detachment and a sense of perspective. However, there are several fundamental features of the period that can be determined. First and most important has been the concern for originality in style and construction; no period of furniture history has been less dependent upon the styles and technology of the past. Second in significance, and closely related to the first feature, has been the use of new materials and technologies which have affected not only the appearance, cost and social status of furniture, but have also altered radically traditional concepts of permanence, value and durability. Third has been the role played by artists and architects in furniture design. At no other period has the painter, sculptor or architect been so involved in the production of furniture, from the point of view of both design and philosophy. A piece of furniture has frequently been produced as an art object, or as the statement of an artistic philosophy. At the same time, the role of the architect as a planner of the total environment has meant that furniture has often been integrated into an overall design. Fourth has been the breaking down of international barriers and the rapid transfer of both style and fashion from one area to another, or from one period to another. This contraction of the time and space barriers is of course an inevitable part of 20th century developments in communication.

During the late 19th and early 20th centuries a succession of European art movements turned the attention of both artists and designers, and the buying public, away from historicism and revivalism. In Britain, Europe and America a major change in design philosophy took place as artists and designers tried to come to terms with industrialization. Some responded by turning their backs on it altogether, and trying to return to a fantasy world based on idealism and an escapist interpretation of hand craftmanship. Others, through the new outlets offered by international exhibitions and trade, and the emerging design-concious shops and department stores, tried to force the processes of industrial production to coincide with advanced ideas of style and design. In Europe and America, as the Arts and Crafts Movement gave away to Art Nouveau, so the problems posed by mixing together an industrialized society with modern design ideas became more apparent. Although it became an international style and the popular expression of modernity, Art Nouveau never really achieved the breakthrough in style and technique that it promised. In fact, its flowing curves and exotic materials were quite impracticable for industrial production on a grand scale. At the same time its links with naturalism, decadence and with specific styles of the past, such as Celtic ornament, made it really the last fling of a Victorian design philosophy.

Left: *Exotic dining room suite in black lacquer, designed by Jon Wealleans during the 1960s. The combination of Mackintosh-style high-backed chairs, table legs of 1930s Lalique glass, cushions with air-brushed decoration and a dado in the spirit of the Vienna Secession well expresses the complexity and stylistic confusion of 20th century design.*

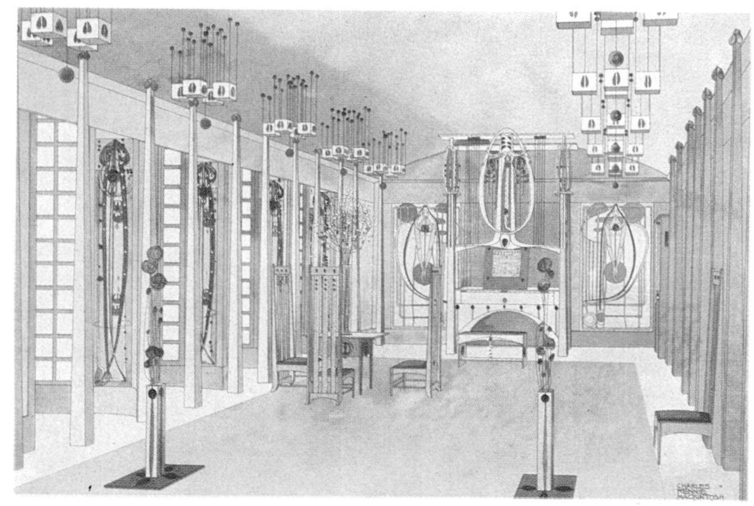

Above: *Scheme for a music room by Charles Rennie Mackintosh, with panels by Margaret Macdonald Mackintosh. This design was entered for the Haus eines Kunstfreunde competition, organized in Darmstadt by the Grand Duke von Hessen.*

However, within this style were many elements of the genuinely modern styles that were to sweep across Europe and America during and after the First World War. In England between 1897 and 1910 Charles Rennie Mackintosh had pushed interior and furniture design beyond the arbitrary limits imposed by function and tradition, and thereby had made the necessary breakthrough into sculptural form. That Mackintosh chairs were grotesquely impractical and uncomfortable, and frequently indifferently made was no longer relevant; what was more important was that they should stand as works of art in their own right, and be part of a total expression of one man's artistic philosophy. In France, Holland and Austria the extremes of Art Nouveau had given way to a genuine desire for modernity, which was to be achieved, not only at

Left: *Cabinet designed by the painter and decorator Sir Frank Brangwyn, 1930. The pottery displayed in the cabinet was also designed by Brangwyn and made by Royal Doulton, c.1935. Brangwyn was well known as a successful designer of articles such as rugs, textiles and stained glass as well as of furniture.*

Right: *Room setting displaying a collection of decorated furniture designed by the Omega Workshops. The bright colours, crude forms and occasionally inept technique reflect the contemporary fascination with primitive art. The Omega Workshops were founded in 1913 by Roger Fry as a centre for the production of well designed objects for daily use, but the pieces made did not always attain this ideal.*

the expense of the past, but also with a general disregard for rules of function or form. A similar movement in America, led by architects such as Frank Lloyd Wright, was elevating interior design to a point where it was on a level with painting and sculpture, a level at which the individual components could only be judged as part of the whole.

All these movements and personalities had one thing in common, namely an awareness of the moves towards abstraction that had affected avant-garde art since the early years of the 20th century. In France, painters such as Gauguin, Matisse, Seurat, and later Delaunay, had dramatically affected popular concepts of colour and form in a way that laid the foundation for the breakthrough to pure abstraction achieved by Braque, Picasso and Duchamp. In Germany, the Expressionists pursued a similar goal, while in England the Vorticists, and in Italy the Futurists, struggled to destroy traditional attitudes to art.

Ultimately it was the First World War and its aftermath that brought these diverse elements together and fused them into a genuine International Modern Style. Four years of cataclysm and chaos finally destroyed the social order of the previous century, and allowed new ideas to sweep across Europe and America. Frontiers were broken down or arbitrarily redrawn, while fundamental changes in social life, affecting for example female emancipation, education, travel and levels of pay, enabled these new ideas to take root. Ironically, many of the avant-garde movements that had flourished immediately before the War did not survive it. Futurism and Vorticism could not cope with international violence and destruction on a scale far beyond anything they might have advocated before the War. Some leading artists and designers actually perished during the conflict, while others were so affected by the experience that they changed totally their artistic direction. In the immediate post-war years Picasso, Braque, Nevinson, Severini and many other pre-war revolutionaries turned to a form of modern Neoclassicism. Others, such as Leger and Le Corbusier, responded very strongly to the new dominance of the machine, but were able to combine this element with a primitive but direct representational style.

In the context of the new post-war world, many of the modern ideas that had seemed revolutionary in 1914 now appeared rather tame. In England, the furniture produced under Roger Fry's direction at the Omega Studios between

Left: *Chair upholstered with fabric designed and sold by the Omega Workshops. The bold, semi-abstract design is in total contrast to the traditional form of the chair, and shows how little Roger Fry and his followers actually understood the avant-garde.*

1913 and 1920 now seemed very traditional; certainly these pieces, designed by Duncan Grant, Vanessa Bell or Fry himself, were decorated with abstract patterns often in dramatic colours, but this was after all no more than surface decoration which did not alter in any way the traditional structure or design of the object. The same could be said of French designer Sonia Delaunay's abstract pattern-making. Similarly the 'brutalist' approach pioneered in France before the War had no lasting effect; in retrospect Duchamp and others seem simply to have questioned the status of a work of art as a whole, without affecting design. They, and others in Europe and America, may have turned simple pieces of furniture into works of art, but this did not radically alter appearance or function in any lasting way.

Design in Russia and Holland

However, in two countries radical ideas did survive the War and were able to affect directly philosophies of design during the 1920s. In Russia the Revolution of 1917 was more than a change in the social order. The new Bolshevik rulers were dedicated to a pursuit of modernism in all its forms with a fervour that was almost religious. So, for a few years until the rise of Stalin brought about the reactionary, formal and 'safe' styles that to this day have characterized Soviet State-approved art, Russian designers and artists were able to develop the first truly modern styles. Lead by Malevich and others, Russian post-revolutionary painting and sculpture became totally abstract, firmly rejecting any lingering connection with representational attitudes. At the same time, post-revolutionary Russia was a totally modern society, firmly wedded to the machine as a means of changing the structure of life. Sculptors and designers were encouraged, even compelled, to use a mechanistic philosophy and pursue new technologies and new materials. Inevitably, little survives from this brief period, but the drawings and designs by Tatlin and others suggest that Russia was able to develop an approach to furniture design that anticipated the functional architect-designed styles of France and Germany that dominated the late 1920s and early 1930s.

Left: *Blue-red chair, designed by Gerrit Rietveld in 1917. The functional nature of Rietveld's design philosophy can be clearly seen in the basic structure of the chair, while the primary colours, used to emphasize the function and form of the chair, associate it closely with the De Stijl movement.*
Right: *Wassily armchair, designed by Marcel Breuer in 1925. This chair, ergonomically designed and with a simple tubular steel frame, expresses the style of industrial design associated with the Bauhaus and at the same time has a dateless modernity that has made it a 20th century classic.*

With post-revolutionary Russia, it is very much a case of 'what might have been'. However, in Holland the situation was quite different. Shortly before and during the War, a group of painters and sculptors, led by Piet Mondrian, had begun to explore the boundaries of art and design and move towards pure abstraction. Like others elsewhere in Europe, this Dutch group, which adopted the name of De Stijl (the style), were determined not only to pursue an international modernism, but also to break down the traditional barriers between fine and applied art. So, while Mondrian, Vantongaloo and other painters and sculptors in the De Stijl group were pursuing the goal of formal abstraction, the cabinetmaker Gerrit Rietveld began in 1916 to alter radically traditional concepts of furniture design. Although strongly aware of the need for a mechanistic approach, Rietveld was a traditional craftsman. He therefore designed furniture that was extremely simple and cheap to produce, being conceived for manufacture with a mixture of traditional woodworking skills combined with a modern modular approach. Wherever possible, pieces were designed to be made from a small number of simple repeating forms, easily cut from readily available timber, and easily assembled.

Another feature of the De Stijl philosophy was the use of basic colour. Following the extensive development of colour theory during the 19th century, the De Stijl artists reduced colour to the three primaries – red, yellow and blue, with black. Apart from believing other colours unnecessary, in that they simply represented mixtures of the primaries, they also used primary colours to create movement. The recessive quality of blue and the advancing quality of red had been recognized for many years, but they had never been applied before in so direct a way. Rietveld therefore painted some of his furniture with colours that would emphasize their features in a basically functional way. His best-known design is the blue-red chair of 1917, one of the cardinal objects in the history of 20th century design. This chair may have been fundamentally uncomfortable, but it was designed with an entirely 'modern' philosophy. The angles were conceived to relate to the geometry of the human body, while the structure and method of manufacture were planned for mass production by the new machine-age. The colour scheme represents the statement of a design philosophy, but at the same time the application of the colours is designed to emphasize the form and function of the chair. Rietveld continued to develop this philosophy and was eventually able to apply it to entire buildings, his Schroder house being the best-known example. His furniture designs are remarkable because they anticipate so much that was to follow. He was limited in one sense by his continued use of traditional materials and techniques. How much more effective would his cantilever Z-Chair of 1934 have been had he used metal or moulded plywood; but ultimately this is not important, for it did not alter the revolutionary nature of his design philosophy. Rietveld and the De Stijl artists were really responsible for laying the foundations upon which all subsequent 20th century designers could build.

The Bauhaus

The most significant developments in the early 1920s took place in Germany. The post-war Weimar Republic was infused with a cult of modernism, similar to, but much more restrained than that which was rampant in Russia. To reject the past was a basic principle in the new Germany, and so this philosophy became an important part of the educational system. In response to this, a new type of art school was founded in 1919 at Weimar, inspired largely by the architect Walter Gropius. Known as the Bauhaus, its principles spread to other centres and greatly influenced concepts of design throughout Europe and America for a decade, before its decline and eventual demise after the rise of Hitler. The Bauhaus philosophy was to reject traditional approaches to art education, and to replace them with a basic form of direct teaching that encouraged an understanding of colour, form, function and technique. Design was seen no longer as a minor part of painting and sculpture but as a major creative and social form in its own right. With its syllabus written largely by architects, it was inevitable that the Bauhaus should concern itself primarily with the environment. Although students were able to gain practical experience in painting, pottery, wood, metal-work, textiles and many other fields, they were trained as

Above: *Armchair designed by Ambrose Heal, 1935. Made from chromium plated steel and upholstered in white leather, this chair represents the blending of traditional form with modern materials, and so shows the continuing impact of the Paris Exhibition of 1925.*

designers first and foremost. In some ways the Bauhaus can claim to have invented the industrial designer. Its students were well trained both technically and artistically and were given a clear understanding of the social significance of design. They knew how to bring together an advanced design philosophy with the demands of a new technological and mechanistic world, and at the same time were aware of the need to obey the requirements of function. A Bauhaus student could therefore design a teapot, a carpet or a table with the certain knowledge that design played a part in the creation of the total object; they were no longer simply ornamenting the surface.

This new approach to design had a very significant impact throughout Europe and America. The revolution it provoked affected not only the appearance of things, but also their social status. Designers trained at the Bauhaus had an inevitable architectural or environmental approach, and so were concerned to produce objects that would impose principles of good design on all levels of society. They therefore concerned themselves deeply with new materials and methods of mass production. This approach naturally affected furniture design far more than any other field.

Marcel Breuer, Mies van der Rohe and others finally threw off the mantle of tradition and so developed the first truly modern furniture designs. New materials such as tubular steel and techniques such as chromium-plating and press-moulding were combined to produce ranges of modern, visually elegant yet relatively cheap furniture designed for mass production, to fit into the newly emerging consumer society. The best known example is the 'Wassily' armchair of 1925, Breuer's first design using tubular steel. Also important were the simple cantilever steel chairs of 1928, among the earliest to use this architectural principle of construction. Inevitably these new ranges were not immediately popular; their overt modernism meant that they were acceptable only to the design conscious. Frequently included by avant-garde architects in modern interior designs, and illustrated by the international art press, the furniture inspired by the Bauhaus took a long time to achieve a general popularity. However, many of the designs were both so rational and so dateless that they are still being produced and sold today. Ironically it was the rise of Hitler that did much to increase their popularity, for many Bauhaus-trained designers fled to America during the 1930s and so were able to exploit a far broader understanding and appreciation of their work. Breuer settled in America in 1937 after spending two years in England.

The influence of the modern furniture inspired by the Bauhaus was international. In France and England the designs were copied and adapted during the 1920s by architects such as Le Corbusier, Mart-Stam and Maxwell Fry, while companies such as PEL and Isokon were set up to develop and exploit the market for mass-produced, modern, tubular steel furniture. In America, the rise of designers such as Charles Eames was based on an appreciation of the Bauhaus philosophy, acquired directly from the designers and architects who had fled across the Atlantic from Nazism.

Scandinavia

However, the greatest impact of the Bauhaus-inspired modernism was in Scandinavia. In the relative political and social calm of Sweden, Denmark and Finland the Bauhaus principles of modern design firmly took root. Here, architects turned themselves into industrial designers to produce furniture that was modern in both style and technology. However, the availability of local raw materials turned the Scandinavian designers towards other techniques. Putting aside tubular steel and other modern industrial materials, they continued to use wood, but developed entirely new methods of mass production. By extensive use of laminates, such as plywood, and an elaboration of the heat moulding technique that Thonet had used so extensively in the 19th century, they were able to produce entirely modern furniture that conformed to Bauhaus principles of modernism and cheap industrial production. Here, as in Germany, architects led the field – men like the Finn Alvar Aalto whose ranges of moulded and laminated wooden furniture were both sculptural in concept and ergonomic in design.

During the 1930s Scandinavian furniture was more advanced in design than at any subsequent period. The Finnish and Danish architects produced designs that were highly acclaimed in Europe and America, and which achieved a greater popularity than their German metal-made souces of inspiration. This was partly because they were popularized and extensively sold through special marketing agencies set up to distribute them. In Scandinavia Futura and in England Finmar did much to establish

Above: *Chair and sideboard by the Finnish designer Alvar Aalto during the 1930s, made of moulded and laminated wood in a simple and functional style.*
Left: *Armchair by Aalto, 1930s. All these pieces, made of traditional materials used in new ways, such as moulded plywood, reveal a clear understanding of contemporary modernity. Influenced both by the Bauhaus and by traditional bentwood furniture, Aalto's work was conceived in essentially human and functional terms, one of the reasons for the long-lasting popularity of Scandinavian design.*

the Scandinavian reputation for modern design. However, this was only part of the story; their popularity was also based on their use of traditional materials and organic forms, albeit in a new style. Scandinavian furniture of the 1930s had a clearly human inspiration, an element frequently lacking in the artistically superb, but rather clinical and mechanistic products of the Bauhaus. Not everyone wanted to live in the perfect environment of the architect's drawing.

Scandinavian styles and techniques were copied extensively in England, France and America, and many designers and manufacturers in those countries were quick to exploit the obvious attraction of the kind of modernism offered by moulded and laminated wood. That Scandinavia rapidly became popularly associated with good modern design was at least in part due to the efforts of designers like Le Corbusier, J. Aronson and William Lescaze, and progressive companies such as Isokon, for whom Marcel Breuer designed a successful range of laminated and moulded wooden chairs in 1935.

The designers of De Stijl, the Bauhaus, Scandinavia and their followers in other countries had effectively turned furniture into an art form. Architects, painters and sculptors had become industrial designers, thereby elevating their products to a fine art status. Many pieces of furniture were bought as examples of modern art, on both public and private levels, and were therefore revered as works of art. By this process their essential function tended to be disregarded, a chair becoming an object to look at, rather than sit on. Functional principles affected the aesthetics of their design and manufacture, because functionalism was an important part of the creed of the designer of the International Modern School. However in many cases the concern for function was only skin deep as the pieces were patently not to be used. This element was taken to extreme lengths during the mid-1930s when the art aspect sometimes took over completely. The fantastic creations of Surrealism deliberately abandoned the already tenuous connection with reality and the requirements of function.

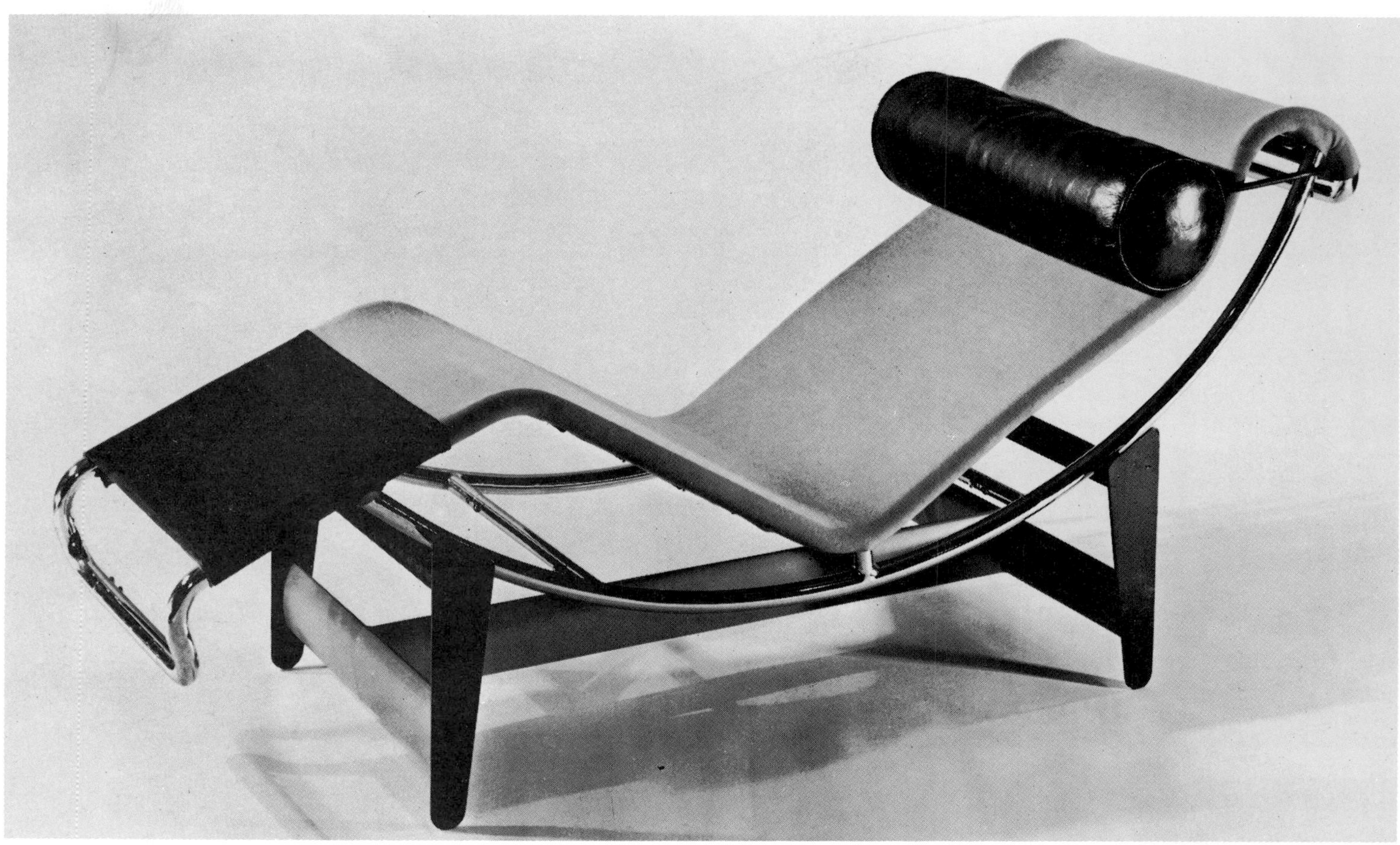

Above: *Adjustable chaise longue, designed by Le Corbusier with Charlotte Perriand and Pierre Jeanneret in 1927. This design, made from tubular steel plated with chromium, is really more a modernistic interpretation of a traditional form rather than a truly modern piece of furniture.*
Below: *Long chair, designed by Marcel Breuer, 1936, and made from moulded plywood by the avant-garde English furniture manufacturer, Isokon. The base and arm rests are made from strips of laminated wood shaped under steam pressure. The upholstery has been removed to reveal the basic form of the seat.*

Salvador Dali's famous Mae West sofa, made in the shape of the star's lips, is no more a piece of furniture than are Oldenburg's soft chairs of the 1960s. They can be sat upon, but that is no longer of any relevance. To promote furniture as an art form with a broad disregard for function was a reflection of the aesthetics of the period, but it is really no more than an entertaining backwater in the history of furniture design.

The survival of tradition

The role played by architects and artists in creating the modern furniture of the period 1918-39 is obviously very important, but it is only one side of the story. The other side is represented by the survival of tradition, despite the continuous assaults of modernism. During the early years of this century, most of Europe and America had undergone a revival of vernacular traditions. In its last fling, the Arts and Crafts Movement had finally succeeded in popularizing the primitive and rural styles of the pre-industrialised world. This revival went beyond the continuous historicism of the Victorian period because it did not actually revive anything.

The vernacular style which appeared between about 1905 and 1915 took many guises, but few of them were based very closely on any particular aspect of furniture design during the past. Instead, a revival of traditional materials and techniques was combined with a fairly dateless style which was, if anything, drawn more from the sophisticated elegance of the 18th century than from the simple styles of any more primitive era.

This new style was successful in many countries, mainly because it could be produced to suit any level of the market.

It was essentially simple in appearance, but well made from good materials, and so could be sold cheaply enough via a retail catalogue, or expensively by the craftsman selling direct to his generally far from rustic patrons. By the outbreak of the First World War, this style had become almost universal. It represented a marvellous compromise between the requirements of modern productive techniques and the general romantic longing for the simple life of the past, a romanticism that requires a level of popular education never obtainable in earlier periods. The mixture of traditional quality with a dateless modernism gave this furniture a lasting appeal that outlived even the chaos of the War. Indeed, it can be argued that the success of Scandinavian design during the 1930s was precisely because it represented a continuity of this happy mixture, but now presented in a more directly avant-garde guise. Scandinavian furniture was descended on one side from the Bauhaus; however the other parent was the popular traditionalism and high quality of Ernest Gimson or Ambrose Heal.

In the years that immediately followed the First World War, there was an outburst of traditional furniture design that was almost universal. In every country traditional

Below: *Wardrobe, designed and made by Heal & Co, 1926. The traditional shape, combined with exotic materials and fine craftsmanship, show that Heals were quick to put into practice the lessons of the Paris Exhibition of 1925.*

manufacturers produced traditional designs in traditional materials. This movement was in part a continuity of pre-war vernacularism and partly a vague desire to maintain pre-war standards in the face of universal revolution and modernism. Some of this furniture was simply pedantic, cumbersome and outmoded, and its design was traditional in a quite barbaric and irrelevant way. The designs were generally of no significance, and the furniture was sold largely by major department stores.

In England and America it took the form of a debased and frequently inaccurate revival of Tudor and Jacobean styles, while in France, Germany, Spain and Italy, the designers took their inspiration from the more extreme styles of the 18th century. Sometimes the designers were not so vulgar, and were simply traditional in a rather unimaginative and academic way: examples were the designs of Malmsten of Stockholm, or Dr J. Frank and Dr O. Wlach of Vienna. Although popular, these styles contributed little to the history of furniture design. However, they are significant because an adventurous use of traditionalism characterized much of the better furniture produced during the early 1920s. In the hands of more inspired designers such as Peter Waals and Gordon Russell, generally traditional styles and materials could be turned into something that was elegant, modern and entirely suitable for the contemporary environment of the 1920's. Sold by stores such as Heal's in London, Macy's in New York and Au Printemps in Paris, this type of traditional-modern furniture achieved considerable popularity. It had no need to be archaic in its use of styles and techniques and was able to take its place in the design-conscious environments of the period, without seeming out of place. At the same time, it enjoyed a traditional feeling of quality that put it apart from the overt modernism of the Bauhaus and its followers.

Perhaps the greatest exponent of this style was the American architect and designer, Frank Lloyd Wright. Trained by the architect Louis Sullivan, he believed firmly in the concept of total environmental design, and insisted on complete responsibility for every aspect of his commissions. A house by Wright is therefore as much an architectural entity as one by Le Corbusier or Mies van der Rohe, but in style they could not be further apart. Wright greatly enjoyed using traditional materials and techniques, but was able to present them in a totally revolutionary manner. However, unlike the structures by Le Corbusier and others which were generally too perfect or too inhuman for normal patterns of life, Wright's buildings were conceived essentially in human terms. They encouraged an adventurous use of space and showed an almost sensuous pleasure in materials and textures, but despite this fact they were still dramatically modern. For example, his rectilinear chairs in wood and metal of 1904 are extraordinarily advanced for their time, and anticipate the 'machine-made' look of the 1920s.

Right: *This sumptuous office was created by Frank Lloyd Wright in 1937 for Edgar Kauffman's department store in Pittsburgh, Pennsylvania. The wood furniture reflects his architectural work in its heavy, square design.*

Art Deco

Traditionalism probably received its greatest boost at the Paris International Exhibition of 1925. This exhibition is cardinal in any study of 20th century design history, for it launched the style that became popularly known as Art Deco. This much abused and maligned term, drawn from the actual title of the exhibition, is frequently used to describe any object, either vaguely or outrageously modern, made between 1920 and 1940. In fact the term has a quite specific meaning, perhaps expressed better by the contemporary term 'Jazz Moderne'. It is an irony that Art Deco has come to mean anything brashly modern, whereas in fact the main characteristic of the Paris Exhibition was its traditionalism.

The 1925 Exhibition was, despite its title, almost entirely a French affair. Although there was a number of international pavilions, from which America was notably

Left: *Combined dressing table and stool, English, 1930s. This essentially ill-conceived and poorly made object shows how debased the Jazz Moderne style became in the hands of the average manufacturer with the department store in mind.*

Below: *Armchair and side table designed by Jacques Ruhlmann, 1930. Made from ebony, with bronze mounts and upholstered in pink satin, these elegant pieces express perfectly the spirit of the Paris Exhibition of 1925 – adventurous but traditional design combined with exotic and luxurious materials. Ruhlmann's high standards of style and execution made him one of the greatest French designers of the period.*

Above: *Chrome table with peach coloured glazed top, c.1935. The designer of this table has learnt some of the lessons of the Modern Movement, particularly in his use of materials. However, the end product is still rather crude by comparison with the elegant Ruhlmann pieces below.*

Above: *Table of inlaid marble and gilt metal. This flamboyant piece is modern in its use of exotic and extravagant materials, but its style echoes the Japanese taste of the late 19th century, particularly in the use made of an extra surface below the table top, and of the corners cut diagonally to give an octagonal shape to the piece.*

Above: *Bureau in pale wood, the drawers and desk top faced with antelope hide, adorned with brass handles and a gilded base. It dates from 1930 and is most probably French in origin. Unlike the table beside it, this bureau is totally exotic in both form and decoration, and so is very expressive of the spirit of Art Deco.*

absent, French styles and products were dominant. The furniture in particular was quite specifically French, and rarely avant-garde. Modernism in the Bauhaus sense was hardly considered, and yet all the French displays were modern in a popular sense. Traditional techniques and traditional materials were flaunted by one designer after another, most of whom clearly saw modernism simply as a surface veneer to be applied to an unchanging fundamental design philosophy. Many styles were drawn consciously from the 18th century, while others luxuriated in the exoticism of their materials. Lacquer, rare woods and leathers, elaborate and essentially decorative carving and tooling, inlay and rich metal mounting were the obvious features of the French furniture, by designers such as Charpentier, Ruhlmann, Dunand and Follot; the exhibition also popularized the design group approach, where all aspects of interior decoration and planning were undertaken by groups such as Atelier or Primavera, in which the individual's contribution was less significant than that of the team as a whole. These groups were frequently based in well known department stores; for example, Primavera operated from Au Printemps under the direction of M. and Mme. Gauchet-Guillard, while Paul Follot ran Pomone at Bon Marché.

Much of the furniture was modern in a decorative, up-to-the-minute way, but its modernity was essentially superficial. This is important, because it explains the popularity of the styles launched by this exhibition. The styles of Art Deco rapidly became universal, because they were presented in a popular format. The influence of Egyptian, South American and other primitive civilizations was readily understood when their decorative features could be applied equally to radio sets, cabinets, clocks, chairs or bathroom fittings. By comparison, the ascetic modernism of the Bauhaus was hard to appreciate, its purity and integrity of design being alien to a culture

Above: *Display cabinet, designed by Paul Follot for Bon Marché, and shown at the Paris Exhibition of 1925. Made from dark wood, enriched with carved foliate decoration and ivory inlay, this luxurious cabinet is still highly functional while retaining the traditional quality and elegance of fine French furniture.*

Above: *Screen designed by Frank Brangwyn in 1920. The marquetry decoration of simplified animal and bird forms is reminiscent of the decorative styles of the late 19th century and so shows the lasting impact which the Arts and Crafts Movement in England had on fashion during the first quarter of this century.*

trained to appreciate and judge its furniture by its attention to decorative detail. Most people were not prepared to make the effort to acquire the trained eye of the architect or industrial designer. It is therefore easy to understand the appeal of the French furniture of 1925, with its deliberate emphasis on luxury and comfort, and its widespread use of a traditionalism that was immediately attractive. It is hardly surprising that Jazz Moderne rapidly became the popular interpretation of the modern style. From Paris the styles of Art Deco spread outwards like ripples on a pool, until a form of decorative modernism, albeit of a very debased nature, was to be found in practically every corner of Europe and America. In fact, one of the few truly modern designers working in Paris at this time was Eileen Gray. Born in England, she spent her working life in Paris,

Above: *Desk, chair and lighting designed in 1932 by Donald Deskey for S. L. Rothafel, the genius behind New York's Radio City Music Hall. This building, a monument to the Art Deco style in America, featured the work of a number of leading designers in a range of new materials, such as aluminium, cork, formica and chrome-plated steel. However, despite its obvious modernism, Deskey's furniture still retains elements of both traditional and even archaic styles.*

designing furniture that combined the French love of exotic styles and materials with a mechanistic Bauhaus-style modernism. Much of the furniture was sold through her own shop, opened in 1922.

The popularity of this form of the modern style was based upon two factors, both of which had only emerged since the First World War. The first was the spread of suburbanism, the tentacles of which were reaching out along every main road during the 1920s and 1930s. Aided by the motor car and the increasing public transport networks, industrialized man had developed the habit of living some distance from his place of work. Cities, towns and villages across the world were spreading outwards, increasing their size with endless varieties of essentially identical semi-detached and detached villas and terraced houses. All these new developments, quickly built by modern techniques, required matching modern furniture.

The second was the growth of advertising and the related emergence of the consumer, a new member of society driven onwards by a desperate need to spend newly earned income on new and frequently unnecessary possessions. These factors, aided by radio, newspapers, department stores, mail order catalogues and the cinema, ensured that there was an insatiable demand for new furniture of a crudely modern style. This in turn stimulated the development of cheaper methods of manufacture and new materials, and resulted inevitably in the emergence of a type of furniture that was ultimately ephemeral. The luxurious and exotic pieces shown in Paris were echoed by cheap and shoddy copies, manufactured in vast quantities all over the world. Despite the aesthetic efforts of the Bauhaus designers and the struggles of craftsmen to maintain traditional qualities, popular modern furniture was, by 1940, something quite different.

The use of new materials

In 1939 the outbreak of war brought about dramatic changes. The designers who had pursued the modernist philosophy were by now scattered around the world, and were applying their industrial design experience in quite

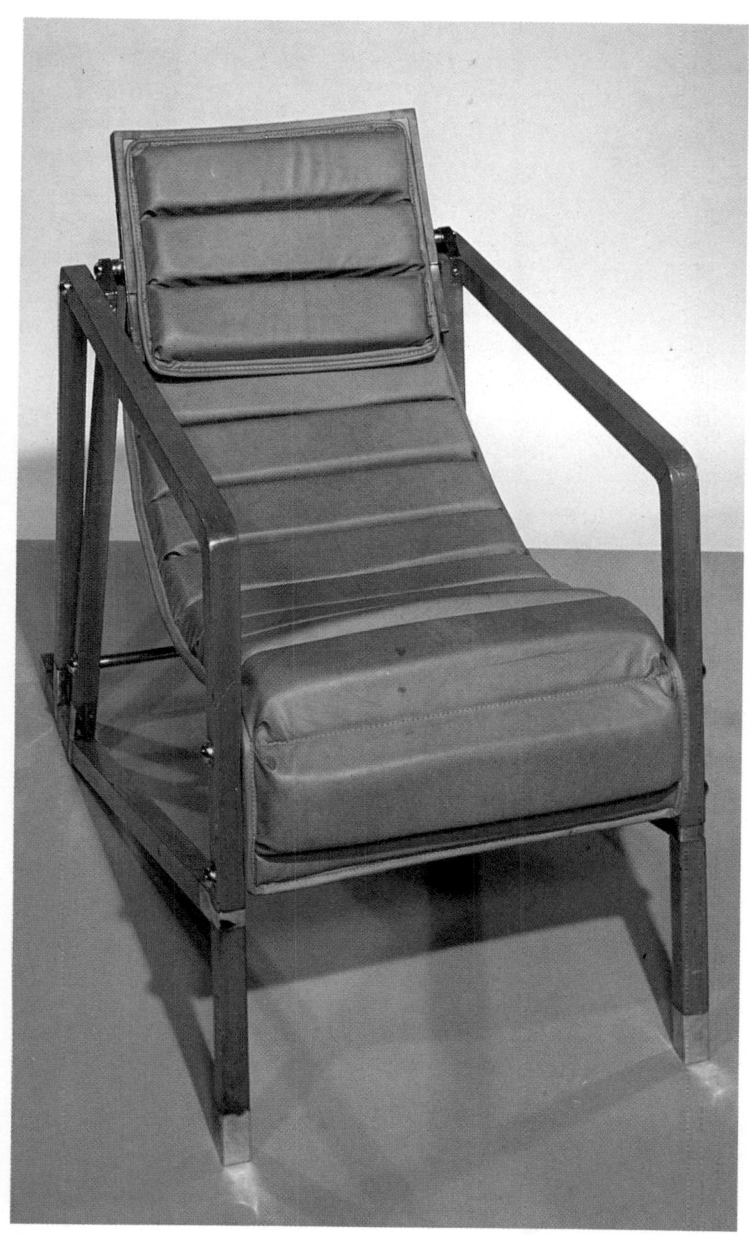

different fields. Factories that had produced laminated and moulded wood furniture were now at work making aeroplanes, while Bauhaus-trained architects were now designing and equipping factories instead of houses for the avant-garde. By the same token traditional craftsmen-designers were now without clients, for the world could no longer afford individual and personalized luxury. During the war the design and production of furniture of original style and quality came virtually to a standstill. Shortages of raw materials and manpower and a greatly restricted consumer society almost closed down the European industry. However, the war had one important effect, namely the development and production of a whole new range of materials. Wood and metals were used in new and more adventurous ways and new types of papers and textiles were developed; but the rapid advances made in the technology of plastics were to have the greatest impact. Many of these new processes and materials were first used extensively in America during the 1940s, and so, by the time the war ended in 1945, the Americans had built up a significant lead in the race to develop peace-time applications of war-time discoveries. The most significant designer to emerge was Charles Eames. Trained as an architect, he worked with Eero Saarinen to exploit the new materials in a modern and organic manner. His first design,

Left: *Chair by Eileen Gray, c.1924. Although lacking the exotic individuality of her early work, chairs such as this show how Eileen Gray was able to adapt her ideas for quantity production. Although clearly influenced by Le Corbusier, this chair combines an obvious modernity with traditional methods of construction.*
Below: *Utility furniture was a government-sponsored attempt to make a range of well-designed modern items available to a mass market. Both new and traditional materials were used in order to produce furniture that was simple, cheap and generally attractive. Inevitably some of the designs have an institutional quality as they lack any form of luxury or ornament.*

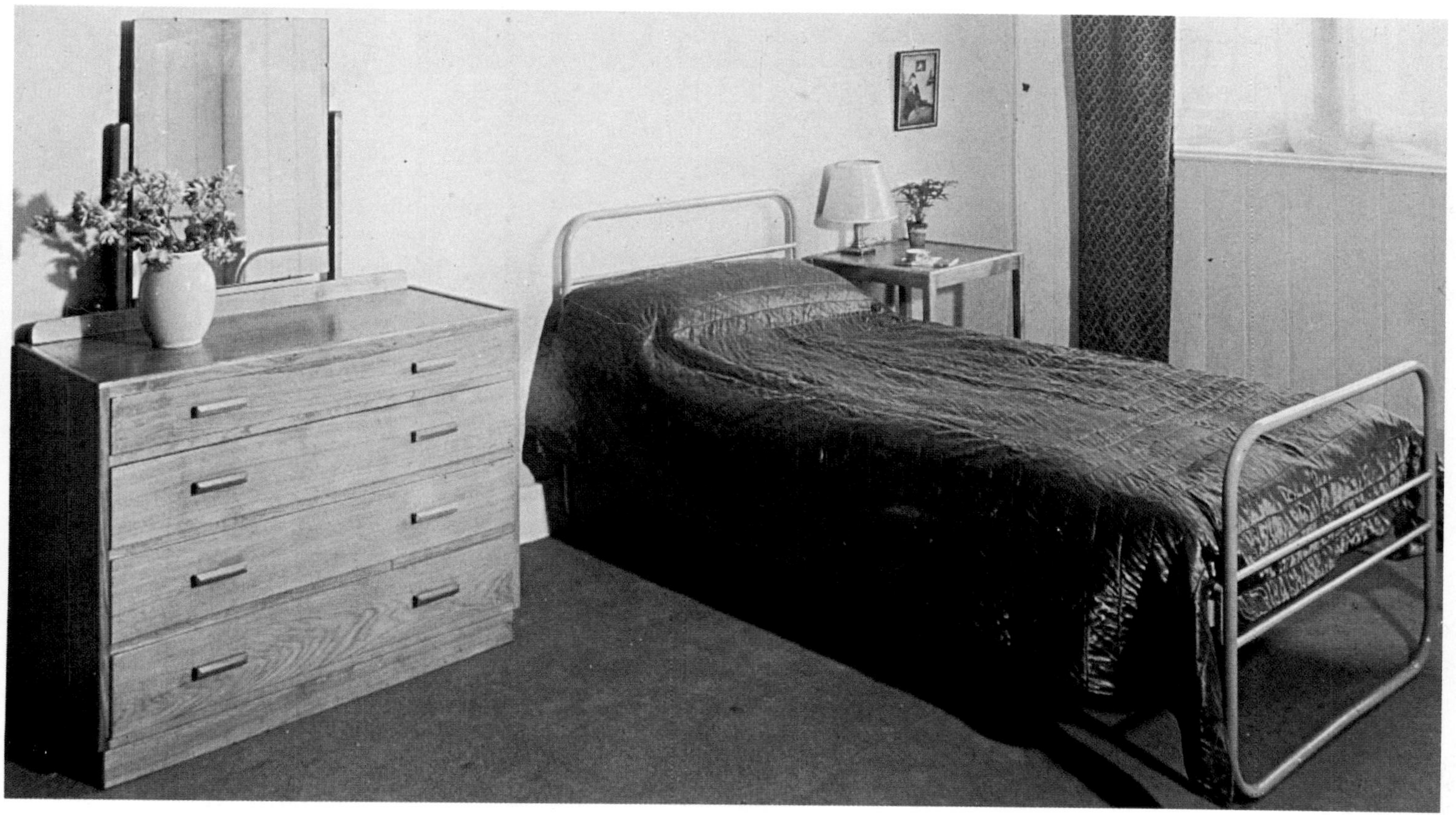

for a chair in moulded plywood and aluminium, appeared in 1940. A year later this was awarded a prize by the Museum of Modern Art in New York. Most important, however, was his DAR chair of 1949, the first to have a seat of moulded glass fibre. In these and similar designs, the seat, back and arms were stamped from one sheet of plastic.

There were many government-sponsored schemes to set the industry in Europe on its feet, but most of them relied on design and production methods that were out of date. In England, established designers such as Gordon Russell were set to work to mastermind the production of the so-called Utility ranges of furniture and textiles. This simple but elegant furniture, designed for easy mass production from good materials by ill-equipped factories, was immediately successful; however, its appeal lay as much in its actual availability, after years of deprivation, as in its appearance. In fact, the range was extremely old-fashioned, and its style and technology represented in some ways the last fling of the craft revival. Similar schemes operated in other countries with similar results. In fact it was in America that the real changes took place. Led by Charles Eames, Pascoe Industries and others,

Left: *Utility chair, 1940s. Although superficially modern in style and the use of materials, this is essentially a traditional armchair of the type for ever to be associated with the three piece suite. Unlike the classic designs of the period, these pieces with their veneer of modernity became dated very quickly and so passed rapidly from fashion.*
Below: *This view of a modern interior in Germany shows a good range of contemporary styles that are now completely international. Traditional materials and forms have been combined with an urbane modernism that well expresses the casual nature of today's social life.*

Above: *Settee and chair made by Vono, c.1972. The contemporary appearance and the use of tubular steel are expressive of a popular acceptance of the machine-made object.*
Right: *The Egg chair, designed by Arne Jacobsen, 1959. Made of upholstered fibreglass and mounted on a chromium plated steel swivel base, this chair is a masterly interpretation of modern technology and traditional elegance.*
Below: *Lounge chair and matching footstool, designed by Charles Eames, 1957. Now accepted as a classic 20th century chair, this design of laminated rosewood and anodised aluminium was considered to be revolutionary when it first appeared.*

Above: *A range of chairs in the British Buoyant series, 1978. The settees reflect the traditional Chesterfield form of the 19th century, revealing a desire to return to comfort at the expense of design. The cantilever chair and footstool is broadly modern in a rather old-fashioned way, but lacks the elegance of the similar Eames design.*
Above left: *A suite of chairs by the French manufacturer Roset, 1977. The soft, shapeless and traditionally upholstered and buttoned forms reveal the contemporary dependence upon plastic foam for both filling and shape. Apart from presenting a serious fire hazard, the widespread use of these materials has ensured that essentially shapeless furniture of this type has no lasting quality. Instead, it is conceived in largely ephemeral terms, although retaining a veneer of luxury.*
Left: *The Ming range of dining room furniture by Tetrad, 1970s. The use of consciously archaic forms combined with modern methods of construction and an impractical covering material reveals the state of confusion of many modern furniture designers and manufacturers.*

American furniture makers began to revolutionize their trade. Extensive use of plastics, laminates and metal produced exciting ranges of furniture that developed further the Scandinavian and Bauhaus-inspired styles of the 1930s. Many Bauhaus designers were now working in America, so they were able to combine their design skills with a technology far more advanced than any other in the world. They also had the advantage of an educated, relatively wealthy public, now trained by the spread of sophisticated communications networks to demand new styles and new technology.

During this period there also developed in America a move to merge together styles of domestic and industrial or office furniture. For the first time the two types were designed and produced to complement each other, or even to be interchangeable. This novel concept, inspired largely by the use of new industrial materials, rapidly gained popular acceptance in other countries, a popularity that has continued to increase. Related to this, because of a similar dependence on new materials and technology, has been the broad acceptance of ephemeral or disposable furniture. Much of the furniture made and sold since the war has been designed to last for 10 or 20 years at the most and to be constantly replaced to satisfy the whims of fashion. As a result, it is now quite hard, and very expensive, to purchase new furniture that is designed to be passed from one generation to another. Ironically, one of the direct results of this has been to make all types and styles of antique furniture more desirable, and so more valuable.

The European furniture industry took the American experience very much to heart and has been following a similar course of development since the war. Aided by exhibitions such as the Festival of Britain of 1951 and the Brussels Exhibition of 1958 and by regular trade shows with their inevitable publicity, European designers and manufacturers gradually recovered their confidence and their pre-war abilities. In England, in particular, the work of government bodies such as the Design Council and, more recently, the Crafts Council have helped to further the cause of modern furniture. The role played by architects was still considerable, however, mainly because of the dramatic changes taking place in the domestic environment. Gradually houses became smaller and clustered increasingly together into estates or tall apartment blocks. The reduction in scale, and the increasing use of building systems made built-in furniture essential. As a result, the architect could frequently design a complete living area which had no need for most of the traditional, individually-made moveable pieces of furniture. The combination of office styles and materials, system structures, built-in furniture and the disposable philosophy has probably altered the interior appearance of the house more radically over the last 30 years than over the previous 300.

Since 1945 there have been several distinct phases in furniture design. The changes from one to another have been prompted largely by fashion, and so the transition has frequently been quick. As a result, styles can have their complete life-cycle within a decade or less, making the products of the 1950s as distinct from those of the 1960s, as those of the 17th century are from the 18th century. During the 1950s, designers began to exploit new materials and techniques, but their lack of experience frequently resulted in furniture that was ill-conceived, badly made and bizarre in appearance and proportion. Traditionalism survived but often took the form of pedantic and over-fussy reproductions of earlier styles. During the 1960s everything changed. By then experience had demonstrated the best use of the new materials and technology, and confidence produced more dynamic, powerful and colourful designs. Plastic became an exciting material in its own right, rather than a means of producing cheap and inferior copies of more costly substances and styles. For reasons that are now quite hard to understand, Scandinavian styles again became quite popular; with their smooth, flowing

Right: *The Coronella range, designed by Michael Tyler in 1977. By the use of materials such as plastics and foam, the structure of the pieces has been reduced to a series of related cubes. The geometric simplicity of this type of furniture makes it a kind of domestic sculpture, for both function and comfort have been disregarded by the designer.*

Below right: *As the lessons of modernity have gradually been learned by furniture designers, the styles of office and domestic furniture have come closer together. This elegant office suite in rosewood and chromium could as well be used in the home, reflecting as it does the varied styles of the Bauhaus, Paris 1925, and Charles Eames.*

Below: *During the 1950s and 1960s detailed space planning was increasingly necessary in the smaller houses and flats being built. This resulted in the appearance of a number of flexible furniture and storage systems. This example, from the early 1970s, has a wide range of interchangeable units and represents a domestic application of industrial or office funiture.*

Above: *Hammock chair, by Paul Kjaerholm, 1965. Made from stainless steel and canework, and with a leather adjustable cushion, this chair represents a curious compromise between the modernist styles of the Bauhaus, and the use of traditional furniture materials. By contrast with the plastic chairs on the left, this underlines how the avant-garde styles of the 1920s and 1930s have now become a widely accepted and established standard modernist form. Variations on many of the classic Bauhaus designs have appeared over and over again since their original introduction.*

Left: *These three chairs, the Pastilli chair (top) by the Finnish designer Eero Arnio, 1968, the Contour chair (centre) by David Colwell, 1968 and the Toga stacking chair (bottom) by Sergio Mazza, also 1968, illustrate the application of new materials and advanced technology to furniture. Made from moulded plastics in bright colours, items such as these represent a total break away from the styles and traditions of the past. Although sculptural in form, they are essentially functional and are designed to be thrown away or replaced when no longer required.*

shapes and decorative uses of traditional materials, the Scandinavian designers appeared to offer something new. In fact, all they were offering were slightly debased revivals of their 1930s styles: elegant, smart, but essentially sterile. However, this lack of originality did not worry the public, and so Scandinavia became briefly the home of modern design.

Also popular during the 1960s was the delicate and carefully balanced Italian furniture, developed from the work of designers such as Ponti, known for his Chiavari chair of 1951. Small, well engineered chairs, with legs to match contemporary stiletto heels, and a highly finished glossy overall colour were the typical products of the period. Many were designed to match the glass or marble-topped coffee tables that accompanied them. More extreme was the furniture formed entirely from moulded plastics, and even paper, whose shapes were once again more closely allied to sculpture, and in whose design form usually took precedence over comfort.

Since then, other changes have occurred. One of the direct results of the great interest in antique furniture has been the popularity of pine. Thousands of pleasant pieces of indeterminate age and period have been divested of their polish to satisfy the apparently insatiable demand for stripped pine furniture, a style popular throughout Europe. Inevitably many manufacturers now produce new pine furniture, in attractive, generally contemporary, but

Above: *English glass and metal dining room suite, early 1970s. The use of modern materials in styles that are elegant but archaic emphasizes the present confused state of furniture design. This suite would be equally at home in the boardroom or the dining room, a loss of identity that shows how the dynamic advances of the inter-war years have been greatly blunted during the last few decades.*

undateable styles, usually finished with a high-gloss varnish seal.

There has also been a revival of traditional techniques and materials, part of a broad craft movement that has affected England, France, Germany and America equally during the last decade. This is still a minority taste so it is hard to tell whether it will develop into a major style or philosophy to affect the nature of furniture design and manufacture during the last years of this century. So far, the characteristic feature of 20th century furniture has been the pursuit of originality in both style and technique. In a revolution led by architects, artists and sculptors, furniture has been changed from something permanent and stable into something ephemeral and immediate; from determining the quality of the domestic environment, it has been absorbed by that environment. Something positive and forceful has gradually been neutralized. Perhaps it is now time to reverse the pattern.

Guide to Museums and Collections

The following list of museums and collections has been listed alphabetically under countries. It is obviously very selective, and has generally been limited to those places which house the most comprehensive collections, or which have an important specialist collection of a particular period of furniture.

AUSTRALIA

Adelaide: Art Gallery of South Australia
Melbourne: National Gallery of Victoria
Sydney: Museum of Applied Arts and Sciences

AUSTRIA

Vienna: Kunsthistorisches Museum
Osterreichisches Museum für angewandte Kunst

BELGIUM

Brussels: Royal Museums of Art and History
Liège: Musée des Beaux Arts

CANADA

Toronto: Royal Ontario Museum
Victoria: Art Gallery of Greater Victoria

CZECHOSLOVAKIA

Prague: Museum of Applied Art

DENMARK

Copenhagen: Kunstindustrimuseet
National Museum
Rosenberg Castle Museum

EIRE

Dublin: National Museum of Ireland

FRANCE

Campiègne: Musée National du Palais de Campiègne
Chantilly: Condé Museum
Fontainebleau: Musée National du Chateau de Fontainebleau
Paris: Louvre Museum
Musée des Arts Decoratifs
Musée Carnavalet
Musée Guimet
Rouen: Musée des Beaux Arts
Rueil-Malmaison: Musée National du Chateau de Malmaison
Versailles: Musée National du Chateau de Versailles

GERMAN DEMOCRATIC REPUBLIC

Berlin: Bode Museum

GERMAN FEDERAL REPUBLIC

Berlin: Charlottenburg Palace Museums
Dahlem Museum
Staatliche Museum Preussischer Kulturbesitz
Kunstgewerbemuseum
Darmstadt: Hessisches Landes Museum
Dusseldorf: Art Museum
Hamburg: Museum für Kunst und Gewerbe
Munich: Residenz Museum
Bayerisches National Museum

GREAT BRITAIN

Bath: American Museum in Britain, Claverton Manor
Bedford: Cecil Higgins Museum
Birmingham: City Museum and Art Gallery
Brighton: Museum and Art Gallery
Royal Pavilion
Bristol: City Art Gallery
Cambridge: Fitzwilliam Museum
Cardiff: National Museum of Wales
Edinburgh: Royal Scottish Museum
Glasgow: Art Gallery and Museum, Kelvingrove
Leeds: Temple Newsam House
Liverpool: Merseyside County Museums
London: Bethnal Green Museum
British Museum
Geffrye Museum
Victoria & Albert Museum
Wallace Collection
William Morris Gallery
Manchester: City Art Gallery
Oxford: Ashmolean Museum
Port Sunlight: Lady Lever Art Gallery

GREECE

Athens: Benaki Museum

HOLLAND
Amsterdam: Rijksmuseum
Haarlem: Frans Hals Museum
Rotterdam: Boymans-van Beuningen Museum

HUNGARY
Budapest: Hungarian National Museum
Museum of Applied Arts

ITALY
Florence: Bargello National Museum
Palazzo Pitti
Milan: Poldi Pezzoli Museum
Naples: Capodimonte National Museum
Rome: National Museum
Turin: Civic Museum of Ancient Art, Palazzo Madama
Venice: Correr Museum

JAPAN
Tokyo: National Museum

NEW ZEALAND
Auckland: City Art Gallery
Wellington: National Art Gallery

NORWAY
Oslo: Kunstindustrimuseet

POLAND
Cracow: Wawelu Castle State Art Collections
Warsaw: Muzeum Narodowe

PORTUGAL
Lisbon: Gulbenkian Foundation

SOUTH AFRICA
Capetown: South African National Gallery
Johannesburg: Art Gallery
Pretoria: Art Museum

SPAIN
Madrid: Museo del Prado

SWEDEN
Stockholm: National Museum
Ostasiatiska Museet

SWITZERLAND
Geneva: Musée d'Art et d'Histoire
Zurich: Kunstgewerke Museum
Landesmuseum

TAIWAN
Taipei: National Palace Museum

THAILAND
Bangkok: National Museum

TURKEY
Istanbul: Topkapi Palace Museum

USA
Boston: Fine Arts Museum
Cambridge, Massachussetts: Fogg Art Museum
Chicago: Art Institute
Cincinnati: Art Museum
Cleveland: Museum of Art
Dearborn: Henry Ford Museum
Detroit: Institute of Fine Arts
Houston: Bayou Bend Collection of Americana
Kansas City: William Rockhill Nelson Collection
Los Angeles: County Museum of Art
John Paul Getty Museum
Minneapolis: Walker Art Center
New Haven: Yale University Art Collection
New York: Frick Collection
Metropolitan Museum
Philadelphia: Museum of Art
San Francisco: M.H. de Young Memorial Museum
Palace of the Legion of Honor
Shaker Heights: Shaker Historical Society
Sturbridge: Old Sturbridge Village
Toledo: Museum of Arts
Washington: Smithsonian Institution
Williamsburg: Colonial Williamsburg
Winterthur: Henry Francis du Pont Winterthur Museum

USSR
Leningrad: Hermitage Museum
Moscow: Tretiakov Gallery

YUGOSLAVIA
Belgrade: National Museum
Ljubljana: Municipal Museum

Glossary

Anthemion: formalized honeysuckle – a form of decoration used especially during the Neoclassical period.

Apron piece: ornamental strip below the seat rail of a chair or sofa, also used on chest-of-drawers, side-tables, etc.

Arabesques: patterns of interlacing foliage and tendrils.

Arcading: decoration formed from a continuous pattern of arches or arcades.

Armoire: large cupboard or wardrobe.

Armoire-à-deux-corps: piece of furniture consisting of an upper and a lower cupboard.

Baluster shape: a turned column-like form, used in furniture for chair-backs and table legs, based on the architectural baluster or balustrade.

Banding: decorative border or edging of wood veneer, with the grain running either across the band (cross-banding) or diagonally to it (herring-bone or feather banding).

Beading: narrow moulding generally semicircular in section.

Bergère: upholstered armchair with a wide seat and rounded back; first developed in 18th century France and much copied in other countries. Early 19th century English examples have caned seats, backs and arms.

Bombé: lit. 'bulging'; a bombé commode is one with convex swelling in the front and sides of the carcase.

Bonnet scrolls: American term for a curved and scrolled pediment on highboys, bookcases etc.

Campaign furniture: portable furniture, designed to fold, unscrew or, in carcase furniture, fitted with sunken carrying handles, for use by officers on military campaigns.

Caquetoire: a ladies' conversation or 'gossip' chair with a narrow back panel and arms set wide apart to accommodate the full skirts of the 16th and early 17th century when this type of chair was prevalent.

Carcase furniture: items with box-like body construction, such as chests of drawers and bookcases.

Cartouche: ornamental panel in the form of an open scroll with curling edges.

Cellaret: wine cooler, or lead-lined vessel for storing bottles of wine.

Certosina: decorative marquetry or intarsia of geometric patterns made with pieces of bone, metal and mother-of-pearl as well as wood.

Chiffonier: small sideboard with a cupboard below and an open shelf or shelves above, introduced in the late 18th century and extremely popular in the early 19th.

Chip carving: shallow carved ornament, usually of geometrical patterns, drawn with mathematical instruments and chipped out.

Composition (or compo): a mixture of whiting, resin and size used for carved or moulded decoration, especially in the 18th century.

Console table: a side-table fixed to the wall and supported by brackets usually carved in scroll form, or by legs only at the front.

Cornucopia: horn of plenty – a decorative motif of a goat's horn filled with ears of wheat, fruit and flowers.

Cresting: decorated top rail of the back of a chair or sofa, or decorated top-piece of a cabinet, usually carved or pierced.

Crockets: hook-shaped leaf ornaments on the angles of pinnacles and canopies in Gothic architecture (and in Gothic furniture).

Dovetail: wedge-shaped tenon which fits into a corresponding mortice to join two pieces of wood at right angles.

Fall-front: movable board at the front of a desk which can be lowered to form a writing surface.

Flemish scroll: double scroll, as in the carving of front legs and stretchers in late 17th century English chairs.

Gesso: a mixture of plaster of Paris and parchment size (and sometimes other substances) used as a base for painted decoration and/or carving and gilding on furniture.

Grisaille: painting in various tints of grey or grey-green to produce a *trompe l'oeil* effect of objects in three dimensions, sometimes used as decoration on furniture.

Housing: the basic constructional framework in a piece of furniture into which other members fit.

Inlay: a decorative pattern composed of contrasting woods set into the solid wood of a piece of furniture, as distinct from marquetry which is veneered decoration.

Intarsia: decoration of wood mosaic in geometric and figurative patterns.

Japanning: European varnished decoration in imitation of oriental lacquer, on wood, metal or papier mâché.

Klismos: type of chair with inward curving sabre-shaped legs, first developed in ancient Greece and revived in the late 18th century.

Loo table: circular table on a pillar support, introduced in the early 19th century specifically for the card game lanterloo but later used for all kinds of purposes.

Marquetry: The decoration of veneered furniture with pictorial designs cut from sheets of contrasting wood veneers and sometimes incorporating slivers of ivory, mother-of-pearl or other materials.

Mortise: slot in a joint which fits the tenon.

Ormolu: the name of the process by which clock cases and other objects, and decorative mounts for furniture, were cast in bronze, chased and fire-gilt. Ormolu was a favourite form of embellishment for 18th century furniture, especially in France.

Oyster veneer: veneers of oyster shape cut from the small branches of trees like laburnum, walnut or lignum vitae and laid side-by-side as a decorative finish on furniture in the 17th and early 18th century.

Palmette: fan-shaped decorative motif.

Papier mâché: hard substance made from pulped paper which was used a great deal especially in the 19th century, for making trays, boxes and other pieces of furniture which were usually varnished and polished to a glossy smoothness and decorated with painting and/or gilding.

Parcel gilt: partly gilt.

Parquetry: the inlaying of veneers in geometric patterns as distinct from the floral and figurative designs of marquetry with which it is sometimes used.

Paterae: circular or oval ornamental discs or rosettes.

Penwork: the decoration of boxes and other small items of furniture with designs, often in the Neoclassical or Chinese manner, in black ink. Usually the background was black and the design 'voided' on it. The technique was originally developed in late 18th century Europe to imitate the ivory inlaid ebony furniture exported from India during the 18th century, and it became a popular ladies' pastime during the first half of the 19th century.

Pier table: a table designed to fit against the pier between the windows of a room, generally in conjunction with a pier glass above.

Pietre dure: hard stones, such as marble, agate, jasper and lapis lazuli inlaid, mosaic-like, into a furniture surface and polished; the technique was also known as Florentine mosaic work.

Quadrant drawer: drawer shaped as a quarter-circle, which swings out on a pivot when opened.

Rebate or rabbet: a rectangular recess cut to receive a corresponding section in the frame of a piece of furniture.

Roundel: ornament circular in shape.

Scagliola: mixture of glue, plaster and small chips of marble, used to imitate pietre dure for table tops etc.

Serpentine front: a curved shape, convex at the centre and concave at the sides, used for chest and table furniture in the 18th century.

Spanish foot: a carved scroll foot with vertical grooves used in English and American furniture in the late 17th and early 18th century; sometimes known as a Braganza toe.

Splat: the central vertical member of a chair back, often a vehicle for decoration.

Strapwork: decorative borders and patterns composed of interlacing scrolls and arabesques, lozenges and cartouches carved in low relief as if cut from parchment.

Stretcher: a horizontal reinforcing member or underbrace at the base of a chair or table.

Stringing: a thin line of wood or metal used as a decorative border in furniture.

Tambour front: strips of wood glued to a canvas backing and used for desk tops or shutters.

Tenon: tongue-piece in a joint, which fits into a mortise.

Tester: wooden canopy, particularly over a bedstead.

Torchère: small portable stand for lamp or candlestick, also known as a guéridon.

Trompe l'oeil: an effect of optical illusion, in painting or inlaid decoration.

Turkey work: upholstery made in imitation of Turkish carpets in the 16th and 17th centuries; it was made by knotting wools into a canvas base.

Turnings: lathe-finished members such as legs, posts, stretchers, balusters and spindles, often give decorative treatment, for example spiral-, ball-, or bobbin-turning.

Vitruvian scrolls: wave-like patterns of convoluted scrolls, on borders and friezes.

Wainscot: a word of Dutch origin meaning wagon-wood, ie. oak, it was eventually used to describe oak furniture of solid, panelled construction: as 'wainscot bed' or 'wainscot chair', as well as the lower panelling of rooms.

Index

References indicating illustrations are shown in *italics*. They are not given, however, for major divisions e.g. Renaissance furniture 25–47. In general 'English' means 'British', except where otherwise indicated.

H

I

J

K

L

M

Acknowledgments

The publishers would like to thank the following individuals and organizations for their kind permission to reproduce the photographs in this book.

Abbotsford, Roxburghshire (Cooper-Bridgeman Library) 172; Agence Top (C. Basnier) 6, (J. Schnapp) 48, (M. Nahmias) 2–3; Amboise Château (Ronald Sheridan) 143 above; American Museum in Britain 215, 221 above, 223 left and right, 229, 230 above, 231 above and below, 232 above, 235 right, 237; Angelo Hornak 44, 99 above right, 298, 256 above right; Antikvarisk Topografiska Arkivet (A.T.A.) 19; Antique Dealer and Collectors' Guide 150; Courtesy of the Art Institute of Chicago 234, 239 above; Art Museum, Princeton University 239 below right, (Gift of Roland Rohlfs) 241; Aston Hall (Birmingham Museum and Art Gallery) 243; Bayerisches Nationalmuseum. Munich 34 left; Bethnal Green Museum 203 above, 204 left and right, 209 above right, (A.C. Cooper) 162 left, (Cooper-Bridgeman Library) 165, (Peter Myers) 169, 190, 199, 200 above and below, 201, 202, 207 above and below; Bonhams Auctioneers and Valuers 42, 72 above, 87; Bowes Museum, Barnard Castle, Co. Durham 257; Brighton Art Gallery and Museum (Angelo Hornak) 300 above right, 301 right; Ca' Rezzonico, Venice (Cooper-Bridgeman Library) 49, 149, (Angelo Hornak) 88 above and below; Cardiff and Chelsea Antiques Fair 86 above; Castello di Racconigi 173 above; Charleston, South Carolina Museum, exhibited in the Heyward Washington House, (Helga Studio photo, courtesy magazine "Antiques") 212; Château de Compiègne (Giraudon) 144 below; Château de Malmaison (Giraudon) 144 above; Château de Versailles (Cooper-Bridgeman Library) 84, (Michael Holford) 78; Chicago Architecture Foundation (Steve Grubman Photography) 233; Christie, Manson and Woods 26, 55 right, 57 above, 58, 65, 80, 86 below, 90, 114 above and below, 115, 134 below, 142 below, 147, 151, 159, (Cooper-Bridgeman Library) 119 below right, 125; Connaissance des Arts 112; Cotehele House, Cornwall (Cooper-Bridgeman Library) 138 below; Craig and Tarlton Inc., Raleigh, N.C. 220 right; Dan Klein, London (Cooper-Bridgeman Library) 300 above left; David Stockwell Inc., Wilmington, Delaware 218 below; 'Deco' Brighton (Cooper-Bridgeman Library) 299 above; Design Council 303 below; Diplomatic Reception Rooms, Dept. of State, Washington, D.C. (Gift of Mr. and Mrs. Mitchell Toradash) 224 above; Elizabeth Whiting 286; Egyptian National Museum (Werner Forman Archive) 12; Mrs. F.L. Griggs Collection (A.C. Cooper) 192 below; Fine Art Society, London 189, (Peter Myers) 195 right; Geffrye Museum (Cooper-Bridgeman Library) 96–97, 152–153, 166; Gemeentesmuseum, Holland 206; Germanisches Nationalmuseum, Nuremberg 34 right; Giraudon 52 below; Graham Dark 91, H. and R. Sandor Inc., New Jersey 221 below; Hamlyn Publishing Group 31, 94, 208 below; Hatfield House (J.R. Freeman) 160; Heal and Son Ltd. 194 below, 306 above and below, 307, 309 above; Heinz Preisig 20; Helga Studio, New York (Private Collection) 225; Henry Francis du Pont Winterthur Museum 214, 217, 220 left, (Cooper-Bridgeman Library) 4–5; Historisches Museum, Basel 35; Hotel de Beauharnais, Paris (Cooper-Bridgeman Library) 140; Houghton Hall, Norfolk (Angelo Hornak) 242; Hunterian Art Galleries, University of Glasgow (Mackintosh Collection) 209, 287; J. de Rothschild Collection (Connaissance des Arts) 1; Jeremy Whitaker 108; King and Chasemore, Pulborough, Saleroom 69, 73, 77; Knole, Kent (Cooper-Bridgeman Library) 245 above; Kunstmuseum, Hamburg (Cooper-Bridgeman Library) 59; Lady Lever Art Gallery, Merseyside 107; Lennox Money, London 158 above, (Cooper-Bridgeman Library) 157 above; Leonard Lassalle, London (Cooper-Bridgeman Library) 40 above; Luton Hoo, Bedfordshire (Cooper-Bridgeman Library) 148; Mallett and Son, London 75, 98, 164 above, 265, (Cooper-Bridgeman Library) 92 below, 269, 276 below, 277 above, 278 right, 281 above; The Mansell Collection 155 above, 156 below, 170, 191, 193; Marquess of Townshend, Norfolk (Cooper-Bridgeman Library) 11 below; Mary Evans Picture Library 136 above and below left and right, 157 below, 184, 192 above; Metropolitan Museum of Art, New York 216, (Gift of Mrs. J. Insley Blair, 1947) 224 below, (Purchased Mrs. Paul Moore. Gift 1965) 230 below, (Gift of Mrs. R. Sage, Bequest of Ethel Yocum, Bequest of Charlotte E. Hoadley, Rogers Fund, by exchange) 228, (Gift of the Samuel H. Kress Foundation, 1958) 254, (Werner Forman Archive) 16; Merseyside County Museum 285; Michael Ridley 263, 266 right, 267, 270 below, 272 above left, 273, 274, 278 above left, 279, 283 above right; Courtesy of Michel Dumez-Onof 27 above and below; Courtesy of Mill House Antiques, Petworth 182; Monastery of Escorial (Michael Holford) 33; Morley Baer (from 'California Design', 1910) 238 below; Munich Residence 145; Musée des Arts Decoratifs, Paris 22, (Giraudon) 141, (Cooper-Bridgeman Library) 205; Musée de L'Ecole, Nancy (Photo Gilbert Mangin) 186, 203 below; Musée Guimet, Paris (Réunion des musées nationaux) 268; Musée National du Château de Fontainebleau 142 above; Museo dell' Arcivescovado (Scala) 18; Museo Nacional de Artes Decorativas, Madrid 63 left; Museo Poldi-Pezzoli, Milan 178; Museu Nacional de Arte Antiga, Lisbon 63 right, 64; Museum of Decorative Art, Copenhagen 11 above; Museum of Modern Art, New York (Gift of Cafe Nicholson) 183, (Gift of Herbert Bayer) 291, (Gift of Thonet Industries Inc.) 294 above; National Gallery, London 25; National Museum, Denmark 92 above; National Trust 30 left, 38, 71, 99 below, 258 above, (John Bethell) 10, 251, (Cooper-Bridgeman Library) 246 above; Noel Riley 135 left, (Peter Myers) 138 above, 156 above; Norman Adams 134 above; Collection of the Oakland Museum, gift of Concours d'Antiques, Art Guild, Oakland Museum Association 240; Objects, London 47; Octopus Books 181 right, 304 above; Osterley Park, London 130–131, 139; Österreichisches Museum für angewandte Kunst, Vienna 210 above left and right, 211; Palazzo Davanzati 28, (Scala) 24; Peter Myers 13; Peter Philp 123; Philadelphia Museum of Art (Purchased from Collab 20th Century Inc.) 305 below, (Given by George Wood Furness) 232 below, (Bequest of Lydia Thompson Morris) 218 above, (Mrs. Samuel H. Ward) 239 below left, (Mrs. Samuel S. Starr) 238 above, (Purchased: Thomas Skelton Harrison Fund) 219, (Given by Mrs. W. Logan Maccoy) 222, (Given by Mr. and Mrs. William T. Carter) 235 left; Phillips and Harris, London 275, 278 below left; Phillips International Fine Art Auctioneers 39 above, 68 above and below, 72 below, 76 above and below, 101, 103 below, 104 above and below, 105, 158 below; Philp and Sons, Cardiff 89, 111, 117; Phoebus Picture Library 161; Photoresources 284; Pingree House, Salem, Mass. (Angelo Hornak) 226–227; Private Collection (A.C. Cooper) 168 above, (Cooper-Bridgeman Library) 8, 41, 74 below, 129, 180 below, 185, 195 left, 246 below, 276 above; Radio City Music Hall, New York (Angelo Hornak) 302; Rijksmuseum, Amsterdam 55 left, 56; Ronald Sheridan 14, 15; Room for Living 308; S.J. Phillips, London (Cooper-Bridgeman Library) 283 below; St James Church, Piccadilly (Angelo Hornak) 74 above; Scala 32; Scotney Castle, Kent (Angelo Hornak) 171; Shaker Museum, Sabbath Bay, Maine 236; Courtesy of Smithsonian Institution, Freer Gallery of Art, Washington 179, 258 below; Sotheby Parke Bernet and Company 51, 83, 99 above left, 100 below, 122; Southwark Cathedral (Peter Myers) 40 below; Spink and Son Ltd. 264 above and below; Staatliche Museum, Berlin 17; Stichting Duivenvoorde 163; Strasbourg Cathedral Museum (Ronald Sheridan) 60; Sybarites Gallery, New York (Angelo Hornak) 301 left; Talavera Antiques, London (Cooper-Bridgeman Library) 62; Temple Newsam House, Leeds 137, 181 left, (Cooper-Bridgeman Library) 29 below, 245 below; Tiroler Volks Kunstmuseum, Innsbruck 127; Tobias Jellinek 43; Uppsala (Cooper-Bridgeman Library) 61; W.F. Greenwood, Yorks 121; W. and R. Harvey and Co. 280; Reproduced by permission of the Trustees, The Wallace Collection, London (J.R. Freeman) 54, 82, 116, 9 above, 85 below right, 255; Werner Forman Archive 262; William Morris Gallery (Woodmansterne Publications Ltd.) 196, 197, 259 above right, 260, (Michael Holford) 198, (Peter Myers) 288 above; Winter Palace, St. Petersburg (Cooper-Bridgeman Library) 164 below; Victoria and Albert Museum, Crown copyright, 9 below, 21, 30 above right, 37, 39 below, 45, 46–47, 50, 53, 57 below, 66–67, 70 left and right, 81 below, 85 below left, 100 above, 102, 103 above, 106, 109 above and below, 118, 119 below left, 120, 124, 126, 132 above and below, 133, 135 right, 153, 154 left and right, 155 below, 167, 168 below, 173 below, 175, 188, 194 above, 208 above left, 244, 247, 248, 249 above and below, 250, 252 above and below, 253, 256 below, 259 above left and below, 303 above, (A.C. Cooper) 162 right, 177 above, 180 above, (Angelo Hornak) 23, 29 above, 52 above, 79, 93, 176, 187, 250 below, 261, 289, 290, 293 above, 295, 305 above right, 310, (Arts Council of Great Britain) 294 below, (C.M. Dixon) 281 below, 282 above, 283 above left, 284, (Cooper-Bridgeman Library) 36, 81 above, 95, 296–297, (Michael Holford) 110, 266 left, 270 above, 271, 272 above right, 277 below, 282 below, (Peter Myers) 174, 177 below, 208 above right, 288 below, 292, 293 below, 299 below; Vono 305 above left, 311; ZEFA (Bloemendal) 128, (K.A.W.) 146, (R. Nuettgens) 304 below.

Index compiled by Valerie Lewis Chandler, B.A., A.L.A.A.

GC 019870 GRIMSBY COLLEGE